BRAND PROTECTION MATTERS

AUSTRALIA
LBC Information Services—Sydney

CANADA AND USA
Carswell—Toronto

NEW ZEALAND
Brooker's—Auckland

SINGAPORE AND MALAYSIA
Sweet & Maxwell Asia
Singapore and Kuala Lumpur

BRAND PROTECTION MATTERS

By

BELINDA ISAAC

Partner, Llewelyn Zietman

LONDON
SWEET & MAXWELL
2000

Published in 2000 by
Sweet & Maxwell Limited of
100 Avenue Road
London NW3 3PF
(http://www.sweetandmaxwell.co.uk)
Typeset by Dataword Services Limited, Chilcompton
Printed and bound in Great Britain by
MPG Books Ltd, Bodmin, Cornwall.

No natural forests were destroyed to make this product,
only farmed timber was used and replanted.

ISBN 0 421 569 301

A CIP catalogue record for this book is available from
the British Library

DEDICATION

For Alan

ACKNOWLEDGMENTS

It has taken longer to complete this book than I like to admit but the fact that it has been completed is itself an acknowledgment of the support and encouragement that I have received from various sources along the way. In particular, I would like to thank Professor Gerald Dworkin for his encouragement to start work on the book and Lionel Bentley for his tireless reading and re-reading of the text and his helpful criticisms of the early drafts. Thanks too are due to Professor Jeremy Phillips and Hugh Brett who read through chapters of the book and provided useful comments. I am indebted to the editors of Sweet & Maxwell, who, without complaint, postponed my deadlines on various occasions.

I would also like to extend particular thanks to my fellow Partners at Llewelyn Zietman for their patience and their recognition of the importance to me of completing the book by giving me time to work on it at the expense of more profitable work. Last, but by no means least, I would like to thank my husband, Alan for his unfailing support and assistance in realising this project.

FOREWORD

English intellectual proerty lawyers, and judges, are regularly criticised for taking an unduly narrow approach to complaints of unfair competition in the marketplace. They are accused of failing to appreciate the value of the brand in modern marketing, and of having failed to develop the law to meet the challenge presented by modern forms of unfair contribution. The counts on the indictment are well known: the emphasis on misrepresentation (or the risk of misrepresentation) as an essential element of impermissible conduct; the reluctance to recognise the mere look-alike as deserving of censure: the problem of the brand. By setting the Trade Marks Act 1994 and the passing-off cases against the wider background of international obligations and developments in the theory of marketing this book aims to provide a rational basis for a law relating to unfair competition by brand misappropriation. It provides a substantial contribution to an important debate which is too often obscured by noisy argument in support of extreme positions, and I welcome it.

Nicholas Pumfrey,
Royal Courts of Justice
April 5, 2000

PREFACE

Numerous marketing books have been written about brands but few legal books aim to address the subject, focusing instead on the individual intellectual property rights that they give rise to. One of the difficulties with this approach for the non specialist, is that there is no single text that addresses the subject. In this book I have endeavoured to address the subject of brand protection holistically, drawing together legal rights and marketing practice. My experience as a trade mark lawyer advising on registration and infringement issues has led to the conclusion that legal protection and marketing are complementary, though distinct, functions. Companies compartmentalise the roles to their disadvantage. The language used by lawyers and marketers may be the same but the meaning is often different. For example, the term "distinctive" to the marketer connotes visual impact (usually in the form of a simple but striking display) and is usually a subjective assessment, whereas to the lawyer it would mean something that was unusual, not at all descriptive, and involves an objective assessment taking into account the activities of competitors. Action taken with the best of intentions within the marketing department may undermine a branded product's legal protection and cause the brand name to be treated as generic. Conversely, an awareness of legal realities as part of an integrated advertising or promotional campaign can improve the prospect of a brand retaining its distinctiveness (in a legal sense), and thus, maintaining its competitive advantage.

The emphasis of this book is on the legal protection of brands from copying and unfair competition. I unashamedly take the perspective of the brand owner, that is the creator, developer or marketer of the product, as opposed to that of the licensee, subsidiary or a competitor. I have done so because it is invariably the brand owner that has the greatest interest in ensuring that its brand has the fullest protection. This approach does not seek to deny the validity of other viewpoints, on the contrary, where appropriate I have sought to include these but my conclusions do support the brand owner.

The hypothesis put forward in this book is that brands are not, as the law currently stands, adequately protected. Change, in terms of statutory protection, needs to take place, and I offer, with due modesty, my suggestions as to how it might be approached. Whilst the adoption of these would be the fullest vindication of this work, I would be satisfied that it had been worthwhile if it makes a contribution to the debate on what is undoubtedly an important and far reaching topic.

In researching for this book I have endeavoured to consider material from a variety of disciplines. Its ambit and objectives have necessarily raised difficult choices of inclusion and omission. References to economic and social history, for example, are unavoidably cursory, however, I have sought to include bibliographical information for follow up reading where my treatment has been limited. Another difficulty encountered is crossing disciplines, is that of the style of writing. Lawyers are accustomed to reading material that is capable of rigorous analysis and criticism. This is not always so in other disciplines, and so, for instance, some of the marketing material does not have the same authority as one might wish for.

Brands have become omnipresent in today's world. Within the past decade the E.U. has embraced significant expansion to the East. China has opened up to Western influences and the old Soviet empire has fragmented. A global marketplace exists as never before. The Internet is increasingly turned to as the vehicle through which goods are advertised, and demand is met. Access is growing and is destined in a short time to become significantly more affordable to use. Competition to serve through it will become intense. A global marketplace requires global recognition of brand names and imagery. Brands and their symbols are thus rapidly becoming the international language of trade. The expansion of the E.U. and the globalisation of trade has also fuelled the move for harmonisation of laws regulating trade. Unfortunately, we have a long way to go until true harmonisation is realised. Consequently, this book only seeks to address the legal position concerning brand protection in the U.K. Perhaps a later edition will be able to adopt a global perspective!

Finally, I should say that whilst I have had assistance from various quarters in writing this book, the errors are, of course, my own. I should also add that, of necessity the principles set out in this book are of a general nature. This book should not be relied upon as the sole basis for establishing your brand protection policy. Brands are, by their nature, individual and appropriate legal advice should therefore be sought that takes into account the individual circumstances pertaining to your brand.

Belinda Isaac
London, February 2000

CONTENTS

Chapter 3: Protecting Product Appearance

Chapter 4: Protecting Product Packaging

TABLE OF CASES

TABLE OF STATUTES

TABLE OF STATUTORY INSTRUMENTS

TABLE OF EUROPEAN MATERIALS

TABLE OF ABBREVIATIONS

Annand and Norman	Annand and Norman, Blackstone's Guide to the Trade Marks Act 1994 (Blackstone Press, London, 1994)
Berne Convention	Berne Convention for the Protection of Literary and Artistic Works
CDPA 1988	Copyright, Designs and Patents Act 1988
Cornish	Cornish Intellectual Property (Sweet & Maxwell, London, 4th ed., 1999)
CTM	Community Trade Mark
CTMO	Community Trade Mark Office (also known as OHIM)
Kerly	Blanco White and Jacob, Kerly's Law of Trade Marks and Trade Names (Sweet & Maxwell, London, 12th ed., 1986 with supplement)
Kotler *et al*	Kotler, Armstrong, Saunders & Wong Principles of Marketing (Prentice Hall, Hemel Hempstead, 2nd European ed., 1999)
Laddie *et al*	Laddie, Prescott and Victoria, The Modern Law of Copyright (Butterworths, London, 2nd ed., 1995)
Madrid Protocol	Protocol (1989) to the Madrid Agreement concerning the International Registration of Marks
McCarthy	McCarthy, Trademarks and Unfair Competition (Clark Boardman, Deerfield, 3rd ed., 1996)
Michaels	Michaels, A Practical Guide to Trade Mark Law (Sweet & Maxwell, London, 2nd ed., 1996
RDA	Registered Designs Act 1949 (as amended)
TMA 1938	Trade Marks Act 1938
TMA 1994	Trade Marks Act 1994
TMA 1994 Rules	Rules under the Trade Marks Act 1994
TRIPS	Agreement on Trade-Related Intellectual Property Rights including Trade in Counterfeit Goods
Wadlow	Wadlow, The Law of Passing Off, (Sweet & Maxwell, London, 2nd ed., 1995, with supplement)
WIPO	World Intellectual Property Organisation

GLOSSARY OF TERMS

Product:	An expression used to refer to goods generally. A product comprises 3 distinct levels, core product; actual product and augmented product.
Core Product:	The most basic level of a product; what might be described as the product concept—the basic idea behind the product. It can be identified by answering the question what is the consumer actually buying.
Core Benefit:	The consumer's perspective of the core product. What benefit does the consumer obtain from buying the product.
Actual Product:	The second level of a product. It comprises the particular product that the consumer buys, packaging, the brand name, logo, colour, quality level, features, design and shape of the product.
Augmented Product:	In addition to the actual product purchased by the consumer, the consumer may receive additional benefits such as after sales service, guarantee, product insurance, a helpline, etc. All these together with the actual product form the augmented product.
Brand name:	That part of a brand which can be vocalised—the utterable.
Brand mark:	That part of a brand which can be recognised but is not utterable, such as a symbol, design (device), distinctive colouring or lettering.
Brand Image:	
Brand:	A mix of tangible and intangible values including the product itself, its shape/configuration, the packaging, the brand name, the promotion advertising and overall presentation. It is a synthesis of all these elements.
Brand Equity:	The marketing effects uniquely attributable to the brand.

CHAPTER 1

The Anatomy of a Brand

INTRODUCTION

1–01 The phenomenal growth in the wealth and cultural influence of multi-national corporations over the past 20 years can arguably be attributed to the development of the modern concept of branding. Indeed, branding has become an integral part of business today across a wide range of industry sectors from consumer goods to financial services, legal services, charities and even to politics, but what exactly is a brand? Is it the same as a product? Marketers constantly refer to their brands whereas lawyers tend to refer to trade marks—but what is the difference? Is a brand the same as a trade mark? Marketing consultants and authors of marketing textbooks no longer appear to discuss marketing *per se* but focus instead upon successful branding. Is it the same process by another name or is there more to it than mere semantics? Is a brand a new phenomenon or is it simply a new name applied to an existing concept?

1–02 This chapter seeks to explore questions such as these in greater detail for the benefit of the legal community. Relying upon traditional marketing theory the chapter begins with a brief analysis of what is meant by the term "product" before moving on to consider what constitutes a brand. From this discussion the formulation of a number of propositions follow concerning the nature and function of a brand and its distinction from trade marks and products. To understand how and why brands evolved to the point of being revered icons of the modern age and as significant financial assets in their own right we will look very briefly at the historical development of the consumer society during the past 100 years. We will see that brands are a recent phenomena whose roots can be traced back to the end of the nineteenth century.

1–03 Many of the issues raised in this chapter will be discussed in greater detail in subsequent chapters. In particular, later chapters will focus on the boundaries between brands, products and trade marks, from a legal perspective and the extent to which brands can be protected in law from unauthorised reproduction and imitation by third parties. The primary purpose of this chapter therefore is to set the scene for subsequent chapters to explore the nature of a brand from a marketing perspective so that the commercial significance of certain issues relating to brands can be appreciated. A secondary aim is to define the terminology central to an understanding of the issues of what constitutes a brand and how brands can be protected by means of intellectual property laws. The principle question with which this book is concerned is whether a brand today is comprehensively protected by law from imitation, and if not, whether protection should be extended, and if so, how.

WHAT IS A PRODUCT?

1–04   We begin our analysis of what constitutes a brand by considering what is a product. It is important to clarify what we mean by the term "product" because the two words, brand and product, are sometimes used interchangeably as if there is no distinction between them. In this book it is important to appreciate that the terms are not considered to be synonymous. On the contrary, as will be seen below, an important distinction can, and should, be drawn between them.

A leading marketing textbook defines a product as[1]:

> "anything that is offered to a market for attention, acquisition, use or consumption and that might satisfy a want or need: products include more than just tangible goods. Broadly defined products include physical objects, services, persons, places, organisations, ideas and mixtures of these entities".

Whilst concurring with the view that, in its broadest sense, a product could include "persons, places, organizations and ideas" for the sake of simplicity, in the context of this book the notion of a product will be limited to physical objects as opposed to intangible services, organisations or ideas. Such products can be considered as comprising three distinct levels which can be illustrated as shown in Figure 1.[2] At the most basic level is what is known as the "core product" or what might be described as the product concept, the basic idea behind the product and in relation to which there may be different ways of implementation. This is the heart of the product and can be identified by asking the question, what is the consumer actually buying? From a consumer perspective the question might be considered as, what is the core benefit of buying the product? By way of illustration, the core product in relation to say a Philishave electric razor, is an electric razor incorporating a flexible head. From a consumer perspective, the core benefit could be described as a quick, close, comfortable shave.

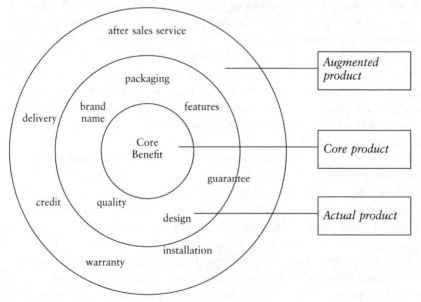

Figure 1—Source: *Kotler et al*

---

[1] Kotler *et al*, p. 561.
[2] Kotler *et al*, p. 562.

1–05 The second level of a product can be described as the "actual product", this includes the packaging, the product name or brand name, logo, colour, quality level, the features of the product, its design and shape as a specific manifestation of the core product. The core product is combined with these additional elements to create an actual product consistent with the core benefit that will satisfy consumer needs. The third level in our analysis of a product, is the "augmented product". In addition to the actual product the manufacturer may provide additional customer services such as an after sales service, a guarantee, product insurance, a helpline and so on. To return to the example of the Philishave razor, these intangible benefits aim to provide the consumer with a complete means of obtaining a quick, close, comfortable shave, consistently. Whereas the core product is essentially tangible, the augmented product can include both tangible and intangible elements.

Thus, whilst in one sense it is true to say that a product is "what the consumer is actually buying", in another sense, when a consumer buys a product such as an electric shaver from a department store, what the consumer actually takes away is more than just the core product. Exactly how much more the consumer receives may depend upon the brand of electric shaver purchased since features of the actual product can vary from one brand to another just as aspects of the augmented product can vary. For example, if the product is purchased from a market stall, the purchaser may not obtain the benefits of any product warranty, guarantee or credit facility and so buys only the actual product.

1–06 The point of differentiating between these different levels of a product is to emphasise that different actual products may provide the same core benefit and to distinguish between the manufacturer's view of the product and the consumer's perspective of what he/she is buying.[2a] As we will see (below) the role of marketing is to present the actual product in terms of the core benefits that consumers seek. Although the core product may be the result of consumer responses to market research, once the actual product has been launched and promoted through advertising it is possible that the core benefit may change. Consumers may attach particular significance to the actual product as a result of societal values attributed to the product associated with ownership. For example, a Filofax personal organiser may offer the core benefit of a more organised way of life but consumers may regard the core benefit as a status symbol, either because the advertising used to promote the actual product positions it as an article possessed by members of a particular social group or, because the article is in fact used by people of a certain social standing.

For the purposes of this book we will need to refer on occasions to the actual product without the brand name, logo or any packaging and we will therefore refer to this as the "naked product". References to the term "product" in the remainder of the book will be to articles in a general sense.[3]

WHAT IS A BRAND?

1–07 A survey of marketing books quickly reveals that there is no universally accepted definition of a brand. Writers concur with the view that brands exist but appear to have great difficulty identifying the characteristics of a brand, preferring

---

[2a] Just how diverse the two perspectives are may depend on the social significance of the product as suggested in the example below relating to the Filofax personal organiser.

[3] For simplicity all future references in this chapter will be to goods but in most cases the principles discussed will apply equally to services unless specified.

instead to focus upon some of the effects that successful branding can engender. For example the authors of one marketing book[4] describe a brand as:

> ". . . a product or service made distinctive by its positioning relative to the competition and by its personality."

A prerequisite to understanding this definition is a knowledge of what is meant by the term "personality" as far as a brand is concerned. All the statement reveals is that a brand is distinctive as against competing products and/or services.

1–08   The different definitions of a brand used by marketers can be regarded as falling within a spectrum with, at the one extreme, brands defined in principally physical terms akin to a definition of a trade mark (as discussed in Chapter 2), with source identification and differentiation as the two key objectives. At the other extreme, brands are defined in terms of intangible values primarily directed at the relationship between the consumer and the manufacturer. In part this diversity of opinion as to what constitutes a brand can be explained in terms of the evolution of the brand concept. Thus older, more established definitions, tend to be based more on the physical attributes associated with a brand, whereas the definitions used by more contemporary writers emphasise intangible values. In order to demonstrate this change in approach we will now look at a number of definitions of a brand, with a view to distilling a working definition that can be used throughout this book to evaluate what level of protection is currently afforded to branded products and to assess whether additional protection is required.

1–09   Professor Philip Kotler, considered by some to be the "prophet" of modern marketing,[5] bases his definition of a brand on that of the traditional 1960 American Marketing Association ("AMA") definition which describes a brand as[5a]:

> "A name, term, sign, symbol, or design, or a combination of these, intended to identify the goods or services of one seller or group of sellers and to differentiate them from those of competitors"

Of the marketing definitions this is the closest to the legal definition of a trade mark as set out in section 1(1) of the Trade Marks Act 1994.

1–10   David Aaker,[6] another acknowledged marketing specialist, defines a brand in a similar manner, adding that:

> "A brand . . . signals to the consumer the source of the product, and protects the customer and the producer from competitors who would attempt to provide products that appear to be identical."

From both the AMA definition and Aaker's interpretation of it, we see that one of the essential requirements of a brand is distinctiveness which can lie in the name, symbol, logo or packaging of the brand. According to Aaker, the requirement of distinctiveness serves two purposes, first, it acts as a means of identifying the source of the product (*i.e.* it serves as an indication of origin function) and secondly, it acts

---

[4] Hankinson & Cowking, *Branding in Action* (McGraw Hill, Maidenhead, 1993), p. 1 ("Hankinson & Cowking").
[5] See Nilson, *Value Added Marketing* (McGraw Hill, Maidenhead, 1992), p. 19 ("Value Added Marketing").
[5a] Kotler *et al*, p. 571.
[6] David Aaker, *Managing Brand Equity* (Macmillan, New York, 1991), p. 7 ("Aaker").

as a means of differentiating the goods of one provider from those of a competitor (*i.e.* a differentiation function). Indeed, Aaker goes on to state that the brand is the only distinguishing element between two otherwise identical articles, thus emphasising the function of differentiation. Both the AMA's and Aaker's definition seek to emphasise the tangible aspects of brands (that is, the product, brand name, logo, packaging, etc.), from what may be termed the "input perspective", that is, from the perspective of brands as manufacturers' creations. Equally, both definitions take account of the legal role fulfilled by a trade mark.

1–11 By way of contrast, John Murphy, the founder of Interbrand, a consultancy working exclusively in the field of branding, has sought to explain what constitutes a brand in terms of both the manufacturers' input and the consumer's output perspectives, observing that[7]:

> ". . . the ways in which branded products or services are distinguished from one another have increasingly come to embrace non-tangible factors, as well as such real factors as size, shape, make-up and price. The brand qualities which consumers rely upon in making a choice between brands have become increasingly subtle and, at times fickle. Cigarette A may be virtually indistinguishable from cigarette B yet outsell it ten to one; a fragrance costing $10 a bottle may be outsold by another fragrance with very similar physical characteristics but which sells at $50 a bottle . . . Thus modern, sophisticated branding is now concerned increasingly with a brands 'gestalt', with assembling together and maintaining a mix of values, both tangible and intangible, which are relevant to consumers and which meaningfully and appropriately distinguish one supplier's brand from that of another."

Murphy thus suggests that a brand is more than the physical aspects of a product (the actual product), in his view it includes a mix of values "both tangible and intangible". Indeed, he goes on to identify the components of a brand as comprising[8]:

> ". . . the product itself, the packaging, the brand name, the promotion, the advertising and the overall presentation. The brand is therefore the synthesis of all these elements, physical, aesthetic, rational and emotional."

Murphy's definition is thus much wider than Aaker's or even that expressed by Hankinson and Cowking because he suggests that it is more than the physical embodiment of the name, logo or packaging (which in themselves form part of the actual product). Murphy argues that the brand also, somehow, encompasses the marketing and promotional activity and the overall presentation that surrounds and sustains sales of the actual product.

1–12 David Arnold goes one step further, observing that[9]:

> "The top 10 brands . . . are virtually all leaders in their markets. This cannot be explained by the weight of their advertising or some inherent product superiority, or the catchiness of their name, even though they all score well on

---

[7] Murphy (Ed.), *Branding: A Key Marketing Tool* (Macmillan, London, 1987), p. 1 ("Murphy").
[8] *ibid.*, p. 3.
[9] Arnold, *The Handbook of Brand Management* (Financial Times Pitman Publishing, London, 1993), p. 14 ("Arnold").

these counts. [Research] suggests that the real key to market leadership is
superior *perceived* quality. Not inherent product quality; only the perception
of the quality by the consumer." *(emphasis added)*

Thus there is, according to both Murphy and Arnold, something over and above
the nature of an actual product that a consumer associates with a brand which
influences the consumer's purchasing decision. Like the augmented product, a
brand is said to comprise both tangible and intangible elements.

1–13   Ambler, a marketing academic, describes a brand in simple terms as
comprising[10]:

> "a product plus added values . . . A brand is a bundle of functional, economic
> and psychological benefits for the end user, more simply known as quality,
> price and image."

This "perceived quality" or "added value" as it is sometimes termed, is a nebulous
concept. It can be based upon the packaging style or the appearance of the product,
the advertising used, the belief that the brand is effective (as in the case of
pharmaceutical products), the sort of people who use the brand (*e.g.* its social
status) or the experience of the brand (*e.g.* where it has been used before).[11] The
value may be actual or emotional: for example, The Body Shop emphasises, as an
emotional brand value, concern for the environment. The importance of these
"added values" leads Arnold to suggest that[12]:

> "Branding is about the way people perceive, and not about the product in
> isolation".

Arnold is not alone in acknowledging the importance of the partially intangible
nature of brands. As Southgate, an advertising executive and author of "Total
Branding", explains[13]:

> "If you think of a brand only as a mark denoting ownership you can slap it on
> anything—and many brand owners still do. But this is to use branding in its
> crudest and simplest form. It is to use branding in the same way as the Wild
> West ranchers used it, simply to say 'this is mine'.
>   To think of a brand as a set of 'intangible values', by contrast, is to
> understand something which is absolutely crucial in the successful develop-
> ment of brands today. And that is that brands do not exist, in any meaningful
> sense, in the factory or even in the marketing department. They exist in the
> consumer's mind."

Not all marketers agree, however, as to the importance of emotional or intangible
aspects of a brand to consumers. Nilson[14] asserts that when reaching a purchasing
decision the consumer is first and foremost concerned about acquiring a product
and is not concerned about emotional or intangible aspects of a brand, in his view:

---

[10] "Building Brand Relationships", *Financial Times,* December 4, 1995.
[11] Jones, *What's in a Name?* (Gower Publishing Co., Aldershot, 1986), p. 30 ("Jones").
[12] Arnold, p. 20.
[13] *Total Branding by Design* (Kogan Page, London, 1994), p. 18.
[14] Nilson, *Value Added Marketing* (McGraw Hill, Maidenhead, 1992), p. 114 ("Value Added
Marketing").

"The physical purchasing action is caused by a decision to acquire a product; the brand is there to serve as a means of identifying the manufacturer. The values of the brand will reflect on the product, but one must not forget that it is the product that is bought".

Whilst it is true that purchasing decisions are often motivated by the desire to acquire a particular product to satisfy a perceived need, buying behaviour is complex and is influenced by many factors.[15] In some circumstances the physical features of a product will be the most important factor for consumers, but in other situations intangible factors may have an important role.[16] For example, when purchasing a car or technical equipment, the consumer may place special emphasis on the image associated with the particular make or style in question, its reliability or social status. The extent to which intangible factors help determine the purchasing decision will vary according to the nature of the consumer, the nature of the product, the channels through which the product is marketed and the level of advertising associated with the product.

1–14   Professor de Chernatony, a marketing academic and frequent writer on issues relating to branding, conducted a survey of "leading edge brand consultants" to determine what they understood by the term "brand" both from a manufacturer and a consumer perspective.[17] The study is of interest because it confirms the divergence of views as to what the nature of a brand is. Based on an initial review of literature, de Chernatony identified nine main themes used in defining the concept of a brand. These include a brand as (i) a legal instrument (ii) a logo, (iii) a company, (iv) an identity system, (v) an image in consumers' minds, (vi) a personality, (vii) a relationship, (viii) as adding value and (ix) as an evolving entity. We have already seen examples of most of these themes in the material quoted above. The idea of a brand changing as part of a natural process, however, is a concept developed by de Chernatony himself[18] in which he sees brands as evolving from a manufacturer's input to a consumer's output perspective. In other words when brands are launched the emphasis is upon the manufacturer's perspective of the brand as a form of legal identification, a logo, etc. but as a brand develops over time and is promoted by means of extensive advertising so the brand becomes embued with advertising imagery and positive associations (especially associations of quality as a result of consumer experience, promotional activity, reputation and so on) such that the emphasis moves towards a consumer perspective of a brand expressed in terms of images, relationships, experience and added values. De Chernatony therefore suggests that the various views of what constitutes a brand should not be considered as contradictory, but rather as evolutionary. Such an understanding is helpful in explaining how established brands have greater symbolic value (and indeed, increased financial value) than new brands, which have not had the benefit of extensive promotional campaigns or customer experience.

---

[15] Chisnall, *Consumer Behaviour* (McGraw Hill, Maidenhead, 1995), p. 11 ("Chisnall").
[16] Franzen & Hoogerbruuge, *The Functions of the Brand* 1995 (unpublished).
[17] De Chernatony. 2 Dall'Olmo Riley, "The Chasm between Managers' and Consumers' Views of Brands: the experts' perspectives" (1997) 5 *Journal of Strategic Marketing* 89–104 at 89; "The Big Brand Challenge" Esomar seminar Berlin, October 9–11, 1996 (Volume 203): see also de Chernatony. 2 McDonald, Creating Powerful Brands (Butterworth Heinemann, Oxford, 2nd ed., 1998).
[18] "Categorising brands: evolutionary processes underpinned by two key dimensions" (1993) 9 *Journal of Marketing Management* 173–88. This evolutionary approach has also been endorsed by Goodyear Ed Birn, Hague, Vangelder, "A Handbook of Market Research Techniques" (Kogan Page, London, 1990) 229–248.

1–15 De Chernatony's survey concluded that brand consultants did not have a single definition of a brand but rather regarded the concept of a brand as:

> "a link between the firms' marketing activities and consumer perceptions of functional and emotional elements".

Such an analysis is considerably broader than the traditional definition of a brand with which we started this section (the AMA definition) but as de Chernatony observes the AMA's perspective of brands as logos is far less appropriate in today's environment. De Chernatony thus endorses the view that the nature of the brand paradigm has changed since the AMA's definition was originally propounded. Changes in, amongst other things, the retail environment (see para. 1–36 below) have given rise to changes in the role of the brand and thus a different explanation of the brand paradigm is needed.

1–16 De Chernatony's analysis maybe an accurate portrayal of the concept of a brand to the consumer but, for the purposes of a legal assessment and analysis his definition is too nebulous to be of practical assistance to us, not only in terms of defining a brand but also in deciding how such a brand can and should be legally protected. De Chernatony's definition is also far removed from the nature of a product relying as it does purely on consumer perception. For the purposes of our consideration of the legal protection of a brand we need a more limited term which can be objectively scrutinised and supported evidentially, not one that is wholly reliant on consumer perceptions. Although the AMA definition would fulfil these criteria it fails to take account of the current role of intangible factors, such as the images portrayed through advertising, in the overall concept of a brand. Thus, for the purposes of this book we need to find a balance between at one extreme, the definition of a brand suggested by the AMA and de Chernatony's definition at the other. As we will see below, marketers tend to concur with the view that brands developed from the legal concept of trade marks which were used primarily to indicate the manufacturing origin of the goods to which the marks were applied. Such trade marks would include the name, logo or aspects of the packaging of the product. In some cases even the shape of the product became synonymous with a particular source. It would therefore be accurate to say that a brand comprises, at the very least the actual product, that is the name, logo and packaging of the goods and also the product shape. As Murphy and Arnold point out, with the growth of advertising, developments in technology and the emergence of affluent societies, manufacturers, or rather consumers, have tended to place greater emphasis on psychological, intangible factors in reaching their purchasing decisions rather than rational considerations. Therefore, for the purposes of this book the brand paradigm will be regarded as comprising a synthesis of these physical and aesthetic features and as far as possible the emotional effects. Our definition is thus closest to that postulated by Murphy. Thus in addition to the actual product and its overall presentation, our definition of a brand can be said to encompass the imagery used in advertising and promotional material. In some cases the brand might also symbolise a philosophy with which the producer or the brand name has become associated (as in the case of the Body Shop with its ethos of ethical trading), depending on how the brand has been positioned.

1–17 It is important to note that not all brands have developed to the same degree. For some brands the emphasis may be upon physical characteristics whereas others may depend more upon intangible aspects (perhaps as a result of the stage of development of the brand in question) or perhaps as a reflection of the market to which the product is directed or a lack of advertising and promotional support. Whatever the reason, it is important to distinguish between products (that is actual products) or nascent brands which do not attain full brand status, because they have no intangible values associated with them but are purchased for their physical characteristics only, and true brands which offer not only tangible but also intangible benefits to the consumer. Not all products may be regarded as brands. Thus the term brand, used in subsequent chapters should be understood to refer to this broader concept of an actual product together with the intangible elements that are associated with it.

1–18   As de Chernatony concludes:

"brands exist because they are of value to consumers. . . . brands act as a shorthand, in consumers' minds, of the set of functional and emotional associations of trust, so that they do not have to think much about their purchase decisions".

The more complex a product, the greater reliance consumers appear to place on the symbolic value or security value afforded by an established brand name. In this way brands (especially the vocal aspect of the brand, the brand name) become guarantees of consumer expectations, repositories for information and symbols of past experience that a consumer has of a brand and thus a shorthand reference that sums up the consumer's perception not just of the augmented product of which the brand name is part but also what the business responsible for that name stands for, especially if the brand name is the corporate name.

1–19   One implication of this understanding of brands as a shorthand in consumers' minds, is that if a new brand can successfully imitate an established brand, such that the consumer associates the set of functional and emotional values of trust, originally created in connection with the established brand, with the new brand, then it can be seen that the new brand will obtain a significant advantage at the cost of the established brand, whose sales will be diminished as a consequence.[19] In Chapter 2 we will consider how the various elements of a brand may be protected against such imitation under the existing framework of intellectual property laws and in subsequent chapters we will consider the effectiveness of such protection. Before turning to consider these issues, however, we first need to consider the nature of a brand and the distinction between marketing and branding, and also to consider briefly the evolution of brands.

The Anatomy of a Brand

1–20   In his analysis of the interrelation between the various elements of a brand, Arnold divides a brand into three constituent parts: essence, benefits and attributes. These can be illustrated as shown in Figure 2.

---

[19] This assumes that the second comer passes on to the consumer the benefit of the cost savings achieved by "free riding" on the back of the established brand. This point is discussed further in Chap. 8.

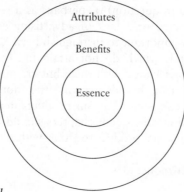

Figure 2—Source: *Arnold*

According to Arnold, the essence of a brand is "a single, simple value, easily understood and valued by consumers".[20] The essence of a brand is sometimes also referred to as "brand personality" and is said to be distinctive of the brand within its market. According to Arnold, it is towards this personality or essence that customers direct their loyalty and which is often the elusive emotional element of a brand.

1–21 The benefits are those aspects of the brand that seek to satisfy consumer "wants" and "needs". The attributes are key physical characteristics of the brand, its packaging and advertising themes. To see how these elements of essence, benefits and attributes blend together—we will consider briefly how these terms might apply to the Marlboro brand of cigarettes (Figure 3).

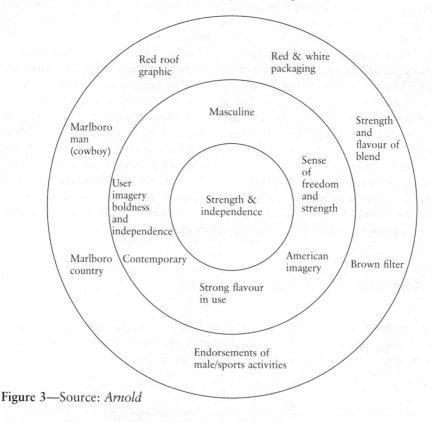

Figure 3—Source: *Arnold*

<hr>

[20] Arnold, p. 27.

From the diagram it can be seen that the fundamental characteristic of the core product (*i.e.* the actual strength and flavour of the cigarette), is only one of the benefits identified. Other benefits derive from the advertising and imagery associated with the promotion of the brand. The attributes have developed from physical aspects of the packaging and product presentation and include key aspects of marketing and promotional material that have remained constant over the life of the brand; such attributes are often referred to as "brand property".

1–22 Like Murphy, Arnold stresses that a brand is a synthesis of the product, packaging, advertising and marketing in addition to the name and logo. To be successful, he argues the theme running through these aspects should be simple, strong and attractive to consumers in the sense of providing benefits (both tangible and intangible) to the consumer, and they must be consistent.

> "A brand must be a blend of complementary physical, rational and emotional appeals. The blend must be distinctive and result in a clear personality which will offer benefits of value to consumers".[21]

The essence of strength and independence is the theme which pervades all promotional activity relating to the Marlboro brand and is cited as one of the reasons that consumers are attracted to it. The Marlboro cigarette itself, has a strong flavour (a functional attribute) and the strength and independence of the cowboy image originally used in advertising form the basis of the emotional attributes. The red and white colour of the packaging reinforces the essence of the brand since they are strong, bold, contrasting colours; the same is true of the mountain scenery used in many of the advertisements. The result is a clear and distinctive personality of strength and independence. This personality is distinct from those of competing brands of cigarettes such as Silk Cut, Benson & Hedges and JPS and thus the brand satisfies the Hankinson and Cowking definition referred to (see para. 1–07). Consistency in all forms of packaging and promotion is an important aspect of maintaining a clear and distinctive personality, if consumer confusion is to be avoided.

1–23 It is submitted that one of the reasons that the Marlboro brand is strong and successful is because the brand does not depend entirely upon the name or logo as a means of distinguishing the core product from competing products. Indeed, the whole pack is distinctive and together with the advertising used to support the brand, it encapsulates the essence of the brand, namely strength and independence.

1–24 Once a brand has become established in the marketplace the brand attributes can become powerful symbols evoking the brand personality. Competitors may seek to emulate the brand personality by creating similar new brands of their own, often imitating the physical brand attributes associated with the successful brand's packaging and advertising themes. The *Pub Squash* case[22] is just one example of such a case and this will be considered in more detail in Chapter 6. In Chapter 4 we will consider the position concerning lookalike products where, this time, retailers have tried to emulate the personality of branded products by adopting similar brand names and packaging with a view to attracting consumers who might otherwise buy the branded product. In such situations it is important to appreciate that those responsible for imitating brands do not simply use a confusing brand name but also endeavours to imitate the imagery and personality associated

---

[21] Arnold, p. 27.
[22] *Cadbury Schweppes Pty Ltd v. The Pub Squash Co. Ltd* [1981] R.P.C. 429.

with the established brand and in particular (as far as this is possible) the associations of trust established with the consumer. How this is achieved will be discussed further in Chapter 4.

THE DIFFERENCE BETWEEN BRANDING AND MARKETING

1–25   Marketing may be said by marketers to involve "a social and managerial position by which individuals and groups obtain what they need and want through creating and exchanging products and value with others."[22a] Traditionally, marketing has not sought to create "needs" or "wants",[23] these are assumed by marketing theory to exist already in our society.[24] What classical marketing seeks to do is to identify these consumer needs and wants, to create products that satisfy those needs and to communicate the availability of products that would satisfy such wants to consumers through effective use of promotional material and product positioning, that is, offering the right value product to meet consumer expectations and so satisfy consumer demands.

> "It is a basic assumption in a competitive economy that the consumer benefits from being able to choose among a wide range in the quality and price of goods and services. But once a range of alternatives is offered, he can choose rationally only if he knows the relevant differences. Acquiring all the appropriate information is in many cases too time-consuming and costly, so risks have to be taken. This is particularly so over qualities that cannot properly be checked or tested before purchase, but have to be taken on trust. How willing a purchaser is to take the risk of buying something unknown in place of something known will depend on many factors: for instance, how satisfied he is with the known, and how serious the consequences will be for him if the unknown turns out unsatisfactory. It is one thing to experiment with a washing powder, but another with a drug . . . "[25]

As this writer makes clear, purchasing a new product for the first time involves taking a risk. To reduce this risk the consumer may rely upon information about the actual product conveyed through advertising material. This material may explain whether the product will be suitable for the purpose the consumer has in mind. The consumer may still be unsure of the suitability of the product (especially if the item is expensive) and may be reassured by the use of a well known brand name, make or manufacturer. The consumer may still be in some doubt as to the suitability of the product and may look to others using it for reassurance of reliability and quality. As one writer noted[26] few people are prepared to trust their

---

[22a] Kotler *et al.*, p. 10.

[23] A human "need" is a state of felt deprivation. Humans have many complex needs including the basic physical need for shelter, clothing, food, safety, warmth, social needs of belongings and affection and personal needs for knowledge and self-expression. These needs are not invented or created by marketers, they are part of human make-up. Human wants can be described in terms of objects that satisfy needs, they can therefore be shaped by culture and personality. As society evolves the wants of its members expand. Kotler *et al.*, p. 10.

[24] In Packard's *The Hidden Persuaders* (Puffin, London, 1960) the author sought to highlight the techniques of "persuasion" through the unconscious, used by marketing companies in the USA in the 1950s and 1960s. The marketers referred to were not creating needs as such but rather exploiting, through psychological means, needs rooted in the subconscious, *e.g.* the need for security and safety, as a means of promoting the sale of new products.

[25] Cornish, p. 613.

[26] D. Cowley, *Understanding Brands*, (Kogan Page, London, 1996) p. 27.

own judgment totally in isolation without some reference to what others in the same situation believe. In each case the purchaser will be seeking to reduce or minimise the risk involved in the purchasing decision. At each stage, the marketing of the product can influence the consumer's decision making process whether it be through the provision of factual information concerning physical characteristics and qualities of the product, through after sales service or product augmentation or from the "added values" associated with a particular brand communicated through use of particular advertising imagery concerning the social status or caché of the product and its effectiveness.[27] The purpose of marketing is to communicate with the consumer about the product—to inform, reassure, and persuade the consumer to buy the product. In short, the aim of the marketing function is to reduce the risks taken by the consumer and to promote sales. Where the risks associated with purchasing many branded items, such as every day consumer goods like food, soap, washing powder etc may be low, the aim of the marketing function is to promote continued loyalty to the brand and to increase the frequency with which the brand is purchased.

1–26 Arnold distinguishes the marketing role from that of branding by reference to demand:

> "Branding is . . . inextricably linked with the central principles of marketing. Marketing is about understanding two levels of demand: needs, which define the boundaries and the critical success factors of a market; and wants, the 'extras' which are valued by consumers and are used by them to differentiate between alternative products. Branding is concerned primarily with this second level, where customer perceptions form the basis of the relationship between customer and product."[28]

Murphy agrees that branding is primarily concerned with differentiation and that branding focuses upon the relationship between the product and the consumer, and thus he seeks to distinguish branding from marketing on the basis that the former is much narrower in scope.

> "Branding consists of the development and maintenance of sets of product attributes and values which are appropriate, distinctive, protectable and coherent. Marketing is a broader function which includes branding and concerns the development and implementation of strategies for moving products from the producer to the consumer in a profitable fashion. Advertising is a narrower function within marketing which is concerned with the use of media to inform and stimulate consumers that products or services, branded or otherwise are available for them to purchase."[29]

Although the role of marketing has changed considerably during the course of the past 100 years or more, it remains a distinct business activity. Branding as such is a function of marketing (as are advertising and sales promotion) and is not synonymous with it. As Chisnall observes[30]:

---

[27] Jones, p. 30.
[28] Arnold, p. 23.
[29] Murphy, p. 3.
[30] Chisnall, p. 3.

"Marketing as an activity is not new: it has been practised in a rudimentary fashion by traders for thousands of years. But in advanced industrial economies, where specialisation of production, labour, managerial talents are widely adopted, marketing has adapted as a distinct and important area of management activity and responsibility. It has assumed the role of the entrepreneur in identifying market opportunities and relating these to the skills, productive capacity and other resources of a company".

Marketing as a separate business function evolved as part of the philosophy that recognised the importance of the consumer to the success of the business. Although such a philosophy may seem *a sine qua non* of business today it has not always been so.[31] The adoption of a consumer driven marketing philosophy resulted from amongst other things, increased competition amongst manufacturers and the change from a sellers to a buyers market. However, changes in the role of marketing and the nature of brands cannot be looked at in isolation if one is to appreciate why changes occurred and what impact they had. Therefore in order to understand how or why marketing as a function has changed we need to broaden our frame of reference.

THE DEVELOPMENT OF THE MASS MARKET

1–27   The difficulty with any analysis of change in markets themselves is that changes can be brought about as the result of many diverse factors which not only impact a market by themselves but also combine with other factors to bring about more significant changes. Such factors can include population growth, the level of employment, standards of living, changes in technology, changes in consumer attitudes, social, political and religious factors, the availability of resources, the global economy and so on. The interrelation of such factors is extremely complex therefore I do not propose to consider them in detail.[32] The aim here is simply to highlight some of the more significant changes that have occurred during the last century which have contributed in some way, to changes in patterns of supply and demand. In the next section we will consider how these changes affected the role of marketing and ultimately helped to establish a society where virtually all goods are branded goods (and most services are too) and even commodity items, such as fresh fruit are often branded (*e.g.* Outspan oranges).

1–28   By focusing upon the changes that took place in the late nineteenth and early twentieth century, I do not intend to suggest that elements of a consumer society did not exist before that date nor that the attitude of the general public

---

[31] Chisnall, p. 5.

[32] Until the 1980s there had been very little interest amongst social historians, sociologists and psychologists regarding the workings of the market and the development of consumer demand although the study of consumption is becoming increasing fashionable. Despite recent interest in the subject there has been little empirical investigation. Although a few historians (such as McKendrick, referred to below) have conducted research into some areas these tend to be limited in scope to particular product areas. For an interesting discussion of social developments see especially Benson, *The Rise of Consumer Society in Britain 1880–1980* (Longman, Harlow, 1994) ("Benson") and Fraser, *The Coming of the Mass Market 1850–1914* (Macmillan, London, 1981) ("Fraser") also McKendrick, *Birth of a Consumer Society* (Europa Publications, London, 1982); Brewer, *Consumption and the World of Goods* (Routledge, London, 1993); Stevenson, *British Society 1914–1945* (Penguin, London, 1984); Marwick, *British Society Since 1945* (Penguin, London, 1996). For an interesting discussion of the changing attitude towards commodities following the Great Exhibition see Richards, *The Commodity Culture of Victorian England* (Verso, London, 1991) ("Richards").

before that date was not at all materialistic. On the contrary, as McKendrick suggests[33]:

> "There was a consumer revolution in eighteenth-century England. More men and women than ever before in human history enjoyed the experience of acquiring material possessions. Objects which for centuries had been the privileged possessions of the rich came, within the space of a few generations, to be within the reach of a larger part of society than ever before, and, for the first time, to be within the legitimate aspirations of almost all of it. Objects which were once acquired as the result of inheritance at best, came to be legitimate pursuit of a whole new class of consumers."

Indeed McKendrick, whilst announcing the birth of a consumer society in the eighteenth century, acknowledged that there was evidence to suggest that there had been commercial change and embryonic growth in the field of consumer behaviour in even earlier periods.[34] He argues, however, that in the eighteenth century there were distinct and qualitative changes in lifestyle sufficient to amount to a commercial revolution. In the same way, I would suggest that the developments that took place during the period from the second half of the nineteenth century to the late twentieth century are important because of the significant impact they had on daily life. Whilst it is true to say that many of the changes in consumer markets and attitudes[35] that took place during this period were the result of evolution rather than revolution, it is also true that many of the developments were indeed unprecedented.[36] As Benson observes,[37] however, there is no agreement amongst historians as to when the consumer revolution came about. Indeed, putting a date on the consumer revolution is an extremely contentious issue. Neither is there any agreement as to what is meant by the term, consumer revolution, or the consequences of it.

1–29   To appreciate something of the nature of the changes that took place during this period and their impact on consumers we will look briefly at some of the changes in supply and demand.

(a) Growing demand

1–30   Benson accounts for the growth in consumer demand during the period 1880 to 1980 in three ways: (i) as a consequence of growth in the size of the population, (ii) growth in the spending power of individuals and (iii) changes in consumer taste or fashion.[38] Between 1851 and 1981 the population of Great Britain more than doubled: it grew from 20.9 million to 54.8 million. Not only did the population expand, the profile of the population also changed and wealth was redistributed following a decline in the aristocracy, and a growth in the middle class and a rise in income of the working class.[39] The trend was for family sizes to

---

[33] McKendrick, p. 1.
[34] McKendrick, p. 3.
[35] Such as the growth in the range of goods available in supermarkets and department stores and the changing consumer attitudes towards possessions and commodities (see Richards, p. 5).
[36] As in the case of the introduction of electricity and the use of mass media such as commercial radio and television. More recently, the introduction of the telephone, facsimile machine and the personal computer and the internet have done much to further the revolution in communication.
[37] Benson, p. 2.
[38] p. 11.
[39] Benson, p. 24–27.

decrease—in part as a response to better education, social conditions and better standards of living.[40] The early part of the nineteenth century witnessed the transition from a rural society to an urban one and by 1851 over 50 per cent of the population was said to live in urban areas.[41]

1-31 The growth in population was accompanied by economic growth with the result that wealth, income and free time also grew significantly.[42] As Fraser observes[43]:

> "The substantial demographic changes of the fifty years before the First World War irrevocably changed society, and undoubtedly influenced demand for goods and services. Firstly there were more people; secondly more and more of them lived in towns, thus increasing the demand for goods and services; thirdly more parents were having smaller families. Living conditions for many of the population improved greatly . . . A higher proportion of the population had homes of their own, and therefore required furnishings and fittings for these. . . . demand grew among the middle class because their expectations of what was a fitting standard for their social class increased."

Consumer demand can also be affected by changes in consumer trends, fashions and expectations.[44] Indeed, Fraser suggests (above) that demand grew among the middle class because of their rise in expectations, he also suggests that with a time lag the working class emulated the ways of the bourgeois. This tendency was encouraged he says because of "the sheer anonymity of urban life . . . Antecedents [was] less important than appearance and style of life".[45] Thus Fraser argues that the desire to emulate others was a significant change in consumer attitude which in turn led to increased demand. In contrast, Benson suggests that there are three possible explanations for changes in consumer attitude namely, manipulation, emulation and amelioration.[46]

> "The first suggests that consumers were manipulated by advertisers and other commercial interests; the second that consumers were satisfying a deep seated need to emulate their fellows; and thirdly that they were satisfying a still more deep seated need to improve the material (and other) circumstances in which they found themselves."

Whilst Benson favours the explanation of amelioration, which takes into account the consumer's desire to improve his/her standard of living, subject to financial constraints, he acknowledges that manipulation and emulation may also play a part in influencing consumer demand.[47] As has been said before, consumer motivation is a very complex subject, accordingly it is more difficult to account for why consumer demand grew than to demonstrate that it did.

---

[40] Fraser, p. 6.
[41] *ibid.*, p. 7.
[42] Benson, p. 11.
[43] p. 12.
[44] For example, until recently no market existed for male cosmetics, however, changes in male consumer attitudes towards cosmetics has given rise to the development of a new market which is now served by many established cosmetic companies.
[45] p. 12.
[46] Benson, p. 27.
[47] *ibid.*, p. 29.

(b) Changes in Supply

1–32 Axiomatic to a discussion of the growth of consumer demand is the suggestion that there must also have been changes in the supply of goods and their means of distribution since otherwise the goods would not have been available to meet the growing demand. To satisfy the increased demand, industry had to expand or be restructured and distribution systems had to become more efficient; taste had to be guided and product preferences stimulated. Changes in the fields of energy supply, manufacturing, transportation, retailing, advertising and mass communication all helped to enable industry to respond to this increased demand. We will consider briefly some of the significant changes in each of these fields.

(i) Energy

1–33 By 1910 electric lighting was just beginning to make an impact on the domestic market. The availability of electricity domestically at an affordable price revolutionised the home and electrical gadgets began to be produced for the domestic market to meet the demand for time saving devices created by the increased number of households without servants.[48] Electricity also had a significant impact on the manufacturing industry, leading to the mechanisation of factories, and was integral to the growth of mass produced goods.

(ii) Transportation

1–34 Since 1875 methods of transportation have changed beyond recognition. Horse drawn vehicles have disappeared from the streets, replaced by motorised transport of all kinds. Together the spread of the railways and the increasing number of motorised vehicles used for commercial purposes enabled manufacturers to deliver their goods direct to their customers at different locations around the country. Therefore instead of operating within a particular locality, manufacturers could begin to supply a much larger market and so take advantage of the economies of scale.[49] A further step forward in transportation came with the development of air transport following World War II. The ability to distribute goods quickly and economically over a wide area further enhanced the growth of new markets and which in turn increased the demand for more goods. Equally, the growth in international travel has led to a homogenisation of markets and tastes.

(iii) Manufacturing

1–35 Insatiable demand stimulated manufacturers to adjust their manufacturing processes so that demands could be met. Production was increased by means of mechanisation and through economies of scale. In the United States manufacturers were quicker to adjust to the growing market conditions than their United Kingdom counterparts.

> "Demand in Britain grew at a much slower rate [than America] and, therefore British Industry's adjustment to the needs of a mass market could be a great deal slower than in the United States . . . The long term result was that mass-produced goods could make their way from the United States to Britain more cheaply than some British goods could be produced, which forced British firms to look for economies of scale and to develop new approaches".[50]

---

[48] Fraser, p. 44.
[49] Stevenson, p. 112.
[50] Fraser, p. 239.

The result was:

> ". . . that, for most of the people, industry was able to offer an ever-widening range of choices for their food, their clothing, their domestic furnishings and for their entertainment . . . By 1914 it was clearly recognised that a mass market had arrived and had to be catered for".[51]

(iv) Retailing

1–36   There have been major developments in retailing since 1875. In the mid-nineteenth century shopping was limited to the corner shop, street markets and fairs, or hawkers, where most goods were purchased as commodities (*i.e.* without individual packaging or any brand name or trade mark). Goods were sold by weight/volume and were taken from unmarked containers (containers bore neither manufacturers' marks nor prices). The reputation for the quality of the goods sold very much attached to the store, and the customer relied upon the relationship of trust established with the shopkeeper as to what to purchase. As supermarkets began to replace corner stores changes took place in the way that goods were sold. The supermarket preferred the goods to be pre-packed and labelled and goods would be clearly priced in store (something that had not happened in the corner shop). The ability to buy goods in bulk from manufacturers enabled owners of chain stores to obtain better, lower prices for basic goods, which in turn enabled them to undercut the corner shop. The location of grocery shops in prime locations to catch passing trade and their long hours enabled them to build up custom quickly. A consequence of their success was the virtual disappearance of street markets, fairs and hawkers and in many cases the corner store as well.[52]

Once established, the grocery stores increased their range of stocks (mainly from imported goods) and developed their own brands of products.[53] Without the trusted shopkeeper to recommend what to purchase consumers began to rely on brand names as a means of identifying products and as signifiers of consistent quality. Although the first brand names were manufacturers names, brand names came to be used as shorthand to identify particular types of product or product features, *e.g.* Ivory became synonymous with soap that floated; Pears with transparent soap[54] It was during the inter war years that brand names such as Kellogg, Heinz, Birds, Bisto and Ovaltine became standard household names.[55]

1–37   As Benson notes[56]:

> "The growth of retailing was central to the growth of supply. It was not just that the number of people employed in trade doubled between 1851 and 1901, and increased by a further 40 per cent between 1901 and 1951. It was also that the development of co-operative, department and multiple stores enables retailing to begin to enjoy some of the economies of scale that had been pioneered by the manufacturing industry".

In relation to clothing, it was not until the turn of the twentieth century that the purchase of ready-made clothing became commonplace. Until then it was either

---

[51] Fraser, p. 239.

[52] *ibid.*, p. 94.

[53] The development of own brand products is discussed in Chap. 4, para. 4–07 *et seq.*

[54] Wilson, *The History of Unilever* (Cassell & Co. Ltd, London, 1954), p. 17.

[55] Stevenson, p. 125.

[56] Benson, p. 40.

tailor made or home made.[57] Today, it is considered exceptional to purchase clothing in a form other than ready to wear.

(v) Advertising and mass communication

1–38   Until 1922, when radio broadcasting first began, the only means of advertising products was by using print media such as posters or press advertisements.[58] Advances in printing techniques meant that posters could be produced relatively cheaply by 1848.[59] Most adverts stressed the functional benefits of the products they featured and the loyalty of customers.

1–39   The other main medium for advertisements was newspapers. Between 1833 and 1853 there was a tax on newspaper advertisements but this was repealed by Gladstone in 1853.[60] As Fraser observes[61]:

> "Newspaper editors showed little awareness of the opportunities that adver- tising offered their papers. Convention had it that nothing must break the regular columns, and there was a general agreement to ban large type. The only way to catch the eye was to repeat the firm's name endlessly or to use slogans . . ."

This is not to suggest that the advertisements used in the first half of the nineteenth century were crude or ineffective. On the contrary, Carlyle noted[62] the quality of advertising would be hard to improve, it was just that at that time the visual impact of advertisements, the graphics used and the images portrayed were rather basic by today's standards. The ability to print good graphics and photographic images of good quality and ultimately to print them in colour has transformed the world of advertising.

The invention of the cinema and later the introduction of television further revolutionised the forms of mass communication available to manufacturers and were largely responsible for the development of mass popular culture:

> "Increasingly, it was a metropolitan or transatlantic culture, based on mass consumerism, uniform products and increasingly persuasive forms of com- munication, principally, the press, radio and cinema with TV waiting in the wings. The paradox of post 1945 Britain would be the expansion and divergence of its 'highbrow' and its mass cultures".[63]

The importance of new and increasingly versatile advertising media to the development of new markets by manufacturers cannot be overstated. Indeed, the combined impact of the development of self-service grocery stores and the manufacture of prepackaged goods meant that advertising was the only means available to manufacturers to communicate directly with the consumer whereas before they had relied on the support of the shopkeeper or travelling salesman to advocate the advantages of their products over those of competitors. Further, as

---

[57] The sewing machine was invented in 1851, before that, all clothes were hand made (Fraser, p. 58).
[58] For a more detailed account of advertising history see Nevett, *Advertising in Britain* (Heinneman, London, 1982).
[59] Fraser, p. 110.
[60] *ibid.*, p. 137.
[61] Fraser, p. 137.
[62] Past and Present (1843).
[63] Stevenson, p. 443.

manufacturers recognised the growth in female purchasing power so they began to advertise their products in new ways.[64]

(vi) The Internet

1–40   Just as the invention of the internal combustion engine was instrumental in opening up new markets beyond the manufacturer's immediate locality so the invention of the personal computer and its subsequent networking through the internet has opened up the frontiers of international trade. Manufacturers can now communicate direct with consumers anywhere in the world and can respond to orders placed over the internet within seconds and, in some cases deliver the goods via the same medium. Whilst the internet does not necessarily increase supply as such it can enable businesses to supply goods to a bigger market without the need for a local presence and in that sense it increases the availability of products.

1–41   It is impossible to recite here all the changes that have taken place during the twentieth century that have contributed to the development of the mass market. The lifting of import barriers; the removal of trade restrictions and the opening up of monopolies and cartels to free market forces, have all contributed to the radical changes in the consumer environment that have undoubtedly taken place. The changes described above provide an indication only of the dramatic nature of some of the developments that have taken place and their impact on the growth of supply and demand for products. Other developments (such as the changing role of women in society, the emergence of a youth culture and the breakdown of institutional religion) although less obvious in their impact on the supply and demand of goods nonetheless had a role to play. The consumer market of the twenty-first century is thus a very different one from that in existence in 1850 and it is in part because of this change that the concept of branding has developed as it has.

THE DEVELOPMENT OF THE MODERN CONCEPT OF BRANDING

1–42   Brands as we know them today, be they Kodak, Coca-Cola, or Disney, have not always existed in their current form, that is, as a mix of tangible and intangible values. Indeed, it is only relatively recently (during the last 30 years or so) that brands, or rather brand owners, have sought to emphasise the intangible or emotional qualities associated with their brands. The historical evolution of brands from products to icons has been a slow process. The role of the brand, and indeed branding, has changed over time with changing social and economic conditions and influences and as a response to the changing role of marketing. To plot its emergence is therefore a complex process if all relevant influences are to be ascertained and understood. Such a study is beyond the scope of this book and accordingly, only a brief synopsis of the evolutionary process can be given here.

1–43   Goods and services have been bartered since human civilisation began.[65] The physical branding of products or animals to distinguish between owners or suppliers also has a long history dating back to pre-Roman civilisation. In contrast

---

[64] For example soap manufacturers began to advertise their products in new ways so that Cuticura soap was said to be a beauty aid, whilst Lifebuoy was said to prevent body odour and Lux kept skin soft and smooth (Benson, p. 48).
[65] Mercer, *Marketing* (Blackwell Publishing, Oxford, 1991), p. 7 ("Mercer").

the concept of a brand as comprising both tangible and intangible values and the emergence of a discourse on brands generally is much more recent, emerging only in the 1980s. To understand why the discourse on brands began we need to step back to look at the changing role of marketing.

1–44 Marketing as an academic discipline only emerged in its modern form with its customer focus in the 1960s.[66] It matured as a discipline in the 1970s as a result of the publication of Philip Kotler's seminal text Marketing Management in 1967. Kotler describes the "marketing management concept" as a business philosophy with a long history although its central tenets did not crystallise until the mid 1950s. It holds that:

> ". . . the key to achieving organisational goals consists in determining the needs and wants of target markets and delivering the desired satisfactions more effectively and efficiently than competitors".[67]

This marketing concept (now simply referred to as "classical marketing") rose to challenge the previous concepts of marketing which tended to focus either on production, the product or the selling process itself. Production focused marketing centres on the premise that consumers will favour those products that are available and low in cost. Supporters of this view direct their efforts to streamlining production and costs so as to be able to produce large quantities of product as widely as possible at low cost and to build market share. Such a concept holds good where demand exceeds supply, or where the product costs are high and the manufacturer is reducing costs to an affordable level. However, where supply exceeds demand as a result of competition and consumers have knowledge of the perspective merits of the products available, sales can be assumed to be lost to other suppliers as criteria other than price operate in the mind of the consumer.

1–45 Sellers that make their focus the product itself rather than the consumer seek to develop new products or improve old ones based on their merits without reference to the commercial reality of whether or not a market exists for the product in question. This philosophy can hold good where buyers are looking for quality and superior performance for some new products but there is a danger that the market will change direction causing sales to fall or new products to fail. This focus on products themselves was described as "marketing myopia" by Levitt, in his classic article on marketing, because it did not take into consideration what the customer needed or wanted.[68]

1–46 As economic conditions have changed and markets have become more saturated, so a consumer-orientated approach to marketing was needed to ensure manufacturers a market for new products that are developed. Thus the marketing management concept which combines a market focus with consumer-orientation developed.

1–47 Although the marketing management concept proved popular in the 1960s as the social and political environment continued to change in the 1970s and 1980s the concept came under criticism[69] in part, this was a result of the fact that there was no longer a competitive advantages to being sensitive to consumer needs as most businesses had adopted a consumer oriented approach, but it was also a

---

[66] Mercer, p. 7.
[67] McKitterick, *What is the Marketing Management Concept? The frontiers of marketing thought and action* (American Marketing Association, Chicago, 1957), p. 71–82.
[68] "Marketing myopia" *Harvard Business Review* July-August 1960, p. 45–56.
[69] Nilson, p. 20.

consequence of significant changes in the social and political environment which made classical marketing less relevant. Unlike the post war markets of the 1950s and 1960s there were fewer opportunities for market growth and the removal of trade barriers meant that competition for existing markets intensified. Most market sectors were considered to be fully developed. This meant that manufacturers placed greater emphasis on obtaining market share from competitors or creating new niches from existing markets. With pressure on manufacturers to increase market share at the expense of competitors (*i.e.* other manufacturers) and retailers,[70] manufacturers not only needed to distinguish their products more from those of competitors but also to defend their ground against competitors.

1–48 Although the customer focus of classical marketing was timeless it required further refinement in response to consumers increasing concern with the environment and social responsibility. It is in this context that a discourse on brands *per se* emerged in the mid to late 1980s. In this context brands were recognised as fulfilling a function beyond their initial role of indicating the origin of a product, to that of signifying product differentiation. As Aaker notes[71]:

> "Although brands have long had a role in commerce, it was not until the twentieth century that branding and brand associations became so central to competitors. In fact, a distinguishing characteristic of modern marketing has been its focus upon the creation of differentiated brands. Market research has been used to help identify and develop bases of brand differentiation. Unique brand associations have been established using product attributes, names, packaging, distribution strategies and advertising. The idea has been to move beyond commodities to branded products—to reduce the primacy of price upon the purchase decision, and accentuate the basis of differentiation."

More recently branding is also being applied to charitable organisations and services.[72]

Today, marketing academics recognise that brands are viewed by consumers as symbols of trustworthiness (more than indicators of source as such) and even describe them as having particular personalities. Indeed a resent survey found that more consumers would trust the manufacturers of the brands Heinz and Kelloggs to be fair and honest than they would trust the police and judiciary![73] The brand paradigm is virtually universally accepted by marketers. The volume of literature on branding in its widest sense has ballooned within the last five years as marketers see them as being a panacea for marketing success and valuable business assets in their own right.[74]

BRAND VALUATION

1–49 The debate concerning the value ascribed to a brand for accounting purposes began in the late 1980s when a number of corporate acquisitions

---

[70] The growth of retailers will be considered in detail in relation to the grocery sector in Chap. 4, para. 4–14.

[71] Aaker, p. 7.

[72] Mercer, p. 274

[73] Survey "Planning for Social Change 1997" carried out by The Henly Centre and quoted in *The Financial Times*, October 13, 1997.

[74] A recent study conducted by Citibank and Interbrand found that branded products can command a price premium of up to 30 per cent or more. *The Financial Times*, October 25, 1997.

involving brand owning companies hit the headlines.[75] The sums paid for the subject companies were significantly greater than the recognised values of the assets of the companies as set out in their respective balance sheets. It was said that the difference represented the value of the brand portfolios that the target companies held and in particular the brand equity. In general terms brand equity is defined in terms of the marketing effects uniquely attributable to the brand name.[76]

1–50 The first company to include on its balance sheet an independent valuation for its brands was Rank Hovis McDougall in 1988, following the failed takeover bid by Goodman Fielder Wattie.[77] In its defence of the bid Rank Hovis McDougall had relied heavily upon the power of its brands stating that the offer did not take into account the real value of these brands which, according to the figure that subsequently appeared in its balance sheet amounted to £678 million. This figure included not only brands that had been developed internally but also those acquired from third parties.

1–51 In January 1988 Grand Metropolitan Plc published its first set of accounts following its acquisition of Heublein Inc. As it did not include brand values on its balance sheet, £565 million of the £800 million paid for Heublein Inc. was written off as goodwill, which was the usual accounting practice following an acquisition. However, this made it look as though Grand Metropolitan had wasted £585 million rather then having invested it in the Smirnoff brand, the principal asset of Heublein. The purchase of Pillsbury the following year gave added cause, if it were needed, for Grand Metropolitan to rethink its practice as regards the treatment of goodwill. The result for Grand Metropolitan was a re-evaluation of value of its brands and their importance to the business of the company. In August 1988 Grand Metropolitan announced that it was intending to value its brands with a view to including these values on its balance sheet. Unlike Rank, Hovis McDougall, however, Grand Metropolitan only included on its balance sheet those brands that it had acquired, not those that had been developed internally.[78] The value of these brands were assessed at the dates of acquisition[79] based upon a discounted capitalisation of cash flow forecasts.[80]

1–52 The inclusion of brand valuations on the balance sheet caused a degree of consternation amongst accountants who regarded the practice with a degree of suspicion for two reasons: first, because the assets that the figures represented were intangible and traditionally intangible assets had been treated as forming part of the goodwill of a business; and secondly, because the capitalisation of internally generated brands "represent[ed] the resurrection of costs already written off to the

---

[75] In 1987 Grand Metropolitan Plc acquired Heublein Inc. whose main asset was the Smirnoff brand. The following year Grand Metropolitan included the brand as an asset on its balance sheet attributing to it a value of £588 million. A few months late Grand Metropolitan acquired Pillsbury for £3.2 billion of which £1.9 billion was attributed to the value of its main brands. (Figures taken from Ed Perrier, *Brand Valuation* (Premier Books, London, 3rd ed., 1997), p. 12–13. ("Brand Valuation"). At about the same time, Nestle acquired Rowntrees for $4.5 billion which represented more than five times the book value of the company (See Interbrand *World's Greatest Brands* (Mercury Books, London, 1992), p. 12.

[76] Keller "Conceptualising, Measuring, and Marketing Customer-Based Brand Equity" (1993) 57 *Journal of Marketing*, p. 1.

[77] Butterfield & Haigh "Understanding the Financial Value of Brands" September 1998, p. 15 (*IPA Report*).

[78] *Brand Valuation,* p. 12–13.

[79] *ibid.,* p. 15.

[80] Other methods of valuation also exist, namely the premium pricing technique and the royalty method. The former look to the premium that the branded product can charge over the equivalent unbranded product the latter considers what a potential licensee would pay for the privilege of using the brand name—p. 20 and following.

profit and loss account. This mean[t] that there [was] scope for creative account-ing".[81] Other objections that have been raised focus on the fact that it is difficult to identify exactly what is or should be covered by the term, brand. Should it for example, only include trade marks or should it include a broader spectrum of Intellectual Property rights? Furthermore, should the brand be separable from other aspects of the proprietor's business if it is to be identified as an asset of the business? Traditionally, accountants only treat resources as assets of a business if they give rise to future economic benefits. Those benefits must, however, be probable and the amount of the benefit must be reliably assessed. Assets are then added to the balance sheet at cost and their value is amortised over the useful life of the resource.[82] Thus the difficulty with brand valuation generally is that the economic benefit that a brand can generate cannot be guaranteed (since fashions can change which adversely affect the popularity of a brand). Indeed, adverse publicity can result in a rapid and dramatic decline in the value of the brand itself as illustrated by the sudden demise of the Ratner's brand following the derogatory comments made by the company's Managing Director.[83] Equally, assessing the value of a brand, even if it was acquired from a third party (rather than developed internally), is not an easy or uncontroversial task, although accountants and investors have developed complex formulae by which to calculate them. Identifying the useful life of the brand has its difficulties too since it is virtually impossible to predict whether a brand will still be in existence 10, 20, 40 or even 100 years from now. The ability of a brand to be stretched[84] beyond its existing product area is also a factor that can affect its value and yet the success of the extended product is by no means guaranteed. But, the desire for businesses to attribute a financial value to the brands as assets in themselves is indicative of the change in attitude that has taken place as regards the role of a brand.

1–53   One of the consequences of formally recognising the financial value of brands has been that it has changed the mindset of investors, analysts and accountants and other business strategists. As one writer observed[85]:

> "The 'brands on the balance sheet' debate has been instrumental in forcing many people in the company—investors, analysts, accountants, followed by general managers and marketers—to focus on those assets which constitute the true worth of many businesses. What began as a narrow balance sheet exercise has developed into techniques that enable companies to effectively manage their major assets—their brands."

Although in the late 1980s many brand-owning companies appointed junior brand managers to take custody of their brands and to make the strategic decisions regarding marketing activities and the future development of the brands in their charge, in the 1990s, as companies have begun to realise the financial value of their brands the responsibility for brand management has moved to more senior managers, often to board directors.

---

[81] *IPA Report,* p. 16.
[82] *Brand Valuation,* p. 74–79.
[83] In April 1991 Gerald Ratner, the Managing Director of the jewellery chain Ratners, made some ill-judged comments about the quality of some of the group's products and customers which led to a significant downturn in the company's business. (*Financial Times,* December 29, 1999).
[84] Brand stretching is discussed further in Chap. 5.
[85] *Brand Valuation,* p. 168.

"One of the recent key shifts in management is ownership and responsibility for the brand or brands. Brand management can no longer be viewed as the sole purpose or responsibility of the marketing department. It makes little sense to hand over responsibility for what are often the 'corporate crown jewels' to a junior brand manager. It is for this reason that chief executive officers . . . are increasingly assuming the charge of being brand stewards . . ."[86]

Such senior brand stewards are also well placed to ensure that corporate strategy is consistent with the ethos of the brand, which in turn can help to reinforce the brand image.

1–54 The Accounting Standards Board (the body responsible for setting the standards used by the accountancy profession in the United Kingdom) has yet to finalise the standard to be set regarding the valuation of goodwill and intangible assets.[87] Despite this, the valuation of brands and the recognition that, in many cases, they represent a company's most significant financial assets has already come a long way since brand valuations were first introduced on balance sheets. However, no agreement has yet been reached as to how brands should be valued and whether brands internally developed should be treated in the same way as those acquired from third parties,[88] there has been growing recognition of the proposition that a brand has a value separate from the goodwill of the business[89] and that, unlike goodwill, the value of a brand should not automatically be written off over time since brands can have an indeterminate life.

CONCLUSION

1–55 A brand is more than an "actual product". Whereas an actual product can be a physical object, a brand can be said to comprise both tangible and intangible elements. A brand can be viewed from the manufacturer's (input) perspective or a consumer's (output) perspective. If viewed from the input perspective, a brand can be said to encompass the name, sign, symbol, shape of the goods or its packaging (or a combination of these features), marketing themes, advertising material and the overall presentation of the product. This holistic understanding of a brand is sometimes described as the brand's "gestalt".

1–56 Traditionally, one function of the brand name was to indicate the source of the goods by acting as a trade mark (in the general sense of the term), but according to research[90] consumers today are not primarily concerned with source as with minimising risk. Whilst this may not hold true of all consumers, and all product types, it is particularly pertinent in situations involving complex products where consumers either do not have the time, or perhaps the inclination or ability,

---

[86] *Brand Valuation*, p. 7.
[87] The proposal is currently in draft form—Financial Reporting Exposure Draft 12.
[88] Both the ASB and the International Accounting Standards Committee are in the process of developing standards to deal with the inclusion of intangible assets, including brands, in financial statements. The process is, however, taking a considerable time. The projects began in 1989 and the proposals are still in draft form! (*Brand Valuation*, p. 73 and following.)
[89] By way of example, Gucci reputedly paid Sanofic $70 million for control of the intellectual property rights (including the YSL brand) in addition to the $1 billion paid for the business which cannot be explained only in terms of the cost of registering such rights. Equally, the sale of the Rolls Royce brand name (separate from the business itself) in July 1998 for £40 million is indicative of the values attributed to brands *per se*.
[90] De Chernatony.

to evaluate product differences. Too great an emphasis on the identification of source *per se* as the primary function of branding distorts the very nature of the brand.

1–57   Consumers more frequently refer to brands as names and logos because they are quick, shorthand reference tools for knowledge and trust enabling the consumer to access holistic entities or images of the brand in their mind and thus to buy brands with little thought.[91] A brand is distinct from a trade mark in that a brand incorporates the total visual and emotional representation of the augmented product and its associated marketing whereas a trade mark is simply (in legal terms) an indication of the manufacturing source of the product albeit that through use, the trade mark becomes a cue for the brand.

1–58   Branding has grown in importance as technology has become more readily available to both large and small enterprises, thus reducing disparities in the quality of the naked product between competing manufacturers. Few companies can therefore maintain their advantage over competitors based upon the superiority of the naked product alone. Thus branding, with its emphasis on consumer wants in terms of both tangible and intangible benefits, offers companies a means of differentiation.

> ". . . with the proliferation of consumer goods in virtually every product-category today, and increasingly in industrial and service sectors as well, brands help us to find what it is we are looking for in a sea of apparent sameness . . . . Brands facilitate product or service specification, and allow customers to simplify choice and, ultimately, their selection. This is particularly important where actual tangible product differences are subtle, almost non-existent or invisible, such as in many areas of high technology, telecommunications, and in the very near future, utilities."[92]

By building brand loyalty through promotional activities, brand owners are able to maintain or even increase market share and as a result maintain or increase profits. This is particularly true of low technology static markets[93] such as fast moving consumer goods (FMCG), especially in the food and drink industry. Whilst in more high technology areas companies have still sought to maintain their competitive advantage by relying upon product quality and innovation, few companies in the food and drink industries have introduced truly innovative products in recent years.[94] The tendency instead has been to develop improvements or variations (line extensions) of existing product lines. The danger for the manufacturer, however, is that these improvements and line extensions can be quickly copied by competitors and the advantage gained is quickly lost.

> ". . . in mature markets in which competitors can easily imitate product developments or packaging improvements branding provides consumers with

---

[91] De Chernatony. 2 Dall'Olmo Riley 'The Chasm between managers' and consumers' views of brands: the experts' perspectives' (1997) 5 *Journal of Strategic Marketing* at p. 99.

[92] *Brand Valuation*, p. 5.

[93] That is, markets where the demand for goods remains reasonably constant as in the case of shampoo say, where the technological differences between different brands of shampoo are small and demand is consistent.

[94] Even in the high technology markets such as computers, manufacturers are finding that the market is so highly competitive that branding is one of the best means available to distinguish the products of one manufacturer from those of another. The computer company Compaq is one company that has shifted its marketing emphasis in recent years from product superiority to brand perception. (*Brand Valuation*, p. 6).

a basis for choice [*i.e.* product differentiation] and companies with an opportunity for sustained competitive advantage."[95]

1–59 The well publicised dispute between the retailer J. Sainsbury plc and the Coca-Cola Company[96–97] has shown that two actual products that are very similar in terms of physical appearance and content can continue to sell with a price differential. If the Coca-Cola brand had no perceived "added value" in the eyes of consumers (*i.e.* intangible benefits) it would not continue to sell at the higher price. Its continued success is testimony to the fact that consumers' believe that the product has a value beyond that of the own label equivalent; a value for which they are prepared to pay a price premium. It may be hard to define what this "added value" is, since each consumer may perceive it differently, but the fact that it does exist cannot be denied.

1–60 Brands are socio-economic phenomena that have evolved rapidly in the last 100 years due to changes *inter alia* in consumer attitudes and in the economic and social climate. Static markets with few opportunities for growth have given rise to increasing competition between manufacturers of ostensibly similar products and branding has developed as a means of both differentiating brands and enhancing the perceived value of products to consumers. Strong brands have established valuable brand equity (separate from the goodwill of the business) which can be (and in many cases have been) valued and identified in company balance sheets.

1–61 Brands are not, however, immortal as some have suggested. Indeed the failure to invest in advertising, promotion and product development or the unfortunate results of adverse publicity can lead to the devaluation of a brand and ultimately to its death, as in the case of the Ratner's brand.

1–62 In the future we are likely to see continued growth in the internationalisation of brands. The operation of the single European market has brought about changes to the way in which brands are presented so that a single brand name is often used throughout the E.U. where before a number of different names would have been used (*e.g.* in relation to the confectionary brand Snickers which was previously known as Marathon in the United Kingdom and Snickers in France). A further factor contributing to the global spread of brands is the erosion of cultural distinctiveness, particularly between the United Kingdom and the United States. The dramatic growth of the internet which provides consumers and businesses with the ability to trade and promote their businesses using a single world-wide forum will increase this process of internationalisation. For the manufacturer able to take advantage of these opportunities for global trade, its market will expand and other manufacturers will lose their market as a consequence. Ultimately, there will be a homogenisation of geographical markets, such that the same brands will be available everywhere. As one writer noted:

"With converging technologies, static markets and increasingly affluent and discriminating consumers, everything points to the intangibles becoming ever more important to the brand equation."[97]

Indeed, recent years have witnessed the expansion of strong brand names from one category of goods to another as brand owners recognise that it can be more cost

---

[95] Hankinson & Cowking, p. 173.
[96–97] Discussed in detail in Chap. 4, para. 4–21 *et seq.*
[98] Arnold, p. 23.

effective to use an existing brand name than to develop a new name for a new product.[99] Brands, it is said, are no longer used simply to sell products; as in the case of Nike or The Body Shop they now offer consumers an "attitude" or a philosophy of life, increasing the emphasis on the intangible nature of the brand concept. Indeed, according to one newspaper report[1]:

> "Nike is much more than a pair of trainers: it is about personal empowerment".

Such is the power associated with brands that even traditional business sectors such as banking and financial services which have in the past ignored overt branding now find themselves in direct competition with more brand conscious businesses. Supermarkets, for example, have expanded their original businesses into new product areas on the strength of the goodwill and the degree of trust associated with their established brand names and all that they symbolise to consumers. Given that for many businesses today their brand is their most valuable asset, no business can afford to ignore the need to protect its brand from either direct imitation or the consequences of dilution.[2] In the next chapter we will consider how brands can be protected from copying and imitation using intellectual property laws.

---

[99] This is discussed further in Chap. 5, para. 5–14.
[1] *The Financial Times*, October 17, 1997.
[2] A concept explored further in Chap. 4, para. 4–66 *et seq.*

CHAPTER 2

The Legal Framework

INTRODUCTION

2–01 In Chapter 1 we looked at the marketing approach to brands and how the concept of branding has developed. In this chapter we move on to consider the legal approach to brands. The chapter is divided into three parts. In Part I, the various legal means by which brands can be protected against unauthorised imitation are set out. We will see that the law does not recognise a brand *per se* and that there is no single, unitary law that provides protection for all aspects of a brand. Despite this, various established intellectual property laws can be relied upon to provide a tapestry of protection for different aspects of a brand. We will, therefore, consider a range of intellectual property rights that offer a measure of protection albeit for differing periods of time and against different activities. A brief account of the historical development of the various rights will be given to indicate how the rights have evolved as this can help to shed light on how the rights are applied and interpreted by the courts.

2–02 The object of Part I is to raise the reader's awareness of the various rights available to the brand owner, to identify their basic principles and key features and to highlight the degree of overlap between them.

As United Kingdom law and its interpretation is increasingly influenced by international agreements and treaty obligations, a brief outline will also be given of the various international agreements that affect brand protection.

2–03 The emphasis in this book is on the application of trade mark law principles to the various facets of brand protection. Accordingly, in Part II we will consider the historical development of trade mark registration. As part of this analysis we will look at the differences between what marketers describe as a "brand" (as defined in Chapter 1) and what lawyers regard as a "trade mark" and discuss the consequences of this distinction. We will see that although the terms trade mark and brand were virtually synonymous in 1875, the notion of a trade mark, and indeed a brand, has changed and the two can no longer be regarded as the same. Furthermore, it is suggested that because of this change in the nature of a brand and the traditional concept of a trade mark there are now shortfalls in the protection available to branded products. These shortfalls will be explored in more detail in subsequent chapters.

2–04 An American lawyer, Frank Schechter, once said that the only rational basis for protecting trade marks was in order to protect the distinctiveness of a mark.[1] In his article analysing trade mark protection, Schechter sought to highlight the various functions of a trade mark concluding that one of several functions worthy of protection, but previously neglected, was an advertising function in relation to which the issue of the distinctiveness of the mark was paramount.

---

[1] "The Rational Basis of Trademark Protection" (1927) 40 Har.L.R. 813 ("Rational Basis").

Despite the passing of more than 70 years since the publication of his seminal article, debate continues as to what is the true function of a trade mark: is it purely to indicate manufacturing source or is there more to it than that? In Part II we will look at the role of a trade mark as understood by the courts and legal writers and consider whether the function of a trade mark has changed since trade marks were first granted legal recognition. We will also look at the extent to which any such changes have been recognised by legislation.

2–05 Continuing with our focus on the registration of trade marks, in Part III we will look in further detail at the essential elements of a trade mark and the threshold required for registration. We will also consider briefly the absolute grounds for refusing to register a trade mark.

2–06 Just as in Chapter 1 the object was to introduce marketing concepts that will be referred to in later chapters, so in this chapter the aim is to introduce legal concepts as they apply to brands and to clarify the distinction between brands and trade marks. This distinction is a product of developments in the marketplace concerning the manner in which branded products are marketed and sold (as discussed in Chapter 1) and changes in what the function of a trade mark is said to be. The consequences of this distinction and its impact on how the courts interpret the various intellectual property rights as they apply to branded products will be explored further in later chapters.

PART I: THE INTELLECTUAL PROPERTY FRAMEWORK

2–07 As Cornish observes,[2] intellectual property is an expanding area of law. Although patents can trace their origins back to the time of Elizabeth I and copyright was first made the subject of statutory protection in 1710 not all intellectual property ("IP") rights have such noble ancestry. Indeed, during the course of the past decade a plethora of other rights have been created.[3] In each case the challenge has been to find an acceptable balance between protecting the position of the proposed right holder whilst retaining a competitive economy. Whether the right balance between adequate protection and effective competition has been achieved is a source of continuing debate in any discussion concerning the enhanced scope of intellectual property rights. In the 1986 White Paper on Intellectual Property and Innovation[4] it was said that:

> ". . . we must ensure that intellectual property rights strike the appropriate balance between, on the one hand, protection which ensures an adequate reward for authors and creators and, on the other hand, access to creative ideas in ways which stimulate competition and allow the use of modern technology."

Intellectual Property laws as a whole are not therefore static but rather a dynamic force evolving over time in response to evidence of over or under protection, taking into account the competing demands of commercial interests as against those of their competitors, as the legislature sees fit. The current state of the law thus

---

[2] Cornish, Chap. 3.
[3] For example, unregistered design rights, database rights, rights in semiconductor chip topographies to name but a few.
[4] Cm. 9712 at para. 3b.

represents a balance reached at a particular point in time. As circumstances change, technology develops and new situations arise so the position needs to be reassessed and as gaps in protection emerge they need to be filled if the balance is to be maintained. It is not simply a question of responding to the demands of industry but as Cornish explains[5] "the prevailing sense of what is just" also needs to be taken into account.

2–08 Whilst focusing on the subject of brand protection it is not necessary (nor does space permit us) to be concerned with the development of all forms of I.P. rights. I will therefore limit our discussion to those rights likely to apply to branded products[6] rather than to particular areas of technology. Our discussion will therefore focus on the primary forms of I.P. protection namely, patents, copyright, designs (registered and unregistered), passing off, registered trade mark law and the law of confidence. In order to aid continuity I will, where possible, mention the international treaties that affect the various national rights as the rights are discussed but will leave discussion of the scope of these international agreements until all the I.P. rights have been introduced. The question of European harmonisation and the emergence of supra-national rights, such as the Community Trade Mark will be considered at the end of this section.

(a) National rights

(i) Patent protection

2–09 Patents can be relied upon to provide monopoly protection in respect of new product innovations where the innovation involves either a development of existing technology or the invention of new technology. The innovation may relate to an article of manufacture or involve a process of manufacture, provided that it meets the requirements of section 1 of the Patents Act 1977 (see para. 2–14).

2–10 Patents for inventions have been granted regularly since the beginning of the sixteenth century but it was not until 1852 that the first major piece of legislation on patents was enacted by Parliament.[7] The grant of letters patent (as they were known), gave the recipient exclusive, monopoly rights, often of unlimited duration. The Statute of Monopolies (1623) attempted to curtail this grant of Court patronage for inventions except for those granted in respect of new inventions, which would continue to be granted but in future would be limited in duration to 14 years. A patent was ordinarily granted to the first inventor of any manner of manufacture.[8] Although the Statute of Monopolies sought to limit the grant of patents to new inventions and methods of manufacture, applicants still sought to obtain patents for existing inventions, and those introduced from abroad. The case of *Darcey v. Allien*[9] concerned the revocation of a patent granted in

---

[5] Cornish, p. 11.
[6] Whilst it is possible that certain I.P. rights, such as the database right, might apply to the technology incorporated in branded products or services such as the Lexis legal database, the issues raised in this regard apply to particular product categories incorporating that particular technology and are of limited application to brands as a whole. I will therefore focus only upon those IP rights that can be said to apply more generally to brands rather than to particular industries or product categories.
[7] For a detailed and interesting account of the history and development of the patent system see Macleod, *Inventing the Industrial Revolution* (Cambridge University Press, Cambridge, 1988) ("Macleod"); for an interesting account of developments relating to patents in the nineteenth century see Coulter, *Property In Ideas: The Patent Question in Mid-Victorian Britain* (The Thomas Jefferson University Press, Kirksville, 1991) ("Coulter"). For a shorter account of patent developments see *Terrell on the Law of Patents* (Sweet & Maxwell, London, 14th Ed., 1994) ("Terrell") at Chap. 3.
[8] s.6.
[9] (1602) 6 *Coke's Reports* by Thomas & Fraser 159.

relation to playing cards on the ground that it was not a new invention at the time that the patent was granted. The application for revocation succeeded.

2–11 The requirement to provide a detailed description of the invention (known as the specification[10]) limiting the scope of the patent developed in the eighteenth century as a result of the practice of depositing descriptions of inventions at the Court of Chancery as a means of proving the date of the invention.[11]

2–12 Despite various unsuccessful attempts to reform the patent laws in the years 1793 to 1826 and throughout the 1830s it was not until 1852 that the law was changed significantly by the passing of the Patent Law Amendment Act. Coulter suggests that the impetus for the passing of the Act in that year was a result of the government's decision to sponsor an international exhibition in 1851 which had given rise to fears that British inventions would be inadequately protected and as a consequence would be copied with impunity by foreign companies.[12] Parliament had, as a consequence, passed legislation in 1851 granting temporary protection to all unpatented items exhibited at the Great Exhibition. The following year the Patent Law Amendment Act was passed. As Coulter observes[13]:

> "The Patent Law Amendment Act of 1852 began the modernization of British patent administration, bringing it from the sixteenth into the nineteenth century."

The Act did not revolutionise the patent system but it did simplify the procedures involved and set in train a number of procedures that remain to this day an integral part of the patent process, for example the requirement to file a formal specification with the application, and also the allocation of a priority date from which the invention is protected once the patent is granted. Although the Act stated that the application would be examined this was simply a formality and did not amount to an assessment of the validity of the invention.[14] The need to examine the invention for the purposes of novelty was recognised in the Patents Act 1902, following the realisation that many of the patents granted at that time were in respect of inventions that were not actually new at all.[15]

2–13 The patent system has been subject to continued reform since 1902 culminating most recently in the Patents Act 1977. The current law of patents is regulated by the Patents Act 1977 (the "1977 Act") which consolidated previous patent law and the Copyright, Designs and Patents Act 1988 which introduced various amendments to procedure in relation to infringement actions.[16] The 1977 Act introduced a number of significant changes into British patent practice. The changes aimed to align the British patent system with those of other European countries in accordance with the terms of the European Patent Convention

---

[10] The Patents Act 1977 states that the specification must disclose the invention in a manner "which is clear enough and complete enough for the invention to be performed by a person skilled in the art" (s.14). It must define the matter for which protection is sought, be clear and concise and be supported by the description.

[11] Coulter, p. 27.

[12] *ibid.*, p. 39.

[13] *ibid.*, p. 71.

[14] *ibid.*

[15] Cornish notes at, p. 114 that in 1901 the Fry Committee demonstrated that 40 per cent of patents granted were in respect of inventions already described in earlier specifications see BPP1901 (Cd506 Cd530) XXIII.

[16] In particular, the CDPA 1988 (ss.287 and 291) enables infringement and revocation actions to be brought in a County Court with special jurisdiction rather than in the High Court.

(discussed below at paras 2–79 to 2–80). It also incorporated the terms of the Patent Co-operation Treaty (discussed below at paras 2–76 *et seq*).

2–14   In accordance with section 1 of the 1977 Act, to be patentable an invention must be new, involve an inventive step, be capable of industrial application and not be excluded by subsections (2) and (3). It is therefore possible to patent both completely new and developing technologies provided that they meet the thresholds of novelty and inventiveness and are not excluded by section 1(2) and (3). Set out in section 1(2) and (3) are non-exhaustive lists of non-patentable material. The lists include, *inter alia*, literary, dramatic, musical and artistic works and any aesthetic creation, and also computer software.[17]

2–15   Once granted a patent is valid for a period of 20 years from the date of publication of the grant, subject to payment of renewal fees. Under certain circumstances it may be possible to extend this period for a further five years following the grant of a Supplementary Protection Certificate.[18]

2–16   Although the term of patent protection is much shorter than that for copyright its scope is much broader in that independent creation of a patented invention in ignorance of the patent's existence will not avoid a finding of infringement whereas it will for copyright. Like copyright, however, it is possible to infringe a patent directly or indirectly, by making, disposing of, or offering to dispose of, using, importing or keeping a patented product or supplying an essential element of the invention.[19] If the invention is a process, use of the process will amount to infringement as will dealings in the products of a process. Once the patent period has expired, competitors are free to exploit the patent provided that they do not infringe any subsequent patent for improvements or modifications.

(ii) Copyright protection

2–17   Copyright laws may be relied upon by a brand owner to prevent, *inter alia*, the copying in a material form of a substantial part of a copyright work but only to the extent that it is expressed in a tangible form. For example in relation to the advertising theme of a brand, its packaging style, label contents, graphics and user imagery, etc.

2–18   Copyright, which is primarily a right against unauthorised reproduction, arises automatically without the need for registration or formalities of any kind and typically lasts for the life of the author plus a further 70 years.[20] The longer period of protection compared to patents is frequently justified on the ground that the scope of protection is much narrower than that for patents.[21]

2–19   The current copyright law has its roots in the Statute of Anne of 1710 although the law has been revised substantially since then.[22] Before the introduction of the statute (which itself was the result of extensive lobbying by members of the

---

[17] These particular works would ordinarily be covered by copyright or design protection.
[18] Patents (Supplementary Protection Certificate for Medicinal Products) Rules 1992 S.I. 1992 No. 3162. The aim of the Supplementary Protection Certificate ("SPC") is to compensate the owner of the patent for lost patent life whilst obtaining regulatory approval of the patented product is sought. For further information on SPCs see Terrell at para. 3.67.
[19] s.60, Patents Act 1977.
[20] s.12, CDPA 1988.
[21] For an impassioned argument against harmonisation of this kind see Jacobs J. "The Stephen Stewart Memorial Lecture: Industrial Property — Industry's Enemy?" [1997] 1 I.P.Q. at 3.
[22] For a more detailed account of the development of copyright law see Cornish, Chap. 9 or Laddie *et al*, pp. 18–24.

book trade[23]) the Stationer's Guild had a royal monopoly on the printing of certain books, but with the removal of the monopoly the booksellers found themselves vulnerable to "pirate" editions of certain works and it was this that led to calls for statutory protection. The current law of copyright is set out in the Copyright Designs and Patent Act 1988 (as amended).

2-20   Copyright arises automatically on the creation *inter alia* of an original literary, dramatic, musical or artistic work, sound recording, film and broadcast.[24] For the purposes of this discussion the primary areas of interest are literary[25] and artistic[26] works as aspects of brand appearance ("get-up"), packaging and advertising can be protected under these categories. Unlike patents, the threshold for copyright protection is very low: all that is required being that the literary or artistic work be "original" in the sense of "not copied"[27] and that either the work be first published in Britain, or its dependent territories or the author be a qualified person as prescribed by section 153 of the CDPA 1988 and Orders in council thereunder. It is also an essential requirement that the work be "fixed" in a tangible form (that is, recorded in writing or otherwise).[28] Broad concepts and general ideas *per se* are not protected by copyright.[29]

2-21   Copyright in a work is infringed, *inter alia*, if a substantial part of the work is reproduced in any material form.[30] Exactly what amounts to a substantial part of a work is a question of fact. It has been said that the question of whether the defendant has taken a substantial part of the plaintiff's work depends more on the quality of what has been taken than the quantity.[31] One approach adopted by the courts when determining whether a substantial part has been taken has been to distinguish between idea and expression and to state that the idea may be copied but not the expression.[32] The difficulty here, however, is differentiating between the two.[33] In relation to a computer program, for example (which is regarded as a literary work), distinguishing between elements of idea and expression can be extremely difficult, leading to complex methods of analysing the original and "infringing" works in order to determine whether or not a substantial part of the original work has been taken.[34] The complexities of such an analysis have led some authors to challenge the entire notion.[35]

2-22   As with other intellectual property rights copyright was originally limited in its application to works of British origin, later however, as a result of international treaties such as the Berne Convention of 1886 foreign works published in Britain, or its dependent territories were accorded the same protection as that given to British works. (This is known as the principle of national treatment).[36]

---

[23] For an interesting account of the birth of copyright law and the struggle concerning the grant of a property right see Rose, *Authors & Owners — The Invention of Copyright* (Harvard University Press, Cambridge, 1993).
[24] ss.1-6 CDPA 1988.
[25] Under s.3(1) CDPA 1988 a literary work means "any work, other than a dramatic or musical work, which is written, spoken or sung, and includes (a) a table or compilation, (b) a computer program, and (c) preparatory design material for a computer program . . .".
[26] s.4 CDPA 1988 states than an artistic work means "(a) a graphic work, photograph, sculpture or collage, irrespective of artistic quality, . . . (c) a work of artistic craftsmanship".
[27] *University of London Press v. University Tutorial Press* [1916] 2 Ch. 601 at 608.
[28] Although this is only necessary for some works.
[29] *LB Plastics Ltd v. Swish Products Ltd* [1979] R.P.C. 551 at 629.
[30] s.17 CDPA 1988.
[31] Lord Reid in *Ladbroke v. William Hill* [1964] 1 W.L.R. 273 at 276.
[32] Cornish, p. 416.
[33] *Nichols v. Universal Pictures* 45 F. 2d. 119 (1930 CA 2nd Cir.).
[34] *Computer Associates Inc v. Altai Inc* 982 F. 2d. 693 (1992 2nd Cir.).
[35] Laddie *et al*, p. 2.
[36] s.160 CDPA 1988; Berne Convention Art. 5.

(iii) Design protection

2–23   The design of an article can be protected in different ways, under different legal regimes, depending upon the nature of the design.[36a] If for example, the design has aesthetic appeal and is applied industrially it may be possible to register the design under the Registered Designs Act 1949 (as amended) ("RDA"). If, on the other hand, the design is purely functional and has no aesthetic appeal it may be possible to rely upon the design right created by the CDPA 1988.[37] Alternatively, if the article is considered to be a work of artistic craftsmanship, it may be possible to obtain protection under section 4(1)(c) of the CDPA 1988. Depending upon which legal regime is applicable so the rights of the owner vary and the scope of protection differs. We will consider each of these rights in turn.

2–24   Registered designs   According to Laddie *et al*[38]:

> "Registered design law is directed at affording reward and protection to those who expend significant time and effort in giving visual, and therefore customer, appeal to articles which would have a function and value even without the design."

Section 1 of the RDA defines what is regarded as a design (for the purposes of registration) and what is excluded from protection under the RDA. A "design" is said to refer to:

> "features of shape, configuration, pattern or ornament applied to an article by any industrial process, being features which in the finished article appear to and are judged by the eye".

The section goes on to exclude from the scope of protection methods or principles of construction, and features of shape or configuration which are either dictated by the function that the article has to perform or are dependent upon the appearance of another article of which the intended article is to form a part (known as the "must match" exception). The section stresses the importance of the aesthetic appeal of the article and in section 1(3) it states that a design shall not be registered if the appearance of the article is not material, that is:

> "if aesthetic considerations are not normally taken into account to material extent by persons acquiring or using articles of that description".

Thus it is not possible to register purely functional articles, that is articles without any aesthetic appeal, or articles that are components since these will fall outside the definition of design unless they form part of the exterior of the article.[39]

2–25   Whilst the nature of a design as comprising features of shape, configuration, pattern or ornament is relatively easy to identify (the terms, shape and configuration being regarded as synonymous[40] as are pattern and ornament), the

---

[36a] For a detailed analysis of design law see Suthersanen, *Design Law in Europe* (Sweet & Maxwell, London, 1999) and Laddie *et al*, pp. 1045–1056.

[37] s.213.

[38] p. 1059.

[39] Although it is possible to protect parts of articles, in order to obtain registration it is necessary that the part be available for sale separately. On what is meant by "made and sold separately", see *Ford Motor Co. Ltd & Iveco Fiat's Design Application* [1994] R.P.C. 545.

[40] Laddie *et al*, p. 1061.

requirement that a design must have aesthetic appeal has challenged judicial thinking. Although the threshold for eye appeal is particularly low in that it does not require an assessment of artistic merit, it can nonetheless be difficult to demonstrate that aesthetic considerations are such that they are normally taken into account to a material extent by consumers of the product in question.

2–26 It is, however, important to remember that the RDA grants a monopoly to the owner of the registration in the design as applied to the article and not in the article itself.[41] A design is therefore often referred to as a capricious addition to an article with visual effect to distinguish it from functional aspects of a design which are those aspects which are intended to enable the article to perform a particular function.

2–27 To obtain the benefit of a design registration the designer, or the person who commissioned the design, must apply to the Design Registry for registration before the design has been made public by commercial exploitation.[42] At the time of filing the application the applicant must indicate the article or set of articles to which the design is applied and must also provide a statement of novelty which acts to limit the scope of the registration by identifying the particular features of the design which are considered to be novel.[43] Once filed, the application is examined for registrability before a certificate is issued granting protection for an initial period of five years extendable (subject to the payment of renewal fees) to a maximum of 25 years.[44]

2–28 A registered design will be infringed by making, importing, selling or offering for sale an article in respect of which the design is registered or a design not substantially different therefrom.[45] Registration of a design will therefore enable the proprietor to prevent not only the importation and sale of identical products but also the sale of products that are not substantially different. Once again the question of substantiality will depend on the facts of each case and, to some extent, depends upon the aesthetic sensibilities of the court determining the issue.[46] In some cases this has meant that the infringer must take virtually all the features of the design to amount to an infringement whereas in others, it may be sufficient if the alleged infringer has only taken a few of the most significant features of the design registration. It is important to appreciate that unlike copyright, designs are infringed by the independent creation of an identical design whereas copyright is only infringed by unauthorised reproduction. Like copyright however, registration of a design does not protect the idea *per se* but only the design as applied to the article referred to in the application.

2–29 From what has been said above, it can be seen that registered designs bear many similarities to patents whilst also having a number of features associated with copyright. In part this can be explained by reference to the historical development of registered designs. As we have already seen the first copyright Act was introduced in 1710 and this provided a measure of protection to literary works. In 1734 it was extended to works of art (engravings only) and in 1787 the first Designs Act was passed.[47] The aim of this Act was to provide limited copyright

---

[41] *Clarke's Design* (1896) 13 R.P.C. 351 at 358.

[42] If the design is made public before the application is filed this can lead to a loss of rights.

[43] The general statement of novelty frequently used in support of design applications is "novelty is claimed in the shape and configuration, pattern and ornament of the design as applied to the article shown in the representation".

[44] s.8 RDA.

[45] s.7 RDA.

[46] Laddie *et al*, p. 1205.

[47] For further information regarding history and development of design protection, see Laddie *et al*, pp. 1045–1056.

protection to those engaged in textile design and printing. The protection was extremely limited.

2–30 Prior to the Designs Act of 1839 there was no requirement to register designs in order to obtain protection. The second Designs Act of 1839[48] not only provided for the establishment of a designs register but also extended protection for the first time to articles of manufacture, and in particular the shape and configuration of any such article.[49]

2–31 In 1842 a further Designs Act was passed replacing earlier legislation. The new statute further refined the registration procedure and the scope of the registered proprietor's rights in the event of infringement. The category of registrable designs was ostensibly the same as that established under the 1839 Act (except that it was confined to designs for the purposes of ornament) with the limitation that designs such as sculptures which were protectable under the Sculpture Copyright Acts of 1797 and 1814 were excluded from the scope of protection. The scope of registration was further extended in 1843 by a new Act which permitted registration of new and original designs for any article having reference to some purpose or utility. This enabled registration of designs composed of functional features and not purely aesthetic designs.

2–32 Design legislation continued to be refined and eventually a new statutory code was introduced in 1883. By this time it had become a requirement of registration that a statement of novelty be filed with the design. Although further refinements were introduced over the course of the next 50 years it was not until 1949 that the law was overhauled completely with the passing of the RDA.

2–33 Although registered design law shared a common origin with copyright, over the years the changes in legislation have drawn more of a distinction between the two forms of protection. For example, the Copyright Act of 1911 attempted to define sharply the boundary between the two rights by excluding from the scope of copyright protection designs capable of being registered (subject to certain exceptions). section 22(1) stated that copyright would not subsist in:

> ". . . designs capable of being registered under the Patents and Designs Act 1907, except designs which, though capable of being so registered, are not used or intended to be used as models or patterns to be multiplied by any industrial process".

Provisions such as these that seek to draw a distinction between what is capable of protection by way of copyright by reference to what was registrable under the Designs Act, are a feature of the Copyright Acts of 1911, 1956 and the Design Copyright Act of 1968. A further feature of such excluding provisions was that they required an assessment of the intention of the original artist in order to ascertain the purpose for which the design was intended.

2–34 One case where the original intention of the artist/designer proved pivotal in securing copyright protection was *King Features Syndicate Inc v. O & M Kleeman*.[50] In this case copyright in the original "Popeye" cartoon strip was relied upon to prevent the sale of three dimensional representations of the character "Popeye" in the form of brooches, etc. The result of this case was that copyright in

---

[48] The first Designs Act of 1839 broadened the scope of the existing system of design protection to include certain types of textiles not previously covered.
[49] As Laddie *et al* notes the wording used to define a design in the current RDA originates from this statute (p. 1046).
[50] (1941) 58 R.P.C. 207.

original two dimensional artistic works could be relied upon to prevent reproductions in three dimensional form. The Copyright Act 1956 sought to rectify this anomaly by excluding from copyright protection designs registrable under the RDA irrespective of whether they were actually registered.[51]

2–35 The impact of this provision was, however, modified by the Design Copyright Act 1968 so that the exclusion of copyright protection for registered or registrable designs only came into effect once the design registration had expired (*i.e.* after 15 years). During this 15-year period dual protection was possible.

2–36 As Laddie *et al* points out, the combined effect of the Copyright Act 1956 and the Design Copyright Act 1968 was to cap copyright protection for registered (or registrable) designs at 15 years, but for designs that were unregistrable (*e.g.* because they were purely functional) protection extended for the full copyright term. This led to a number of cases in which functional articles obtained greater protection than aesthetic articles.[52] A watershed was reached in *British Leyland Motor Corporation v. Armstrong Patents Co. Ltd*[53] where the plaintiff sought relief against the manufacturer of exhaust pipes as spare parts on the basis of infringement of copyright in the original engineering drawings. Although the House of Lords acknowledged that the drawing of the exhaust pipe received the benefit of copyright protection (as it was not registrable as a design) and that the copyright in the drawing had been infringed by making the exhaust pipe it disapproved so strongly of British Leyland's actions in controlling the spare parts' market in its own parts by means of copyright that it introduced a new defence based on non-derogation from grant.[54] The House of Lords called upon the Government to change the law to avoid further abuse of the copyright system. This the Government did by enacting the CDPA 1988 which severely restricted copyright protection of design drawings *per se*, introducing instead a new *sui generis* right known as the unregistered design right.

2–37 The CDPA 1988 also amended the Registered Designs Act 1949 in a number of ways, in particular by extending the duration of protection to 25 years and by excluding from the scope of registration features of shape or configuration dictated solely by the function the article is to perform. Articles without aesthetic appeal are no longer registrable under the RDA. Functional designs may, however, qualify for protection under the unregistered design right regime.[55]

2–38 **The unregistered design right** The structure of and terminology used in the CDPA 1988 in connection with the creation of the then new (unregistered)[56] design right was derived from an earlier piece of legislation concerning the protection of semiconductor chip topographies,[57] which itself was based upon an European Council Directive.[58] According to Laddie *et al*[59] the genesis of the unregistered design right was really the 1987 Regulation or rather the Directive on

---

[51] s.10 Copyright Act 1956.
[52] For example, *Amp v. Utilux* [1972] R.P.C. 103.
[53] [1986] R.P.C. 279.
[54] The decision in this case is discussed in more detail in Chap 3.
[55] For further information regarding history and development of design protection, see Laddie *et al*, pp. 1045–1056.
[56] The new right is referred to in the CDPA 1988 as "design right" the term "unregistered design right" is used here to distinguish the new right from registered designs.
[57] The Semiconductor Products (Protection of Topography) Regulations 1987 S.I. 1987 No. 1497 ("the 1987 Regulation").
[58] 87/54 EEC O.J. No. L24.
[59] p. 1266.

which it was based. The CDPA 1988 only expanded those designs to which it would apply. Support for this view may be gained from the fact that certain phrases used in the Directive appear in connection with the UDR, for example the exclusion of protection for "commonplace" designs/topographies. Further the topography right came under the umbrella of design right when the 1987 Regulations were replaced by the Design Right (Topographies) Regulations 1989.[60]

2–39 The definition of "design" in the context of the unregistered design right (UDR) is quite different from that used in the RDA. Section 213 of the CDPA 1988 states that "design" means the "design of any aspect of the shape or configuration (whether internal or external) of the whole or part of an article". The section goes on to provide that:

> "Design right does not subsist in—
>
>   (a) a method or principle of construction,
>   (b) features of shape or configuration of an article which—
>
>   (i)   enable the article to be connected to, or placed in around or against another article so that either article may perform its function or
>   (ii) are dependent upon the appearance of another article of which the article is intended by the designer to form an integral part, or
>
>   (c) surface decoration".

An important feature of the UDR is the fact that it has no requirement of aesthetic appeal, it can therefore be relied upon to protect functional and industrial articles provided that they do not fall within the exclusions. A further prerequisite to obtaining design right protection is that the design must be original, that is, not commonplace.[61] This test of originality is more reminiscent of copyright than of patents in that it requires the independent work of designer and not simply copying the design of an earlier article.[62] Whether or not the design may be regarded as commonplace requires an objective assessment of similar articles in the same field, taking into account expert evidence. The judgment is one of fact and degree. Like copyright, the UDR[63] subsists automatically without the need for registration, subject to the design qualifying for protection by reference to the designer or the country of first marketing.[64]

As Pumfrey J. notes,[65] it was the intention of those responsible for drafting the CDPA 1988 to exclude from copyright protection "ordinary functional commercial articles". Instead, such articles would benefit from the UDR. Section 51 of the CDPA 1988 defines the boundary between the respective fields of copyright and

---

[60] S.I. 1989 No. 1100. For further information regarding history and development of design protection, see Laddie *et al,* p. 1265–1266; see also *Ocular Sciences Ltd v. Aspect Vision Care Ltd* [1997] R.P.C. 289 at 421.
[61] s.213(4) CDPA 1988. This is discussed in further detail in Chap. 3.
[62] *Farmers Build Ltd v. Carrier Ltd* [1997] R.P.C. 461 CA at 481.
[63] *ibid.* at 482.
[64] s.213(5) CDPA 1988. The requirements as to qualification for designers, commissioners and first marketing are set out in ss.217–200 CDPA 1988. Design right protection is limited to EEA citizens and corporations or products first marketed in the EEA or countries offering reciprocal protection.
[65] *Mackie Designs Inc. v. Behringer* [1999] R.P.C. 717 at 723.

design protection and section 236 sets out a mutual exclusivity of UDR and copyright protection.

2–40   Whilst it is possible for a design to have the benefit of protection under both the UDR and the RDA it is not possible to receive dual protection under copyright and the UDR.[66] Thus industrial articles devoid of aesthetic appeal (and so unregistrable from a RDA perspective) may nonetheless receive protection under the UDR system.[67] Protection extends for a maximum period of 15 years from making the article, or 10 years from first marketing, subject to compulsory licensing in the final five years.[68]

2–41   As with copyright the UDR is a right against copying, rather than an absolute monopoly. Thus the UDR is infringed by copying the design "so as to produce articles exactly or substantially to that design" without the authority of the owner of the design.[69] It is also an infringement to import or sell an infringing article.[70] Independent creation of the same design will not therefore infringe the UDR.

2–42   The enactment of the CDPA 1988 and the creation of the UDR have helped to clarify the boundary between industrially applied aesthetic and non-aesthetic designs ensuring that the former have the benefit of greater protection under the RDA whilst the latter have the benefit of the more limited UDR. Section 51 of the CDPA 1988 undoubtedly excludes from copyright infringement much that would have been covered under the previous law. Whether this has caused the balance to shift from over protection (which existed prior to 1988) to under protection for non-aesthetic articles remains to be seen.

2–43   Works of artistic craftsmanship   Aspects of a brand (other than literary aspects) that do not fall within the definition of artistic work under section 4(1)(a) of CDPA 1988 may fall within section 4(1)(c) as works of "artistic craftsmanship". This may be significant if the element in question does not have the benefit of protection under the RDA or UDR. The term "work of artistic craftsmanship" is not further defined although there have been a few cases that have sought to explore its meaning. Essentially, it involves some notion of craftsmanship and requires the article to have some artistic appeal.[71] In *Hensher v. Restawile*[72] the court refused to grant protection to a prototype piece of furniture on the basis that it was not sufficiently artistic. The House of Lords could not, however, agree on an interpretation of what was meant by the term "artistic", nor could they agree whether the artist's intuition to create something artistic was more important than the perception of artistic quality by members of the public.

2–44   Assuming that the necessary qualities of artistic skill and craftsmanship (whatever they may be) can be shown, a plaintiff will also need to show that the work is original if he is to obtain the benefit of copyright protection as described above. As Laddie *et al* note, there have been few claims to works of artistic craftsmanship in recent years and this may be because of the lack of guidance given by the House of Lords in the *Hensher v. Restawile* case.

---

[66] See ss.51 and 236 CDPA 1988.
[67] Provided they satisfy the requirements of ss.213 and 214 CDPA 1988.
[68] ss.216 and 237 CDPA 1988.
[69] s.226 CDPA 1988.
[70] s.227 CDPA 1988.
[71] Whilst drawings or other original artistic works may on the face of it obtain the benefit of copyright protection ss.51 and 52 CDPA 1988 act to restrict the scope of copyright protection see Laddie *et al*, pp. 205–206 and *BBC Worldwide Limited v. Pally Screen Printing Limited* [1998] F.S.R. 665.
[72] [1976] A.C. 64, HL.

2–45   In general terms, a brand (or more particularly, the naked product) will not be regarded as a work of artistic craftsmanship because of the level of artistry and craftsmanship involved in creating it. It may be possible for prototypes of brands to be considered works of artistic craftsmanship and so obtain the benefit of full copyright protection but this is likely to be so only in exceptional cases, for example in relation to prototypes of elaborate perfume bottles, etc. Where an artistic work has been exploited by making copies by an industrial process then copyright protection is limited to a period of 25 years from the end of the calendar year in which the articles are first marketed.[73] Thus if the original artistic work was a drawing of an electric razor say, the copyright protection in the article would be reduced to 25 years, (albeit that a prototype model might be regarded as a work of artistic craftsmanship). The consequence is that after the expiration of the copyright period the article (that is, the three dimensional article) can be copied without infringing the copyright in the original work.[74] Although potentially artistic works such as label designs and packaging designs are also industrially applied and so could be caught by this section as well, the Secretary of State has in accordance with section 52(4) excluded these items from the scope of section 52.[75] Thus labels and packaging materials continue to receive the full term of copyright protection. The loss of copyright protection for industrial articles is, to some extent, mitigated by the existence of the unregistered design right (discussed above).

(iv) The law of passing off

2–46   The common law tort of passing off developed to protect the goodwill of a trader. Cornish argues[76] that early English case law suggests that the courts of equity would intervene where it could be shown that one trader represented to the public that he was selling goods of another. Cornish relies not only on *Southern v. How* (a case whose reliability has been questioned—see below at para. 2–95) to support this claim but also on *Blanchard v. Hill,*[77] *Hogg v. Kirby,*[78] *Longman v. Winchester*[79] and also *Sykes v. Sykes*[80] as examples of cases where demands for legal protection in respect of the imitation of marks were being made out and the basic principles of what was to be known as "passing off", established.

2–47   The courts of equity would only intervene and provide injunctive relief to protect property rights. Plaintiffs therefore had to demonstrate a property interest. This they did by characterising the goodwill of a business as property. To succeed at common law the action had to be based on deceit which required proof of fraud. Plaintiffs sought to satisfy this requirement by pointing to the deception of the public as proof of the fraud.[81] It was not necessary for a plaintiff to show that the public knew or could even identify the producer from the mark used in order to obtain protection, it was sufficient if the plaintiff could show that the public relied on the mark as a sign of quality.[82] Although the requirement to prove deceit no longer remains, plaintiffs still need to provide evidence of misrepresentation if they are to succeed.

---

[73] s.52(2) CDPA 1988.
[74] *ibid.*
[75] S.I. 1989 No. 1070.
[76] p. 517.
[77] (1742) 2 Atk 485.
[78] (1803) 8 Ves. 215.
[79] (1809) 16 Ves. Jun 269.
[80] (1824) 3B & C 541.
[81] Cornish, p. 599.
[82] *Hall v. Barrows* (1863) 4 De. G.J. & S. 150 at 157.

2–48   In some respects, the tort has operated to give wider protection than that offered by registration of a trade mark since it has been possible not only to bring actions in respect of signs that were not, at the time of the action, registrable as trade marks (as in the case of the *Jif Lemon*[83]), but also in relation to marks used in connection with goods or services different from those for which the plaintiff's mark was used.[84] The *raison d'être* for providing such a comparatively broad form of relief has not just been the protection of the trader's goodwill but also protection of the public against deception as a result of a third party's use of a deceptively similar mark.

2–49   The three essential ingredients for a successful passing off action were succinctly enumerated in the *Parma Ham* case.[85] It requires (i) a misrepresentation in the course of trade, to a third party, (ii) giving rise to damage to the (iii) plaintiff's goodwill. It is not sufficient for the public to be confused as to the source of the product or service. There must be a misrepresentation giving rise to deception or a likelihood of deception. In other words, the consumer must buy goods from "A" believing them to come from "B". If it can be shown that in reality the consumer is indifferent as to the source of the goods (*i.e.* the consumer does not mind whether the goods come from "A" or "B") then the claim will fail.[86]

2–50   Although passing off actions have been relied upon to prevent copying of product shape, packaging, colours and advertising format such actions have not always proved successful.[87] In such cases, the courts have been eager to emphasise the fact that whilst passing off protects the goodwill of the trader from deception/ confusion with other traders, it does not insulate the trader from competition *per se*. The courts have therefore on occasions denied protection to plaintiffs who have previously benefited from protection under patents or registered designs on the basis that the plaintiffs have not established the necessary goodwill or distinctiveness in the mark concerned.[88]

2–51   Cases where it has been shown that consumers are actually motivated by source and are deceived as to the origin have very often turned on their own facts and it is therefore difficult here to add further gloss to the three basic ingredients of an action for passing off as described above, except to say that it is possible for an action for passing off to be brought in relation to any imitation of a brand or even an aspect of a brand provided that it can be shown that there has been deception in fact and that the particular element(s) of the brand in question were distinctive and not previously the subject of patents or registered designs.

2–52   As noted above, proof of damage beyond *de minimus* is an essential element of the tort. As a result of two recent decisions it has been suggested that the courts are now ready to accept dilution of trade marks or trade dress as a form of damage sufficient to warrant relief (assuming all other aspects of the tort are made out) but this remains unclear.[89]

[83] *Reckitt & Colman (Products) Ltd v. Border Inc* [1990] R.P.C. 340, HL.
[84] *Lego Systems A/S v. Lego M Lemelstritch Ltd* [1983] F.S.R. 155.
[85] *Conzorzio del Prosciutto di Parma v. Marks & Spencer plc* [1991] R.P.C. 351.
[86] *Hodgkinson and Corby Ltd v. Words Mobility Services Ltd* [1995] F.S.R. 169 (the "*Roho* case").
[87] See the *Roho* case, *RizlaLtd v. Bryant & May* [1986] R.P.C. 389 and *Cadbury Schweppes Pty Ltd v. The Pub Squash co Ltd* [1981] R.P.C. 429.
[88] See for example *Canadian Shredded Wheat Co v. Kellogg* (1938) R.P.C. 125.
[89] See *Taittinger v. Allbev* [1993] F.S.R. 641, CA and *Harrods v. Harrodian School Ltd* [1996] R.P.C. 697, CA. The latter case is discussed in further detail in Chap. 5.

(v) Registered trade marks

2–53 The Trade Marks Act 1994[90–91] is the current United Kingdom statute governing trade mark registration. Under section 1(1) of the TMA 1994, it is possible to register as a trade mark:

> "any sign capable of being represented graphically which is capable of distinguishing goods or services of one undertaking from those of other undertakings. A trade mark may, in particular, consist of words (including personal names), designs, letters, numerals or the shape of goods or their packaging."

The meaning of this provision will be discussed in detail in Part III, suffice to say that it is now possible to register, *inter alia*, words, numerals, designs, combinations of these, colours, fragrances, sounds and three dimensional objects as trade marks, provided that the signs[92] are capable of distinguishing and are not excluded from registration by virtue of Sections 3 and 4 (specially protected emblems).

2–54 Section 3 sets out the absolute grounds for refusing to register certain types of sign, namely those which[93]:

- do not satisfy the requirements of section 1(1);

- are devoid of any distinctive character;

- consist exclusively of signs or indications which are descriptive;

- consist exclusively of signs or indications customary in the trade.

If, however, the applicant can show that, in relation to the last three items listed above, before the date of the application the sign had acquired a distinctive character through use then it will not be refused registration. Evidence of use of the mark will not, however, enable the proprietor to overcome the requirement that the sign be capable of graphic representation and capable of distinguishing the goods or services of the applicant.

2–55 Also excluded from registration are signs consisting exclusively of the shape which results from the nature of the goods, shapes necessary to obtain a technical effect, and shapes that give a substantial value to the goods.[94] The application of these provisions are discussed in further detail in Chapter 3 in relation to the protection of the product shape.

Section 9 of the TMA 1994 sets out the scope of the rights conferred by registration, that is, the exclusive rights in the trade mark, which are infringed by use of the mark without the owner's consent. The infringement provisions are set out in section 10 of the TMA 1994 and are considerably broader in scope than those provided under previous statutes.[95]

[90–91] The Act implements the terms of the E.C. Directive 89/104/EEC (December 21, 1988) ("the Directive") which aims to harmonise the trade mark laws of the various member states of the E.U. The Directive did not, however, provide for complete harmonisation since the implementation of some of its provisions were mandatory where as others were optional, for example Art. 5(2).
[92] The term "sign" is used in some sections of the TMA 1994 to distinguish between marks that are registered and those that are not.
[93] s.3(1).
[94] s.3(2)
[95] s.10(2). The scope of the infringement provisions are discussed in detail in Chaps 3, 4 and 5, see paras 24–43 and following respectively.

2–56   In general terms a registered trade mark may be infringed by the use in the course of trade of an identical sign in relation to identical goods to those for which the mark is registered[96] or by the use of an identical or similar sign in relation to identical or similar goods if there exists a likelihood of confusion.[97] The latter provision represents a broadening of the scope of trade mark rights from the position under the Trade Marks Act 1938 ("TMA 1938") where a mark was only infringed if an identical mark or one so nearly resembling it as to be likely to deceive or cause confusion was used on goods the same as those covered by the registration, or goods of the same description.[98] Under the TMA 1994 it is also possible to bring an action for infringement against a third party using an identical or similar trade mark in relation to dissimilar goods in certain circumstances.[99]

2–57   One of the advantages of trade mark registration is that the registration acts as *prima facie* proof of the proprietor's entitlement to the mark. A registration also enables an action for infringement to be brought without evidence that the proprietor has suffered damage as a result of the alleged infringer's use (if the sign is used on identical or similar goods).[1] This is a significant advantage over actions for passing off and helps to reduce the cost of bringing an infringement action as against an action for passing off.

2–58   To obtain the benefits of trade mark registration an application must be made to the Registrar at the United Kingdom Trade Marks Office.[2] The application must set out *inter alia* details of the mark to be registered and details of the goods/ services to be covered.[3] The application must be accompanied by the requisite fee and should state that the trade mark is being used by the applicant, or with his consent, or that the applicant has a bona fide intention to do so.[4] Once the application has been filed, it is allocated a filing date which, when accepted for registration, will be the date from which renewal of the mark will be calculated and from which any infringement of the mark will be actionable (albeit that the trade mark owner will not be able to initiate proceedings until the mark is entered on the Register).

2–59   Once filed, the application is examined for registrability and if no objections are raised the mark will be published for opposition purposes. The mark is published in the Trade Marks Journal, following which a third party may oppose the registration of the mark within three months of the date of publication on certain specified grounds.[5] Once registered, the mark is valid for an initial period of 10 years and may be renewed for successive 10 year periods.[6] The mark will continue to be valid provided that renewal fees are paid and the mark continues to be used in relation to the goods for which it is registered. If the mark is not used for a continuous period of five years from the date of the entry in the Trade Marks

---

[96] s.10(1).
[97] The scope of these provisions are discussed in detail in Chap. 4.
[98] s.4 and s.68. The significance of this increased scope is discussed further in Chap. 4.
[99] The circumstances in question are identified and discussed further in Chap. 5 at para. 5–62 *et seq.*
[1] Annand and Norman, p. 16.
[2] s.32(1) TMA 1994.
[3] s.32(2). Goods and services are divided into 42 classes; classes 1–34 cover goods, classes 35–42 cover services. An applicant must specify in which classes protection is sought and for which goods or services within each class.
[4] s.32(3).
[5] These are set out in s.5 and are equivalent to the infringement provisions set out in s.10 which are discussed in detail in Chaps 4 and 5 at paras 4–43 and following and 5.62 and following.
[6] s.42.
[7] s.46. This section is discussed further in Chap. 5.

Register or for any successive period of five years then it is open to a third party to apply to revoke the registration on the grounds of non-use.[7]

2–60 A registered trade mark, and indeed an application to register a trade mark, can be assigned, disposed of by will or by law either with or without the goodwill of the business to which it is attached[8]; it may also be licensed in respect of all the goods/services covered by the registration or in respect of only some of them.[9]

(vi) The law of confidence

2–61 The law of confidence, like the tort of passing off, is a common law doctrine that has its roots in the equitable jurisdiction of the court. The law of confidence is not limited in its subject-matter but may cover all sorts of information provided that it is imparted or gathered in confidence and is not public knowledge. The requirements of an actionable breach of confidence were set out by Megarry J. in *Coco v. Clark*[10] where he said:

> "First, the information itself . . . must 'have the necessary quality of confidence about it' secondly, that information must be imparted in circumstances importing an obligation of confidence. Thirdly, there must be an unauthorised use of that information . . . to the detriment of the party communicating it".

Whilst it is possible for inventions such as those the subject of a patent application to be regarded as material protected under the law of confidence, once these are set out in a patent application which is published, the information can no longer be regarded as confidential. Equally, whilst it is possible for confidential information that has been expressed in a tangible form to obtain the benefit of copyright protection, once such material has been disclosed (other than in circumstances importing an obligation of confidence) the nature of the information as confidential is lost. Thus, in the context of branded products the law of confidence will only be of relevance in relation to material that is not disclosed as a result of the launch and sale of a branded product, for example, a recipe setting out the formulation of a particular drink product or the chemical constituents of a particular compound. However, if the product itself can be analysed[10a] in such a way that this information becomes apparent then the information may no longer be regarded as confidential (or reversed engineered).

2–62 As has been said before, a breach of confidence action may lie in respect of technical commercial, personal or other information irrespective of subject matter. An idea for a new project may obtain the benefit of legal protection as confidential information even if there is no underlying copyright or other intellectual property rights. However, like copyright there is a requirement to show specific expression of the idea and not simply a vague concept.[11]

2–63 Information will not be regarded as confidential if it was freely available to the public before it was disclosed in confidence or once the disclosure has been made and before the action for breach of confidence has been heard. It is therefore imperative that if a brand owner wishes to maintain the secrecy of a formulation or

---

[8] s.24(1).
[9] s.28.
[10] 1969 [RPC] 41 at 47.
[10a] *Marslik Ltd v. Teknowledge Ltd* [2000] F.S.R. 138.
[11] *Talbot v. General Television* [1981] R.P.C. 1 (Supreme Court of Victoria).

recipe that it should ensure that the information does not get into the public domain. Thus if and when disclosures are necessary they need to be made in circumstances importing an obligation of confidence, for example in circumstances where the person disclosing the information advises the recipient that the information is confidential and the recipient agrees to keep the information confidential.[12]

2-64   One area that often causes particular concern is that involving former employees especially where, as an employee, the person had access to confidential information and subsequent to the termination of the employment, the information is either used or disclosed to third parties. In *Faccenda Chicken v. Fowler*[13] the Court of Appeal stated that the employer may only seek to protect two interests namely his trade secrets and the goodwill existing with his customers. These principles were first developed in connection with express covenants contained within the employee's contract of employment and are enforceable only if considered to be reasonably necessary to protect the employer's interests. Once again it is important for brand owners to appreciate that if they chose to rely on the law of confidence to protect information such as formulations and recipes or trade secrets concerning methods of production, they should ensure that employees are bound by similar covenants not to use or disclose the information following termination of their employment.[14]

(b) The international dimension

2-65   So far in this section we have been considering the various forms of protection available in the United Kingdom. We will now turn to consider the various international agreements that exist that enable owners of intellectual property rights in the United Kingdom to obtain corresponding protection in other countries. We will start by looking briefly at the main international agreements as they relate to the various IP rights referred to above.

(i) The Paris Convention

2-66   The Paris Convention for the Protection of Industrial Property concluded in 1883 (the "Paris Convention") was the first international convention relating to industrial property. The Convention has been revised on a number of occasions.[15] As its name suggests the Paris Convention applies to all forms of industrial property which, in Article 1(2) is said to include "patents, utility models, industrial designs, trade marks, service marks, trade names, indications of source or appellations of origin, and the repression of unfair competition". The Convention does not therefore cover copyright works but it does cover most other types of intellectual property.

2-67   The Paris Convention provides for a minimum level of protection in countries that are members of the Union. It also provides a basis for non-discrimination against nationals of any country that is a member of the Union. This is known as the principle of "national treatment". The Paris Convention also provides for national treatment for nationals of non-member countries where it can be said that the person or organisation has a real and effective business establishment in one of the member countries.[16] The exact scope of this provision, however, remains uncertain.

---

[12] *Coco v. Clark* [1969] R.P.C. 41 at 47.
[13] [1986] 1 All E.R. 617.
[14] For further information regarding law of confidence see Cornish, Chap. 8, at p. 263.
[15] In particular, in 1900, 1925, 1934, 1958, 1967 and most recently in 1979. As at October 1997 more than 140 states were members of the Paris Convention including the U.K. and most other developed countries.
[16] Art. 3.

2–68   Although the Paris Convention sets out a minimum standard of protection it does not do so in a prescriptive form. For example in Article 5 it states that "industrial designs should be protected in all countries of the Union". The convention does not go on to say how such designs should be protected or what the scope of protection should be.

2–69   One of the advantages of the Paris Convention is that it provides for a system of obtaining what is known as "convention priority" in connection with applications for industrial property protection. In Article 4(A) it states that where an application for a patent, design, utility model, trade mark, etc., is for more than one member country, the applicant can take advantage of the same priority date in other member countries if applications are filed in those other member countries within the period of six months for designs, trade marks and utility models, and within 12 months for patents. This facility can be extremely useful where the brand owner seeks protection in a number of jurisdictions but where, for financial reasons it may wish to spread the cost of the filing programme by filing applications in one country at the outset, following this up with further applications at intervals in other countries within the six-month period. Although the Convention also states that members of the Union are "bound to assure nationals of such countries effective protection against unfair competition" what amounts to unfair competition is not made clear.[17]

2–70   One of the weaknesses of the Paris Convention is that it does not make any provision for sanctions against a member country that does not provide the minimum level of protection laid down by the Convention.

(ii) The Berne Convention

2–71   Like the Paris Convention, the Berne Convention seeks to establish a minimum standard of protection throughout members of the Union. Its sphere of application relates to the rights of authors in their literary and artistic works, although the expression "literary and artistic works" is very wide and is said to encompass "every production in the literary, scientific and artistic domain, whatever may be the mode or form of its expression".[18] The Convention provides that literary and artistic works shall be protected in all countries of the Union to the extent that their respective laws allow, but the enjoyment and exercise of those rights must not be subject to any formality (e.g. registration).[19] The provisions of the Berne Convention enable the author, inter alia, of copyright material created in the United Kingdom to take action for infringement in other countries that are members of the Berne Convention to the extent that the laws in the country where the infringement takes place allow, without the need for the copyright owner to register his copyright interest or take any other action in order to secure his rights. This is a considerable benefit to owners of literary and artistic works, who, unlike trade mark owners, do not need to embark upon a programme of international registration in order to protect their intellectual property.

(iii) The Madrid Agreement

2–72   The Madrid Agreement concerning the international registration of marks was first established in 1891. Like the Paris Convention it has been revised on a

---

[17] Art. 10.
[18] Art. 2.
[19] Art. 5(2).

number of occasions, most recently in 1979. The Madrid Agreement provides for a system of obtaining the international registration of trade mark rights (known as "international registrations"). The procedure prescribed by the Agreement is as follows: a national of a member country of the Agreement can apply for registration of a trade mark in its home territory ("the home" registration). Once this application matures to registration the applicant can apply to the World Intellectual Property Organisation (WIPO) in Geneva to extend this home registration to a number of designated countries, each designated country being a member of the Agreement. The application is registered at the International Bureau at WIPO and the mark is published in the WIPO Gazette. Details of the application are sent to the various Trade Marks Offices in the designated countries who then either register, or refuse, the mark, according the rules existing in their countries at that time. Once all the designated countries have either registered or refused the mark the applicant has in effect a number of national registrations.

2–73 The advantage of the international system of registration is that it provides a simplified administrative procedure, such that, when the marks are due for renewal, the owner of the marks need only pay the renewal fees at the International Bureau rather than deal with the various registrations separately. One of the weaknesses of the system, however, is that of "central attack". In other words, if for any reason, the home registration is cancelled within the first five years of registration then all the international registrations connected with the home registration are also cancelled.

2–74 Despite the success of the Madrid Agreement,[20] a number of significant countries were not members of the Agreement because they regarded it as unattractive. In particular, designated countries within the Madrid Agreement are only allowed a 12-month period within which to refuse protection to an application, a number of non-member countries felt that this period was too short. Furthermore, the system of central attack was also regarded as unattractive. The Madrid Protocol which was established in 1997 aimed to overcome these shortcomings.

2–75 The United Kingdom is signatory to the Madrid Protocol and the European Community is expected to accede to the Madrid Protocol this year. Members of the Madrid Protocol are able to apply for international protection of trade marks based on a national application (as opposed to a registration under the Madrid Agreement). An applicant can extend protection to those countries that are members of the Madrid Protocol only (but not to members of the Madrid Agreement). As with the Madrid Agreement, the international application is filed at WIPO, who examines the application. Assuming that that application is in order it is published in the WIPO Gazette and the various designated countries then examine the application for registrability subject to their national laws. The time limit for notification of refusal of the application is one year from the date on which WIPO notifies the designated state of the original application. Unlike the Madrid Agreement however, the designated country can extend the period up to 18 months or even longer where the extension is the result of an opposition.[21] Unlike international applications under the Madrid Agreement, registrations under the Madrid Protocol can be converted to national registrations in the event of central

---

[20] Since it came in force in 1892 over 600,000 international registrations have been made with each registration covering an average of 10 countries. See Annand & Norman, *Blackstone's Guide to the Community Trade Mark* (Blackstone Press Limited, London, 1998), p. 260 ("Community Trade Mark").
[21] *ibid.*, p. 269.

attack on the home registration. The Madrid Protocol therefore is a much more attractive proposition to trade mark owners who can obtain protection in a number of countries more cost effectively without fear of losing all their protection if the home registration is challenged.

(iv) The Patent Co-operation Treaty

2–76   The Patent Co-operation Treaty ("PCT") came into effect in June 1978. Prior to this treaty there was no equivalent international agreement relating to patent protection that could be described as an international patent system. The main provisions of the PCT concern the submission of a single patent application designating countries that are members to the Treaty where protection is sought. The first part of the Treaty creates an international search which can be conducted by one of a number of search authorities. The second part establishes an international preliminary examination. Participating states are not obliged to adhere to both parts of the Treaty nor is an applicant obliged to have the preliminary examination.

2–77   The main advantage of the Treaty is a practical one in that it allows an applicant to institute applications in a number of countries via a single application (similar to the Madrid Agreement relating to trade marks) but to delay the final decision as to where to extend protection. The Treaty does not, however, provide for an international patent, rather the protection granted is in the form of national patent rights and it is down to each individual regional office to decide whether or not to grant a patent covering its own territory.[22]

2–78   One of the aims of the PCT is to simplify the administrative procedures for obtaining patent protection in several countries.[23] It does this by enabling a patentee to file a single international application in one Member State at a receiving office (usually the applicant's local national office) and giving the applicant a right of priority from that filing date. The application is then accepted, searches are carried out and the mark is examined on an international basis before proceeding to the grant of national patent rights. Thus a United Kingdom patentee seeking protection of his invention in the United Kingdom can file an application either directly at the United Kingdom Patent Office[24] or at the European Patent Office in Munich, designating the United Kingdom in his application[25] along with other European countries in which protection is sought.

(v) European Patent Convention

2–79   The European Patent Convention (EPC) (1973) established a European Patent Office and a centralised procedure for obtaining patent protection in various countries in Western Europe. The aim of the EPC was to reduce bureaucracy and duplication of searches by centralising the application process and also providing a substantial examination of the application, something that not all Member States carried out at that time. The system acted as an alternative for, and not a replacement of national patents systems.

2–80   The European Patent Office receives applications from would be patentees and examines them in accordance with the rules laid down in the

---

[22] In 1995, 78 states were participating in the PCT. In 1987 more than 9,000 international applications were filed and the number has increased since then. See Cornish, p. 121.
[23] Cornish, p. 121 et seq.
[24] ss.14–21, 1977 Act, Patent Rules rr.16–38.
[25] EPC Arts 75–85 & 90–98, European Patent Rules, rr.24–37 & 39–54.

Convention. The applicant must designate those countries in which protection is sought and pay the appropriate fee. Once the EPO has accepted the application it grants a European patent for each of the designated Member States. Each European patent granted is equivalent to a national patent granted in that particular state. Thus a European Patent designating the United Kingdom is equivalent to a national United Kingdom patent.[26]

(vi) GATT-TRIPS

2–81 In 1994 as part of the re-negotiation of the General Agreement on Tariffs and Trade ("GATT") an agreement was concluded specifically relating to international aspects of intellectual property rights. The Agreement, entitled "Trade Related Aspects of Intellectual Property Rights" ("TRIPS") not only incorporates the Paris Convention and Berne Convention but also seeks to establish links between the WIPO and a new organisation established under the Agreement known as the Word Trade Organisation ("WTO"). The WTO provides a forum for enforcing obligations under the TRIPS Agreement. The TRIPS Agreement also combines the principle of national treatment found in the Paris Convention with that of the "most favoured nation treatment" found in the WTO Agreement.

2–82 The aim of the GATT-TRIPS Agreement is to promote minimum standards of IP protection and to ensure that IP rights in themselves do not become barriers to trade.[27] As noted above neither the Paris Convention nor the Berne Convention provide sanctions against member countries that fail to comply with the terms of each Convention. These weaknesses have, to some extent, been overcome by incorporating the two Conventions into the TRIPS Agreement which does provide for the enforcement of sanctions against countries in default through the aegis of the WTO.

(c) Supra-national rights

(i) E.U. Harmonisation

2–83 Much of the legislation introduced in England in the past 10 or more years in the field of intellectual property has been introduced as a result of initiatives that began in Brussels, the seat of the European Commission. Membership of the European Community has brought with it initiatives to harmonise intellectual property legislation in all the Member States in order to eliminate barriers to trade and promote the free movement of goods within the single market. In connection with the IP rights discussed here, the main initiatives have been the Trade Mark Harmonisation Directive,[28] the Copyright Term Directive,[29] the Database Directive,[30] the Computer Software Directive,[31] the Community Trade Marks Regulation[32] and the Design Directive[33] In addition various proposals for future directives and regulations have been put forward although these have yet to

---

[26] s.77(1) PA 1977.
[27] For further information concerning the impact of the TRIPS Agreement see Blakeney *Trade Related Aspects of Intellectual Property* (Sweet & Maxwell, London, 1996).
[28] 89/104 O.J. 1985 C351/1 (the "Directive").
[29] 93/98 O.J. 1993 L290/9.
[30] 96/9 O.J. 1996 L77/20.
[31] 91/250.
[32] 40/94.
[33] 98/71 of O.J. 1998 L289. The deadline for implementation is Octoer 28, 2001 but so far, no Member State has implemented it.

be adopted or implemented, they include the Community Patent Convention,[34] the Community Design,[35] the Community Utility Model.[36]

2–84 In many instances the approach adopted by the European Commission has not only been to seek to harmonise existing laws but also to introduce separate supra-national rights and systems of registration as a further tier of protection. In time it is expected that these supranational rights will replace the national rights and registration systems.

2–85 In 1989 the European Parliament adopted the Directive which aimed to harmonise the trade mark laws of the various Member States. This was not an easy task bearing in mind the different legal traditions of the various countries concerned, the fact that they had independently developed IP laws based on different traditions and rationales, and involved different procedures. For example the English registration system involved the examination of the trade mark applications for distinctiveness and conflicts with prior registrations, whereas the French and Benelux systems were deposit systems with no examination process. As a result of the implementation of the Directive, concepts have been introduced into United Kingdom trade mark law that were previously unknown.[37] It therefore comes as no surprise to find members of the judiciary wrestling to interpret and implement its terms in a manner consistent with English legal theory[38] and in line with the expressed principle objective of the single market, namely the freedom of movement of goods.

2–86 In view of the fact that the Benelux countries (that is, Belgium, Netherlands and Luxembourg) already operated a supranational trade mark registration system[39] and its law was more recent than that of other E.U. Member States it had been expected that the Benelux model would not only influence the drafting of the Directive but also its interpretation.[40] However, recent decisions of the English High Court[41] and the European Court of Justice (the "ECJ"),[42] the ultimate arbiter as to the meaning of the Directive, suggest that this is not the case. The following chapters will nonetheless compare the interpretation of the TMA 1994 and the Directive with the Benelux law where the approach adopted in relation to the former is at variance with the latter.

2–87 Unfortunately for the United Kingdom, the European style of proposing legislation, its consensus approach to drafting and the subsequent adoption of directives without expressing definitive principles of legal theory, all militate against producing documents that are exhaustive in their definitions or comprehensive in their terms. Also, the different legal traditions of the various Member States demand different approaches to the question of how explicit the text must be in

---

[34] O.J. 1976 L17/1.

[35] O.J. 1994 C29/20.

[36] O.J. 1998 C36/13.

[37] For example the concept of a "likelihood of association" in s.10(2) TMA 1994.

[38] See for example the comments of Laddie J. in *Wagamama Ltd v. City Centre Restaurants Plc* [1995] F.S.R. 713 (the "*Wagamama*" case), discussed in Chap. 4 at para. 4–44.

[39] That is, a combined system whereby registration at a central office in the Hague is effective in each of the contracting states. The contracting states do not operate their own independent registration systems of trade mark laws but rely upon the unified law.

[40] See, by way of example, Annand and Norman, p. 156 where reference is made to the Benelux law as an aid to interpreting s.10(3) TMA 1994; Cornish, p. 570 and Kamperman Sanders "Some Frequently Asked Questions About The Trade Marks Act 1994" [1995] E.I.P.R. 3.

[41] In particular, *Wagamama*, and *The Baywatch Production Company Inc v. The Home Video Channel Ltd* [1997] F.S.R. 22 discussed in Chap. 5.

[42] *Sabel BV v. Puma AG* [1998] E.T.M.R. 1; [1998] C.M.L.R. 445.

order to implement harmonisation effectively within the various Member States.[43] Whereas the English legal tradition is to analyse carefully the text of each clause and sub-clause and to study the nuance of each article, countries with a civil law tradition are content to accept the directive at face value and to implement the terms in accordance with what is thought to be the philosophy behind them rather than analyse the detailed wording of the section. Thus as Strowel points out, in a civil code country the expansion of rights is achieved through judicial interpretation whereas in a common law system such as that in the United Kingdom the role of the judiciary is more limited and new rights are only introduced by the legislators (not the judiciary). As Strowel concludes[44] (in the context of his examination of copyright and *droit d'auteur*):

> "we need, particularly in times of the harmonisation . . . within Europe, to ask new questions such as: what are the problems that will be created when the logic of a closed system is transplanted into an open one; and are our legislators aware of the risks that this transplantation may engender? In other words, we need to focus attention not only on the detailed technicalities of . . . law, but upon the interpretative framework within which the different European systems take on their meaning and gain their distinctive shapes."

Such comments apply equally to the field of trade mark harmonisation. Indeed until those responsible for drafting E.U. legislation (and those responsible for its interpretation) take into account factors such as these it is likely that the United Kingdom will continue to stand apart from other Member States with regard to the interpretation and implementation of E.U. regulations and directives.[45]

(ii) The Community Trade Mark

2–88   In addition to the Directive, the E.U. has adopted a Regulation creating the Community Trade Mark ("CTM")[46] and establishing the Office for the Harmonisation of the Internal Market ("OHIM") based in Alicante, the registry for the CTM. The CTM is a unitary registration system whereby an applicant can apply for registration and if granted the proprietor will receive a single registration which is effective throughout the Member States of the E.U. It is a single trade mark registration which is maintained centrally. Use of the mark in one country will be sufficient to maintain the registration.[47]

---

[43] Strowel (p. 250–1) considers the different approaches adopted in relation to copyright in the U.K. and *droit d'auteur* in France and concludes that the U.K. adopts a "closed system" approach based on the premise that copyright is a monopoly right and the statute must therefore set out comprehensively all the rights that are granted and the acts that constitute infringement. This makes the U.K. law less flexible than its French counterpart. In contrast, the French approach to *droit d'auteur* regards the rights as a natural law property right and the approach taken to the law is that of an "open system" setting out basic principles which are subsequently developed by the judiciary thus making it much more flexible. Although Strowel's examination and analysis is based on copyright protection it can equally be applied to trade mark protection.

[44] *ibid.*, p. 253.

[45] In the *Sabel v. Puma* case the governments of the Benelux countries submitted arguments in favour of a broad interpretation of the infringement provisions of the Directive whereas the U.K. government and the Commission advocated a narrower interpretation. The U.K. government was alone in suggesting that a likelihood of association should be limited to all instances involving confusion (*i.e.* direct confusion).

[46] Regulation 40/94 of December 20, 1993.

[47] As Annand and Norman note in Community Trade Mark, p. 139, this advantage is not mentioned specifically in the Regulation but it was confirmed in the minutes of the Council meeting at which the Regulation was adopted.

2–89   The CTM has proved to be much more popular that initially expected.[48] Although OHIM opened its doors to receive applications on April 1, 1996 the first CTMs emerged in 1998. CTM applications, like national applications, are examined and advertised for opposition purposes. If opposed successfully, for example on the basis of prior use or registration of a conflicting mark in any country of the E.U., registration will be refused. Given the number of marks registered in each Member State it is expected that only arbitrary, or invented marks and those already registered separately in all Member States will proceed to registration unchallenged. However, the potential savings in terms of filing fees and the advantage of a single registration from an administrative point of view make the CTM an attractive proposition.

2–90   What remains unclear and uncertain is how the enforcement of CTM's will work in practice. Despite the fact that the infringement provisions of the Regulation mirror those of the Directive the ways in which the various Member States interpret them will no doubt lead to inconsistencies until such time as the ECJ is able to provide clearer direction on a case-by-case basis.

2–91   In view of the fact that the infringement provisions are the same as those of the Directive the remainder of this book will focus on the position under the Directive rather than under the Regulation. Only when there are differences in approach will the Regulation be referred to separately.

(iii) Community Patent Convention

2–92   As a second part of the EPC arrangement, a further convention was signed in Luxembourg in 1975 known as the Community Patent Convention ("CPC"). The principal object of this Convention is to establish a Community Patent, that is, a single patent right that covers the whole of the European Ecomomic Area ("EEA"). Despite the signing of the CPC in 1975 no community patent yet exists. The reasons are both complex and political.[49] Suffice it to say that however desirable such a unitary system may be its implementation is far from straightforward. Considerable progress has, however, been made and it should not be too long before the Community Patent becomes a reality.[50]

PART II

(a) The historical development of the law relating to trade marks

2–93   According to Schechter[51] the modern law of trade marks has two roots. First, in the form of a regulatory mark compulsorily affixed to goods to indicate the craftsman responsible for making the product. His mark would comprise a "guild mark" to indicate that "guild" or trade association to which he belonged, and a second unique mark to identify his workmanship. Each guild would keep a record of those craftsmen that were authorised to apply to the guild mark and would also keep a record of each individual craftsman's mark. The purpose of this was to enable the craftsman to be identified in the event that the article was considered to be defective in any way. Thus the regulatory mark, or craftsman's mark, was compulsory and more of a liability than an asset.[52]

---

[48] Community Trade Mark, p. 1.
[49] Cornish, pp. 124–125.
[50] The Green Paper (COM(97) 314) on Community Patents and the Patent System in Europe was adopted by the Commission on June 24, 1997.
[51] Schechter, *The Historical Foundation of the Law Relating to Trade Marks* (Columbia. University Press, USA, 1925), p. 78 ("Historical Foundations").
[52] Schechter, *Historical Foundations* Chap. III.

2–94 The second root can be traced back to the use of a proprietary mark by merchants or traders for the benefit of illiterate clerks or as a means of identifying ownership of goods in the event of piracy or shipwreck.[53] This second form of mark, was not compulsory, was more of an asset than a liability, and tended to be used to indicate ownership in the form of possession or entitlement to goods rather than the source of manufacture. It was possible for both forms of mark to be used together, as in the case of two marks, or the same mark could be used to perform both functions.

2–95 The starting point of the present law of trade marks is usually regarded as the case of *Southern v. How*,[54] however, Schechter challenges this ancestry arguing that "the sole contribution of that case was at best an irrelevant dictum of a reminiscent judge that he remembered an action in II Elizabeth by one clothier against another for the mis-use of the former's trade mark".[55] It is at best, he says, a fragile link between the Middle Ages and the modern commercial world. Instead, Schechter traces the development of trade marks as assets of commercial importance back to the second half of the nineteenth century.

2–96 Calls for a law against the use of false marks, names and imitation of brands increased during the second half of the nineteenth century with the growth of cheap imports from abroad and concern about the quality of such goods.[56] These calls were in addition to those of commercial interests who argued that their prices were being undercut by cheap imports that did not clearly label their contents and imitated established brand names and trade marks.[57] The Merchandise Marks Act 1862 was the first specific piece of legislation to target "forging of a trade mark" as well as falsely marking goods generally. It was a criminal statute and therefore did not enable a plaintiff to bring a civil action against a competitor.[58]

2–97 Despite opposition from those who were suspicious of granting a new "property" in respect of trade marks and concern that such a right might restrict the ability of traders in the future to select and apply marks, traders continued their demands for legislation to increase the protection of their trade marks. These demands were met to some extent in the passing of the Trade Marks Registration Act 1875. This Act established the first Trade Marks Register in England and permitted the registration of trade marks for particular goods, subject to examination by the Registry. Only a limited range of marks could, however, be registered as trade marks, in particular a "trade mark" had to consist of one or more of the following[59]:

(i) a name of an individual, or firm printed in a particular and distinctive manner;

(ii) a signature of an individual or firm;

(iii) a distinctive device, mark, heading, label or ticket;

(iv) any special and distinctive word or words or combination thereof used before the Act came into force.

Although the Act stated that a trade mark had to be registered in connection with particular goods[60] and could be transferred only with the goodwill of the business,

---

[53] *Historical Foundations*, Chap. IV and *Rational Basis*, p. 813.
[54] (1618) *Popham* 144.
[55] *Historical Foundations*, p. 123.
[56] Cornish, p. 600.
[57] See, Report of the Trade Marks Bill Select Committee, p. 1862 (212) XII.
[58] Cornish, p. 600.
[59] s.10 Trade Marks Registration Act 1875.
[60] Services were not covered by registration until 1986.

the Act did not specify what function the trade mark was meant to perform or what prominence it should have on the goods concerned. It is clear from the wording of section 10 that one of the primary requirements for registration was that the mark be distinctive either in itself or that as a result of the use of the mark, it had acquired distinctiveness though exactly what was meant by this term was not specified.

2–98   The list of elements that a mark might comprise may seem particularly limited compared to TMA 1994 but it could be said that it reflected the ways in which traders identified and distinguished their products from those of competitors at that time. However, cases such as *Re James's Trade Mark Application*[61] indicate that traders also used shapes as marks even in 1886. In this case the courts refused an application to register a dome shaped lead block. In refusing registration Lindley L.J. stated:

> "One must be careful to avoid confusion. I take it that a mark cannot be a mark of itself, but here we have got a thing, and we have got a mark on the thing, and the question is whether that mark on the thing is or is not a distinctive mark within the meaning of the Trade Marks Act. Of course it is obvious to all lawyers that the Plaintiffs in this case have no monopoly in black lead or this shape. Anybody may mark black lead of this shape, provided they do not wrap it up and represent it as the Plaintiff's black lead. There is no monopoly in the shape and I cannot help thinking that that has not been quite kept in mind".

Thus, it was not possible to register shapes as trade marks, and as Lindley L.J. observed there had to be a distinction between a mark and "the thing marked". Such a distinction remains today although it is not always a straightforward task to separate the two.[62]

2–99   The Trade Mark Registration Act 1875 was amended in 1876 and 1877 and was replaced in 1883 by the Patents, Designs and Trade Marks Act. Amongst other things, the 1883 Act used the word "brand" for the first time in relation to trade marks. Section 64 set out the essential requirements of a mark for the purposes of registration. In addition to the type of marks included in the Act 1875 (identified in points (i), (ii) and (iv)) it was also possible for a mark to consist of "A distinctive device, mark, *brand*, heading, label, ticket or fancy word or words not in common use" (*emphasis added*).[63]

2–100   The use of the word "brand" in this context has not attracted particular comment from either writers[64] or the courts and its juxtaposition with "headings, labels and tickets" suggests that the term was understood to refer to the name of a product or a device mark rather than the broader definition of a brand that as discussed in Chapter 1. If that were not true, and the term was intended to refer to a broader concept then its inclusion in such a list would be tautologous since, as we saw earlier, a brand includes a name, device, possibly a heading, etc. Furthermore, we know that a brand includes the shape of goods and their packaging and yet shapes *per se* were not registrable under the 1883 Act or indeed, in the case of

---

[61] (1886) 3 R.P.C. 240.
[62] Some shape marks registered under the TMA 1994 appear to fall foul of this distinction (*e.g.* the registration of the Morgan sports car — Number 2008299) but until an application for infringement of the mark, or an action for revocation or invalidity is considered by the court the question will remain open to speculation.
[63] s.64(1).
[64] See Kerly, *The Law of Trade Marks* (Sweet & Maxwell, London, 12th Ed., 1984), p. 5 ("Kerly").

containers such as the Coca-Cola bottle were not registrable until 1994. It would therefore appear that the term "brand" in this context referred only to the name of a product, such as Sunlight soap, or Coca-Cola rather than the broader concept of a brand as we understand it today.

2–101 This interpretation is supported by the fact that the Trade Marks (Amendment) Act of 1984 (which introduced for the first time protection for service marks equivalent to that existing under the 1938 Act in respect of trade marks), did not include a reference to "brand" within the definition of a mark, even though services today are branded in just the same way as products.

2–102 Whilst the definition of a trade mark in the TMA 1994 is considerably broader than under previous statutes specifically including as it does the shape of goods or their packaging, the reference to "brand" has disappeared entirely, supporting the view that either a brand is considered to be greater than a trade mark (*i.e.* a trade mark is a subset of a brand) or that the term is understood to be synonymous with the other elements of which a trade mark may consist. Aspects of a brand, such as the brand name, logo, get-up, etc., may of course be registered as trade marks and, as has been stated above, there are attractive reasons for seeking registration of as many elements as possible. However, it should be borne in mind that despite the fact that the TMA 1994 makes it possible to register elements that were previously unregistrable, registration is only permitted if such elements function as trade marks. As we will see in later chapters, features of a brand such as the product's shape, packaging, label design, etc., that do not function in this way will be refused registration or be removed from the Register if already registered.[65]

(b) The function of a trade mark

2–103 The function of a trade mark is the subject of continuing speculation and debate amongst legal academics[66] and is frequently said to be the determining factor in assessing questions of trade mark validity and infringement.[67] Legal writers have suggested[68] that trade marks fulfil as many as six different functions which include the identification of the product, identification of the physical source, or an anonymous source, a guarantee as to quality, as well as an advertising function and a merchandising role. For the purposes of this discussion we will consider these various functions within four broad categories, namely:

    (i) as an indication of origin;

    (ii) as a means of differentiation;

    (iii) as a guarantee of quality;

    (iv) as an advertising or investment function.

---

[65] See for example the *Philips* case where a registration of the face plate of a three headed razor was described as a limping mark and was eventually removed from the Register. This case is discussed in Chap. 3, para. 3–37. See also *Proctor & Gamble Ltd's Trade Marks Applications* [1999] R.P.C. 673, CA discussed in Chap. 4, at para. 4–39.

[66] See, for example, Cornish, p. 612; Annand and Norman, pp. 13–17, Wilkof *Trade Mark Licensing* (Sweet & Maxwell, London, 1995) Chap. 2; Schechter Rational Basis and Historical Foundations; Sanders/Maniatis "A Consumer Trade Mark: Protection Based on Origin and Quality" [1993] 11 E.I.P.R. 406.

[67] Case 102/77 *Hoffman-La Roche, Centrafarm v. American Home Products; Deutsche Renault AG v. Audi AG* [1995] 1 C.M.L.R. 461 at 483/4. See for example the Advocate General's Opinion in *Sabel BV v. Puma AG* [1997] T.M.R. 283 at 301 and *Wagamama Ltd v. City Centre Restaurants Plc* [1995] F.S.R. 713 at 730.

[68] See Wilkof, p. 19.

(i) Trade marks as indicators of origin

2-104   As Schechter acknowledged, one of the earliest uses of trade marks was by members of trade associations or guilds for the purposes of identifying the person responsible for making them. As commercial trade has developed, however, and international trade has grown the use of trade marks as a shorthand identifier of the person or company responsible for manufacturing goods has also increased. Whilst early trade marks may well have included a reference to the name of an individual or company this was not necessarily the case and indeed with the development of branded products it became more common for brand names to be registered as trade marks without reference to the name of the company that was responsible for making it. Today, consumers are encouraged to rely upon brand names as a means of distinguishing between products and, even where it can be shown that consumers do not know the identity of the company that owns the brand name it is still possible for the brand owner to obtain relief against a competitor using a similar mark.[69] In today's market place where many household trade marks are in fact owned by organisations with which consumers are unfamiliar, the recognition of trade marks as indicators of source (albeit of an anonymous source) is still important. It is unlikely, however, that consumers equate a particular trade mark with a particular place of manufacture and indeed reliance on a trade mark as the source of manufacture may actually be misleading since with increased licensing and subcontracting it is quite possible that the owner of the mark and the manufacturer are not the same organisation or even based in the same continent. It was for these reasons and others that Schechter argued that the origin function of trade marks should be regarded as historic and that other functions of trade marks, most notably the advertising function, should be acknowledged. Despite his arguments the United Kingdom TMA 1938 still identified the function of a trade mark as being to indicate origin. This was set out in section 68(1) where it was said that a trade mark meant:

> "a mark used or proposed to be used in relation to goods for the purpose of indicating, or so as to indicate, a connection in the course of trade between the goods and some person having the right either as proprietor or as registered user to use the mark . . .".

As Annand and Norman note[70] this definition:

> "came to permeate every aspect of the 1938 Act, and consequently had a restrictive effect."

This was especially true of the infringement provisions where a mark was held not to infringe a registered trade mark if it was not used "as a trade mark" as defined by section 68(1).[71] Although the TMA 1994 does not include an express provision stating that the function of a trade mark is to indicate origin the same limited interpretation of the function of a trade mark remains. This has been confirmed on a number of occasions and in particular in *Philips Electronics NV v. Remington Consumer Products Ltd,*[72] in the *Wagamama* case[73] and in *Zino Davidoff SA v.*

---

[69] Reference to *Birmingham Vinegar Co Limited v. Powell* [1897] A.C. 710.
[70] p. 15.
[71] See *Mars GB Ltd v. Cadbury Ltd* [1987] R.P.C. 387.
[72] [1999] E.T.M.R. 816, CA.
[73] At 729–731.

A & G Imports Ltd[74] where Laddie J. emphasised that a trade mark is designed to identify properly the trade origin of goods and not the novelty, design, nature or quality of the goods. He based his analysis on the jurisprudence of the ECJ.[75]

2–105   Even before the Directive was adopted, the ECJ had emphasised in its judgments that the identification of origin function of trade marks was the fundamental basis upon which trade mark protection was granted. Although there have been calls to acknowledge other important functions which trade marks serve (discussed below) the courts and legislature have so far resisted them.[76]

(ii) Product differentiation function

2–106   The definition of a trade mark as set out in section 1(1) of the TMA 1994 describes a trade mark in terms of its power to distinguish the goods (or services) of one trade from those of another. Certainly this function of distinguishing goods is at the heart of trade mark protection. If a mark cannot be relied upon to distinguish between traders it cannot fulfil any other role except perhaps as a description of the goods or decoration of them. Those that have analysed trade marks from an economic point of view, justify the grant of trade mark protection (and the rights attendant to it) on the basis that trade marks enable consumers to distinguish between products (not just products from different sources but also variations from the same source), and that trade marks can thus reduce the searching costs of customers.[77] Although this function has been acknowledged by legal writers[78] it has yet to receive judicial recognition.

(iii) The quality function

2–107   One of the functions of a trade mark is said to be that of guaranteeing the quality of goods to the consumer. Although this guarantee is not legally binding it is in the trade mark owner's interest to maintain the quality of the goods to which the mark is applied, if not to improve them. A customer buying goods marked with a particular trade mark has an expectation that all goods bearing the same mark will be of the same quality. If a third party is able to use the same mark on an inferior quality product this would damage the reputation of the true trade mark owner and consumers would feel that they could no longer rely upon the mark as an indicator of the quality of the product.

2–108   Trade marks, unlike hallmarks, are not guarantees of quality in the strict sense although if a trade mark owner uses his mark in such a way that it becomes liable to mislead the public it is possible for a third party to apply to have the registration revoked.[79]

---

[74] [1999] E.T.M.R. 700.
[75] *Hoffman-La Roche & Co AG v. Centrafarm* [1978] E.C.R. 1139 and *IHT Internationale Heiztechnik v. Ideal Standard* [1994] E.C.R. 1–2789.
[76] It has been argued that the advertising function of trade marks has to some extent been acknowledged in the Directive as a result of references to "dilution" of a distinctiveness of a mark. The subject of dilution is discussed below and in Chaps 4 and 5. In *Parfums Christian Dior SA v. Evora BV* [1998] E.T.M.R. 26 the ECJ accepted that inferior quality advertising could damage the reputation of a trade marked product. This case is discussed further in Chap. 6.
[77] This is discussed in further detail in Chap. 8, at paras 8–12—8–21.
[78] For example Annand and Norman, p. 15.
[79] s.46(1)(d) TMA 1994.

The quantity or guarantee function of a trade mark has received some judicial endorsement particularly by the ECJ which referred to the guarantee function (like the origin function) as the "essential function of a trade mark".[80]

> "Trade marks . . . act as a guarantee, to the consumer, that all goods bearing a particular mark have been produced by, or under the control of, the same manufacturer and are therefore likely to be of similar quality. The guarantee of quality offered by a trade mark is not of course absolute, for the manufacturer is at liberty to vary the quality; however, he does so at his own risk and he—not his competitors—will suffer the consequences if he allows the quality to decline. Thus, although trade marks do not provide any form of *legal* guarantee of quality—the absence of which may have misled some to underestimate their significance—they do in economic terms provide such a guarantee, which is acted upon daily by consumers."[81]

(iv) Investment or advertising function

2–109   ". . . [T]oday the trade mark is not merely the symbol of goodwill but often the most effective agent for the creation of goodwill, imprinting upon the public mind an anonymous and impersonal guarantee of satisfaction, creating a desire for further satisfaction. The mark actually sells the goods. And, self-evidently, the more distinctive the mark, the more effective is its selling power."[82]

Following his analysis of the functions of trade marks, Schechter concluded that as a consequence of the extensive use of advertising to promote trade marked goods such trade marks increasingly came to signify more than just the commercial origin of the goods. Schechter argued that as a result of extensive advertising trade marks acquired a particular value apart from the goods to which they were applied. Such was the value of established marks and the goodwill they engendered, he said, that third parties would seek to use the marks in relation to unrelated product areas, for example, use of the name Kodak in connection with bicycles.[83] Schechter went on to argue that the use of well known marks in this way diluted the distinctiveness of the original mark. He said that coined or unique trade marks (that is inherently distinctive trade marks) should be protected from this "gradual whittling away or dispersion of the identity and hold upon the public mind" resulting from the use of such trade marks on non-competing goods.[84] His assertion that the true value of a trade mark depended on its advertising function was not, however, universally accepted at the time, although support for his views has since grown.[85]

2–110   Section 10(3) of the TMA 1994 (equivalent to Article 5 of the Directive)[86] grants trade mark owners protection against the use of an identical or similar mark on dissimilar goods in certain circumstances if the use "takes unfair

---

[80] *Hoffman-La Roche & Co. AG v. Centrafarm* (case 192/77) [1978] E.C.R. 1139; *SA CNL-Sucal NV v. Hag GF AG* (Case C–10/89) [1990] 3 C.M.L.R. 571 ("Hag II"); and also *IHT Internationale Heiztechnik GmbH v. Ideal Standard GmbH* [1994] E.C.R. 1–2789.
[81] *Hag II* at 583 quoted by Laddie J. in *Wagamama* at 729.
[82] Rational Basis, p. 819.
[83] *Eastman Photographic v. Griffiths* (1898) 15 R.P.C. 105.
[84] Rational Basis, p. 825.
[85] In 1995 the U.S. introduced the Federal Trademark Dilution Act to protect well known trade marks against dilution. The subject of dilution is discussed further in Chap. 5.
[86] This provision is discussed in detail in Chap. 5.

advantage of or is detrimental to, the distinctive character or repute of the trade mark". It has been said[87] that references to taking of "unfair advantage" and "detrimental use" signify an acknowledgment of the advertising function of trade mark since there is no mention of confusion as to origin. Whilst this may be true, it is suggested that these provisions are more likely to be interpreted in line with the role of trade marks as indictors of origin or guarantees of quality as this is consistent with the approach adopted by the ECJ to date. Trade marks will not be able to perform these functions if they become devalued or common place. Having said that, in the recent case of *Dior v. Evora*[88] concerning the use of registered trade marks by a third party in advertising material, the Advocate General acknowledged that, in certain circumstances, the manner in which the mark is used in advertisements can affect the esteem in which the mark is held and this in turn could damage the mark as a whole. Whilst accepting that use of a trade mark by a third party in poor quality advertising could detract from the image created around the trade mark, the ECJ refused to grant relief unless it could be shown that the advertising was seriously damaging. Although this case goes some way towards recognising the importance of imagery associated with a trade mark, the difficulty for the trade mark owner will be demonstrating the true impact of such poor quality advertising on the trade mark.

2–111   In his analysis of the functions of a trade mark Cornish suggests that the measure of whether the new E.C. law protects the "investment function" of marks will turn upon the trade mark owners ability to prevent parallel imports or grey market goods, that is, the importation of goods into the EEA when the goods were originally marketed in a country outside the EEA.[89] However, in the recent *Silhouette*[90] case whilst upholding the trade mark owner's right to prevent imports into the E.U. of goods first sold with the trade mark owner's consent outside the EEA, the ECJ was silent on the question of the functions of a trade mark. The ECJ's decision was, however, regarded as influenced more by political interests than concerns about the proper functions of trade marks.[91] Nevertheless, in the context of parallel imports within the community the ECJ has continued to stress in cases relating to the repackaging of pharmaceutical products that the specific purpose of a trade mark is to guarantee to the end user the identity of the trade-marked product's origin.[92] It has not therefore granted protection to the advertising function of a trade mark.

2–112   The Directive does not indicate that a trade mark may serve only one function. In fact, recital 10 of the Directive merely states that the function of a trade mark is "*in particular* to guarantee the trade mark as an indication of origin . . ." (*emphasis added*) which suggests a recognition that this is not the only function of a trade mark but rather one of a number of functions. Such an interpretation would allow the ECJ scope to acknowledge other functions of trade marks as circumstances of particular cases allow.

2–113   As it is, the persistent assertion that the proper function of a trade mark is to indicate origin by implication suggests that other functions of trade marks are

---

[87] Annand and Norman, p. 15.
[88] *Parfums Christian Dior v. Evora BV* [1997] E.T.M.R. 323.
[89] s.12 TMA 1994.
[90] *Silhouette International v. Hartlauer* [1998] E.T.M.R. 286.
[91] For an impassioned discussion of the ECJ's decision see Cornish "Trade Mark: Portcullis for the EEA" [1998] 5 E.I.P.R. 172.
[92] See by way of example the Advocate-General's Opinion in this case in *Pharmarcia & Upjohn SA v. Paranova A/S* [1999] E.T.M.R. 937.

not recognised by the courts and so will not be protected under the TMA 1994. This limitation of the function of trade marks to that of source indication, will as we shall see, influence how the TMA 1994 is interpreted, and accordingly, how brands are protected.

PART III: ESSENTIAL ELEMENTS OF A TRADE MARK

2–114   Section 1(1) of the TMA 1994 sets out the definition of a trade mark:

> ". . . a 'trade mark' means any sign capable of being represented graphically which is capable of distinguishing goods or services of one undertaking from those of other undertakings.
>   A trade mark may, in particular, consist of words (including personal names), designs, letters, numerals or the shape of goods or their packaging."

It can be seen from this definition that to be regarded as a trade mark a sign must fulfil two conditions:

(i)   it must be capable of being represented graphically; and

(ii) it must be capable of distinguishing the goods or services of one undertaking from those of other undertakings.

The White Paper[93] indicates that the term "sign" is to be interpreted broadly and that no forms of sign are to be automatically excluded from the scope of the Act. Indeed, Jacob J. noted in *Philips v. Remington*[93a] that a "sign" is "anything which can convey information" and the only qualification is that it must be capable of being represented graphically. Thus as the Act itself suggests it is possible for signs to consist of words (including personal names), designs, letters, numerals or the shape of goods or their packaging, as well as sounds and fragrances. Furthermore, such signs can be registered provided that they satisfy the further condition that they are capable of distinguishing, or in other words are distinctive. Although the requirement for graphic representation would on the face of it appear relatively straightforward[94]) in fact it has given rise to a number of decisions regarding the acceptability of descriptions, formulae or other technical information as a means of representing the mask,[94a] in essence, people searching the register must be able to identify precisely what the sign is from the graphic representation. If the representation is in any way ambiguous, or if it requires the person reading it to undertake further steps to identify the mark then it will be unacceptable. The issue of distinctiveness is rather more complex. Thus as Kitchin and Mellor observe[95]:

> "Academically, it may be interesting to debate the ways in which those things [sounds, smells and tastes] may be represented graphically, . . . the real point is whether those things actually perform any trade mark function in practice. Does a smell which is being considered for registration actually distinguish in trade? . . ."

---

[93] Cmnd 1203, 1990 para 2.06.
[93a] [1998] E.T.M.R. 124 at 139.
[94] *Ty Nant Spring Water Ltd's Trade Mark Application* [1999] R.P.C. 392.
[94a] See *Swizzel Mat Low Ltd's Application* [1999] R.P.C. 55; *Ty Nant Spring Water Ltd's Application* [2000]; *Venootschap onder firma Senta Aromatic Marketing's Application* [1999] E.T.M.R. 429.
[95] Kitchin & Mellor *The Trade Marks Act 1994* (London: Sweet and Maxwell, 1995), p. 26–11 ("Kitchin").

The issue of distinctiveness is not a new one but is one that has been at the heart of the debate concerning the level of protection that should be granted to trade marks.[96] According to Kitchin, it is not possible to consider the question of distinctiveness in isolation, one must also bear in mind section 3 of the TMA 1994 which sets out the absolute grounds for refusing registration of a trade mark. Regard should also be had to the function of a trade mark as it is only by considering the function of a mark that the capacity to distinguish can be fully appreciated.

2–115   As we have seen above, historically the most important function of a trade mark was to distinguish the goods of one manufacturer or supplier from those of another. If the mark is wholly descriptive of the product, for example, "Tyres" for tyres or "Chocolate confectionery" for confectionery products coated in chocolate, then the mark cannot be relied upon to distinguish the source of the goods as opposed to merely describing the goods.[96a]

2–116   The question of distinctiveness can be considered as a scale, at one end of which are marks that are considered to be wholly descriptive whilst at the other, marks are considered to be inherently distinctive.[97] Between these two extremes marks can be more or less distinctive. The ability of a mark to distinguish products may vary depending upon the nature of the goods to which the mark is applied and whether or not the mark has actually been used.

2–117   Under the TMA 1938 Act those marks that were considered inherently capable of distinguishing were registered in what was known as Part A of the Register whilst those marks which were considered capable of distinguishing were registrable in Part B only.[98] Frequently, marks that were not considered to be inherently distinctive were accepted as registrable within Part B of the Register as a result of the use that had been made of the mark which demonstrated that the mark had become distinctive in fact. Some marks however, were considered incapable of achieving the necessary level of distinctiveness for registration, or for policy reasons, were refused registration. For example, marks that were regarded as purely descriptive or consisted of terms customary in the trade were refused registration despite the level of use of the mark, as in the case of the mark "York" which was refused registration because of its reference to the geographical origin of the products concerned.[99] Although the threshold for registration in Part B of the register under the TMA 1938 involved similar criteria to those set out in section 1(1) it is unlikely that the cases determined under the Act will prove very influential in determining what may be accepted under the TMA 1994 since the latter sets out in section 3 further requirements concerning distinctiveness and because the definition of a trade mark is itself different to that under consideration in earlier cases.[1]

2–118   Once an application for registration of a trade mark has been filed the Trade Marks Office can raise any of the absolute grounds set out in section 3 as a basis for refusing to register the trade mark. Signs that do not meet the

---

[96] Under the TMA 1938 the level of distinctiveness of a mark determined whether the mark could be registered in Part A or Part B of the Register. This division of the register was significant in the context of infringement where a lower level of protection was afforded to marks registered in Part B (see s.5 TMA 1938). The TMA 1994 removed this division. It remains to be seen, however, whether all marks will receive the benefit of the same level of protection irrespective of the distinctiveness of the mark.

[96a] *Philips Electronics NV v. Remington Consumer Products* [1999] E.T.M.R. 816, CA; *Bach and Bach Flower Remedies Trade Marks* [1999] R.P.C. 1; *The Times*, December 1999, CA.

[97] Invented words such as Kodak and Zeneca are good examples of marks that are inherently distinctive.

[98] ss.9 and 10.

[99] *York* [1984] R.P.C. 231, HL.

[1] In Chap. 3 (paras 3–40 and following), further consideration will be given to the relationship between ss.1 and 3 TMA 1994.

requirements of section 1(1) will be refused as will marks that are devoid of any distinctive character[2]; marks that are wholly descriptive,[3] and marks that are customary in the language or in the trade,[4] although such marks may acquire the necessary distinctiveness as a result of use.[5]

2–119   In his analysis of the meaning of section 3 Geoffrey Hobbs Q.C., acting as the Lord Chancellor's Appointed Person to hear an appeal from the Trade Marks Office concerning the refusal to register the trade mark *AD2000*,[6] explained that the refusal to register trade marks that meet the threshold of section 1(1) but fail section 3 stems from the fact that trade marks are primarily protected because of their function to indicate the source of the goods to which the mark is applied. Basing his analysis upon the wording of the Directive and the jurisprudence of the ECJ as reviewed by Laddie J. in the *Wagamama* case,[7] he concluded that the protection afforded to a trade mark "is in particular to guarantee the trade mark as an indication of origin." Trade marks without the capacity to communicate to consumers that the goods in question come from a particular source lack sufficient distinctiveness to be registered and protected as a badge of origin. As the ECJ noted in *Hag II*[8]:

> "Trade mark rights . . . constitute an essential element in the system of undistorted competition which the Treaty is intended to establish. In such a system, undertakings must be able to attract and retain customers by the quality of their products and services, which is possible only thanks to the existence of distinctive signs allowing them to be identified. For the trade mark to be able to fulfil that function, it must constitute a guarantee that all products which bear it have been manufactured under the control of a single undertaking to which responsibility for their quality may be attributed."

Thus when a sign serves only to describe the goods, or characteristics of them, or has no distinctive character "people exposed to the use of it are not generally likely to regard it as something which provides an indication as to the provenance of the goods or services with reference to which it is used".[9]

Thus the function of a trade mark as an indication of the source of goods is pivotal in determining whether the mark is sufficiently distinctive to be accepted for registration.

Conclusion

2–120   To conclude, United Kingdom I.P. laws have developed on an ad hoc basis, often in response to lobbying and political pressure. In recent years the United Kingdom has come under particular pressure to change its laws to harmonise them with those of other E.U. Member States in the interests of the common market and the free movement of goods. Harmonisation is an ambitious goal bearing in mind the different legal approaches to IP that have evolved over the years.

---

[2] s.3(1)(b) TMA 1994.
[3] s.3(1)(c) TMA 1994.
[4] s.31(d) TMA 1994.
[5] See s.3 proviso and the comments of Jacob J. in *British Sugar Plc v. James Robertson & Sons Ltd* [1996] R.P.C. 281 at 305–306.
[6] *Allied Domecq Plc's Application* (AD2000) [1997] E.T.M.R. 259 (the *"Allied Domecq"* case) at 259–262.
[7] [1995] F.S.R. 713 at 729–731.
[8] [1990] 3 C.M.L.R. 571.
[9] *Allied Domecq* at 261.

2–121 As can be seen from the brief outline of the historical development of the various IP rights set out above, there have been no clear guiding principles justifying the creation of new rights or the expansion of existing ones and the boundaries between one right and another are sometimes ill defined. In the main, the rights have developed in response to a perceived market need, more often in response to continued lobbying than to academic argument. Although legal theories have been advanced to justify the grant of IP rights none have been universally accepted and many remain open to criticism.[10]

2–122 We have seen that patent protection is granted to protect new inventions and is justified on the basis that an incentive is needed to encourage inventors to disclose their ideas and as a reward for inventiveness and that copyright exists to protect expressions of ideas and is justified on a similar basis. These two forms of protection form what is known as the patent/copyright paradigm. Other forms of protection such as design protection and trade mark protection are not justified on the same basis and, perhaps as a consequence, are not protected to the same degree.

Trade mark protection is traditionally justified as a means of protecting the trade with which the mark is associated, as an incentive to manufacturers to develop new products and maintain the quality of existing ones. Trade marks also act as guarantees (in economic terms) of quality and origin to consumers. Protection from confusion as to origin is thus in the interests of both the consumer and the manufacturer and is regarded as one of the central tenets of trade mark protection. Brands like designs are social phenomena that have evolved as a consequence of developments in the market place. Whereas brands to marketers are an entity, to lawyers they are not so much of an entity as a collection of attributes each of which may to be protection by different I.P. rights. Where third parties seek to imitate aspects of a brand lawyers are left grappling for the rights out of traditions developed for completely different purposes. As we have seen, IP rights are very much the product of their own histories. Although trade mark registration may initially have been designed to protect branded products the manner in which brands have developed since 1875 has meant that there is now a significant difference between a registered trade mark and a branded product. Despite attempts by Schechter and others to argue for an enhanced understanding of the role of trade marks (more akin to that of a brand) the courts have remained stoic in their assertion that the proper function of a trade mark is to indicate origin.

2–123 In the chapters that follow we will consider the different aspects of branded products and examine exactly how the framework of legal rights outlined above can be applied to protect brands from unauthorised copying and imitation. Some of the rights, such as registered trade marks, will prove more adept than others although it will be seen that each right has its limitations. Ultimately, we will see that not all aspects of a brand are protected to the same degree and indeed in some areas the protection is very limited.

The grant of exclusive rights, however, has to be balanced against society's desire for free and unfettered competition. If the balance is not right it can, as we have seen, lead to cycles of over and under protection which are themselves counter productive. As Cornish observes,[11] the question of whether the balance is appropriate needs to be continually reviewed in the light of the "economic needs of the country and the prevailing sense of what is just". It is with this in mind that we now turn to consider how brands are currently protected in practice in the United Kingdom.

---

[10] These are considered further in Chap. 8, at paras to 8–09 to 8–43.
[11] Cornish, p. 6.

CHAPTER 3

Protecting Product Appearance

"Nowhere is the real essence of a brand more powerfully and definitively expressed than in its visual presentation."[1]

IS PRODUCT APPEARANCE IMPORTANT?

3–01 It is axiomatic in the fashion and sports industries that appearance can make or break a product (or even its manufacturer). What may be surprising, however, is the importance of product appearance in other fields where factors other than design are commonly expected to play a decisive role in the customer's decision making process.[2] As one English judge observed[3]:

"Those who wish to purchase an article for use are often influenced in their choice not only by practical efficiency but by appearance. Common experience shows that not all are influenced in the same way. Some look for artistic merit. Some are attracted by a design which is strange or bizarre. Many simply choose the article which catches their eye. Whatever the reason may be one article with a particular design may sell better than one without it: then it is profitable to use the design. And much thought, time and expense may have been incurred in finding a design which will increase sales."

3–02 One example of a simple but profitable change in design was the change in Tetley tea bag which was square and became round. Following the change the brand became the number one tea bag brand in England.[4] Sales were also boosted for another product, the Toilet Duck lavatory cleaner, when its packaging was given a new twist (in the neck of the bottle). Such was its success that a flood of similar looking cleaners soon appeared on supermarket shelves. Why? Because consumers were attracted to the Toilet Duck by its appearance. Although some might argue that the Toilet Duck packaging was functional (that is, the shape of the packaging was dictated by the function it was to perform), it was not the only design that could have been selected. There were clearly elements of the design that had aesthetic appeal alone, as with the "round" tea bag. As John Towers, Chief Executive of Rover Group, noted[5]:

---

[1] J. Hall "Brand development: How design can add value" *The Journal of Brand Management* ("Hall").
[2] Medical equipment is a sector where design has become paramount in part because of competitive pressures which make it difficult for Western medical businesses to compete with Far Eastern products based on price alone. See Rassam *Design & Corporate Success* (Gower Publishing, Aldershot, 1995), p. 32 ("Design & Corporate Success").
[3] Whitford J. *Interlego AG v. Alex Foley (Vic) Ltd* [1987] F.S.R. 283 at 295 (hereafter "*Interlego v. Alex Foley*").
[4] *The Times*, November 29, 1995.
[5] *Design & Corporate Success*, p. ix.

"Today's customers are faced by an avalanche of choice in every product sector, from toasters and televisions to cameras and cars. For producers, success in the market no longer rests on technical issues of quality and reliability. These are assumed to be of a high standard and indeed are now the price of entry to the shop window or showroom. The role of design in determining a product's commercial success is therefore becoming more important and is as central to a progressive manufacturer's strategy as it is in determining which product sells instead of another . . . Good designs are successful not simply as a result of their function; they should also represent value through emotive elements of style and character."

In 1990 the French company Allègre Puériculture, maker of baby bottles and feeding utensils, made a strategic decision to break free from its traditional approach to product promotion whereby its brand name and packaging were what distinguished its products from those of its competitors. Instead, it brought design to the forefront of its business activities. Its goal was product differentiation by design. By differentiating its products by means of design it was able to increase its turnover over the next few years by 77 per cent.[6]

3–03 Allègre Puériculture is not alone in recognising the importance of product design as a means of product differentiation. Indeed, research conducted by American academics[7] has shown that in United States/West German trade, non-price features are the dominant cause of trade success rather than price advantage. Similar research in the United Kingdom endorsed the view that consumers do not make purchasing decisions based solely on price grounds.[8]

3–04 Although there has not been extensive research into the effects of investment in design in small and medium sized enterprises, what there has been has shown that there is a greater financial benefit to businesses investing in design than is commonly thought to be the case.[9] This may account for the level of spending each year on design royalties and fees which, according to research carried out by the Netherlands Design Institute, amounted to 7.3 billion ECU in Europe alone, in 1993.[10] An analysis of design-leading companies (that is, those companies that have a high number of Design Council citations and awards and receive a high evaluation from their competitors) confirms that such firms are significantly more profitable than other companies,[11] confirming the view that differentiation by design is associated with competitive advantage. As John McArthur, Dean of Harvard Business School observed[12]:

"As global competition becomes more intense, new dimensions of competitive strategy have received increasing attention. One of the most important is

[6] J. Thackara Winners! How Today's Successful Companies Innovate by Design (Gower Publishing, Aldershot, 1997) ("Winners"), p. 60.
[7] Design & Corporate Success, p. 31 (quoting research published by Kravis & Lipsey in Price Competitiveness and World Trade).
[8] ibid., p. 31 (quoting research published by Schott and Pick published in 1983).
[9] ibid., p. 33 (quoting research results produced by Open University/UMIST Design Innovation Group, 1990).
[10] Winners, p. 33. The leading Japanese companies are said to invest significantly more in professional product design than their U.S. or European counterparts. (See Blaich Product Design and Corporate Strategy (McGraw Hill, USA, 1993), p. 27.
[11] Design & Corporate Success, p. 35 (quoting from the research results produced by Open University/UMIST Design Innovation Group, 1990).
[12] Foreword Designing for Product Success essays and case studies from the TRIAD design project exhibition, Design Management Institute, Boston 1989.

design and the management of design. Even as recently as five years ago, most managers considered good design almost frivolous. They viewed designers as people who simply determine the colour and overall appearance of design. When the success of companies like Braun in Germany or Sony in Japan is analysed, however, the significance of design to their company's reputation and profitability becomes clear. Design—from reliance performance to quality appearance—is indeed a crucial competitive weapon."

Having achieved a distinctive or striking appearance for a new product,[13] it is essential to consider how best to protect these features, if any attempt is to be made to safeguard their exclusivity and restrain unauthorised copying or product imitation. As both the makers of the Tetley tea bag and the Toilet Duck discovered, a successful and well differentiated product will inevitably be imitated by competitors. If no steps are taken to protect the product's appearance, prior to launch, it will be too late to do so once others have followed suit. Frequently, the consequence is that the unique and distinctive appearance of the innovative product is lost forever and the investment in the development of the design which enabled the product to stand out from the competition is effectively written off. Thus product appearance forms an integral part of a brand's anatomy.

3–05   The aim of this chapter therefore is to consider how, from a legal point of view, the appearance of a product can be protected in the United Kingdom and how effective such protection can be when imitations begin to appear on the market and litigation ensues. For the purposes of illustration and discussion, the legal issues will be considered by comparing and contrasting two distinctive products, namely the Rubik's Cube puzzle, which became the subject of a world-wide craze in the 1980's, and the Lego building brick which is an enormously successful product. Little protection had been sought for the Rubik's Cube puzzle prior to its launch whereas extensive legal protection has been sought throughout the world in relation to the Lego brick. Attention will initially focus upon the manner in which such products can be protected (prior to launch) before considering the weakness in protection.

3–06   It should be stated at the outset that the comments and recommendations made in this chapter regarding the level of legal protection are those applicable in an ideal situation where the budget for protection is unlimited. It is acknowledged that in reality no product has such unlimited spending power behind its launch, for this is the moment when the capital invested in the development of the project already heavily outweighs the immediate returns. Only products with a significant expected life span and virtually guaranteed success (which must be the exception rather than the rule) will justify such legal protection at this early stage. Thus, for most product owners, there is a difficult balance to strike between the resources spent on legal protection and those spent on marketing and promotion. It is therefore hoped that this chapter will illustrate how a wise allocation of funds at the outset will result in long term benefits both in terms of product life and market share, which will in turn, convince those responsible for the allocation of resources that investing in marketing and promotion rather than legal protection is nothing short of marketing myopia.

---

[13] This chapter is primarily concerned with product appearance *per se* as opposed to the appearance or get-up of packaging where other factors may be pertinent. The protection of product packaging is discussed in detail in Chap. 4.

3–07   As one design consultant observed[14]:

"With little distinction between many competitive products at point-of-sale, packaging [and product shape generally] has become an important means of differentiation. . . . Greater emphasis is being placed on the shape of packaging, its functionality and its role in the marketing process."

Product shape (as well as packaging shape) can play an important role in product differentiation, not least in enabling the product to stand out from its competitors. It can also add to the perceived value of the product as a whole. The physical pack can also become a key element in building a strong brand identity that is easily distinguished from those of competing products as in the case of the Coca-Cola bottle, the Jif lemon and the Toblerone triangular comb.[15] Some brands have gone beyond this even, becoming almost synonymous with the shape of the product as in the case of the Frisbee or the Yo-yo.[16] Given that product appearance can affect the long term success of a product, steps need to be taken to assess the value of the appearance of such products and ensure that they are properly protected, before they are launched.

THE LEGAL PROTECTION OF PRODUCT APPEARANCE

3–08   When considering how to protect a product it is important to remember that intellectual property laws (that is, trade mark, copyright, design and patent laws) provide a variety of means for protecting different aspects of a naked product.[17] To see how these different laws may be relied upon in practice to provide a framework of legal protection against unauthorised copying or product imitation, we need to consider each right in turn as it applies to the different facets of a product's physical appearance using the Lego building brick and the Rubik's Cube puzzle as examples. I have assumed, for the purposes of this section, that the two products have not yet been launched on the market. Where in practice, these two products and their associated legal rights have been the subject of judicial examination the findings of the court will be indicated.

Lego bricks

3–09   Lego, as a toy, consists of a range of brick pieces of different shapes and sizes. The essential features of a typical brick are brightly coloured plastic with a number of round studs on the upper surface and corresponding tubes on the lower surface protected by a thin skirt. The sides of a typical brick are smooth with square corners.[18] Each Lego brick is sold as part of a construction set; the aim is to construct an object by connecting the various different pieces together using the stud and tube mechanism.

---

[14] Hall, p. 99.
[15] This will be considered further in Chap. 4.
[16] Although instinctively one might think that these shapes are functional the fact is that although elements of them are functional, *e.g.* the central spindle of the Yo-yo other elements are not, *e.g.* the external appearance of the two sides.
[17] The basic principles of each of these laws are set out in Chap. 2, at para. 2–09—2–64.
[18] See Appendix C, photograph 1.

Rubik's Cube puzzle

3-10   The Rubik's Cube puzzle is a puzzle in the shape of a cube with each side subdivided into nine smaller cubes; each of the small cubes has a coloured sticker affixed to it such that one side of the puzzle appears to be all blue, another red, still another all yellow and so on.[19] The colours themselves are quite striking especially against the black background of the cube itself. The sides of the cube can be rotated around a central axis such that the smaller cubes change the colour pattern. The aim of the puzzle is, by a series of rotating movements, to mix up the colour pattern and then to return the puzzle to its original appearance with one colour only on each of the six sides.[20]

(i) Design registration

3-11   As we saw in Chapter 2, the shape and configuration of products such as the Lego brick and the Rubik's Cube puzzle can be protected by means of design registrations under section 1(1) of the Registered Designs Act 1949 (RDA) as amended by the Copyright, Designs and Patents Act 1988 (CDPA). Protection will not, however, extend to features that "must match" those of another article or to methods or principles of construction.[21] Thus the interlocking system of studs and tubes that enables Lego bricks to be connected one to another cannot be protected by means of design registration. These features are more accurately described as a method or principle of construction and as such are more appropriately protected by means of a patent, assuming that it is novel and inventive, etc.[22] Thus in relation to the Lego brick, design protection can only be sought in relation to the overall shape and configuration of the brick (excluding the functional features). Any application for registration of a design must be filed before the product is made public otherwise protection will be denied.[23]

3-12   The Rubik's Cube puzzle is striking in its appearance with its distinctive colouring and apparent simplicity of design. As the external appearance of the cube is integral to its appeal it would be appropriate to consider registration of the puzzle as a design. The actual method of operating the puzzle, however, would not be protectable by design registration but might be protected by means of a patent.

3-13   The Rubik's Cube puzzle may qualify for design registration in respect of its shape and configuration (that is, the six-sided cube with each side consisting of nine cubes). It might also qualify for registration in respect of the pattern or ornament applied to the surface, *i.e.* the arrangement of colours on different faces of the cube and the black background. Although at first one might be tempted to think that the wording of section 1(1) is tautologous (*e.g.* shape and configuration, pattern and ornament) case law has confirmed that it is not so much tautologous but rather "a belt and braces" approach. It is said,[24] for example, that configuration will normally be taken to refer to the contour of the surface moulding/decoration whereas shape could be said to refer to the outline of the product itself. Thus, in relation to a hot water bottle for example, "shape" refers to the outline of the hot

---

[19] See Appendix C, photograph 2.
[20] "Simple though it sounds, it has driven sundry men grey-haired and occupied some children I believe as little as 40 seconds" (*Politechnika Ipari Szovetkezet & Others v. Situls (Kensington) Ltd* March 25, 1982, CA (unreported) Templeman L.J.).
[21] s.1(1)(a) RDA.
[22] The requirements for patent protection are set out in Chap. 2.
[23] s.1(4)(b) RDA.
[24] See, for example, Fellner, *Industrial Designs Law* (Sweet & Maxwell, London, 1995), p. 18.

water bottle whereas "configuration" refers to the fins that are part of the moulding of the surface of the bottle.[25] Generally, pattern and ornament are taken to refer to two dimensional, surface decoration.

3–14 It will be recalled that a statement of novelty is required to support an application for design registration. In the case of the Rubik's Cube puzzle, novelty should be claimed in respect of the shape and configuration, pattern and ornament of the article. Although it would be possible to limit the statement of novelty to shape and configuration only, on the basis that any imitation of the shape of the cube would thus amount to an infringement irrespective of the surface colouring, it would also mean that a cube of different dimensions or of a different shape but with the same colour scheme might not be regarded as an infringement. Given the relatively small cost of design applications,[26] it would be prudent to submit applications for both aspects (*i.e.* one with a statement of novelty referring to pattern and ornament, the other referring to shape and configuration).

3–15 As we saw in the previous chapter, to qualify for design registration, the article must have, *inter alia*, features of shape, configuration, pattern or ornament applied by an industrial process which "in the finished article appeals to and are judged by the eye".[27] In *Interlego AG v. Tyco Industries*[28] the court considered in detail the views expressed by the House of Lords in *Amp Inc v. Utilux Pty Ltd*,[29] the leading authority on the question of "eye appeal". The principles set forth in *Amp v. Utilux* were that in order to be registered as a design an article should have eye-appeal and "in this context (a) the eye is that of the prospective customer and (b) the appeal is that created by a distinctiveness of shape . . . calculated to influence the customer's choice".[30]

3–16 Furthermore, if the shape is determined solely by the function that the article has to perform then it will be disqualified from registration. In determining whether the shape is dictated solely by function it was held that it is not sufficient simply to show that the function could have been performed by an article of some other shape. On the contrary, what is needed, is to demonstrate that the features concerned resulted from attempts to make the article more appealing to consumers rather than attempts to make the article perform a function. Further, if every feature of the shape is attributable to the function that the article is to perform then, according to Lord Reid, the article will not qualify for design registration.[31]

Lord Oliver, in *Interlego v. Tyco*, confirmed that the right to protection would not be conferred where every feature of a design is dictated by the function that the article has to perform. If, however, some features are included for aesthetic reasons then:

> "The incorporation into the shape as a whole of some (perhaps a majority of) features dictated solely by functional requirements will not bring the

---

[25] *Cow & Co. Ltd v. Cannon Rubber Manufacturers Ltd* [1959] R.P.C. 240.
[26] Approximately £300 in the U.K.
[27] s.1 RDA. This requirement of "eye appeal" is a modification of the wording used in earlier legislation which stated that the design must have "features which . . . appeal to and are judged *solely* by the eye" (emphasis added). The initial impression is that the modification in the current statute has relaxed the requirement for "eye appeal" but as Aldous J. noted in *Valeo Vision SA v. Flexible Lamps Ltd* ([1995] R.P.C. 205 at 214) but this is not, in fact the case. The test remains the same.
[28] [1989] A.C. 217 (the "*Interlego v. Tyco*" case).
[29] [1972] R.P.C. 103 (the "*Amp v. Utilux*" case).
[30] *per* Lord Oliver in *Interlego v. Tyco* (pp. 243–244), paraphrasing the findings of the House of Lords in *Amp v. Utilux* at, pp. 243–244.
[31] *Amp v. Utilux* at p. 110.

exclusion into operation so as to deprive it of protection, if there are also some features of the shape which are not attributable solely to function."[32]

As a result, a design as a whole may be capable of registration even though it comprises both features appealing to and judged by the eye and features dictated solely by function. Thus, a Lego brick would qualify for protection as a registered design if it could be shown that the brick includes features (such as the proportions, smooth sides, squared corners etc) that were specifically chosen for aesthetic reasons. Indeed, this was the interpretation applied in *Interlego v. Alex Foley* and in *Interlego v. Tyco*.[33]

3–17 The Rubik's Cube puzzle certainly does have a measure of "eye appeal" and on the basis of *Interlego v. Tyco* would also be *prima facie* acceptable for registration, unless all the features were held to be dictated by function. If such an objection were raised on the basis of the cubes function to rotate it could be argued that the shape and configuration of this particular puzzle are not dependant upon the function to rotate but rather to amuse, challenge and entertain and that specific aspects of the product's appearance were included in order to enhance its eye appeal, *e.g.* the rounded corners of each cube, the chamfered edges and the colour scheme. Although games are not bought for their aesthetic appeal, the appearance of the product can be a motivating factor in reaching a purchasing decision.

3–18 The "must match" provision[34] is a new addition to the RDA, introduced by amendment in 1988. Essentially it was included to deal with the spare parts trade where articles were manufactured industrially to match existing parts as in the case of an exhaust pipe or body panel of a car. In such situations registration is denied. The Rubik's Cube puzzle would not be caught by this exception as the provision would not apply to a stand alone toy. It might, however, prevent some toys (such as children's construction kits) or parts of them from being registered as designs.

3–19 A further requirement of the RDA is that of relative novelty. This means that at the date of the application for registration the design must not have been published in the United Kingdom, or registered in respect of the same or a similar article.[35] It is here that many potential applicants founder because over enthusiastic marketing departments have decided to press ahead with test marketing the product before ensuring that all the necessary legal steps have been taken to protect exclusivity. Such a step completely undermines a design application unless it can be shown that the disclosure was confidential.[36] Although a "focus group" might fall into this category (depending on the circumstances), testing marketing to members of the public will not.

3–20 The RDA does not elaborate upon the novelty threshold for registration except to say[37] that if a design is already registered in respect of the same article or if it differs only in immaterial details, or in features which are variants commonly used in the trade, it will not be registrable. Thus both the Lego brick and Rubik's Cube puzzle would arguably qualify for protection if details of the products have not been made public in the United Kingdom prior to the application date and there were no previous design registrations for these products at the time that the original applications were filed.

---

[32] *Amp v. Utilix* at 245.
[33] [1987] F.S.R. 283.
[34] s.1(b)(ii) RDA.
[35] s.4 RDA.
[36] See ss.1(4), 4 and 6 RDA.
[37] s.1(4) RDA.

(ii) Unregistered design right

3-21 The unregistered design right arises without the need for registration and belongs to the creator of a design; a design is said to include features of shape and configuration, but not surface decoration or ornamentation.[38] The right provides a degree of protection for industrial articles that would not otherwise qualify for design registration by virtue of their lack of eye appeal as well as providing an additional layer of legal protection for aesthetic articles that are (or could be) registered as designs. Excluded from protection under the unregistered design right are methods or principles of construction (as with their registered counterparts), "must fit" and "must match" articles or parts thereof where the design of the article is dependent upon another article.[39]

3-22 Assuming for the moment that the Rubik's Cube puzzle and the Lego brick were designed after August 1, 1989 (the date of implementation of the CDPA) then design rights would subsist in the shape and configuration of the puzzle (but not the surface decoration) and the brick provided that they are "original" that is, not commonplace in the design field in question.[40] According to the Court of Appeal in the *Farmers Build* case[41] the term "commonplace" does not equate to the requirement of novelty associated with other intellectual property rights although it is meant to be construed narrowly, and objectively by comparing the article to other similar articles in the field. If the same feature does not appear in the other articles then it will not be regarded as commonplace.

3-23 It is also necessary for the designer or the country of first marketing to meet the requirements of section 213(5) of the CDPA. This section states that the designer—which by virtue of section 214(1) means the person who creates the design (if not in pursuance of a commission or in the course of employment)—must be a qualifying individual.[42] A qualifying individual or qualifying person is defined as a citizen, or person habitually resident in a qualifying country (*i.e.* the United Kingdom, EEA or a country covered by a statutory instrument).[43]

3-24 The importance of these provisions is that if the designer does not satisfy these requirements no protection will be available in respect of the design unless the product is first marketed in the E.U.[43a] Thus, if (as in the case of the original Rubik's Cube puzzle) the product was designed in Hungary, then no design right protection would be granted to the designer of the puzzle unless it was first marketed in the United Kingdom. Unless deliberate efforts are made to ensure first marketing of the article in the United Kingdom through a qualifying company or individual[44] who is exclusively authorised to market the article by the person who would have been first owner of the design right,[44a] no design rights will arise.

3-25 As there is no registration or examination system for the unregistered design right the existence and scope of the right is not confirmed until action is taken for infringement. At this point the owner may seek to rely upon his/her design rights but will have nothing to prove to potential infringers that the right

---

[38] s.213 CDPA 1998.
[39] s.213(3) CDPA 1988.
[40] s.213(4) CPDA 1988.
[41] *Farmers Build Ltd v. Carrier Bulk Materials Handing* Ltd [1999] R.P.C. 461, CA.
[42] s.218 CDPA 1988.
[43] s.217(1) CDPA 1988; see also Design Right (Reciprocal Protection) (No. 2) Order 1989 (S.I. 1989 No. 1294).
[43a] This was found to be the position in *Mackie Designs Inc. v. Behringer* [1999] R.P.C. 717.
[44] That is, a resident of the U.K., EEA or country covered by statutory instrument—s.220 CDPA 1988.
[44a] To comply with section 220 CDPA 1988 and so obtain the benefit of UDR the exclusivity must be capable of being enforced in the United Kingdom by legal proceedings (s.220(4)).

actually subsists[45] especially if it is alleged by the defendant that the design is commonplace.[46] Although the right may prove to be a useful safety net if, for example, design registration was either overlooked or not possible, the protection offered is limited to exact reproductions or those substantially similar to the design.[47] If the design is particularly unusual or unique this may be sufficient but the danger for the design owner is that a small modification may be sufficient to avoid infringement.

(iii) Copyright

3–26   As we saw in Chapter 2, copyright will automatically subsist in relation to sketches and drawings from which the Lego building bricks are made. In some cases models (in the form of prototypes), might also qualify for protection as artistic works in their own right[48] assuming that they are not transitory.[49] Equally, the drawings and sketches of the Rubik's Cube puzzle will be protected by copyright.

3–27   Prior to August 1, 1989 proprietors of three dimensional articles could (with a few exceptions) rely upon copyright existing in the drawings of the article as the basis of an action for infringement, however, the historic House of Lords decision in *British Leyland Motor Corp v. Armstrong Patents Co*[50] heralded a change in fortune for "utilitarian" articles (that is, articles that are purely functional and non aesthetic). In that case, which concerned drawings of an exhaust pipe, it was argued that granting copyright protection to utilitarian articles was an abuse of the monopolistic powers granted under copyright law. Copyright law, it was argued, aimed to encourage learning and stimulate human advancement but it was being used in such a way as to stifle competition by restricting the ability of others to compete, amongst other things, the aftermarket for spare parts. The period of protection for copyright works (which at that stage was 50 years beyond the life of the author) meant that no competitor could successfully compete with the original manufacturer in the spare parts market without either taking a licence from the original author or infringing his copyright. The House of Lords in the *British Leyland* case relied upon the legal principle of non derogation from grant to justify its breaking the hold of manufacturers over the subsequent manufacture and supply of spare parts.

3–28   As noted in Chapter 2, the CDPA 1988 draws a distinction between design documents embodying designs for artistic works and those for something other than an artistic work.[51] In respect of the latter, although copyright subsists in the designs document itself it cannot be relied upon to give copyright protection to the design in question. Instead the owner must look to the UDR as the means of

---

[45] Whilst a design registration does not prove that a right actually subsists it is persuasive evidence since before registration is granted the design is examined for registrability and a search of prior rights is undertaken.

[46] *Farmers Build Ltd v. Carrier Bulk Materials Handling Ltd* [1999] R.P.C. 461, CA and *Ocular Sciences Ltd v. Aspect Vision Care Ltd* [1997] R.P.C. 289.

[47] s.226(2) CDPA 1988.

[48] In *Wham-O Mfg v. Lincoln Industries Ltd* [1981] 2 N.Z.L.R. 629 the prototype for the "Frisbee" was held to be a sculpture and thus qualified for artistic copyright protection. See also *Breville Europe plc & Othrs v. Thorn EMI Domestic Appliances Ltd* [1995] F.S.R. 77 where plaster moulds for a sandwich toaster were held to be sculptures.

[49] *Davis (JES) (Holdings) Ltd v. Wright Health Group Ltd* [1998] R.P.C. 403. In *Metix (UK) Ltd v. Maughan (Plastics) Ltd* [1997] F.S.R. 718, Laddie J. indicated that he had difficulty in agreeing with Whitford J. (in *Davis v. Wright*) that a work which has a transient existence cannot be a work of sculpture.

[50] [1986] A.C. 577.

[51] s.51(1).

redress.[52] For design documents for artistic works, it remains the case that copying, including dimensional shift changes (*i.e.* a change from two dimensional to three dimensional or *vice versa*) will infringe copyright.[53]

3–29   Section 51(1) states that:

> "It is not an infringement of any copyright in a design document or model recording or embodying a design for anything other than an artistic work . . . to make an article to the design or to copy an article made to the design".

Section 51(3) defines what is meant by "design" as:

> ". . . the design of any aspect of the shape or configuration . . ."

and "design document" is said to mean:

> ". . . any record of a design, whether in the form of a drawing, a written description, a photograph . . ."

The meaning of section 51(1) is far from clear, but it is thought that unless the design in question relates to an artistic work or a typeface, copying the design or making an article to the design will not be considered an infringement of copyright.[54] Thus if a third party was to copy the Rubik's Cube puzzle it would not, by virtue of section 51(1), amount to infringement of the copyright in the drawings of the cube itself because the cube is not an artistic work.

3–30   As Laddie J. noted in *BBC Worldwide Ltd v. Pally Screen Printing Ltd*[55]:

> ". . . many will think that the type of infringement alleged here should be treated as wrongful. But the legislature has chosen a simple and perhaps blunt, way of excluding some types of reproduction from the scope of copyright infringement."

In this case the plaintiff was the owner of copyright in a television programme featuring characters known as the "Teletubbies". These characters were lifesize three dimensional puppets. It was alleged that the defendant had produced T-shirts bearing pictures of the Teletubbies by either reproducing a picture of the puppets that had appeared in a children's magazine, or by copying the puppets as seen on television. Whilst the judge took the view that the illustrations on the T-shirt were a substantial reproduction of the original copyright work the case centred on whether copying the three dimensional puppets constituted an infringement in light of section 51(1). Although counsel for the plaintiff argued that the intention of the legislature was to remove from copyright protection only that material which was properly within the scope of design right and no further. Laddie J. acknowledged that whatever the intention of the legislature may have been the fact was that the wording of section 51(1) did not limit its sphere of application to the making of three dimensional reproductions. As a consequence, it was held that the defendant

---

[52] Laddie *et al*, p. 1350.
[53] s.17(3).
[54] This was the interpretation put forward in *BBC Worldwide Ltd v. Pally Screen Printing Ltd* [1998] F.S.R. 665 (an application for summary judgment) and was supported in *Mackie Designs Inc. v. Behringer* [1999] R.P.C. 717.
[55] [1998] F.S.R. 665.

had an arguable defence to the claim of copyright infringement and summary judgment was refused. Thus despite the defendant's obvious copying of the plaintiff's characters, the plaintiff was unable to obtain relief at this juncture.

3–31 Copyright protection is thus of more limited value now for protecting articles that are industrially produced unless it can be shown that the drawings themselves have been reproduced. To this extent authors should preserve their original drawings and sketches etc and ensure that these are clearly dated and bear copyright notices, for future reference. In the event that copies of the cube or brick are produced the authors should aim, to obtain copies of the potential defendant's production drawings. If these are copies of their own drawings (albeit the product of reverse engineering) a copyright action may be possible. If, however, the replica cubes and bricks were made without production drawings then it will not be possible for the authors of the original cube or brick to rely upon copyright for protection.

(iv) Trade mark registration

3–32 Applications could be filed to protect the respective shapes of the Lego brick and Rubik's Cube products as three dimensional trade marks. In the case of the Lego brick, as indeed with any product that comprises a set of many parts with different shapes, colours and sizes, etc., it would be necessary to consider exactly how (*i.e.* in what form) to register the mark. Ideally, the manufacturer or promoter of the product should decide exactly what the actual product will look like and what element(s) will be relied upon to indicate the unique source of the product. The eight stud brick has been identified by the producers of Lego toys as being the most well known and distinctive aspect of its building system and it has therefore chosen to use an illustration of this brick when seeking trade mark registration in a number of countries.[56]

3–33 Under the Trade Marks Act 1938 it was not possible to register three dimensional objects as trade marks although it was possible to register two dimensional line drawings of the three dimensional objects. This was confirmed by the House of Lords in the celebrated case refusing registration of the Coca-Cola bottle,[57] in which it was held that the bottle, a container, was not a trade mark within the meaning of the Act,[58] and that a mark should be something that distinguishes goods rather than comprises the goods themselves. The principal concerns of the House were summarised by Lord Templeman[59]:

> "It is not sufficient for the Coca-Cola bottle to be distinctive. The Coca-Cola Company must succeed in the startling proposition that a bottle is a trade mark. If so, then any other container or article of a distinctive shape is capable of being a trade mark. This raises the spectre of a total and perpetual monopoly in containers and articles achieved by means of the Act of 1938.

---

[56] Admittedly, this decision was made with the benefit of hindsight but it should still be possible for someone working closely with a product before launch to identify the key features of the product where it is not practical to register every single unit as a separate trade mark. Although in the U.K. it may be possible to cover a series of representations in the same trade mark application this is only possible where the series differ only in relation to non-distinctive matter (s.41 TMA). See for example, *Dualit Ltd's (Toaster Shapes) Trade Mark Applications* [1999] R.P.C. 890 at 903/4.

[57] *Re Coca-Cola Trade Marks* [1986] R.P.C. 421.

[58] This was despite the fact that the House had previously allowed the registration of a mark comprising a pharmaceutical in capsule form, in *Smith, Kline and French Laboratories Ltd v. Sterling Winthrop Group Ltd* [1976] R.P.C. 511, which it was said was decided on its own special facts.

[59] [1986] R.P.C. 421 at 457.

Once the container or article has become associated with the manufacturer and distinctiveness has been established, with or without the help of the monopolies created by the Patents Act, the Registered Designs Act or the Copyright Act, the perpetual trade mark monopoly in the container or article can be achieved. In my opinion the Act of 1938 was not intended to confer on the manufacturer of a container or on the manufacturer of an article, a statutory monopoly on the ground that the manufacturer has in the eyes of the public established a connection between the shape of the container or article and the manufacturer. A rival manufacturer must be free to sell any container or article of similar shape provided the container or article is labelled or packaged in a manner which avoids confusion as to the origin of the goods in the container or the origin of the article. The . . . registrar of trade marks has always taken the view that the function of trade mark legislation is to protect the mark but not the article which is marked. I agree."

3–34   Although it is now possible under the TMA 1994[60] to register three dimensional objects as trade marks, concern still exists in some quarters that such a provision will be abused by those who would seek to obtain a monopoly in the appearance of an article to the detriment of fellow traders.[61] As Annand and Norman observe[62]:

". . . when trade mark protection is extended to three dimensional product shapes, as it has been by section 1(1) of the 1994 Act, the line between free and fair competition becomes less easy to define. Trade mark registration for a product shape can mean withdrawal of the product from the public domain. The absolute grounds for refusal in section 3(2) of the 1994 Act represent an attempt to reconcile the different objectives of free and fair competition with regard to the registration as trade marks of products shapes, and to ensure that the monopoly conferred by a copyright, patent or design is not abused by indefinite extension."

The White Paper[63] which prepared the way for the TMA 1994 justified the extension of trade mark protection to shapes on the basis that some shapes are already recognised by consumers as indicating the source of a product:

"It is a fact of the marketplace . . . that some shapes are recognised by consumers as distinctive of the products of a particular trader. Allowing registration of such shapes would therefore not be *conferring* a monopoly—it would merely be recognising a *de facto* monopoly already exists."

3–35   Thus, it seems that the intention (at least as expressed in the White Paper) was to grant protection in respect of *de facto* monopolies rather than to confer protection in circumstances where articles or containers had not been used prior to the date of the application. Cornish, despite his concern that trade mark protection

---

[60] Three dimensional marks that have already been registered under TMA 1994 include the Coca-Cola bottle (number 2000548); the Morgan motor car (number 2008299); the Toblerone chocolate bar and its packaging (numbers 2000005 and 2000986 respectively).
[61] See for example Cornish commenting upon the registration of the Lego brick in the Netherlands—Cornish, p. 593.
[62] Annand & Norman, p. 84.
[63] Reform of Trade Marks Law (1990), para. 2.18.

will confer monopoly protection on products *per se*, appears willing to accept an extension of the registration system to shapes where "secondary meaning is clear from usage", on the grounds that traders should first and foremost rely upon labelling to indicate the source of goods rather than rely upon the shape of the goods to indicate origin.[64] He states that as a general principle shapes are not inherently distinctive and should not therefore be registrable without extensive evidence of use.[65]

3–36 The requirements for registration We saw in Chapter 2 that a trade mark can consist of "any sign capable of being represented graphically which is capable of distinguishing goods . . . of one undertaking from those of other undertakings".[66] Notwithstanding the fact that marks fulfil the requirements of section 1(1), the registration of certain marks are excluded,[67] under section 3(1), if:

- the mark is devoid of any distinctive character;
- the mark consists exclusively of descriptive material (*e.g.* as to place of manufacture, kind, quality or type of goods, etc.);
- the mark consists exclusively of signs that have become customary in the trade.

Also excluded from registration, by virtue of section 3(2), are trade marks that consist exclusively of:

(a) the shape which results from the nature of the goods themselves;

(b) the shape of goods which is necessary to obtain a technical result; or

(c) the shape which gives substantial value to the goods.

Whereas there should be no difficulty in satisfying the requirement in section 1(1) that the Lego brick be represented graphically, the question of the Lego brick's capacity to distinguish goods of one trader from those of another is more problematic.

3–37 In *Philips Electronics NV v. Remington Consumer Products Ltd*[68] Aldous L.J. stressed that the capacity of a mark to distinguish the goods depended on the inherent features of the mark itself rather than on the extent of its use and that the more the trade mark described the goods the less likely it would be to distinguish those goods from similar goods of other traders. It was said that in order to be capable of distinguishing the goods the mark had to be more than a description, there must be a capricious addition to the goods. It was held that shape marks that depict a product (or an aspect of it) are merely pictorial descriptions of the products and accordingly are not capable of distinguishing the goods represented from those of other traders. For this reason the mark in question, depicting the

---

[64] Cornish, p. 593.
[65] *ibid.*, p. 592.
[66] s.1(1) TMA 1994.
[67] As Mr Geoffrey Hobbs, Q.C. explained in *Allied Domecq Plc's Application* ([1997] R.P.C. 168 at p. 172 (the "*Allied Domecq*" case) in connection with the mark AD2000, "[i]n order to be eligible for registration under the Act a sign must possess the qualities identified in s.1(1) and none of the defects identified in s.3".
[68] [1999] E.T.M.R. 816, CA (the "*Philips*" case).

Philips 3 headed rotary shaver, was held to be invalid. The case has, however, been referred to the ECJ for a ruling on the question of whether use of a mark representing the shape of goods by a monopoly supplier such that the relevant trade and public associate the goods with the trader can ever be sufficient to satisfy section 1(1).

3–37/1   In the slightly later case of *Dualit's Toasters*[68a] it was said that the toaster shapes in question were not generic of a class of toaster, and indeed Lloyd J. conceded that it would not be impossible to show that at least some features of the shape had trade mark significance (thus satisfying section 3(1)(a)). However, Lloyd J. upheld the decision of the Hearing Officer to refuse registration on the grounds that the shapes were not inherently distinctive and distinctiveness had not been shown to have been acquired through use.

3–38   Like the pictorial mark in the *Philips* case, there is a danger that representations of both the Rubik's Cube and the Lego brick would fall foul of section 3(1)(a). If so, according to the proviso in section 3, no amount of use of the mark will enable it to overcome this objection (subject to the determination of the ECJ) although the manner of use may be relevant in determining whether the sign is in fact capable of distinguishing the goods.[68b] If, on the other hand, it can be shown that the representation of the mark does include a "capricious addition" sufficient to enable it to acquire a secondary meaning (and the example given by the Court of Appeal suggests that the addition does not need to be great), then this requirement may be overcome.

3–39   In relation to the Rubik's Cube puzzle and the Lego brick it is hard to imagine the form that such an addition might take, except perhaps the inclusion of the brand name. But such an addition would bring with it the danger that the protection gained would essentially be limited to the brand name, or at least the combined use of brand name and shape. This may not be particularly advantageous since third parties who might seek to copy the product are unlikely to copy the brand name as well.

3–40   **Distinctiveness**   Although it can be argued that the Lego brick has the potential to distinguish goods (at least to the limited extent that it is not incapable of distinguishing the source of the goods[69]), whether the mark can be said to be distinctive is another matter. There is thus a risk that an objection to registration could be raised based on section 3(1)(b), on the grounds that the mark is devoid of any distinctive character. In *British Sugar Plc v. James Robertson & Sons Ltd*,[70] Jacob J. stressed the fact that marks that were devoid of any distinctive character were unregistrable unless they had acquired a distinctive character through use. He went on to explain what he thought the words "distinctive character" meant[71]:

> "I think the phrase requires consideration of the mark on its own, assuming no use. Is it the sort of word (or other sign) which cannot do the job of distinguishing without first educating the public that it is a trade mark?"

Jacob J.'s explanation of what was meant by the term "distinctive character" is akin to the notion under the old law of "inherently distinctive". Marks that lack any

---

[68a] *Dualit's (Toaster Shapes) Trade Mark Applications* [1999] R.P.C. 890 ("*Dualit*").
[68b] *Healing Herbs Ltd v. Bach Flower Remedies Ltd*, CA, *The Times*, December 1, 1999.
[69] *Allied Domecq* at 173.
[70] [1996] R.P.C. 281.
[71] *ibid.* at 305–306.

inherent distinctiveness, such as purely descriptive marks (*e.g.* the mark "soap" for soap products), are not registrable because they cannot act to distinguish the goods of one manufacturer from those of another and are thus excluded under section 3(1)(a) and 3(1)(b). Marks that over time can act so as to distinguish the goods of one source from those of another are said to become distinctive by nurture, by educating the public as to their trade mark significance. In the *Allied Domecq* case, referred to above, Mr Geoffrey Hobbs Q.C., reconciled the apparent contradiction between the requirements of section 1(1) and those of section 3(1)(b), by finding that[72]:

> "The proviso to section 3(1) indicates that the essence of the objection to registration under section 3(1)(b) is immaturity: the sign in question is not incapable of distinguishing goods or services of one undertaking from those of other undertakings, but it is not distinctive by nature and has not become distinctive by nurture."

3–41   An assessment of distinctiveness in relation to word marks or device marks is something that the courts and the Trade Marks Office have had to grapple with under previous legislation and have subsequently refined their approach under current legislation.[72a] General principles have therefore already been established as to what may or may not, be regarded as distinctive and further guidance has also been provided by the ECJ as to what factors should be taken into account.[72b] In relation to shapes, however, case law is only beginning to develop in the United Kingdom.[73] Although in the *Philips* case, at first instance, Jacob J. sought to extend the comments he made in the *Treat* case relating to descriptive words to marks comprising a picture of an article *per se* he did not provide any further indication as to what might constitute a distinctive shape[74] and no assistance was given on this point by the Court of Appeal either.[75] In the *Proctor & Gamble* case, Walker L.J., with whom the other judges agreed, stressed the need for a visible sign or combination of signs which could readily distinguish one trader's product from another's. The absence of a distinctive product name or device as part of the mark applied for was fatal in this case. There is therefore limited material available to indicate how shape marks will generally be assessed. For example, will a polygon be regarded as more distinctive than a sphere or a cube; a spiral as more distinctive than a tube?

3–42   According to the Trade Mark Registry Work Manual[76] (which provides guidance both to Trade Mark Examiners and practitioners on matters of registration) the appropriate test for *prima facie* acceptance of a shape mark is whether because (a) the shape in question immediately strikes the eye as different and therefore memorable; and (b) the differences between the shape in question and

---

[72] [1997] E.T.M.R. 253 at 259.
[72a] *W&G ducros' Application* (1913) 30 R.P.C. 660; *York Trade Mark* [1982] 1 W.L.R. 195; *Healing Herbs Ltd v. Bach Flower Remedies*, CA, *The Times*, December 1, 1999.
[72b] *Windsurfing Chiemsee Produktions v. Huber* [1999] E.T.M.R. 585 at 599 to 600; *Lloyd Schuhfabrik Meyer v. Klijsen Handel BV* [1999] E.T.M.R. 690.
[73] *Proctor & Gamble Ltd's Trade Mark Applications* [1999] R.P.C. 673, CA; *Philips Electronics NV v. Remington Consumer Products Ltd* [1999] E.T.M.R. 816, CA; *Dualit Ltd's (Toaster Shapes) Trade Mark Applications* [1999] R.P.C. 890. For an interesting discussion of the need to develop appropriate means for assessing the inherent distinctiveness of product shapes distinct from those created in connection with marks see Dinwoodie, "Reconceptualising the Inherent Distinctiveness of Product Design Trade Dress" [1997] 75 *North Carolina Law Rev.* 47.
[74] *Philips Electronics NV v. Remington Consumer Products* [1998] R.P.C. 283 at 302.
[75] *Philips Electronics NV v. Remington Consumer Products* [1999] E.T.M.R. 816.
[76] Chap. 6, p. 58.

those of other trader's are arbitrary and not dictated by function or some other non-trade mark purpose; the public are likely to assume that the goods with reference to which the shape is used recurrently are those of the same undertaking.

3–43 Thus to be *prima facie* registrable as a shape trade mark, we would need to show that the Lego brick shape itself was "different and therefore memorable" and that this was not due to aspects of the function of the brick. This is a difficult hurdle to overcome since arguably the distinctive aspects of the shape of the Lego brick are the studs and tubes that enable the brick to connect with other bricks. Thus it is unlikely that an objection based on the fact that the mark is devoid of "any distinctive character" under section 3(1)(b) could be overcome at the outset based on the above test. It is possible, however, that if the mark was used extensively, evidence of secondary meaning could be established, in which case it would be possible for an objection based on section 3(1)(b) to be overcome, although other objections may then be raised to registration under section 3(2) (discussed below).

3–44 As far as the Rubik's cube puzzle is concerned, it would be possible to represent the mark graphically and it should be possible to show that the appearance of the product is sufficiently distinctive to overcome any objection that might be raised under section 3(1)(b), since it is unusual in its appearance both in terms of the shape and colour and these features are not due to function alone, accordingly it should be regarded as memorable and therefore *prima facie* acceptable.[77]

3–45 Evidence of distinctiveness Where evidence of distinctiveness is required, it should in theory be possible to build up such evidence during the period that design and patent registrations are in place. There is, however, a danger that the validity of a registration accepted on the basis of such use may be challenged at a later date when the design and patent registrations expire and third parties are able to produce similar competing products. This was the case in *The Canadian Shredded Wheat Co. Ltd v. Kellogg Co of Canada Ltd*[78] in connection with the use of the words "Shredded Wheat" and in the *Philips* case.[79] In the latter case at first instance, it was held that use during the period when the mark was protected by a patent or design amounted to use in a protected market rather than use in a real market situation and accordingly should be discounted.[80] As was noted in the Court of Appeal:

> "Philips' case is based on the fallacy that extensive use of a purely descriptive mark such that it becomes associated with a trader means that the trade mark has a distinctive character."

The court went on to find that without any feature that had a trade mark significance and which could become distinctive through use the mark was devoid of distinctive character within the meaning of section 3(1)(b) and so unregistrable.

---

[77] The puzzle was distinctive and memorable when it was first launched; assuming that that is still the case now the mark should be regarded as distinctive, if, however, the mark is no longer distinctive because of third party use of similar marks then this objection could be maintained.

[78] (1938) 55 R.P.C. 125.

[79] [1998] R.P.C. 283 (first instance decision); [1999] E.T.M.R. 816, CA.

[80] Further, in the *Philips case* the judge referred to the trade mark as a "limping mark" in that in was only used by the proprietor in conjunction with the word mark Philishave—this is discussed further below.

3–46 Accordingly, in the absence of clear evidence to show that the mark is regarded as an indication of origin by consumers, and not simply a representation or description of the product, the use was not sufficient to support the registration.[80a] To avoid the possibility of such a challenge to a registration of the Lego shape mark, the proprietor would need to ensure that emphasis was placed upon the significance of the shape as a source identifier in advertising and marketing materials during the period of design protection so that consumers are educated to regard the shape of the goods as indicative of source. Without taking deliberate steps to educate the public in this way it is unlikely that a sufficient degree of awareness of the shape as an indicator of source would be established to support the mark if challenged.[80b]

3–47 **Exclusions from registration** Assuming that, for both products the hurdle of distinctiveness required by section 3(1)(b) can be overcome, it is still possible that further objections to registration may be raised by the Trade Marks Office against both marks on the grounds of section 3(2) of the TMA 1994. Whereas section 1(1) specifically includes the shape of goods or their packaging within the definition of what may constitute a trade mark, section 3(2) specifically excludes shapes which result from the nature of the goods themselves, shapes which are necessary to obtain a technical benefit and shapes that give value to the goods.[81] In this way the TMA 1994 seeks to strike a balance between allowing the registration of shapes which function as trade marks and preventing the grant of monopolies for articles or containers *per se*.[82] Exactly where the dividing line will fall will depend on how narrowly section 3(2) is interpreted by the Trade Marks Office and by the courts.

3–48 The wording of section 3(2) is taken straight from Article 3(1)(e) of the EC Trade Marks Harmonisation Directive[83] ("the Directive") which, like many other sections of the Directive is reputedly derived from the Uniform Benelux Trademark Law 1971 (Article 1(2)). Under Benelux law whether a shape can be registered as a trade mark depends *inter alia* on whether the goods perform a function by virtue of their shape.

3–49 Commenting on the interpretation of the TMA 1994 some writers[84] have suggested that the United Kingdom courts will look to the Benelux model to see how the equivalent provision to section 3(2) is implemented there before applying it in the United Kingdom. There have also been suggestions that the courts should look to the United States approach to the registration of three dimensional trade marks when interpreting the United Kingdom statute. However appealing or attractive such approaches may seem, the comments made by Laddie J. in the *Wagamama* case,[85] suggest that whilst the United Kingdom courts may look to the Benelux and other E.U. countries or even to the United States to see how they approach the subject, it is highly unlikely that they will rely on them as giving an

---

[80a] As regards the importance of the nature of the use, see *Healing Herbs Ltd v. Bach Remedies Ltd*, *The Times*, December 1, 1999, CA.
[80b] As illustrated by the results of the survey evidence in the *Dualit* case.
[81] Or as Aldous L.J. put it "excludes from registration certain shapes which are protectable under patents, registered designs and other such intellectual property rights" (*Philips* case [1999] E.T.M.R. 816 at 824).
[82] Kitchen & Mellor *The Trade Marks Act 1994* (Sweet & Maxwell, London, 1995) at 26–22 ("Kitchen & Mellor").
[83] 89/104/EEC.
[84] See for example Strowel "Benelux: A Guide to the Validity of Three dimensional Trade Marks in Europe" [1995] E.I.P.R. 154.
[85] *Wagamama Ltd v. City Centre Restaurants Plc* [1995] F.S.R. 713 (the "Wagamama" case).

authoritative interpretation. Whilst Laddie J. acknowledged that the purpose of the Directive was to ensure a measure of uniformity between the trade mark laws of member states he stressed that[86]:

". . . the obligation of the English court is to decide what the proper construction is. If that construction differs from that adopted in the Benelux countries, one, at least, is wrong. It would not be right for an English court to follow the route adopted by the courts of another member state if it is firmly of a different view simply because the other court expressed a view first."

3–50   As in the *Wagamama case*, it is far more probable (when it comes to infringement at least) that the courts will look back at relevant dicta expressed under the old law.[87] For assistance in interpreting the new Act and in so doing will import concepts into the new law that were established under previous legislation. In the *Philips case*,[88] in response to the challenge that the old law had been swept away and so should not be regarded as affording any form of assistance to the interpretation of the new law, Jacob J. acknowledged that to be the case but sought to justify his reliance on old jurisprudence on the grounds that the problems addressed by both laws were the same:

"We now have a new European law and one cannot get any help from the details of the old law of any particular European country. But it does not follow that the sort of concepts and safeguards provided for in the old laws (or indeed the laws of countries outside the European Union) have no place under the law. On the contrary one is bound to bump up against the same sort of problem under the new law as under other laws. For some matters are basic to any rational law of trade marks. I believe this case involves such a problem, involving as it does the question of the extent to which trade mark law, conferring a perpetual monopoly, can interfere with the freedom within the European union of manufacturers to make an artefact of a desirable and good engineering design."

His comments were approved by Walker L.J. in the *Proctor & Gamble* case.[88a] It is therefore likely that section 3(2) will be construed broadly and that there will be judicial reluctance, or at least caution, in permitting the registration of shapes as trade marks.[89] Ultimately, of course, it will be the ECJ that will have to resolve the issue as to how broadly to interpret Article 3(1)(e) and the *Philips* case may well provide the opportunity for it to do so. At present there is little to suggest what its approach will be to three dimensional marks for registration other than its frequent reaffirmation of the fact that one of the primary functions of a trade mark is to indicate origin.[90] Whether this means that the ECJ will adopt an approach similar to that of the United Kingdom court remains open to speculation.

---

[86] *ibid.* at 728.
[87] Such as that of Templeman L.J. in *Re Coca Cola Trade Mark* [1986] 1 W.L.R. 695. Which concerned an application to register the Coco Cola bottle as a trade mark. In that case registration was refused in part as a matter of policy in that it would grant a perpetual monopoly in the article itself.
[88] The *Philips* case at 299.
[88a] *Proctor & Gamble Ltd's Trade Mark Applications* [1999] R.P.C. 673, CA at 680.
[89] The need to show that the shape functions as a mark of trade origin was stressed by the Registrar in *Dualit Ltd's Trade Mark Applications* [1999] R.P.C. 304 at 313/4, and by Lloyd J. when the case went to the High Court on appeal. *Dualit Ltd's (Toaster Shapes) Applications* [1999] R.P.C. 890 at 902.
[90] *IHT Internationale Heiztechnik v. Ideal Standard* [1994] E.C.R. 1–2789.

3–51   Despite the reluctance of English courts to endorse three dimensional trade marks the Trade Marks Office has now accepted certain well known marks for registration including the famous Coca-Cola bottle[91] which confirms that it is not impossible to secure a three dimensional trade mark registration.

3–52   In the case of the Lego brick mark and the Rubik's cube mark, it is likely that objections to registration will be raised based on each of the grounds identified in section 3(2), that is, that the mark consists exclusively of the shape (a) which results from the nature of the goods themselves, (b) which is necessary to obtain a technical result, or (c) which gives substantial value to the goods. These are absolute grounds for refusal, which means that if the objections are not overcome at the outset, no amount of use of the mark or reputation will assist in overcoming the Registry's objections, unless perhaps the volume and type of use was such that either the perception of the nature of the goods themselves changed as a consequence of the use, or that the evidence shows that the shape is not functional or that the value of the goods is not derived from the shape but some other aspect of the product.

3–53   *The nature of the goods.*   In the cases that we are considering, the marks are representations of a Lego brick and the Rubik's cube and the goods for which the registrations are sought are, in a broad sense, toys. If the term "nature" is interpreted narrowly and a wide specification is accepted, then arguably since toys do not have a particular shape, the shape of the marks do not consist exclusively of a shape which results from the nature of the goods.[92] If, however, the goods are defined more precisely (*e.g.* toy bricks and cube puzzles) then it is possible to concede that both marks consist exclusively of shapes which result from the nature of the goods themselves. Thus, as Kitchen & Mellor note,[93] when considering the application of this exclusion it is important to give careful consideration to both the mark and the goods for which it is applied. Whilst this may be true, as Aldous L.J. pointed out in the *Philips* case "the goods" refers to any of the goods covered by the application, thus the fact that some toys are of that shape is sufficient. The purpose of the subsection is "to prevent traders monopolising shapes of particular goods".[94] Thus, subsection 2(a) needs to be considered in conjunction with subsections (b) and (c) which seek to exclude from registration basic shapes that should be available to the public. In interpreting subsection 2(a) therefore, Aldous L.J. applied a narrow test suggesting that only shapes produced by nature should be excluded. As toys and puzzles are not restricted to the shapes adopted by Lego and the Rubik's Cube puzzle, no objection should be raised under this lead.

3–54   *Necessary to obtain a technical effect.*   Under this provision shapes that are merely functional are excluded from registration. The important point is that the mark will be refused registration if it consists exclusively of a shape that is functional or the result of technical considerations. Under Benelux law it is possible to overcome this objection by showing that a number of other forms exist that perform the same technical function.[95] The fact that other means exist for obtaining

---

[91] Registration number 2000548 granted on October 25, 1995.
[92] Cornish, for example, notes how the Dutch court held that the particular shape of the Lego brick was not considered part of its nature, apparently because there were other shapes that could be used to make a toy building system—see Cornish at 689.
[93] Kitchen & Mellor at 26–23.
[94] *Per* Aldous L.J. in the *Philips* case.
[95] Strowel, "Benelux: A Guide to the Validity of Three-dimensional Trade Marks in Europe" [1995] E.I.P.R. 154 at 158.

the same technical effect ensures that the proprietor of the mark does not obtain an unfair monopoly over a functional advantage to the detriment of fellow traders, thus maintaining a competitive balance. However, this narrow interpretation of the subsection was rejected by the Court of Appeal in the *Philips* case where it was held that it was sufficient to show that the essential features of the shape are attributable only to the technical result in order for the exclusion to apply. Thus, it matters not whether there are alternative ways of achieving the same technical effect. As Aldous L.J. noted in that case, the purpose of the subsection is to exclude from registration those shapes motivated by function and the result of technical considerations.[95a] To be registrable the mark must have some additional characteristic which is capable of and does, denote origin.[95b]

3–55   As noted above, the Lego brick mark consists exclusively of a functional shape in that the studs and tubes serve the function of interconnection with other bricks and the brick shape itself must be of a particular shape in order to enable it to used as part of a construction kit. Equally, it is possible that the Rubik's cube mark will be regarded as functional if its function is perceived as being to rotate around a central axis as opposed to entertain. If the Benelux approach were followed, it would be sufficient for the proprietors of these marks to show that other means exist of obtaining the same technical result in order to overcome this objection.[96] However, this is not the approach that has been adopted in the United Kingdom now, and unless the ECJ provides further guidance when it considers the *Philips* case it is unlikely that the approach will change. As a result, both the Lego brick mark and the Rubik's Cube mark are likely to be rejected on this ground albeit that the marks include other elements such as colour, their essential features are likely to be regarded as functional.

3–56   *The value of the goods.*   The rationale for this provision has been said to be that if it is the shape that gives substantial value to the goods then that aspect of shape should perhaps be protected by way of design legislation rather than by trade mark legislation.[97] The difficulty with this provision, as with the previous subsections, is that it is not always clear in practice whether the shape gives substantial value to the goods or not.[98] One approach may be to enquire whether the goods are purchased primarily for the function they perform or for their shape as such.[99] If they are purchased by reason of the former then arguably the shape is incidental. The difficulty with this approach is that it requires an assessment of the motivations

---

[95a] The *Philips* case at 830.

[95b] Although, as expressed by Aldous L.J., the test under subsection 2(b) appears to be similar to the test of registrability under the RDA, in fact the threshold under the TMA is higher because of the requirement that the "additional characteristic" be capable of indicating origin rather than simply appeal to the eye as needed under the RDA.

[96] The Commercial Court in Namur, Belgium in its judgment of September 4, 1995 relating to the registration of the Lego brick mark (Case No. 2641/92) held that the shape of the Lego brick was not necessary to obtain a technical benefit since various other building systems existed in the market place—cited by Helbling "Shapes as Trade Marks?—The Struggle to Register Three Dimensional Signs: A Comparative Study of U.K. and Swiss Law" [1997] I.P.Q. No 4, 413 at, 428.

[97] Kitchen & Mellor, p. 26–23.

[98] See for example the trade mark opposition case *Dualit Ltd's Trade Mark Applications* [1999] R.P.C. 304 at 319–322 where the Registrar had to consider this point and concluded that the weight of evidence referring, amongst other things, to the appearance of a product as a "design classic" supported the view that the appearance of the product (the mark) gave substantial value to the goods. On appeal Lloyd L.J. did not need to address the section 3(2) objection order to decide the case. Had it been necessary to address it, he said he would have referred the matter to the ECJ. *Dualit Ltd's (Toaster Shapes) Trade Mark Applications* [1999] R.P.C. at 903.

[99] Michaels, p. 22.

of the buyer which may be influenced by a number of factors and not simply the function of the product. An alternative approach, and one suggested in the *Philips* case, is to compare the shape sought to be registered with shapes of equivalent articles. Only if the shape has substantial value will it be excluded from registration.

3–57 Whilst both the shape marks that we are considering can be said to give substantial value to the goods, it can be argued, in the case of the Lego brick, that the primary reason for purchasing the product will be to use it as a construction toy and a comparison with other construction toys is unlikely to indicate that the shape has substantial value. It is difficult to see how such an objection could be overcome in relation to the Rubik's Cube puzzle since the shape is such an integral part of the product. If, perhaps, the goods were made of materials other than plastic it might be possible to argue that the value is derived from some aspect other than the shape but this is tenuous.

3–58 As with the other exclusions under section 3(2) there is potential for both of two marks we are considering to be excluded from registration depending upon how broadly the provisions are interpreted. Until such time as the Act has been more fully tried and tested, particularly in relation to these provisions and guidelines have been established by the ECJ as to what may or may not be registered as a result of the application of section 3(2), it will be extremely difficult to predict the outcome of three dimensional trade mark applications except to say that registration is likely to be exceptional, especially if the mark is a representation of the goods themselves rather than the packaging, etc.

3–59 In 1988 applications were filed in the United Kingdom to register the Lego brick as a trade mark[1] (under the previous law). The applications were, however, rejected on the basis that the marks were considered to be functional and not distinctive. Despite an appeal to the court, the decision was upheld by Neuberger J.[2] Neuberger J. began his analysis of the issue of registrability by considering the practical effect of granting registration, the effective monopoly that it would confer on the applicant and how the absence of registration would not preclude protection at common law. After reviewing the extensive evidence filed by the applicant, Neuberger J. concluded that in his view the bricks did not constitute a trade mark. His reasoning was based on that of Lord Templeman in the *Coca-Cola case*.[3] Indeed, he went as far as to say that[4-6]:

> ". . . [Interlego] are not so much seeking a permanent monopoly in their mark, but more a permanent monopoly in their bricks. This is, at least in general, contrary to principle and objectionable in practice. A trade mark is, after all, the mark which enables the public to identify the source or origin of the article so marked. The function of the trade mark legislation is not to enable the manufacturer of the article to have a monopoly in the article itself."

As Neuberger J. considered the question of registration under the 1938 Act, it is open to Lego to apply for registration under the 1994 Act, although the introduction of competing products in the intervening years (*i.e.* between 1988 and 1994) could well have diluted the distinctiveness of the brick thus making

---

[1] Application numbers 1355423/27/33 & 1357479 filed on August 16, 1988.
[2] *Interlego AG's Trade Mark Applications* [1998] R.P.C. 69.
[3] *Re Coca-Cola Trade Mark* [1986] R.P.C. 421 at 457.
[4-6] [1998] R.P.C. 69 at 110.

registration even more difficult to show that the shape of the brick does function in practice as an indication of origin.

3–60   At this point it is worth noting that an application to register the brick as a Community Trade Mark was accepted (in principle) and advertised in the Community Trade Mark Bulletin on November 23, 1998 (application number 000107029).

(v) Passing off

3–61   As we saw in Chapter 2 the tort of passing off developed to protect the goodwill of a business. Prior to the launch of a new product there will be no goodwill associated with the shape of the product *per se* (assuming that there has been no pre-launch publicity). Consequently, it would not be possible to base an action on passing off if the product launch was pre-empted by a third party. However, once the product has been launched preferably with advertising and promotional support, goodwill will begin to accrue which may then be protectable by means of an action for passing off. One of the difficulties with passing off actions in the context of product appearance, is demonstrating that the product shape alone (rather than any trade mark or brand name) is recognised by consumers as denoting a particular source of the goods (*i.e.* is distinctive) such that, when a competitor launches an imitation of the product, consumers are confused as to the source of the newcomer's goods. The courts have frequently asserted that copying alone does not amount to passing off.[7] Any trader is free to copy (*i.e.* to misappropriate) the shape of another's product provided that he does not infringe any patent, copyright, design or trade mark and does not directly or indirectly misrepresent his goods as being those of the plaintiff.

3–62   The basic requirements of the tort of passing off are those of distinctiveness (or secondary meaning) giving rise to goodwill and a misrepresentation (not misappropriation) causing damage.[8] In cases involving the appearance of a product or its packaging (loosely referred to as "get-up"), the plaintiff must show that customers associate uniquely with the plaintiff those features of the get-up that have been reproduced by the defendant. The courts have not, however, clearly differentiated between get-up cases that involve packaging from those involving product simulation. This has given rise to a degree of confusion as to how far the courts are prepared to go to protect the goodwill associated with distinctive features of a product that are also functional features. Fletcher Moulton L.J. in *J. B. Williams v. Bronnley & Co. Ltd*[9] said that:

> "The get-up of an article means a capricious addition to the article itself—the colour, or shape, it may be the wrapper, or anything of that kind; but I strongly object to look at anything that has a value in use, as part of the get-up of the article. Anything which is in itself useful appears to me rightly to belong to the article itself."

3–63   According to Fletcher Moulton, functional features should not be protected by means of an action for passing off, only non functional features can be

---

[7] *British American Glass Co. Ltd v. Winton Products (Blackpool) Ltd* [1962] R.P.C. 230 at 232; *Benchairs Ltd v. Chair Centre Ltd* [1974] R.P.C. 429 at 435; *Kemtron Properties Pty Ltd v. Jimmy's Co. Ltd* [1979] F.S.R. 86 at 88; *Hodgkinson & Colby Ltd v. Wards Mobility Services Ltd* [1995] F.S.R. 169 at 177 (the "*Roho*" case).
[8] *Hensher Ltd v. Restawhile Upholstery (Lancs) Ltd* [1973] 1 W.L.R. 144.
[9] (1909) 26 R.P.C. 765 at 773.

protected in this way. Where cases have concerned the imitation of the shape of packaging[10] it has been relatively easy to show that the get-up is a "capricious addition to the article" once the distinction has been made between the article itself and the packaging.[11] However, in relation to the goods themselves the test is much harder to apply. In the Hong Kong case of *Kemtron Properties Pty Ltd v. Jimmy's Co. Ltd*[12] which concerned the appearance of an electric fan known as the Mistral fan, the court held that there was passing off even though the distinctive features of the fan that were reproduced by the defendant constituted the article rather than a capricious addition for the purpose of identifying the plaintiff's product. As Lahore notes in his comment on the *Mistral fan* case[13]:

> "The distinction between article and get up is reminiscent of the distinction in registered design law between article and design features of shape or pattern. Neither distinction makes much sense in the context of modern product design. The real question is whether it is an unjustified extension of monopoly to give protection against copying the product itself outside the statutory monopolies and for an indefinite term."

In the *Mistral fan* case, the court found that the combination of a number of functional features could amount to get-up and so would be protectable by means of passing off. The meaning of the word "get-up" in this context, however, does not equate to that used by Fletcher Moulton L.J. since he expressly stated the need to identify non functional features—the use of the same term is therefore misleading. In effect the court in the *Mistral fan* case provided protection against product simulation where there was evidence of direct copying—thereby providing a remedy for unfair competition or misappropriation. The result was to grant the plaintiff an injunction against further sales of the infringing product that was not limited as to time.

3–64 In the *Jif Lemon* case the House of Lords granted protection under passing off to the shape of a plastic lemon as a container for selling lemon juice. Although the case primarily concerned the protection of product packaging as opposed to product simulation, Lord Jauncey did state that "the general principle that no man may sell his goods under the pretence that they are the goods of another" applies equally to the goods themselves as to their get-up. The crucial determinant is the extent to which customers are deceived into believing that the goods of the newcomer are those of the original manufacturer as a result of the simulation of product features alone.[14] If the defendant can distinguish his product from the original product by means of a label or some other distinguishing feature so as to avoid deception then this would be sufficient to avoid a passing off action.

3–65 In the *Roho* case, which concerned the simulation of an orthopaedic cushion, the court denied protection, on the grounds that purchasers of the product did not regard the shape as indicative of source but rather as a functional feature. Accordingly, it was held that there was no misrepresentation by the defendant as to

---

[10] See for example *Coca Cola Co v. AG Barr & Co. Ltd* [1961] R.P.C. 367; *John Haig & Co. Ltd v. Forth Blending Co. Ltd* [1953] 70 R.P.C. 259; *Reckitt & Colman Products Ltd v. Borden Inc* [1990] R.P.C. 341.

[11] *Hoffman-La Roche & Co v. DDSA Pharmaceuticals Ltd* [1972] R.P.C. 1, CA; *Reckitt & Colman Products Ltd v. Borden Inc* [1990] R.P.C. 341 (the "*Jif Lemon*" case).

[12] [1979] F.S.R. 86 (the "*Mistral fan*" case).

[13] "Product simulation and copying the Get up of Goods" [1979] E.I.P.R. 146.

[14] See also *Tots Toys Ltd v. Mitchell* [1993] 1 N.Z.L.R. 325 and an interesting article discussing the case by Jeremiah "Passing Off the 'Buzzy Bee': When Get-up Can Be Functional" [1994] E.I.P.R. 355.

the source of its goods as a result of simulating the plaintiff's product.[15] As Jacob J. observed[16]:

> "The plaintiff's problems of proof when there is no manifest badge of trade origin such as a trade mark becomes hard. This is so in the case of descriptive or semi-descriptive words such as 'Camel Hair'! It is perhaps even more so where one is concerned with no self evident trade origin frill or embellishment for people are likely to buy the article because of what it is, not in reliance on any belief of any particular trade origin. This is so whether they buy it for eye appeal (*e.g.* glass dogs) or for what it does . . ."

3–66   Given that in England at least, the protection of product shape by means of an action for passing off will only be successful if it can be shown that the features in question serve to indicate the origin of products and are recognised as emanating from a particular source, proprietors of products that have a distinctive appearance should ensure that all promotional material emphasises the shape aspect of the product as being indicative of source rather than primarily functional. This can be done by ensuring that all advertisements and/or point of sale material include a reference or by-line along the lines of "Look for the . . ." and specify the product feature, so, for example, in relation to the Rubik's Cube puzzle the tag line could read "Look for the multicoloured cube". Such techniques can prove effective when seeking to build up awareness of source identifying features. Indeed the makers of Levi jeans have used advertising slogans such as "We keep tabs on everything" and "Look for the LEVI"S tab on the pocket" for many years and as a result have been able to establish sufficient secondary meaning associated with the orange tab device to enable it to protect its pocket tab in actions for passing off or trade mark infringement in a number of countries.[17] The Levi's tab also features prominently in all advertisements and point of sale material which provides additional emphasis to the tabs significance as an indication of source. Television advertising with its ability to zoom in on products can also be used very effectively to this end to highlight, for example, particular features of product shape. Once again, Levi Strauss have used this zooming technique to draw attention to its orange tab device.

(vi) Patent protection

3–67   The Rubik's Cube product is designed as a puzzle and its novelty lies in the way in which the smaller cubes rotate around a main central axis. In relation to the Lego brick the novelty lies in the stud and tube connections. To the extent that either of these inventions incorporate any principle of construction that is novel, or any aspect of their method of manufacture is novel (for example if some new technology for injection moulding is involved in the manufacture of the puzzle or the bricks) then, assuming that it also involves an inventive step and is capable of

---

[15] A similar line of reasoning was followed in the earlier case of *British American Glass Co. Ltd v. Winton (Blackpool) Ltd* [1962] R.P.C. 230 which concerned the appearance of ornamental glass dogs where it was said that the articles were purchased for their ornamental appearance rather than with reference to their source.

[16] *Hodgkinson & Corby Ltd v. Words Mobility Services Ltd* [1995] F.S.R. 169 at 177.

[17] *Levi Strauss & Co v. Shah & Anthr* [1985] R.P.C. 371; *Levi Strauss & Co v. Kimbyr Investments Ltd* [1994] 1 N.Z.L.R. 332; *Levi Strauss & Co v. Robertson Ltd* (1993) (unreported). See B. Sullivan "Further New Zealand Decision on Levi's Pocket Tab Trade Mark" [1994] E.I.P.R. 170; *Levi Strauss & Co v. Blue Bell Inc* 632 F. 2d. 817 (9th Cir. 1980).

industrial application, patent applications may be filed to protect those aspects of novelty in relation to the products thereby obtaining an effective monopoly on their production.[18] Patent protection does not, however, extend to the appearance of an article *per se*. A reference to "patent pending" on the products and/or the packaging (or the patent number once granted) may have a useful deterrent effect on would be copiers and so should be incorporated if at all possible but wrongful masking is a criminal offence.[18a] From a legal point of view such notices are of value because they put third parties on notice of the rights claimed and accordingly can affect the patent holders ability to claim relief in the event of infringement.[19]

3–68   If no patent protection is available to protect the mechanics of the puzzle or the construction principle of the bricks perhaps due to a lack of novelty, then greater reliance will need to be placed upon design and trade mark registrations as providing the only means of protecting the outward appearance of the products beyond the scope of copyright and unregistered design rights which arise automatically. In any event, patent protection will not extend to the appearance of a product in terms of its colour or surface decoration and so other legal regimes will need to be relied upon to protect these aspects.

PRODUCT SUCCESS

3–69   The Lego brick was originally designed by an Englishman, Hilary Page, who marketed it under the name "Kiddicraft". It was the subject of United Kingdom patents which expired in 1954 and 1959. The Lego brick was, to all intents and purposes, a copy of the Hilary Page design (which was not protected in Denmark where the Lego company was based). Lego bought any remaining copyright from Page's executors. Lego made various alterations and modifications to the original Page design resulting in a second and then a third generation of "brick". The third generation brick devised in 1958 was a significant step forward and was protected both by patent and design registrations which expired in 1975. The Lego group have consistently invested in marketing and advertising the product and developing the product range. Product quality and safety have also been key features of their promotional campaigns.

> "Although other manufacturers have attempted to launch and market competing products operating on broadly similar principles, none has achieved anything like the success of the Lego . . . range which, for the past 30 years or more, have completely dominated the market in children's model building systems."[20]

In contrast to the Lego brick, the Rubik's Cube puzzle's success was much more sudden and dramatic. The original Rubik's Cube puzzle was invented in 1975 in Hungary and production commenced in 1976. Professor Rubik, through the state co-operative enterprise Politechnika Ipari Szovetkezet applied for patent protection in Hungary[21] but not elsewhere.[22] Trade mark applications were subsequently filed

---

[18] It is not possible to obtain a patent in respect of aesthetic creations because aesthetic creations are not regarded as inventions for the purposes of the Patent Act 1977 (s.1(2)(b)).
[18a] s.111 Patents Act 1977.
[19] s.62(1) Patents Act 1977.
[20] Lord Oliver of Aylmerton in *Interlego v. Tyco* (n.28, p. 237).
[21] Patent No. HU170062 (1975).
[22] Without patent protection in Hungary it was not possible for inventors to obtains royalties for the licensing of their inventions. It is believed that the primary aim of patent protection for Professor Rubik was to enable him to subsequently licence the manufacture of the cube to third parties and obtain royalties.

in a number of countries and a design registration[23] was granted in the United Kingdom in May 1979.

3–70 In 1979 the Rubik's Cube puzzle, which had already been on sale in Hungary was launched in the United Kingdom and later that year and the following year it was exported internationally. Whilst the original copyright was retained by Professor Rubik the rights to the three dimensional cube, the ability to license it and the ownership of the trade mark itself were transferred to a company by the name of Seven Towns Limited ("Seven Towns"). Seven Towns granted licences to a number of companies to manufacture the cube including, in June 1980, the Ideal Toy Corp ("Ideal") and their various subsidiaries.

3–71 The promotion of the product in the United Kingdom was rather unusual in that:

> "instead of the usual massively expensive television advertisements linking the product with the name of the distributor, what was done was to send samples of the cube to local newspapers throughout the country and to those in charge of local radio stations and to certain national newspapers . . . in the hope that the intrinsic qualities of the cube as a puzzle would sufficiently intrigue the newspapers to give coverage and publicity to the cube."[24]

This proved to be a successful way of communicating the products Unique Selling Proposition ("USP") which might otherwise have proved difficult to communicate using static displays and promotional material. In 1980 the cube won the Toy of the Year Award.

3–72 The cube itself was promoted along with the name of Professor Rubik but for the most part the names of the manufacturer and distributor were never mentioned. One particular television programme showed the puzzle being completed by a schoolboy in less than 40 seconds and this sealed the launch of what became first a nation-wide and then a world-wide craze.

3–73 Between June 1980 when Ideal first began selling the puzzle in the United Kingdom and January 1981 205,000 units were sold which was "a very large number of sales for a toy or puzzle".[25] During the course of the next two months a further 200,000 were sold confirming the cubes phenomenal success. Indeed the cube was so successful that the manufacturers were unable to cope with the demand.

THE WEAKNESSES IN LEGAL PROTECTION

(a) In relation to the Rubik's Cube Puzzle

3–74 Such was the success of the Rubik's Cube puzzle that imitations of the puzzle flooded into all markets from Taiwan. At one point it was believed that as many as forty different companies were manufacturing copies of the puzzle in Taiwan.[26] This led to a series of legal battles concerning the alleged infringement of intellectual property rights in various jurisdictions including the United Kingdom, France, Benelux, Denmark, Austria, Canada, Australia, Japan and the United States.

[23] Registration No. 990060.
[24] *Politechnika Ipari Szovetkezet & Others v. Dallas Print Transfers Ltd* [1982] F.S.R. 529 at 534 Dillon J.
[25] *per* Dillon J. *ibid.* at 534.
[26] *Politechnika Ipari Szovetkezet v. Dallas Print Transfers Ltd* [1982] F.S.R. 529.

The copies were often sold under the name the "Wonderful Puzzler" or the "Magic Puzzle". In appearance they were virtually identical to the Rubik's Cube puzzle with minor differences in shade discernible only when the two products were placed side by side. The proportions were also identical. The operation of the Wonderful Puzzler was not as smooth as that of the Rubik's Cube puzzle nor was it as robust. Its chief attraction was that it was significantly cheaper and for this reason it was extremely popular and proved to be a serious challenge to the genuine Rubik's Cube puzzle.

3–75 The distributors of the Rubik's Cube puzzle relied on various intellectual property rights in their attempts to prevent the sale of the Taiwanese imitation, The "Wonderful Puzzler". In the Netherlands case[27] the action was based upon copyright infringement. The court of first instance found that there was no infringement as the puzzle was held not to embody sufficient artistic endeavour to justify copyright protection. However, the Court of Appeal of Amsterdam reversed this decision on the basis that the cube was a work of applied art. The test of artistic endeavour in relation to works of applied art was held to be very low. An injunction was therefore granted.

3–76 In England the action was based on copyright infringement and passing off.[28] Although there was a design registration in the United Kingdom, the plaintiff chose not to rely upon it and subsequently allowed the design registration to lapse. This may have been because the registration was inherently defective (having been applied for after publication) or because it would potentially have dis-entitled the owner to protection under copyright law.

3–77 As the English case was heard in 1982, the Copyright Act 1956 (the old Act) applied under which it was possible to obtain protection of three dimensional articles from two dimensional drawings. The production drawings used to make the original Rubik's Cube puzzle were the subject of artistic copyright; their indirect copying by reverse engineering a Rubik's Cube puzzle to make drawings from which the defendant could make its cube, was held to infringe copyright. The court had no difficulty in regarding the drawings as copyright works or finding that they had been infringed. An injunction against copyright infringement and the continued sale of the cubes was therefore granted.[29] Had the same proceedings been initiated today, such a judgment might not have been so easily obtained because of the changes to copyright protection and, in particular, the boundary with the unregistered design right which means that design drawings for articles other than artistic works are not infringed by making articles to the same design.[30]

3–78 The plaintiffs also based their action on passing off but, unlike their claim for copyright infringement, the action for passing off failed because the plaintiffs could not show that they had an established goodwill and that a misrepresentation had been made by the defendant. According to Dillon J., that the plaintiffs had not identified themselves in the mind of the public as the source of the product consequently when customers purchased the defendant's product it could not be shown that they did so believing that the product was that of the plaintiffs thus the action failed. Dillon J. noted that[31]:

---

[27] H. C. Jehoram, *Rubik's Cube—Copyright in Rubik's Cube Under Dutch Law* [1982] 4 E.I.P.R. 117.
[28] *Politechnika Ipari Szovetkezet v. Dallas Print Transfers Ltd* [1982] F.S.R. 529.
[29] *ibid.*
[30] Discussed above in relation to s.51 CDPA 1988.
[31] *Politechnika Ipari Szovetkezet v. Dallas Print Transfers Ltd* [1982] F.S.R. 529 at 538.

"[the evidence from witnesses] in particular, convinces me that most people at that stage wanted the cube as a puzzle to enjoy or to try their wits on, without regard to what source it came from. This was perhaps a consequence of the style of publicity campaign . . . People were interested in the cube itself as a puzzle rather than its source. If indeed a long period had elapsed before Taiwanese cubes came onto the market it may be that . . . the public would have come to associate the cubes with the source, but by the time of the issue of the writ in this action they had not done so."

The difficulties of establishing a goodwill sufficient to form the basis of an action for passing off and that a misrepresentation has been made are all too common in actions relating to the appearance or shape of goods generally.[32] This is because, consumers buy certain products by reference to the nature of the product itself without any thought as to the name of the manufacturer or source of the product. Promoting the generic product without reference to the source of the product may initially appear attractive but it effectively undermines already weak legal protection. If, however, the marketing campaign accompanying the Rubik's Cube launch had drawn particular attention to unique features of the product appearance as indicating source, or referred to the product as being available only from a particular manufacturer then this might have proved sufficient to educate consumers such that when a competing product found its way onto the market consumers would be sufficiently aware of the source of the original to know that the newcomer was from a different stable. Whilst this would go some way to helping the proprietor establish goodwill in the appearance of the product it might still not help in demonstrating that a misrepresentation has been made if, knowing that the product is from a different stable the consumer still purchasers it! This was said to be what happened in the *Roho* case which concerned an orthopaedic cushion of a distinctive shape.

3–79   England was not the only country in which the manner of marketing the cube received judicial criticism. In Australia, the distributors of the Rubik's Cube puzzle (Ideal) were involved in an action against the Australian distributors of the Wonderful Puzzler. The action was based on passing off, on copyright infringement (although this was not pursued at trial), and section 52 and section 53 of the Trade Practices Act 1974. Fox J. observed[33]:

"Before putting its puzzle on the market, Ideal Toy and Ideal Leisure [their Australian subsidiary] engaged in a substantial advertising campaign for the article 'Rubik's Cube'. However, much of the literature appearing at about that time referred to the cube and its fascination without reference to Ideal Leisure or Ideal Toy, or any mark or either of them, or for that matter, to their being only one source."

Fox J. concluded that the words "Rubik's Cube" were generic (that is, that it had become descriptive of the name of the product generally rather than indicative of source) and that there was no confusion or deception amongst the public or the trade in relation to the toy produced and sold by Ideal and the modified get-up of the Wonderful Puzzler.[34] No injunction was granted since confusion is a prerequisite for

---

[32] See for example the *Roho* case and *British American Glass Co. Ltd v. Winton (Blackpool) Ltd* [1962] R.P.C. 230 both referred to above at para. 3–61.
[33] *John Engelander & Co Pty Ltd v. Ideal Toy Corporation & Anthr* [1981] 54 F.L.R. 227 at 229.
[34] Before the commencement of the court action the distributor of the Wonderful Puzzler agreed to change the background colour of their puzzle from black to white. All other features remained the same.

actions under the Trade Practices Act and passing off. Although the judge conceded that the visual presentation of the Wonderful Puzzler and its packaging was very similar to that of the Rubik's Cube puzzle which was said to be distinctive by the time of the hearing the defendants had agreed to modify the packaging to ensure that there was no confusion and this was considered sufficient.

3–80   The plaintiff's position in Australia was not helped by the fact that it had provided its consent to the use of a photograph of its puzzle on the front cover of a book on how to solve the puzzle that was published at about the same time as the product launch. The book did not distinguish between the name of the cube, its author and the generic product and there was no reference to the plaintiff or to its having granted permission to use the photograph of the cube. The book therefore gave the impression that "Rubik's Cube" was the generic name of the product instead of an exclusive trade mark.

3–81   Registration of "Rubik's Cube" as a trade mark and careful policing of its use would have avoided the finding that the words were generic of the product. In such situations it is imperative that the proprietor not only monitors references to the article in publications and trade press but that it also ensures that an acknowledgment is given to the trade mark and copyright, for example in the form "Rubik's Cube is a trade mark of . . . and is used with permission (or under licence)" whenever permission is given to reproduce it. Sony undertakes a strict market watch on the use of its trade mark "Walkman" to guard against its generic use. Registration of the design in Australia might also have assisted in stopping the Wonderful Puzzler, even with its modified get up.

3–82   In the United States,[35] France,[36] Austria,[37] and Japan[38] proceedings were issued on the basis of unfair competition. In each case an injunction was granted on the grounds that the defendant had adopted not only functional features of the cube's design but also the non- functional features such as the colour combination, the size and the proportions of the cube. Arguments that the appearance of the article was functional were rejected by all four courts.

3–83   In the United States the actions were based on section 43(a) of the Lanham Act, under which use of a trade mark or trade dress that is likely to cause confusion or mistake as to the origin of the product amounts to infringement whether or not the trade mark or trade dress is registered. In determining whether the trade dress is entitled to protection it is necessary to establish secondary meaning, that is, that the primary significance of the product feature relied upon is to identify source.[39] When determining the issue of secondary meaning the court may consider such factors as length of use, extent of sales and advertising and the fact of copying.[40] In one of the Rubik's Cube cases, which involved a number of defendants, it was held that although the Plaintiff could not demonstrate secondary meaning based on the extent of sales or length of use, the number of imitators and the accuracy of the copying of the plaintiff's trade dress were persuasive evidence that the trade dress had acquired the necessary secondary meaning to create confusion if used by someone other than the original manufacturer. (Similar evidence would not be persuasive to an English court.)

---

[35] *Ideal Toy Corporation v. Chinese Arts & Crafts Inc.* 530 F.supp. 375 (SDNY 1981) and *Ideal Toy Corporation v. Plawner Toy Mfg Corp* 685 F. 2d. 78 (3rd Cir. 1982).
[36] *Ideal Loisirs v. Edimay* [1982] E.I.P.R. D–75.
[37] Poch "Rubik's Cube—The Austrian Decision" [1982] E.I.P.R. 231.
[38] *Tsukuda Original Inc v. Hayakawa Toys Inc* [1982] E.I.P.R. D–138.
[39] *Inwood laboratories v. Ives Laboratories* 102 S.Ct. 2182 (1982).
[40] *Faberge Inc v. Saxony Products Inc* 605 F. 2d. 426 (9th Cir. 1979).

3-84 In *Ideal Toy Corporation v. Plawner Toy Mfg Corp.* the plaintiff established the existence of consumer confusion by means of a consumer survey which showed that 40 per cent of respondents wrongly identified the defendant's product as a "Rubik's Cube" puzzle. The defendant also admitted copying which the court regarded as persuasive evidence of secondary meaning. Accordingly, injunctions were granted in favour of Ideal, the distributor.

3-85 Although the manner of marketing the puzzle was not substantially different in these four markets the approach of the courts towards copying differed significantly from those of the English and Australian courts. Furthermore, the existence of laws on unfair competition and, (in the case of Austria and to a lesser extent France) a public policy against condoning deliberate acts of copying creating a danger of confusion, made it easier for the plaintiffs to obtain redress. The action in the United States and the other markets (excluding Japan[41]) might have been easier still if the puzzle had been registered as a trade mark in its three dimensional form as this would have reduced the evidential burden on the plaintiff.

3-86 In Denmark[42] the plaintiff effectively had exclusive distribution of the Rubik's Cube puzzle and held a strong market position. Action was taken against the importer of the Taiwanese cube on the basis that it had not acted "in accordance with proper marketing practices". In other words the defendant was taking unfair advantage of the advertising and marketing efforts of the plaintiff. The action, based on unfair trade practices and in particular violation of Danish marketing laws, was thus effectively a claim of unfair competition and in particular misappropriation of the plaintiff's effort. An injunction was granted in favour of the plaintiff.

3-87 Once again, registration of the three dimensional article as a trade mark would perhaps have avoided the need to rely upon the Danish marketing laws.

(b) In relation to the Lego brick

3-88 Compared to the Rubik's Cube puzzle, the success of the Lego brick has been much more gradual resulting from the continued development and improvement of both the product and its reputation and continued investment in its marketing and promotion. As with any successful product it has been copied by a number of competitors and has been the subject of litigation in the Benelux, Denmark, Hong Kong, Norway, the United Kingdom and United States amongst others.

3-89 In a recent case in the Benelux, action was taken by Lego against Blomsen.[43] The case involved a slavish copy of the Lego brick. Lego had registered a number of its toy bricks as three dimensional trade marks and sought to rely upon these registrations in the action against Blomsen. Blomsen argued that the marks should not have been registered because, in its view, the shape of the trade mark was dictated by function. The District Court rejected this argument indicating that different dimensions and other forms could be used with equal technical benefit.[43a] The registrations were therefore held to be valid and Blomsen held to have

---

[41] At that time Japan did not accept three dimensional trade mark registrations.

[42] "Unfair Trade Practices—Rubik's Cube under the Marketing Act" [1982] E.I.P.R. D–164.

[43] District Court, Harlem December 14, 1993 (unreported).

[43a] The approach of the Benelux court should be contrasted with that of the English High Court which considers the existence of alternative arrangements as irrelevant in determining functionality. See *Philips Electronics NV v. Remington Consumer Products Ltd* [1999] E.T.M.R. 816, CA at 830 (discussed at para. 3–54—3–55 *supra*).

infringed them. Lego therefore has a *de facto* monopoly, in the Benelux at least, on all toy bricks corresponding to the shape and dimensions registered.

3–90 Although in Denmark Lego was also successful in its action against an alleged infringer, Byggis, the court refused to accept that the shape of the Lego brick could be protected by trade mark law.[44] According to the Danish court, the shape of the brick was mainly dictated by its technical function and for this reason was not entitled to trade mark protection.[45] An injunction was nonetheless granted against the copier, Byggis on the basis that the marketing of the Byggis product amounted to unfair copying contrary to the Marketing Practices Act. The court held that the extent of the similarity between the Byggis brick and the Lego brick went beyond what was necessary to achieve the technical effect described in the patent (now expired) and the claim that this was to enable the product to be interoperable was not regarded as a defence, but rather a fact in support of a finding of unfair copying!

3–91 By way of contrast, the Norwegian Supreme Court held[46] that the issue of compatibility was relevant in that it encouraged competition as to price and quality. It is a general rule of law that once patents have expired it is open to a defendant to use the invention. The court stated that, in the absence of confusion, the similarity of features which results from the compatibility of products should not be regarded as infringement. Furthermore, the fact that Lego had been on the market for a long time and had a wide reputation should, in the court's view, justify a lesser degree of protection. This particular judgment appears to place greater emphasis on competition policy, than on the protection of intellectual property rights *per se*.

3–92 In the United States, the shape of the Lego brick was held to be functional and for this reason not entitled to trade mark protection.[47] In the words of District Judge Brown:

> "A product whose shape incorporates both functional and non-functional features may raise conflicting considerations of free competition and trade mark protection. In such a case, the courts generally resolve these rival interests by determining whether numerous, equally acceptable alternate configurations are available to competitors. In the case of the Lego 2 × 4 block, however, alternative configurations are of little relevance because the shape of the block does not comprise or incorporate any arbitrary, decorative or other non-utilitarian feature which would raise conflicting considerations. Thus, in this case there are no rival interests to be resolved."

Quoting the earlier case of *Ideal Toy Corp v. Plawner Toy Manufacturing Corp.*[48] which concerned the Rubik's Cube puzzle, District Judge Brown said that:

> "a product feature is functional if it is essential to the use or purpose of the article or if it affects the cost or quality of the article . . . a feature . . . is considered non-functional if the element of the product serves no purpose other than identification" (*omitting references*).

District Judge Brown concluded that since the stud and tube mechanism served a purpose other than as identification, and indeed was an essential part of the Lego

---

[44] See *Lego Systemer A/S v. Byggis AB June 1994* [1995] E.I.P.R. D-65.
[45] It should be noted that the Danish trade mark law is based upon the EC Directive.
[46] *Lego System AS & Lego Norge AS v. Brio AS* [1995] E.I.P.R. D-339.
[47] *Tyco Industries Inc v. Lego Systems Inc* 853 F2d 921 (3rd Cir. 1988).
[48] 685 F. 2d. 78 (3rd Cir. 1982).

building brick, it was functional. Although Lego tried to argue that alternative possibilities existed in terms of the shape of the brick as a whole and the stud and tube mechanism it did not deny that the configuration of its bricks was precisely determined by the bricks function, so that rearranging the elements was not possible. Further, on the evidence, the proposed alternatives were not considered by the court to be of the same standard of utility and would be more expensive to manufacture, making them unattractive to competitors.

3–93   In England and Hong Kong, the actions against alleged copiers centred on copyright infringement. In both cases it was necessary for the plaintiff to show that the Lego brick was not entitled to protection as a registered design, as this would have precluded the possibility of copyright protection, the two rights not being cumulative under section 10 of the Copyright Act 1956. If Lego had chosen to rely upon its design registrations there would have been no opportunity to rely upon the potentially stronger claim of copyright infringement.[49]

3–94   In the *Hong Kong* case[50] before the court could determine whether or not there had been copyright infringement it first had to construe section 10 of the Copyright Act 1956 and determine, whether the bricks qualified for design protection. It was held that copyright protection was only available for designs that did not qualify for design registration. Lego therefore had to argue that its bricks were incorrectly registered as designs so that it could obtain the benefit of copyright protection which was of longer duration. In determining whether the Lego brick would have qualified for design registration the courts considered the test of eye appeal (discussed above) and concluded that there did exist sufficient aesthetic appeal apart from the functional elements to enable the designs to be registered. In considering the issue of functionality, it was said that the question of whether a design was functional was not the same as whether there were other ways of performing the same function. In both the *English* and *Hong Kong* cases it was held that the bricks did not qualify for copyright protection because they qualified for design protection. As the design registrations and patents had expired this left the owner unable to stop the sale of copy products.

3–95   In Italy,[51] the distributor of a competing manufacturer of toy bricks sought a declaration of non-infringement against the producers of the Lego brick. The Lego company contested the claim and brought separate proceedings alleging unfair competition and an action for servile imitation under Article 2598(i) of the Civil Code. The case was appealed to the Supreme Court of Cassation where it was held that although it was lawful to copy another's functional idea it was not lawful to do so in such a way as to render the two products indistinguishable on the market for, it said, to do so would be to enable the newcomer to take advantage of the other's commercial goodwill. The court accepted that whilst:

> "the law must seek to avoid the perpetuation of a monopoly beyond the lifetime of a patent, it may not . . . as a mater of principle, permit . . . the siphoning off of the profits of another's investment. Should it condone such a position it would end up stifling competition. It would remove a fundamental

---

[49] Furthermore, at that time design registrations were only valid for a period of 15 years whereas artistic copyright was valid for 50 years beyond the life of the author. Although the Design Copyright Act 1968 sought to amend s.10 thereby limiting copyright protection to 15 years from first marketing for industrial articles, the court in *Sifam v. Sangamo* [1971] F.S.R. 337 continued to apply the pre 1968 test with the consequence that the full term of artistic copyright was granted.
[50] *Interlego AG v. Tyco Industries* [1989] A.C. 217.
[51] *Lego System A/S and Lego Spa v. Tyco Industries In & Arco Falc Srl* [1999] E.T.M.R. 250.

principle of a competitive market that is, the possibility of winning over one's own clientele in accordance with rules of communication propriety."

3–96 Thus the copier was obliged to make changes to the product in order to distinguish it from the original. A similar approach was adopted by the Utrecht District Court, in the Netherlands in relation to a claim of unfair competition against a servile copy of the Lego brick.[52] This approach, however, is in stark contrast to that of the English court.

3–97 Although the proprietor of the Lego brick found its ability to stop competing products severely restricted by the English and Hong Kong judgments[53] it did receive a favourable judgment in relation to the use of the Lego name itself[54] and the colourful get-up of the bricks themselves. Indeed, although it took action against a manufacturer of agricultural equipment using the name Lego based on passing off, it was successful because it could show that the name Lego was so well known in conjunction with colourful plastic bricks that there was a likelihood of deception as a result of the use of the name on colourful plastic irrigation equipment despite the fact that the Lego brick company did not, at that stage, operate outside the field of children's toys.

(c) Lessons from the Lego and Rubik's Cube litigation

3–98 At the time of its launch the proprietor of the Rubik's Cube puzzle had invested relatively little in the legal protection of its product. It was fortunate in being able to rely successfully upon copyright in a number of jurisdictions which subsists without the need for registration. Although it had a patent in Hungary this was of no assistance because reproductions were made in the Far East and sold in the United States and western Europe. It did have a design registration in the United Kingdom but this proved to be defective and was not relied upon. Many of the trade mark applications that it had filed had not been registered by the time that the infringements occurred and legal action taken and so could not be relied upon. Had there been design registrations in the countries where litigation took place this would almost certainly have avoided the criticisms levelled against the proprietor as to the method of marketing the puzzle and may have obviated the need to rely upon passing off or unfair competition laws.

3–99 If the legal action in England had taken place after the commencement of the Copyright, Designs and Patents Act 1988 (that is after August 1989) it is doubtful that the proprietor of the Rubik's Cube puzzle would have been successful. Although the unregistered design right was introduced to provide a degree of protection to mass produce articles irrespective of artistic merit, Professor Rubik would not have been eligible to take advantage of these provisions because he would not be a qualifying person and the puzzle was not first marketed exclusively in the United Kingdom as required by section 218 and section 220 of the CDPA 1988.

3–100 At the time the cases referred to above were heard, the owners of the Rubik's Cube puzzle were extremely fortunate in being able to rely upon a combination of copyright laws and unfair competition laws which enabled them to obtain protection in most markets without the initial investment in trade mark,

---

[52] *Lego v. Oku Hobby Speelgoed BV/Frits de Vries Agenturen BV/Lima Srl* (September 10, 1998) [1999] E.I.P.R. D-83. An appeal against this decision has been filed.
[53] The *Hong Kong* case was actually determined by the Privy Council, an English court.
[54] *Lego System A/S v. Lego M Lemelstrich Ltd* [1983] F.S.R. 155.

design or patent registrations.[55] Such an investment may, however, have avoided the need for such extensive litigation and helped to sustain the exclusivity of the product until it became a time honoured classic. Furthermore, registrations could have had an added deterrent effect by identifying the proprietary rights of the owner. The outcome of litigation is always uncertain, especially where unregistered rights are relied upon, but it is a brave business that proceeds with the adoption of a trade mark or uses a design to launch a new product where an identical or similar mark or design has already been registered by a competitor. Although the Rubik's Cube puzzle was phenomenally successful in its first few years it disappeared within five years of its launch not to return to the shelves for a further six years or so. In part this can be accounted for by the fact that it was something of a craze and the product (and the copies) flooded the market. Had the copies not existed, however, it is possible that the proprietor's could have met the demand through licensed channels and so sustained a longer term consumer interest.

3–101   It is interesting to note that although the defendant in each case was different it was understood that many of the copies of the Rubik's Cube puzzle emanated from Taiwan.[56] Had the producer of the puzzle initiated legal action in Taiwan it might have been possible to stop the copies at source without the need to take action on a market by market basis. It is acknowledged that at that time Taiwan was not as co-operative as it has now become in relation to unauthorised product imitation. Under the terms of Article 20 of the Taiwanese Fair Trade Law 1991, however, action could be taken to stop the manufacture of infringing products on the basis of their appearance. As Dillon J.[57] noted:

> "It is well known in the toy trade, on the evidence I have had that Far Eastern copies are made of popular toys which can be sold in the United Kingdom market at cheaper prices than the prototypes which have been copied are marketed at."

This being the case the producer of the Rubik's Cube puzzle would have been well advised to seek protection of the cube in South East Asia or Taiwan at least, if nowhere else. Alternatively, the producers could have considered making use of the various customs procedures that now exist to prevent the importation of goods bearing infringing trade marks. All that is needed is an existing trade mark or design registration copies of which need to be supplied to the relevant customs authorities.[58] This is an inexpensive way to ensure that infringing products do not enter a particular market especially if the source of manufacture or supply of the copies is known. Customs officials can then focus upon imports from that particular country. The procedure is relatively simple and if information is available as to where supplies are expected to arrive it can be very effective and relatively inexpensive.[59]

---

[55] Trade mark registration in each of the nine countries would cost approximately £9,000 and design registration £4,500. Patent registration costs significantly more. A conservative estimate of the litigation cost is approximately £20,000 per country.

[56] *Politechnika Ipari Szovetkezet v. Dallas Print Transfers Ltd* [1982] F.S.R. 529.

[57] *ibid.* at p. 535.

[58] s.89 TMA 1994. The form of notice required varies depending on the expected county of export. If the goods are expected to arrive in the U.K. from outside the EEA the form required is set out in the Schedule to the Trade Marks (Customs) Regulations 1994 (S.I. 1994 No. 2625). If the goods are expected to arrive from within the EEA Form C1340 is to be completed as specified by Council Regulation (E.C.) No. 3295/94 (as amended by (E.C.) 241/1999).

[59] Once the application has been accepted by Customs the applicant is legally obliged to keep Customs indemnified against any liability or expense which might be incurred but this is usually minimal compared to the cost of litigation for trade mark infringement or passing off.

3–102 By way of contrast the producer of the Lego brick had spent significant sums on the protection of its intellectual property rights. It invested in all forms of protection to the extent that it even had to argue that protection should not have been granted to it—as in the case of the United Kingdom design registrations—in order to obtain the maximum benefit of other intellectual property rights. Although the cases referred to above may not at first glance appear to endorse the view that it is worth investing in intellectual property rights it should be remembered that the Lego product was protected first by patent, then by copyright for a number of years before forming the subject of trade mark registrations. The proprietor has thus retained an element of exclusivity in relation to the product appearance for almost sixty years. The careful marketing of the Lego brand over many years coupled with investment in legal protection has enabled the product to build a strong brand identity, secure a large market share and a strong international presence in the face of serious competition. Although the legal armour has not proved impenetrable in terms of completely preventing unauthorised copying it has made it significantly more difficult for competitors to imitate the Lego brick particularly in jurisdictions other than the United Kingdom.

3–103 As both of these products illustrate, all aspects of a product's appearance should be considered from the point of view of protection before the product is launched, and the protection reviewed periodically as the product becomes more established. Through careful use of a combination of trade mark, design, copyright and patent laws, a matrix of defensive armour can be established to protect key features of product appearance. Where registration of intellectual property rights is needed to secure protection key markets for the product need to be identified at the outset (and continually reviewed) and applications filed as early as possible.

3–104 Marketers should develop promotional activities that reinforce the source identification purpose of product attributes rather than emphasise the utilitarian function of particular features since this may render them purely functional and so deprive the owner of any claim to exclusivity on the basis of their ability to act as trade marks. Careful distinction between the brand name and the generic name of the product enhances consumer perception of the brand and helps to avoid the brand name being rendered descriptive.

CONCLUSION — THE GAPS IN LEGAL PROTECTION

3–105 In this chapter we have considered the importance of product appearance and seen how businesses that invest in product design can reap significant benefits in terms of increased market share and profitability. Product design is an important competitive weapon in today's market place. It can be a powerful and tangible facet of a brand and the protection of its exclusivity is a serious matter that needs to be considered at the outset (*i.e.* before the product is launched) and which requires investment in various forms of legal protection.

3–106 Whilst some forms of legal protection are cumulative (*e.g.* registered designs, passing off and copyright) others are not (*e.g.* copyright and unregistered design right). The traditional boundaries between trade marks, patents and designs are being eroded with the introduction into United Kingdom law of three dimensional trade marks and the distinctions are now much more nebulous. There is something of a legal conundrum as to whether protection should, as matter of policy, be granted in the form of trade mark registration to product shapes that may already have had the benefit of patent and/or design protection. There have been a number of decisions in support of the view that once the proprietor of a particular product has received the benefit of patent protection, the further benefits of trade mark registration, or design rights should be denied and competitors allowed to use the shape with impunity.[60]

3-107   Others argue[61] that where the proprietor of a product has established a reputation or goodwill in relation to a particular product feature that proprietor should be entitled to protect its reputation by means of three dimensional trade marks and that to hold otherwise is to permit competitors to take advantage of the first comer's established investment. Whilst this may be true it raises the question of whether the goodwill was established at a time when the product had the benefit of design or patent protection, whether the features relied upon really do indicate origin, whether they are associated with that type of product,[62] or with aspects of functionality. But are these distinctions appropriate?

3-108   At present, the United Kingdom Trade Marks Registry will only accept three dimensional marks for registration if they are inherently distinctive or sufficient evidence of use can be shown to establish secondary meaning (*i.e.* that the relevant features are indicative of trade origin) and the shape does not fall within any of the exclusions set out in section 3(2) of the TMA. This approach has been reinforced by the Court of Appeal which expressed its support for the view that three dimensional shapes that are motivated by or are the result of technical considerations should not be monopolised for an unlimited period of time by trade mark registration. In its view it is only those characteristics that operate to denote trade origin that should be protected in this way.[63]

3-109   Given the constraints on what can be registered as a trade mark, it is likely that registration of three dimensional marks will be the exception, rather than the rule. This means that in general terms, to protect the appearance of what in Chapter 1 were called naked products most proprietors in the United Kingdom will be forced to rely primarily on design legislation or passing off as the basis of any action to prevent product simulation. If the proprietor of the naked product is forced to rely on design rights these will only if at all, provide protection for a limited period of time.[64] Given the commercial importance of design in terms of competitiveness and the scale of financial investment made in the development of products, particularly where design is a key element, such limited legal protection will be a significant disadvantage and may well prove to be a disincentive to further investment in design in the longer term.

3-110   Clearly, if no restrictions are placed on the newcomer to differentiate his product from the original he will be taking a free ride on the back of the investment in research and development made by the original manufacturer. Although the law of passing off can assist the need to show that consumers not only identify the configuration uniquely with the plaintiff but also that buying a product with a similar appearance from a third party constitutes a misrepresentation. Given that it is rare for products to be sold without labels or packaging denoting a brand name and/or manufacturer, it is hard, in practice, to prove a misrepresentation has indeed

---

[60] See for example *Canadian Shredded Wheat Co v. Kellogg* (1938) R.P.C. 125 and the *Philips* case.

[61] See for example Dinwoodie "Reconceptualising the Inherent Distinctiveness of Product Design Trade Dress" (1997) 75 *North Carolina Law Review* 471 and Swann, "The Configuration Quagmine: Is Protection Anticompetitive or Beneficial to consumers, and The Need to Synthesize Extremes" 1997 87 T.M.R. 253.

[62] An argument raised in the *Philips* case.

[63] *Philips Electronics NV v. Remington Consumer Products Ltd* [1999] E.T.M.R. 816, CA.

[64] 25 years if the design is registered (s.8 RDA) or 10 years from first marketing if unregistered (s.216 CDPA 1988). UDR protection is only available for qualifying individuals or products first marketed in the U.K.

been made. Even if a brand owner can show the product shape is distinctive of origin, there is still authority to suggest that if the defendant takes steps to distinguish his product from that of the plaintiff, that will be sufficient.[64a]

3–110/1 The Lego brick and Rubik's Cube puzzle were chosen as the subject for the case studies in this chapter because of the importance of the physical appearance of the products to each brand and their international success and consequent involvement in litigation in a number of countries. What the various cases referred to above involving these two products show, however, is that there are gaps in the level of legal protection available to product configurations in the United Kingdom that do not exist elsewhere. Although copyright was relied on in the past to provide protection against copying of design drawings, such protection is no longer available as a result of changes in the copyright law. The UDR was introduced to provide a more limited form of protection for mass produced articles but these rights are not available to everyone and the Rubik's Cube puzzle would not have benefited from this.

3–111 In the English case of *Edge v. Niccolls*[65] it was acknowledged that the plaintiff's get up was distinctive but it was said that the defendant must take steps to distinguish its product from that of the plaintiff, not that it must not reproduce the get up at all. Thus if the distinctive features of the product's appearance are used by the newcomer in connection with a word mark or company name which is not associated with the original manufacturer, this will be sufficient to avoid a finding of passing off. As mentioned above, in the recent Lego cases in Italy and the Netherlands the courts went further than this holding that where a distinctive product appearance had been copied it was not sufficient to ensure that the packaging alone distinguished the source of the products. These courts accepted that servile imitations of the product itself took unfair advantage of the goodwill established by the original manufacturer, even in the absence of exclusive intellectual property rights. This approach is in sharp contrast to that followed in the United Kingdom. Thus the existence of laws of unfair competition in other jurisdictions means that brand owners are able to obtain redress in circumstances of servile imitation where copying the appearance of a product means benefiting from the existing goodwill of the product owner. In England no equivalent law exists and the tort of passing off presents too high a threshold for the average manufacturer to reach in the context of product appearance.

3–112 Should the manufacturer of a successful product have to endure such competition from a fellow trader who has reproduced its design and undercut its pricing? The prevailing assumption that competition is the overriding concern fails to take account of the fact that "... *it may be just as inimical to competition and to consumers to deny protection to a differentiating design as it is to protect a common one*".[66] Distinctive or unique configurations that operate to distinguish the goods of one producer from those of another whether they are taken by consumers to indicate source or not should be protectable from imitation from the outset (and for the entire life of the product) to encourage investment in alternative configurations that configurations that consumers value.[67]

[64a] *Edge v. Niccolls* [1911] A.C. 693.

[65] [1911] A.C. 693.

[66] Swann, "The Configuration Quagmine: Is Protection Anticompetitive or Beneficial to consumers, and The Need to Synthesize Extremes" 87 T.M.R. 253 at 264.

[67] As Tichane notes, consumers may be less willing to purchase products with distinctive appearances unless the exclusivity can be preserved. Tichane "The Maturing Trademark Doctrine of Post-Sales Confusion" 85 T.M.R. 399 (1995).

3–113 The debate concerning the proper scope of protection for product configurations is not a new one but the significance of providing adequate protection takes on new meaning as design becomes increasingly important in the commercial arena. The free market's opposition to the grant of exclusive rights exists in tension with the countervailing tradition of granting rights to encourage creativity and investment. The balance between these competing demands has, in times past, swung in favour of the original creator, but with the restrictions in the scope of artistic copyright introduced in the CDPA 1988, producers of products with distinctive and innovative configurations unable to rely on unregistered design rights have found themselves exposed to unauthorised copying and imitation of their form. Even those that are able to obtain design right protection may only rely on it for a maximum of 15 years. Given the life of some brands (such as Lego and Coca-Cola) this is a very short period of protection especially against servile imitations. The position therefore needs to be re-assessed and the balance restored.[68]

---

[68] This will be discussed further in Chap. 8.

CHAPTER 4

Protecting Product Packaging

INTRODUCTION

4–01 In the previous chapter we considered the manner in which the appearance of a product could be protected. In this chapter we turn our attention to product packaging and consider the importance of selecting and maintaining distinctive packaging or, as it is sometime called, trade dress.[1] Unlike other forms of promotional material, which are by nature temporary, a product's trade dress can act as a permanent advertisement for the brand in the consumer's home. From a commercial perspective therefore, it is important at the time of repeating the purchase that the consumer can easily identify the brand that he or she has come to trust (the preferred brand). If the consumer cannot recognise the preferred brand or selects a different brand (either by mistake or as a result of the belief that the products in question share a common origin), then not only has the owner of the preferred brand lost that particular sale but it may also lose subsequent sales (discussed further below).

4–02 It is axiomatic that successful brands are copied. This applies equally to trade dress as to the product itself. The development of own label brands is a good example of the continuing evolution of rival products driven by competition in the market place. Very often the rival product starts life as a cheaper version of the brand leader within a particular product sector, using packaging that is reminiscent of the established brand but with the emphasis at point of sale on the price differential rather than the quality of the competing product/brand. As the product becomes more established and as technology advances (such that the quality of the product can be improved at lower cost), the quality of the product is enhanced. More money is then spent on the promotion and trade dress of the enhanced product until ultimately the successful imitation becomes a brand in its own right. Examples of market sectors where this evolution has taken place include the Irish cream liqueur market which was created with the launch of Bailey's Irish Cream Liqueur and was followed by the launch of a number of cheaper imitations produced by various manufacturers. Ultimately, some of these "me-too" products developed to become established brands in their own right as in the case of Carolans. In the gin sector, the Larios brand of gin which began life as a "me-too" in Spain following behind Gordon's gin, has developed to become an international brand.

4–03 The danger for the brand owner in relation to the development of competing products is not the competition *per se*, but rather the confusion (in the broadest sense of the word) suffered by members of the public and the loss of

---

[1] The term "trade dress" is used in the United States to refer not only to the appearance of the packaging *per se* but also to the appearance of articles themselves, as in the case of greeting cards, etc., or a particular sales technique, or a performance style of a rock group (see McCarthy, para. 8–01). However, for the purposes of this book the term will be used simply to refer to the overall appearance of a product's packaging.

distinctiveness of the original brand or more particularly the loss of distinctiveness of the packaging engendered by the use of "lookalike" packaging, that is packaging that is reminiscent of the original brand. As one commentator observed:

"If you are in the business of making something that has become indistinguishable from its rivals, it has in effect turned into a commodity and will therefore sell chiefly on price."[1a]

In the battle of the supermarket shelves between branded and own label products, brand owners know only too well the dangers of their brands becoming indistinguishable from those of the retailer and thus being regarded as commodities. Once branded products lose their ability to stand out from other products, either as a result of their distinctive trade dress or as a result of their brand image, consumers will no longer be willing to pay a price premium to acquire them and as a consequence their market share will fall. If, however, the brand owner can maintain the distinctiveness of the brand's trade dress and the brand's image then consumers will continue to pay a price premium to acquire the brand of their choice even in the face of tough price competition.[2]

4–04 The legal issues concerning the protection of trade dress, and the lacunae that exist under the current legal regime, can usefully be illustrated by reference to the own label phenomenon where the issue of lookalikes has reached its zenith. In 1997 own label products accounted for 37 per cent of the total grocery market in the United Kingdom and this figure is expected to increase to 40 per cent by 2001.[3] Own label products therefore represent a significant proportion of the grocery market. We will begin by looking at some of the marketing issues relating to the nature of own label products before turning to consider the psychological principles underlying brand imitation. The second section will address the legal issues relating to lookalikes and will include an analysis of the different causes of action that might be available to the brand owner. Proving confusion exists, or that there is a likelihood of confusion, is central to a successful action for trade mark infringement where lookalike products are concerned but it can often elude the brand owner, especially where the retailer's own name appears prominently on the product label. Demonstrating that a misrepresentation has been made for the purposes of a passing off action can prove equally arduous.

We will consider what the nature of the harm is that brand owners' suffer when a lookalike brand is launched with a view to identifying what might be a more appropriate cause of action. We will see that dilution (which does not require confusion) and/or misappropriation (with its emphasis on business ethics) might provide more appropriate means for protecting trade dress, although neither of these currently exist as distinct causes of action in the United Kingdom.

MARKETING ISSUES

(a) What are "own label" products?

4–05 Before discussing the subject of own label products in any detail it is first necessary to be clear what is meant by the expression. The terms "own label",

---

[1a] *The Economist*, July 2, 1994.
[2] In the year ending June 1996 Tesco cut the price of its budget own label baked beans from 16p to 3p per tin. During the same period Heinz increased the price of its beans from 30p to 32p per tin. Despite the significant price difference Heinz share of market revenue remained stable. 1997 (Buck "The Continuing Grocery Revolution" 4 *The Journal of Brand Management* 227 at 237.)
[3] *The Financial Times* April 26–27, 1997.

"private label", "own brand" and "retailer brand" are often used interchangeably. Nielsen[4] defines an own brand as:

> "A brand name owned by a retailer or a wholesaler for a line or variety of items under exclusive or controlled distribution."

Whereas Morris[5] defines own label products as:

> "Consumer products produced by, or on behalf of, distributors and sold under the distributor's own name or trade mark through the distributor's own outlet."

The key factor in both definitions is the control of the distribution chain. It is this fact that sets own label products apart from manufacturers' branded products which are available to all retailers and where the manufacturer has comparatively little control over the distribution or the retail sale of the product. Although many brand owners are increasing their investment in distribution networks the fact that, in general terms, they are not involved in the retail sector denies them ultimate control over the sale of their products in terms of price, shelf space, presentation, positioning and environment and in terms of consumer information and feedback.

4–06   When discussing own brand products attention is often focused upon the food sector and supermarkets in particular. The concept is not, however, confined to the supermarket shelf. Indeed in some respects it has developed more in other market sectors. In most countries clothing and footwear form the second biggest market for own label goods although the proportion of own label products in the health and beauty sector is increasing in size. Stores such as Marks & Spencer, Next, Jaegar, Halfords, Wicks, John Lewis and Liberty's (to name but a few) display as many, if not more, own label products than supermarkets. For the purposes of this discussion, however, examples will be given principally from the food sector although the comments made will apply equally to other market sectors.

(i) Types of own label products

4–07   In his paper entitled "Own Brands in Food Retailing Across Europe"[6] Laaksonen identified four main categories of own brand: generic brands; store brands; non-store brands, and exclusive or private brands.

4–08   **Generic brands**   Generic brands have been described as[7]:

> "Retailer controlled items which are packed in such a way that the prime concern with the packaging is product protection with minimal concern for aesthetic appeal, and displaying only the legal minimum amount of information."

---

[4] Nielsen Marketing Research is part of Dun & Bradstreet Corporation and is the world's largest marketing research organisation. It is the authoritative voice on market trends in the fast moving consumer goods (FMCG) sector.
[5] Morris, "The Strategy of Own Brands" (1971) 2 *European Journal of Marketing* 13.
[6] Published by The Oxford Institute of Retail Management, 1994 ("Laaksonen").
[7] De Chernatony "Prospects for Grocery Brands in the Single European Market" a study prepared for the Coca-Cola Retailing Research Group Europe, London, p. 28 ("De Chernatony").

Goods such as rice, milk, sugar, cereal and other commodity items usually form the basis of generic brands. Consumers are encouraged to make their purchasing decision based purely on price considerations. The price is intended to be the key issue, and will be designed to be the cheapest available in the store for that product type. Some stores will name their range of generic goods as, for example, their "Savers" range (Safeway's generic brand) or "Value" range (Tesco's equivalent) (See Appendix C, photograph 3). Simple packaging with little overt branding, the Savers pack bears a simple but distinctive logo and uses Safeway's corporate colours. There is usually limited wording on the pack; the product name is usually descriptive; and the packaging itself is usually simple, often transparent. Although the packaging may be of low quality and unsophisticated compared to premium brand products, it can be equally distinctive in that it is readily recognisable to consumers.

4–09 Generic brands are sometimes referred to as first generation own brands because they are often the first form of own label goods that retailers produce. In general terms generic brands do not seek to look like or resemble the leading brand in the category in any way.

4–10 Store brands In the context of Lookalikes store brands are the most important form of own label product. They are products that bear the name of the retailer as the brand name, *e.g.* Sainbury's Orange Juice, or Tesco Lemonade, a Next jacket. Like generic brands, their packaging can be extremely important as a means of communicating product quality and in projecting the image of the store. Unlike the basic appearance of generic brands, the trade dress of store brands is more sophisticated and is often designed to compete directly with that of the brand leader in the particular product sector concerned.[8] It is these store brands that are at the centre of controversy in the lookalike debate, as will be seen below.

4–11 Non-store brands The classic example of a non-store brand is the own label brand of Marks & Spencer plc, St Michael. The name appears on the label of all clothing sold within Marks & Spencer stores but it is not the retailer's own name.[9] Consumers unfamiliar with the store may not recognise these non-store brands as own label products.

4–12 One of the important differences between store brands and non-store brands is that the former compete with branded goods relying upon the retailers image and reputation (amongst other things), whilst the latter compete without that support. Non-store brands do not, generally speaking, tend to bear too close a resemblance to their branded counterparts. They have not, however, escaped criticism from brand owners.

4–13 Private/exclusive brands A non-store brand should not be confused with a private or exclusive brand which is a brand manufactured by a company using a name or trade mark (not including the store name) exclusively for one customer/

---

[8] In the absence of objective information concerning the quality of a product the consumer looks for "cues" as to quality given by the appearance of the product packaging. Although simple packaging can denote a quality product this is usually so where the quality of the packaging materials themselves are high and the design of the packaging is more sophisticated as in the case of some cosmetic products. The packaging of generic products, by contrast, often features poorer quality materials in an effort to keep production costs as low as possible.

[9] The St. Michael brand is unusual in that it is so well known today that it has become virtually synonymous with the store name of Marks & Spencer. This would not have been the case, however, when the brand was first launched.

distributor and often supplying the same product to other distributors using different brand names. No7 cosmetics manufactured for, and sold only at, Boots stores is an example of an exclusive brand. Like their branded counterparts, exclusive or private brands include a price premium and may employ distinctive names and packaging that may be suitable for design and/or trade mark registration. Indeed No7 cosmetics are protected in this way. Private brands may also be advertised and promoted in the same manner as their branded counterparts and indeed the No7 brand is regularly featured in full page colour advertisements in womens' magazines in direct competition with cosmetic brands such as Lancôme and Christian Dior. Private brands have, so far, avoided criticism from brand owners based on their packaging appearance.

4–14 Although own label products have been on sale for over 100 years only in the last 10 years or so has their existence provoked significant debate. The recession in the United Kingdom in the 1970's coupled with the abandoning of price controls and market restraints provided a unique opportunity for growth in the own label market unparalleled in retailing history.[10] The United Kingdom witnessed tremendous growth in the concentration and power of supermarkets such that by 1992 the top five stores (Sainsbury, Safeway, Tesco, Gateway and Asda) accounted for 64 per cent of the £42.6 billion grocery sector and sold 80 per cent of all own brand grocery products sold. By 1992 Sainsbury had the biggest single share of the market with 17.8 per cent[11] but Tesco has since overtaken it. Own brand sales have for a long time accounted for over 50 per cent of Sainsbury's total sales, as opposed to 42 per cent of Tesco's (1992) and 31 per cent at Asda (1990).[11a]

4–15 During the period 1991—1996 own label sales grew on average 7.5 per cent a year compared to 3.5 per cent for overall retail sales growth. In 1996, the total market of own label products in Europe was estimated to be worth £160 billion and was said to be capable of growing by a further 23 per cent in real terms by the end of 1999.[12] Own label products are therefore particularly important both commercially and in terms of their impact on marketing practice. If retailers are free to adopted lookalike packaging then this can have serious consequences for brand owners given the size of the own label market.

(b) Own label quality and packaging—"lookalikes"

4–16 One a retailer has decided to introduce an own label range of goods, the next important decision for the retailer is whether to promote the own label goods relying solely upon the price advantage with no claims being made as to the quality of the product (a price-led strategy), or whether to differentiate the own label product based on quality, *i.e.* producing quality products that compete in terms of quality with the branded equivalent—where the margins to be made are greater.[13] In the case of the former the competition is based on price alone whereas in the latter there may be competition both in terms of quality and price (*i.e.* value for money). Although some retailers do choose to compete on price alone (*e.g.* notably

---

[10] For a more detailed account of the evolution of own label products see Laaksonen, p. 9.

[11] Figures are taken from *The Grocer* April 23, 1994 quoting Corporate Intelligence. According to figures quoted in *The Times* February 8, 1996 grocery own label sales accounted for more than 40 per cent of all grocery sales in 1994.

[11a] Laaksonen, p. 55.

[12] These figures are taken from a Euromonitor report entitled "Private Label in Europe" (1996) reported in *The Times* February 8, 1996.

[13] Second and third generation own brands tend to be positioned by reference to their quality as opposed to their price.

Kwiksave and Co-Op) many of the larger retail chains choose to compete on the basis of value for money.

4–17 Whilst brand owners were used to the occasional instance of a competitor imitating a successful brand, the growing number of lookalike own label products in the 1990s caused considerable consternation. Two particular events in 1993–94 sparked unprecedented comment and protest from brand owners and manufacturers on the issue of own brands and lookalikes. The introduction of the Trade Marks Bill in the House of Lords in December 1993 was the first incident that led brand owners to voice their concerns regarding lookalikes. The second was the launch of Sainsbury's Classic Cola, an own brand cola with a trade dress reminiscent of the Coca Cola brand.

4–18 Although the Trade Marks Bill[14] itself had been expected for some time— and an uneventful passage through parliament was predicted—an amendment was tabled at a late stage which provoked lively debate. The amendment,[15] as tabled, was said to address:

> "The growing problem of own brand lookalikes; that is to say, major retailers marketing their products for their own shelves in packaging designed to resemble that of a famous brand name or brand leader."[16]

Brand owners sought to amend the law to deal specifically with the issue of own brand products imitating the trade dress of branded products. The amendment was not preceded by any particular incidence of "copying", nor had there been previous public debate on the subject. Indeed, manufacturers seemed strangely silent in the face of the growing trend of own label "copies". According to the British Producers and Brand Owners Group (BPBOG), (the lobby group representing the interests of brand owners) manufacturers felt unable to tackle the issue directly with retailers because of the power of the retailer to "de-list" (*i.e.* to cease stocking) the brand in question and since the retail stores were very often the manufacturers' biggest customer this made confrontation "commercial suicide". It was argued that the amendment to the Bill was needed as existing laws were too uncertain and difficult to enforce. In particular, since it was not possible to register three dimensional objects as trade marks, brand owners had found it virtually impossible to retain exclusivity of a brand's trade dress relying on trade mark registration.

4–19 Brand owners emphasised that their objection lay not with the competition from retailers *per se*, but with the growing tendency for the retailer to give customers:

> "The general impression that their product is the same as that of the famous brand by combining several characteristic features of the packaging that consumers associate with that product [as part of the packaging on the own label product]."[17]

Or as it was put in *The Times*[18]:

[14] The Bill aimed to implement the Trade Marks Directive No 89/104/EEC 1988 (hereafter the "Trade Marks Directive").
[15] Amendment 25, January 18, 1994.
[16] Lord Reay, House of Lords Parliamentary Debate, February 24, 1994.
[17] *ibid.*, January 18, 1994.
[18] "Brand of Logic" *The Times* April 20, 1994.

"The . . . subtle goal of 'lookalike' packaging is to hijack the reputation and symbolism of the famous brand. To give two products a virtually identical visual appearance is to imply a similarity of quality, taste or efficiency."

Manufacturers of branded goods continued to assert that own brand products were inferior in quality to branded products. It goes without saying therefore that they strongly resisted the implication that own label products were as good as branded products if they bore the same or similar packaging.[19]

4-20   In the early days of own brand products the quality was typically inferior to the branded equivalent because the main selling point was one of price and not quality. The retailer was aiming to deliver goods at a significantly cheaper price. But, as better technology became available at lower cost, the retailer began to address the issue of quality. This, combined with the brand owners obsession with new product development (at the cost of the development and improvement of existing product lines), provided the retailer with an opportunity to improve product quality to such an extent that consumer perception of own brand products underwent a complete revolution.

"The consumer perception of own brands has changed and they are no longer perceived to be cheaper copies of manufacturer's brands. Besides price, quality is increasingly important."[20]

Indeed, according to the results of a survey[21] the majority of shoppers believed own label quality to be as good as proprietary brands. At Asda 75 per cent of shoppers thought its own label was as good as the branded equivalent, 21 per cent thought it was worse, and 4 per cent thought it was better. The figures for Gateway were 67 per cent, 31 per cent and 2 per cent. Sainsbury scored 78 per cent, 15 per cent and 7 per cent.

"During the late 1980's the evolution of own brands has been rapid. As large multiple retailers started to compete against each other less on price and more on quality and service, the quality and sophistication of own labels generally rose to the standards set by manufacturers' brands. As a part of their increasing sophistication, retailers started to introduce more sophisticated lines moving away from the basic staple products."[22]

Although the pricing differential between branded and own label products reduced, the own brand was still positioned lower than its branded rival. The effect upon branded products was clearly demonstrated by the well publicised and controversial launch of Sainsbury's Classic Cola.

4-21   Sainsbury's Classic Cola was launched on April 18, 1994 and was controversial from the outset because of the product's appearance. It consisted of a can coloured a metallic red with white italic lettering partly horizontal and partly vertical. The overall effect was reminiscent of a can of Coca-Cola, its intended rival.[22a] During the weeks that followed the launch the national press (not to

---

[19] See Appendix C, photographs 4, 5 and 6 which illustrate some of the packaging at the centre of the complaint.
[20] Laaksonen, p. 2.
[21] *The Independent on Sunday*, February 20, 1994.
[22] Laaksonen, p. 15.
[22a] See Appendix C, photograph 7.

mention the trade press) was full of articles comparing the performance and look of the two products. According to published figures,[23] Sainsbury's previous version of their own brand cola (made to a different recipe and using a different packaging style) accounted for an average of 15 per cent of the stores cola sales (in March). In April, the new Sainsbury's Classic Cola took this share of total cola sales to a staggering 60 per cent, whilst sales of Coca-Cola fell from 60 per cent to 33 per cent. It should, however, be stressed that during this same period total sales of cola grew by almost two thirds—giving a final drop to Coca-Cola of 20 per cent.[24] According to newspaper surveys the success of Classic Cola was not only due to the price (25p for Classic Cola as opposed to 32p for Coca-Cola) but also due to product quality. Although most of the surveys can be regarded as little more than street polls, the general impression was that the repackaged Sainsbury's own brand was as good, if not better than the "the Real Thing".

4–22   According to brand owners, the copying of product trade dress by retailers such as Sainsbury caused damage to the value of the manufacturer's brand—value that has been built up by considerable investment in advertising and marketing. They alleged that the retailer was taking advantage of the goodwill generated through the advertising and promotion of the branded product. Or as *The Times* newspaper put it[25]:

> "The major manufacturers argue that supermarkets' clever use of packaging, logos and colour unfairly exploits the consumer loyalty which they have built up over the years through ingenuity and investment."

Further, brand owners argued that consumers were misled into believing that the own brand product was made by the brand leader. (An argument relied upon in the *Marmite* case referred to below). This argument stems from the supermarket's original practice of selling firstly branded goods (and exclusive brands) and then store brands, sourced by manufacturers of branded products or third party manufacturers. In addition, comments made by the retailers themselves positively encourage this view, as can be seen from this extract from a letter from a senior employee at Sainsbury in response to a letter from a customer concerning own label goods.[26]

> "Regarding the branded manufacturers, I must mention that, in many instances, they supply us with our own-label lines."

Whilst this may be true, the consumer has no way of knowing which own brands are made by the manufacturers of branded goods and which are not. United Biscuits, for example, produces Jaffa cakes for Sainsbury under the Sainsbury name as well as under the McVities brand name. This has led to the erroneous assumption by consumers that many own brand products are manufactured by brand owning companies. This, in turn, has caused some brand manufacturers to put warning notices on their packets in an effort to educate consumers to the fact that they do not manufacture own label products, *e.g.* Kellogg.[27]

---

[23] *The Times* May 11, 1994.
[24] According to industry sources from April 1994 to April 1995 Coca-Cola's share of supermarket sales dropped from 44 per cent to 32 per cent whilst those of Pepsi dropped from 18 per cent to 13 per cent. During the same period own label sales increased their share of the market from 20 per cent to 36 per cent and Virgin cola introduced through Tesco stores took 9 per cent of the market.
[25] *The Times*, April 20, 1994.
[26] *The Grocer*, September 10, 1994
[27] See Appendix C, photograph 8.

(c) The psychological basis of brand imitation

4–23 The Stimulus generalisation theory helps to provide an explanation as to why consumers react similarly to imitation products as to the original brand. It also explains, to some extent, why supermarkets want their brands to look like leading branded products. Stimulus generalisation theory is based on the proposition that individuals generalise from object or incidence to another similar object or incidence as part of the learning process. Zaichkowsky[28] explains how the original experiments by Ivan Pavlov concerning conditioned responses (involving dogs learning to salivate at the sound of a bell) also showed that if the stimulus, in this case the sound of the bell, was subsequently replaced by a similar sound, such as that of jangling keys, a buzzer or even a metronome, the same result was achieved. This illustrates the ability of the dogs to generalise the sound of the stimulus.

4–24 Just as Pavlov's dogs learned to generalise from the bell sound to the jangling keys so research in the USA[29] has shown that perceptions as to whether there is a common origin as between a branded product and an imitator are significantly affected by the similarity in physical appearance of the two products. The researchers speculated that consumers used the external package cues, such as colour, to evaluate the product attributes and to motivate purchase. Support for their speculation was provided by subsequent research.[30]

4–25 Consumer buying behaviour is a complex process and much of it is conducted subconsciously making it difficult to analyse and to repeat in experimental or artificial situations as in the case of a consumer survey for the purposes of litigation. However, it is important to have a basic understanding of the process in order to appreciate how those responsible for developing packaging that imitates that of a competitor seek to trade off associations and mistakes that consumers make as part of the buying process. The first step in the decision-making process is perception of the stimulus or object. In order to perceive an object or stimulus the consumer must pay attention to it. Attention involves bother intensity and direction. Intensity is the time spent actually looking at the object. The longer the consumer looks at the object the greater the chance that it will be perceived. Direction refers to the object being in focus. Obviously to perceive an object the consumer must both focus on the object and spend time looking at it.

4–26 In directing the attention of the consumer, visual (as opposed to semantic) information has a significant impact, thus the size and colour of the object can affect its ability to attract attention. When a consumer first perceives a stimulus (that is within the first 200 milliseconds) he/she views it holistically to determine where to focus his/her attention, in order to find the information that he/she is searching for.

4–27 As Zaichkowsky notes,[31] an individual's processing capacity is limited and so the individual is looking for the easiest way to achieve his/her goal with least effort. By means of selective attention (that is the differential processing of simultaneous sources of information), the individual determines where to focus his/her attention to find the information that he/she is searching for (*e.g.* brand name,

---

[28] Zaichkowsky, *Defending Your Brand Against Imitation* (Quorum Books, Westport), 1995, ("Zaichkowsky") p. 34.

[29] Loken, Ross & Hinkle "Consumer confusion of origin and brand similarity perceptions" (1986) 5 *Journal of Public Policy and Marketing* 195.

[30] Wad, Loken, Ross & Hasapopoulos, "The influence of physical similarity on generalisation of affect and attribute perceptions from national brands to private label brands" in Shrimp *et al* (Eds), *American Educator's Proceedings*, Series No. 52 (American Marketing Association, Chicago) 1986, p. 51.

[31] *ibid.* at p. 38.

price, weight, etc.). The subsequent pattern of looking will depend on the consumer's goal—that is, what the consumer is looking for. In the process of selective attention, sensory rather than semantic cues tend to be more important since they tend to be more accurate and require less effort. Spatial cues (*i.e.* those relating to the shape of a product) are particularly effective.[32] Stimuli outside the field of focus undergo little, if any sensory or semantic processing during the selective attention process. Thus the individual narrowly focuses attention and does it as simply as possible. For this reason, consumers sometimes mistake or confuse branded products and imitations particularly where the trade dress of both products incorporate visual and spatial elements that are very similar even if the semantic content is different.

4–28   Having perceived an object or stimulus, these perceptions are then interpreted by the individual subconsciously, based on the individual's previous experience and in the light of what he/she expects to see. Thus what is actually perceived is different for different people. As Zaichkowsky notes[33]:

> "We may cognitively rearrange what is actually seen to coincide with what we think we would most likely logically see."

The principles underlying perceptual organisation (the process of how we see things) are sometimes referred to as "gestalt psychology". The basic premise of gestalt psychology is that people do not experience the numerous stimuli they select from the environment as discrete sensations but rather they tend to organise them into groups and see them as wholes. Thus a single stimulus is viewed as a function of the whole to which the stimulus belongs.[34] The organisation of the stimuli into groups also helps to memorise and recall them. Consumers therefore tend to remember the overall "look" of a product, rather then individual details of the packaging such as font, colour, text, etc. As Zaichkowsky observes,

> "Gestalt psychology explains why objects can be detailed differently but still look the same to the observer."[35]

This may explain why a product with a similar trade dress may be "mistaken" for a branded product even where a number of differences exist in the detail of the packaging.[35a]

4–29   Zaichkowsky also suggests[36] that the social psychology concept of balance theory might explain the retailer's desire to associate a successful brand with a new or lesser known own label brand. Balance theory is based on the premise that individuals are motivated by a desire to keep their attitudes and feelings consistent with their objective thoughts and beliefs. Thus if a consumer has a positive attitude to say a particular celebrity, then linking that celebrity with an object through product endorsement leads to a positive connection between the object endorsed and the consumer because of the consumer's desire to maintain a state of balance.

---

[32] *ibid.* at p. 39.
[33] *ibid.* at p. 43.
[34] *ibid.* at p. 44.
[35] *ibid.* at p. 45, although suggestions are not directed at lookalikes *per se*.
[35a] Research undertaken by the Consumer Association in 1998 (unpublished) found that in the 6 months prior to the date of the survey 27 per cent of shoppers had brought or selected the "wrong" product and most people attributed the mistake to the design of the pack and in particular the colour.
[36] *ibid.* at p. 45.

> "Getting consumers to have a positive attitude toward their product or service is a major task for [retailers]. While there are several complex, time-consuming, and expensive ways to build positive attitudes based on the creation of good products and images, a very simple way is to associate the [new product] with an object that consumers already have a positive attitude towards."[37]

The linking of the new brand to the established brand causes the consumer to transfer the values of quality established in relation to the first brand to the new brand.

4–29/1   From this brief look at the process of perception and decision making we can see that consumers generalise from one stimulus to another, that they initially view objects holistically and then focus narrowly on the information they are searching for. We have also seen that sensory information (especially information about shape) is more important than semantic content during the selective attention process. Gestalt theory, with its emphasis on the whole rather than on individual stimuli, suggests that when consumers identify one cue on product packaging that they are likely to call to mind the overall look of the pack previously seen. This perception, combined with the interpretation of the customer's expectations, suggests that in practice consumers may well mistake a lookalike product for the original branded product.

> "Theories from psychology help to explain why imitation, as a marketing strategy, is a threat to the selection and perception of the original brand. Consumers generalise expectations from experiences with original brands to similar looking brands goods and devices in the marketplace. Due to fleeting attention and perceptual biases, individuals often make mistakes in their perception of similar but different brand in the market place."[38]

These theories also help to explain why in consumer surveys it can be so difficult to gather evidence to support the view that consumers confuse two particular brands given that the consumer search and decision making process usually takes place in a fraction of a second and depends on what information the consumer is searching for. Consumer surveys are generally carried out in a much more considered environment where the consumer's "goal" is quite different.

THE LEGAL ISSUES

4–30   Having considered the marketing issues surrounding lookalike products and the psychology of brand imitation generally, we will now turn to consider the legal issues that arise when brand owners contemplate taking legal action to stop the use of lookalike packaging by retailers or competitors generally. Accordingly, for the purposes of this next section a lookalike brand should be understood as encompassing any competing brand that imitates the trade dress of a successful brand and not just those produced by retailers. Once we have looked at the forms of legal action that currently exist, we will turn to consider possible alternative causes of action that might be relevant in these circumstances.

---

[37] *ibid.* at p. .45.
[38] *ibid.* at p. 48.

4–31   There are three possible causes of action open to the brand owner—copyright infringement, trade mark infringement and passing off. Whether all, or indeed any, of these can be relied upon very much depends on the facts of each particular case. In general terms, as we will see, there are difficulties and limitations inherent in each form of action. This can result in the brand owner being unable to bring a successful action even when it is clear that the business responsible for the lookalike intended to imitate the established brand to the point that visual cues from the packaging of the established brand have been incorporated in the packaging of the lookalike. To understand how this can happen we will us look at each cause of action in turn.

(a) Copyright infringement

4–32   Copyright arises automatically in relation to *inter alia* an original literary or artistic work which includes a graphic work[39] assuming that the author is a qualifying person[40] or that the work was first published in a qualifying country,[41] such as the United Kingdom. The author of the work will be the first owner of copyright unless the author is an employee in which case the employer will be the first owner subject to the contrary.[42] The effect of these provisions is that copyright will subsist in original artwork relating to a product's packaging design or label and it will belong to the design agency that created it unless there is an assignment transferring ownership to the brand owner.

4–33   The term of copyright protection extends to 70 years after the death of the author.[43] Although at first this would appear to be a very long period of protection one needs to bear in mind that some products have been on the market for over a hundred years (*e.g.* Coca-Cola). Whilst it is true that brands regularly update their packaging design it is questionable whether merely updating a label, as opposed to redesigning it, would be sufficient to create a new copyright.[44] Assuming, however, that the packaging design still has the benefit of copyright protection will the holder of the copyright be able to rely on it to stop the use of lookalike packaging?

4–34   As we saw in Chapter 2, to bring a successful claim for copyright infringement the copyright owner must show that there has been a substantial reproduction of the copyright work in a material form without the copyright holders consent.[45] Although it has been held that the test of substantiality is a qualitative and not a quantitative one[46] it has also been said that if the plaintiff's labour, skill and judgment was only just enough to earn copyright protection there will need to be an almost exact imitation to be any infringement.[47] Whilst the trade dress of branded products generally calls for more labour, skill and judgment than the simple drawing of a hand at issue in that case, if the trade dress is of a simple nature (such as that of the fragrance CK One produced by Calvin Klein which comprises a frosted glass bottle with a silver screw top and the brand name) there will need to be an almost exact reproduction before infringement will be found.

---

[39] ss.1 and 4 CDPA.
[40] s.154 CDPA.
[41] s.153 CDPA.
[42] s.11 CDPA.
[43] s.12 CDPA.
[44] *Interlego AG v. Tyco Industries* [1988] R.P.C. 343, PC.
[45] s.17 CDPA.
[46] Lord Reid, *Ladbroke v. William Hill* [1964] 1 W.L.R. 273 at 276, HL.
[47] *Kenrick v. Lawrence* (1890) 25 Q.B.D. 99.

Equally, if the trade dress consists of a number of aspects that are commonly used in the trade for those type of goods then arguably closer imitation will be required than if the original packaging design was very unusual.

4–35   As it is, most lookalike brands do not actually reproduce the detail of the trade dress of the brand they seek to imitate but rather use a similar coloured background with lettering of a similar colour albeit that the text itself is different to the original.[48] Although the overall scheme of the packaging may be similar in the sense that there are common features of style there is usually insufficient resemblance to give rise to a successful action for infringement.

4–36   One of the few examples of a successful action for infringement of a label design is *Tavener Rutledge Ltd v. Spectre Ltd*[49] where the defendant copied the plaintiff's label for a sweet tin. The background of the label, which comprised an array of sweets, was copied exactly except where the name Tavener had appeared Spectre appeared instead. The centre of the original label featured a circle bordered by flowers with a white band across the centre of the circle. Although the defendant's label had a more elaborate device in the centre, it too was bordered by flowers and included a white band. The judge held that it was a clear case of infringement on the basis that the defendant had copied the plaintiff's label and the small differences it had made to the design did not make any substantial difference.

4–37   The difficulty arises where the work undertaken by the defendant does make a difference. In *Elanco Products Ltd v. Mandops (Agrochemical Specialists) Ltd*[50] the defendant, who had copied the packaging of the plaintiff's product but had subsequently modified it when the plaintiff complained, had not gone far enough according to the court. The question is whether the defendant has gone far enough to create a fresh copyright or whether a substantial amount of the plaintiff's work remains in the defendant's work. In the *Schlurppes* case,[51] the defendant produced what it claimed was a parody of the plaintiff's label using the word Schlurppes in place of the plaintiff's trade mark Schweppes. Falconer J. noted that[52]:

> ". . . one only has to look at the two side by side to see that there is no possibility of any other conclusion than that a very substantial part has been reproduced. The labels are from an artistic point of view, particularly the layout, virtually identical."

As has been said before, although there have not been many cases in this area in relation to lookalikes it is likely that most lookalikes would not be regarded as infringements of the corresponding branded product as they do not reproduce the text or artwork from the original product, and in many cases do not replicate the exact design either—rather it is more a question of the overall look or impression of the packaging that is replicated (see Appendix C, photograph 9).

(b) Trade mark infringement

4–38   As we saw in Chapter 3, prior to the enactment of the Trade Marks Act 1994 ("TMA") it was not possible to register three dimensional articles as trade

---

[48] For example Asda supermarket produced an own brand fragrance called "George 1" which was sold in a frosted glass bottle with a silver top—*The Sunday Times*, December 22, 1996.
[49] (1959) R.P.C. 83.
[50] [1980] R.P.C. 213, CA.
[51] *Schweppes Ltd v. Wellington Ltd* [1984] F.S.R. 210 (the "*Schlurppes*" case).
[52] *ibid.* at, p. 211.

marks. This meant that from a practical point of view, brand owners were only able to register as trade marks words, logos and labels. Although it was possible to register as a trade mark a two dimensional representation of three dimensional packaging[53] the effectiveness of such a registration was in some doubt. Brand owners were therefore unable to rely on trade mark law to provide protection for a product's overall appearance, or trade dress. This in turn meant that brand owners would often rely on both actions, trade mark infringement (in respect of any names or labels imitated) and passing off (as regards the product's trade dress).

4–39   Under the TMA it is possible to register a product's trade dress provided that it meets the criteria set out in section 1 of the TMA and does not fall foul of section 3.[54] The first hurdle for the brand owner is to demonstrate that the trade dress itself is a trade mark and is distinctive. The rejection of trade mark applications such as those filed by Proctor & Gamble Limited[55] in respect of the trade dress of Flash cleaning fluid on the grounds that the mark was devoid of any distinctive character under section 3(1)(b) of the Act, highlights the difficulties faced by brand owners in achieving registration. In relation to that, the Hearing Officer rejected the application mark registration concluding that neither the shape of the container, nor the matter appearing on the label nor the colour of the container were distinctive either separately or in combination (see Appendix C, photograph 10). As no evidence of use of the mark had been filed to overcome the objections raised, the application was rejected. This decision was affirmed by the Court of Appeal. Admittedly this was an unusual case in that Proctor & Gamble had removed the wording actually used (including the brand name) from the label leaving a form of "ghosting" as to where the words would have been. As Walker L.J. noted, the "ghosting" of the labels was at the heart of the appeal.[56] Proctor & Gamble were, according to the judge, seeking to go beyond the registration of a particular name or logo to achieve registration of the "get-up" of the goods. He agreed, as did his fellow judges, with the Hearing Officer that nothing about the bottle could be regarded as inherently distinctive, rather he found that it was typical of the get-up of products used for household cleaning purposes—except that it bore no name or logo. Accordingly, registration was refused.

4–40   The result of this decision is that brand owners seeking registration of brand packaging must either develop more inherently distinctive packaging, or include the brand name on the packaging if the trade dress is to be accepted for registration. However, as we shall see, including the brand name as part of the trade mark brings with it certain disadvantages when it comes to infringement.

4–41   For the brand owner that does manage to register its brand's trade dress, the Act introduces in section 10 two tests for infringement that could *prima facie* apply to lookalike products. The first test is set out in section 10(1), which states that:

> "A person infringes a registered trade mark if he uses in the course of trade a sign which is identical with the trade mark in relation to goods or services which are identical with those for which it is registered."

To succeed under this section a comparison must first be made between the registered trade mark and the "sign" used on the lookalike product,[57] and then a

---

[53] See for example *Re Coca-Cola Trade Marks* [1986] R.P.C. 421.
[54] As discussed in Chap. 3.
[55] *Proctor & Gamble Limited's Trade Mark Applications* [1999] R.P.C. 673, CA.
[56] *ibid.* at p. 676.
[57] *Origins Natural Resources v. Origin Clothing* [1995] F.S.R. 280.

comparison is made of the alleged infringing products and the goods covered by the registration. If there is identity of marks and goods then liability is strict (subject to there being any defence under section 11, for example that the mark is descriptive, etc.). There is no need to show any likelihood of confusion.

4–42 Although, in the context of lookalikes, the comparison of the goods is likely to be straightforward[58] (the goods are, generally speaking, identical to those of the brand owner), that of the trade mark and the sign are not. Whilst it may be clear what the mark is, namely that which is registered, it is not always so obvious what the sign is. In the case of *British Sugar Plc v. James Robertson & Sons Ltd*,[59] for example, it was held that the defendant's sign was "Treat" and not "Robertson's Toffee Treat" which was the name that appeared on the label. According to Jacob J., the first two words were "added matter" and should therefore be disregarded. This approach followed that established in *Saville Perfumery v. June Perfect*,[60] a case decided under the 1938 Act. Thus to show that the defendant has used an identical mark the plaintiff must find the entirety of its registered mark in the trade dress used by the defendant. The defendant can not escape liability by including on its packaging additional material, as this will be disregarded. As noted above, however, in practice it is rare for lookalike products to incorporate the exact words and designs used on the branded product (as illustrated in Appendix C, photographs 4, 5, 6, 7, 9 and 11). It is therefore unlikely that the brand owner will be in a position to bring proceedings based on section 10(1). This is especially true if the brand owner has included the brand name as part of the registered trade mark. In which case the brand owner will need to turn to the second test for infringement set out in section 10(2) if action is to be taken against the lookalike product.

4–43 Section 10(2) states that:

"A person infringes a registered trade mark if he uses in the course of trade a sign where because —

(a) the sign is identical with the trade mark and is used in relation to goods or services similar to those for which the trade mark is registered, or

(b) the sign is similar to the trade mark and is used in relation to goods or services identical with or similar to those for which the trade mark is registered,

there exists a likelihood of confusion on the part of the public, which includes the likelihood of association with the trade mark."

This provision is taken straight from the Directive,[61] although its ultimate provenance remains open to speculation and debate. It has been argued[62] that this section owes its origin to the Uniform Benelux Trademark Law 1971. Under Benelux law, the likelihood of association is a very wide concept, much broader in scope than the likelihood of confusion. It includes any mental connection, or calling to mind, that is made between the registered mark and the junior user even if there is no

---

[58] What will be considered as "similar" is discussed in detail in Chap. 5, at paras 5–66 *et seq.*
[59] [1997] E.T.M.R. 118 (the "*Treat*" case).
[60] (1941) 58 R.P.C. 147, HL.
[61] Art. 5 Trade Marks Directive.
[62] Annand & Norman, p. 154–155 and Geilen "European Trade Mark Legislation: The Statements" [1996] E.I.P.R. 83.

confusion as to the source of the product. Indeed in the case of *Always v. Regina*[63] (a case involving lookalike products) the Benelux Court held that the trade mark Always for sanitary towels was infringed by the use of the own brand product named Regina, despite the different brand names. The packaging of the own brand was similar to that of Always and the court held that there was a likelihood of association because of this similarity.

4–44   If this precedent had been followed in the United Kingdom it would have provided brand owners with the results that they were looking for without resorting to dilution or misappropriation (discussed below at para. 4–62 *et seq.*). However, in *Wagamama Limited v. City Centre Restaurants Plc*,[64] the first United Kingdom case to test the meaning of this provision, Laddie J. refused to give such a wide interpretation to section 10(2) on the basis that both the Directive and the Trade Marks Act 1994 referred to a "likelihood of confusion" as including a "likelihood of association". If confusion was not an essential element then both statutes would, said Laddie J., refer to a likelihood of association as including a likelihood of confusion and not the other way around. Accordingly, it was held that a "likelihood of confusion" was as an essential ingredient in establishing trade mark infringement under section 10(2). Despite arguments submitted by the plaintiff to the effect that the Council had intended to adopt the Benelux approach these arguments were dismissed as being based on no more than "Chinese whispers".[65]

4–45   To determine whether a brand owner might succeed under section 10(2) a comparison needs to be made between (i) the registered mark and the sign used, (ii) the goods for which the mark is registered and those on which the sign is used, and finally an assessment must be made as to the likelihood of confusion. In the *Treat* case Jacob J. said that the test was a threefold one and that care should be taken to ensure that one did not elide the questions. However, the ECJ criticised this view,[66] stating firmly that the likelihood of confusion must be treated globally, taking into account all factors relevant to the circumstances of the case. That global appreciation of the visual, aural or conceptual similarity of the marks in question must be based on the overall impression given by the marks, bearing in mind their distinctive and dominant components.[67] The ECJ acknowledged that the more distinctive the earlier mark the greater the likelihood of confusion.

4–46   In *Sabel BV v. Puma AG*[68] the ECJ had an opportunity to comment on the meaning of section 10(2), or rather Article 4 of the Directive (on which section 10(2) is based). It stated that the "mere association which the public might make between two trade marks as a result of their analogous semantic content is not itself a sufficient ground for concluding that there is a likelihood of association". Thus it endorsed the Advocate General's Opinion which itself was a ringing endorsement of Laddie J.'s decision in *Wagamama*. However, the Advocate General in his Opinion stressed that the words "likelihood of association" were not redundant. They could, he said, operate in situations where there was no confusion as to source as such, but where there is confusion in the sense that there is a mistaken assumption that there is an organisational or economic link between the two undertakings concerned.

[63] *The Proctor & Gamble Company v. NV Regina* (1993) Intellectuele Eigendom en Reclamerecht.
[64] [1995] F.S.R. 713.
[65] [1995] F.S.R. 713 at 726.
[66] The criticisms were in fact made by the Advocate General in *Canon Kabushiki Kaisha v. Metro-Goldwyn-Mayer Inc.* [1999] E.T.M.R. 1.
[67] *Sabel BV v. Puma AG* [1998] E.T.M.R. 1 at 8.
[68] *ibid.*

4-47   Thus in determining whether the trade dress of a lookalike product infringes a brand owner's trade mark registration, a comparison needs to be made of the relevant registration and the lookalike product in visual, aural and conceptual terms taking into account their distinctive components. The nature of the defendant's product and the goods covered by the plaintiff's registration also need to be assessed, and finally an assessment should be made of the likelihood of confusion on the part of the public bearing in mind all the surrounding circumstances but remembering that it is not sufficient for consumers to be prompted merely to think of the branded product when they see the lookalike, they must go further than that and believe, at the very least, that a trade connection or economic link exists as a consequence of the use of the offending packaging.

4-47/1   In assessing the distinctive character of the mark, account needs to be taken of its inherent characteristics, whether it contains any descriptive elements, the market share held by the mark, how intensive, geographically widespread and longstanding the use of the mark has been; the amount invested in advertising in promoting the mark; the proportion of the relevant section of the public which identifies the goods as originating from a particular source (manufacturer) because of the mark and statements of traders.[68a]

4-47/2   As noted in the *Lloyds* case[69] the assessment of the marks in the mind of the average consumer of the category of goods plays a decisive role in the global appreciation of the likelihood of confusion. For the purposes of that global appreciation, the average consumer of that category of goods is deemed to be reasonably well informed and reasonably observant and circumspect. However, account also has to be taken of the fact that the consumer rarely has a chance to make a side by side comparison and has an imperfect recollection of the goods in his mind.

Thus the test is by no means an easy one for the courts to apply since the assessment of whether or not a likelihood of confusion exists is a matter on which the minds of intelligent people are prone to differ.

4-48   For the brand owner, it can be seen that obtaining a registration of a brand's trade dress, even without the brand name on the pack, does not guarantee success in an action for trade mark infringement since the manner in which the court currently approaches the assessment of similarity finds place greater emphasis on semantic content. The analysis, carried out in the cold light of the court room during the course of a trial, may last for several days and is far removed from the supermarket aisle where purchasing decisions are made by members of the public in a matter of seconds. Although in the *Lloyds* case the ECJ acknowledged that consumers carry with them an imperfect recollection of the mark, the requirement that the average consumer be regarded as "well informed and reasonably observant and circumspect" may raise the threshold too high for lookalike products to be caught by it. Whilst the notion of the average consumer as the proverbial moron in a hurry may put the test too low, it perhaps more accurately reflects consumer supermarket shopping patterns.

4-49   Whilst the comments of the ECJ that the assessment of similarity of the marks should include a global appreciation of the overall impression of the marks, it is difficult to see how this will be adhered to by the courts whose nature is to focus on the detail. However, unless the courts begin to adopt a more holistic approach to the overall look of the plaintiff's registration and the defendant's trade

---

[68a] *Windsurferchiemsee v. Huber and Attenberger* [1999] E.T.M.R. 585.
[69] *Lloyd Schuhfabrik Meyer L Co v. Klijsen Handel* [1999] E.T.M.R. 690 at 698.

dress it is unlikely that any of the lookalikes that have appeared thus far will be regarded as infringements.[70]

(c) Passing off

4–50   As noted in Chapter 2, the essential elements of an action for passing off can be summarised as a need to show a misrepresentation causing damage to goodwill.[71] However, these cherished notions are a fertile source of inconsistency.

4–51   Whilst many brand owners may be able to show goodwill attached to their products with relative ease, proving the distinctiveness of a product's trade dress as a whole can be rather more complex. The main hurdle though, and one where most cases of this kind fall, is the requirement to show a misrepresentation.

4–52   From as early as 1915 the courts have sought to clarify what amounts to an actionable misrepresentation. In *Spalding (AG) & Bros v. AW Gamage Ltd*,[72] Lord Parker stated that:

> "[T]he basis of a passing off action being a false representation by the defendant, it must be proved in each case as a fact that the false representation was made. It may, of course, have been made in express words, but cases of express misrepresentation of this sort are rare. The more common case is where the representation is implied in the use or imitation of a mark, trade name or get up with which the goods of another are associated in the minds of the public, or a particular class of the public. In such cases the point to be decided is whether, having regard to all the circumstances of the case, the use by the defendant in connection with the goods of the mark, name or get up in question impliedly represents such goods to be the goods of the plaintiff, or the goods of the plaintiff of a particular class or quality, or, as it is sometimes put, whether the defendant's use of such mark, name or get up is *calculated to deceive*" (*emphasis added*).

Thus to succeed in an action for passing off the plaintiff must show not merely that confusion of the two products is possible, but that there is deception such that the consumer is deceived into believing that the goods of the defendant are actually those of the plaintiff—or in the context of own label products, that the own label is really the branded product. Confusion alone is not sufficient unless that confusion is the product of a misrepresentation: for example, where the product holds itself out as being something that it is not.

> "In the absence of any patent or trade mark infringement, it [is] only unlawful for a trader to copy and market a rival's product if that rival could show that purchasers were being or would be deceived into buying the copy in mistake for the original."[73]

4–53   In the *JPS*[74] case, the plaintiffs, Imperial Group plc, brought a passing off action against Philip Morris Ltd, following the latter's launch of a new brand of

[70] Annand, in her article focusing on lookalikes agrees that the widest interpretation of "similarity" is required if effective protection is to be obtained against lookalikes (Annand, "Lookalikes under the new U.K. Trademarks Act 1994" (1996) T.M.R. Vol. 86, 143 at p. 155.
[71] *Reckitt & Colman v. Borden* [1990] R.P.C. 341, HL.
[72] (1915) 32 R.P.C. 273 at 284.
[73] *Hodgkinson & Corby Ltd v. Wards Mobility Services Ltd,* [1994] 1 W.L.R. 1564, *The Times* August 3, 1994.
[74] *Imperial Group Plc & Another v. Philip Morris Ltd & Another* [1984] R.P.C. 293 ("*Imperial v. Philip Morris*").

cigarettes named Raffles, sold in a black packet with gold lettering (see Appendix C, photograph 12). The plaintiffs had for many years sold JPS cigarettes in a black packet using a monogram in gold. JPS had drawn attention to the appearance of the black pack in its advertising although the letters JPS were also used prominently. The court, however, refused to grant an injunction and the action was ultimately dismissed on the basis that nobody seeing or buying a packet of Raffles cigarettes would think that they were seeing or buying a packet of JPS (*i.e.* there would be no deception) despite obvious similarities in the packaging. Indeed Whitford J., commenting upon the advertising and promotion of the JPS brand observed that[75]:

> "The plaintiffs' case, which is a case of passing off by get-up, must succeed if at all, on reputation acquired by the very large sales of JPS International and Kingsize in the [black] packs . . . and in their very extensive advertising for those brands. In their advertising attention has been focused upon the production of an association of the word "black" with this particular brand. The advertising has been on an extraordinarily large scale and cannot have failed to make its impact upon smokers in this country and indeed upon a very large number of persons who are not smokers. The sale of the JPS cigarettes in black packs with the gold monogram and the words "John Players" have been enormous."

And yet, he continued, quoting from an earlier case[76] involving similarities in the get up of two brands of coffee bearing wholly dissimilar brand names:

> "[to succeed the plaintiffs] must make out that the defendants' goods are calculated to be mistaken for the plaintiffs' and where, as in this case, the goods of the plaintiff and defendant unquestionably resemble each other, but where the features in which they resemble each other are common to the trade, what has the defendant to make out? He must make out not that the defendants' are like his by reason of those features common to them and other people, but he must make out that the defendants' are like his by reason of something peculiar to him, and by reason of the defendants having adopted some mark, or device or label, or something of that kind which distinguishes the plaintiffs' from other goods which have like his, the features common to the trade. Unless the plaintiffs can bring his case up to that he fails."

Whitford J. continued:

> "In my judgment the plaintiffs' case fails at the outset. They were never in a position to establish that black alone or black with gold embellishments in the field of packs of cigarettes could be distinctive of them selling their cigarettes made under the brand name John Players."

If this was true of JPS cigarettes whose pack design was simple in style and distinctive, as compared to other leading brands of cigarettes, and whose advertising had for years stressed its distinctive black pack design, how much more so does it apply to the packaging of groceries that generally bear pack designs that are less distinctive (in a marketing sense—incorporating several different colours as part of

---

[75] *Imperial v. Philip Morris* at 296.
[76] *Paynton v. Snelling Lampard & Co. Ltd* (1900) 17 R.P.C. 48 at 52.

the surface graphics some of which may be common to the trade, together with descriptive text (see Appendix C, photographs 9 and 11).

4–54   One of the significant differences between the *JPS* case (where the plaintiffs lost) and the *Jiff Lemon*[77] case (where the plaintiff obtained an injunction to protect the distinctive packaging of its lemon juice) was that at the time of launching the JPS brand a few other minor brands of cigarettes also existed in black packs although by the time of the dispute concerning the Raffles brand none of the other brands were as well known as JPS.

4–55   The *Jif Lemon* case concerned the packaging for lemon juice. The plaintiff's packaging comprised a yellow, plastic lemon approximately the size and shape of a real lemon. Although during the early years of its use other brands of lemon juice existed using similar packaging, the plaintiff had either taken steps to stop the continued use of the packaging or had acquired the company concerned and so effectively obtained exclusivity of its packaging design in the market place. The defendant sought to introduce a brand of lemon juice in a plastic lemon shaped container different in appearance from that of the plaintiff's product both in size and shape (so far as this was possible whilst still retaining the look of a real lemon). The plaintiff initiated legal action to stop the defendant, pursuing its claim to the House of Lords. The plaintiff argued that use of such packaging by the defendant amounted to passing off and that consumers would be deceived into believing that the defendant's goods were really those of the plaintiff. To support this view the plaintiff relied upon survey evidence indicating that consumers still believed the defendant's product to be that of the plaintiff despite labels on the goods stating that they were not! The outcome was surprising given that the packaging in question was essentially descriptive (in a trade mark sense) even though it had been used by the plaintiff for approximately thirty years. Few brands can, however, point to such a long period of exclusive use of their trade dress in terms of the colour or shape. For brands that have not been established very long (*i.e.* less than five years) it is difficult to demonstrate such a clear association in the minds of consumers between the product and the shape and colour of their trade dress so as to be regarded as synonymous.

4–56   In the light of the *JPS* and *Jif Lemon* cases, it is small wonder that brand owners were reluctant to challenge lookalikes in the English courts. One of the few cases challenging retailers that did reach the courts was the *Marmite*[78] case. In this case the plaintiffs applied for an interlocutory injunction to stop the defendant's adoption of packaging that was similar in appearance to their well known brands, Marmite and Bovril (see Appendix C, photograph 13). In the words of Whitford J., the plaintiffs submitted that, on the basis of survey evidence:

> "When these new jars appeared in the Sainsbury shops customers were being led to believe that this was an own label product of Sainsbury, made by the makers of Marmite and Bovril. [They do] not suggest, and indeed nobody at any time suggested, that anybody is going to take the Sainsbury's product as being Marmite or Bovril."

The plaintiffs argued that the defendant had sold its own brand of yeast extract in a cylindrical container for several years and that its only object in changing the packaging to resemble the plaintiffs' brands was to trade off their reputation and

---

[77] *Reckitt & Colman Products Ltd v. Borden Inc* [1990] R.P.C. 341 (the *"Jif Lemon"* case).
[78] *Beecham Group Plc & Another v. J Sainsbury plc* (1987) (unreported) (the *"Marmite"* case).

goodwill, why else would the defendant change its pack to be so similar to that of the plaintiff?

4–57 There was no allegation that consumers would be deceived or misled into thinking that the own label product was Bovril or Marmite—but there was a risk (according to the plaintiffs) that consumers would associate the two products—believing them to emanate from the same source. No injunction was, however, granted, despite Whitford J.'s acknowledgment that the shapes of the plaintiffs' brands were distinctive and had been used by the plaintiffs alone for at least 20 years—requirements that he had indicated as being essential (and lacking) in the JPS case. Instead Whitford J. concluded (at the interlocutory stage) that:

> "In view of the fact that I can see no immediate damage and serious accruing, and no damage to the plaintiffs which cannot be made good, it is best to let the matter stand at this stage and to go to trial."

The judge failed to appreciate the damage caused to the distinctiveness of the plaintiffs' packaging and the fact that this could not be made good at trial if they succeeded.

4–58 It would seem that the judge did not wish to become embroiled at an interlocutory stage in a battle that would have serious commercial ramifications without evidence of any real misrepresentation and on the basis of survey evidence that was not without its shortcomings. It is disappointing that the case did not progress further as many of the issues raised remain unresolved.

4–59 One of the few successful cases concerning lookalike products to reach the courts after the enactment of the TMA was *United Biscuits (U.K.) Limited v. Asda Stores Limited*[79] which concerned the trade dress of Penguin chocolate biscuits and that of Asda's Puffin biscuit (see Appendix C, photograph 14). Although United Biscuits was unsuccessful in its claim of trade mark infringement under section 10(2) in connection with its registration of the word mark Penguin, it was successful in its claim for passing off. The outcome was surprising given that the trade mark action failed. Although both packs used the same background colouring and had brand names depicted in black lettering (bordered with white) that was the extent of the similarity. In reaching his decision it seems likely that the judge was influenced by the defendant's conduct in seeking to copy the plaintiff's pack design as closely as it could without being challenged for copying. Commenting on the defendants behaviour Walker J. noted[80]:

> "I cannot escape the conclusion that, while aiming to avoid what the law would characterise as deception, they were taking a conscious decision to live dangerously. That is not in my judgment something that the court is bound to disregard."

The judge concluded that the Puffin packaging was deceptively similar to the Penguin trade dress in that a substantial number of people would, he said believe that the two products were made by the same manufacturer because of the similarity in the packaging style. It is hard to say whether this decision indicates a sea change in the court's approach to passing off in lookalike cases or whether the judge was so greatly influenced by the conduct of the defendant that the case can be

---

[79] [1997] R.P.C. 513 (the *"Penguin"* case).
[80] *ibid.* at, p. 531.

distinguished on that ground alone. Certainly the judge's appreciation that customers would view the trade dress as a whole and not analyse the individual
components is a step forward.

4–60   Whether the judge in reaching his conclusion that customers might think
there was a connection between the two manufacturers, was influenced by the fact
that United Biscuits manufactured some own label products as well as branded
products is unclear. If he was, then it would be much harder for say Kellogg to rely
on consumers making such a connection in view of the fact that it states on its
packaging that it does not make own label products. Unlike other judges who are
often at pains to point out that in the absence of a registered trade mark, patent or
copyright competitors are entitled to copy provided that they do not encroach
upon the goodwill of another trader,[81] Walker J. stressed the obligation of the
court to determine what is fair or unfair saying that[82]:

> "The importance of brands and the emergence of competing own-brands
> means that the law's tests of what is fair and what is unfair competition have
> to be applied in new and changing conditions."

Whilst endorsing the judge's sentiments I would venture to suggest that the law of
passing off, with its strict adherence to the need to show a misrepresentation, is
limited in its ability to function as a means or regulating unfair competition. Whilst
it can certainly kerb its wildest excesses it cannot provide a remedy in the face of
misappropriation (discussed below), in the absence of a misrepresentation. Accordingly, unless the court regards misappropriation as fair competition it will indeed
need to review its process of determining what is fair and what is not.

The Real Nature of the Harm

4–61   From the above analysis of the different forms of intellectual property
right that brand owner's might seek to rely on in support of an action against the
producers of lookalike brands we see that it is hard for brand owners to
demonstrate that consumer's are "confused" in the classic sense, that is, that they
are confused as to the origin of the allegedly infringing product. The essence of the
brand owner's complaint is essentially twofold:

   (i) that owners of lookalike brands are taking unfair advantage of their
       investment, labour, skill and judgment in the design of the own brand's
       trade dress ("misappropriation"); and

   (ii) that the use of similar looking packaging reduces the overall distinctive-
        ness of the original brand owner's packaging design ("dilution").

We will consider each of these claims in turn.

(a) Misappropriation

4–62   This concept has principally (though not exclusively) developed in civil
law countries with a law of unfair competition and has been largely neglected in the

---

[81] See for example Jacob J. in *Hodgkinson & Corby v. Wards Mobility* [1995] F.S.R. 169.
[82] The *Penguin* case at, 537.

United Kingdom. Instead of looking at the issue of confusion (which is fundamental to misrepresentation), misappropriation is concerned with the wrongful taking of a proprietary right.[82a] In other words, in the context of lookalike products, when comparing two similar looking products the test would not be one of deceptive similarity but whether the manufacturer of the second product took the expressed idea (the intellectual property) from the first, *i.e.* did the creator of the second product base its artwork or design upon the first product? If it could be shown that it was independently created then there would be no misappropriation, but if, on the other hand, it could be shown that the second manufacturer's starting point for the design of artwork/packaging was the property of the first owner then it could be said that the second manufacturer had reaped the benefit of the time and effort invested in the design and creation of the first product by using it as stepping stone from which to develop its own product. "Feeding upon the intellectual or economic investment of another" as the French law describes it.

4–63   Misappropriation would tackle the problem of lookalike packaging from a completely different angle to misrepresentation. Confusion would no longer be an issue, instead the question would be one of business ethics, questioning the honesty and integrity surrounding the design of new products. This is the approach taken in France, for example, in relation to unfair competition and "parasitism"—or slavish imitation, where the court will look at features of packaging as they appear on the second product to see whether they are taken from the first. In the case of Classic Cola (had the action been brought in France) it is likely that the Coca-Cola Company would have had a successful case based upon parasitism given that the colouring was similar to its own as was the lettering style and positioning.[83]

4–64   It would seem inappropriate, however, to limit the development of misappropriation (based as it is on business ethics generally) to the field of trade marks and get up and so it is no surprise to find that the recent proposals to this effect seeking amendment of the United Kingdom Trade Marks Bill were rejected by the Government. The Government did, however, indicate that it would consider the matter carefully for future legislation in which case it would do well to take on board the calls for a United Kingdom law of unfair competition that have been made by academics, professionals and industry alike in a bid to reintroduce standards of morality and integrity into the business world by providing incentives for investment in the use of creative skill and labour and not by apparently encouraging competitors to trade off the work and investment of others.

4–65   In a market economy, economic competition has often been described as a game where the best team should win. This assumes of course that rules (indicating conduct that is not acceptable) exist to regulate the game and that all competitors play by the rules:

> "Violations of the basic rules of economic competition can take various forms, ranging from illegal but harmless acts . . . to malicious fouls intended to harm competitors or mislead consumers. They may consist in a direct attack on an individual competitor or in surreptitious deception of the 'referee', who in economic competition typically is the consumer. Whatever

---

[82a] See Kamperman Sanders, *Unfair Competition* (Clarendon Press, Oxford, 1997) in particular at 113 *et seq.*
[83] Although Lord Scarman refers to misappropriation in the context of passing off confirming that a plaintiff in the U.K. may bring a successful action where it can show that what has been taken is distinctive in fact, this is not the same as the approach taken in France where factual distinctiveness is not a pre-requisite—*Cadbury Schweppes Pty Ltd v. The Pub Squash Co. Ltd* [1981] R.P.C. 429 at 496

form such violations may take, it is in the interest of the honest entrepreneur, the consumer and the public at large that they should be prevented as early and effectively as possible . . . Experience has shown that there is little hope of fairness in competition being achieved solely by the *free play of market forces.*"[84]

(b) Dilution

4–66   In addition to taking unfair advantage of the brand owner's efforts, developing lookalike packaging also reduces the distinctiveness of the brand owner's original pack design. This whittling away of the distinctiveness is generally referred to as the doctrine of dilution. Callman, the United States academic, described it as:

> "The continuous use of a mark similar to the plaintiff's [which] works an inexorably adverse effect upon the distinctiveness of the plaintiff's mark, and . . . if he is powerless to prevent such use, his mark will lose its distinctiveness entirely. This injury differs materially from that arising out of the orthodox confusion . . . Such confusion leads to immediate injury, while dilution is an infection which if allowed to spread, will inevitably destroy the advertising value of the mark."[85]

Although his explanation postulates dilution in respect of a trade mark there is no reason to limit the concept to a mark as opposed to trade dress generally. The important point is that it does not involve confusion, it is simply concerned with the preservation of the plaintiff's trade dress and its ability to stand out from those of its competitors. If, as in fact happened in the case of Coca-Cola, first one retailer launches a lookalike (in this case Sainsbury) and then others follow in no time at all. Within six months of the launch of Classic Cola by Sainsbury there were at least six other lookalikes all in red cans with white lettering. As a consequence it is much harder for consumers to distinguish a can of Coca-Cola from these other cans. Whilst it is true that not all these brands will be on display at the same store it does mean that consumers have to be more astute when they shop if they want to be sure to select the right brand and it will be that much harder for individual branded products like Coca-Cola to attract consumer attention in the store.

4–67   The consequences of dilution were recognised by the Court of Appeal in the *Elderflower* case where it was acknowledged that use of the word champagne on products not from that appellation would devalue the distinctive name champagne. In the words of Sir Thomas Bingham M.R.[86]:

> "Any product which is not Champagne but is allowed to describe itself as such must inevitably, in my view, erode the singularity and exclusiveness of the description Champagne and so cause the . . . plaintiffs damage of an insidious but serious kind."

A brand's trade dress has significant advertising value because of its power to call to mind a particular product and evoke an association of desirability and satisfaction

[84] WIPO "Protection Against Unfair Competition", p. 11.
[85] Callmann, *The Law of Unfair Competition and Trademarks* (2nd ed., 1950) p. 1643.
[86] *Taittinger SA v. Allbev Ltd* [1993] F.S.R. 641 at 678 (the "*Elderflower*" case).

with that product. If other brands are allowed to develop using the same or similar trade dress then the power of the first brand to be associated with a particular product is weakened and the investment in its creation, development, promotion and marketing thereby significantly reduced. The dilution doctrine established in the United States seeks to protect the valuable interest embodied in the advertising function of a trade mark or trade dress. This function, and its value as an asset, were also specifically acknowledged by the German Supreme Court[87]:

"The consideration underlying this special anti-dilution protection is that the owner of such a distinctive mark has a legitimate interest in continuing to maintain the position of exclusivity he acquired through large expenditures of time and money and that everything which could impair the originality and distinctive character of his distinctive mark, as well as the advertising effectiveness derived from its uniqueness, is to be avoided . . . Its basic purpose is not to prevent any form of confusion but to protect an acquired asset against impairment."

4–68 The doctrine of dilution has developed principally in the context of dissimilar goods where a well known brand name associated with one type of product is used by another trade on an unrelated product area, for example the mark Polaroid originally used on camera equipment might be used by a trader on refrigeration equipment.[88] There is no reason, however, why the doctrine should be limited to the use of a similar mark on dissimilar goods. The principle danger in allowing claims for dilution in respect of competing goods is that some will no doubt argue that such an extension of the rights of brand owners to non confusion based claims will reduce competitors' ability to compete by allowing manufacturers to monopolise what might be regarded as generic styles of trade dress. Whenever there is discussion of expanding the scope of intellectual property rights there are always claims that such a move will be anti-competitive. However, provided there are controls on the application of the doctrine, that is, qualifying criteria as regards the distinctiveness of the original design this should prove sufficient to allay fears.[89] The real difficulty in seeking to establish some form of protection for brand owners based on the doctrine of dilution is that it will be difficult to assess the extent to which a lookalike brand is actually diluting the trade dress of a branded product if the trade dress of the original brand comprises a number of features that are common to that particular market sector.

4–69 The difficulties in establishing suitably distinctive trade dress and assessing whether or not lookalike brands are diluting them may make misappropriation a more attractive cause of action.[90]

CONCLUSION

4–70 Despite announcements made by some retailers[90a] that lookalikes would stop, efforts by brand owners to persuade the Government to introduce appropriate

---

[87] Quick, BGH 1959GRUR182,186 (Translation taken from G Schricker, "Protection of Famous Trademarks Against Dilution in Germany" (1979) 11 I.I.C. 166 171.
[88] *Polaroid v. Polaraid Inc* 319 F. 2d. 830 (1963).
[89] We will return to the issue of dilution in Chap. 5 when we consider the issue of brand stretching.
[90] Whether or not misappropriation would be the most appropriate cause of action and what form such a law might take is explored further in Chap. 8, at para. 8–64 and following.
[90a] Tesco was reported as having agreed to stop imitating branded packaging in *The Financial Times*, April 26-27, 1997. Sainsbury's announced it was to stop lookalikes in *Marketing*, April 24, 1997.

legislation to protect their brands from imitation continue. On January 20, 2000 the Copyright and Trade Marks Bill was introduced in the House of Lords. Clause 3 of the Bill seeks to introduce a statutory duty not to imitate features of packaging, marketing or labelling in such a way as to lead the public to attribute the reputation of one trader's goods to those of another. This Bill is unlikely to be passed in its current form and Clause 3 will, in all probability, be dropped. The clause itself has been drafted using vague terms and so gives rise to a very broad protection. The duty appears to be one of strict liability with no defence available for a manufacturer whose use is inadvertent or without knowledge of the plaintiff's use and/or reputation. There is no requirement that the first trader's marketing or packaging be distinctive or even unique, and many of the terms used in the clause are themselves undefined.

4–71 The fact that this proposal is likely to fail does not mean that additional protection is unwarranted. On the contrary, as noted above, gaps in the protection of product packaging do exist. In particular, The "straight jacket" of passing off with its requirement of deception generally means that no brand owner can realistically rely upon it in order to stop a retailer mimicking its brand's trade dress. The strength of the retailer's store name is often such that consumers will realise that the product is made for the retailer and to its specification, although they may think there is some connection between the two. Alternatively, the consumer may realise there is no connection but will nonetheless associate the attributes of one product with the other.[90b] Although the *Penguin* case offers some hope to brand owners that it is sufficient to show that consumers believe that the own label product is made by the manufacturer of the equivalent branded product this is of little comfort to companies such as Kellogg bearing mind the words of Millet L.J. in the *Harrods* case[91]:

> "It is not in my opinion sufficient to demonstrate that there must be a connection of some kind between the defendant and the plaintiff, if it is not a connection which would lead the public to suppose that the plaintiff has made himself responsible for the quality of the defendant's goods."

4–72 This means that when confronted with competing products using look-alike packaging brand owners cannot be sure of redress based on passing off. An action for trade mark infringement is equally precarious. Brand owners can generally only obtain registration of their brands' trade dress by including the brand name as part of the sign to be registered. This means that they are unlikely to succeed in an action for infringement against a lookalike using a different brand name but with a similar get up because of the emphasis placed on the semantic context of the mark, and the absence of a likelihood of confusion as to origin.

4–73 Thus, to provide adequate means of protection any new cause of action needs to take into account the conduct of the defendant and in particular the misappropriation of the trade dress, or elements of it. We will return to the question of the form that such a cause of action might take in Chapter 8.

[90b] In the United States this is referred to as "subliminal confusion" and is recognised in some circuits as a basis for relief under unfair competition. For a discussion of the theory of subliminal confusion see Coleman, "National Brands, Private Labels and Unfair Competition" (1997) T.M.R. Vol. 87 at 98.
[91] *Harrods Limited v. Harrodian School Limited* [1996] R.P.C. 697, CA at 713.

CHAPTER 5

Brand Stretching and Merchandising

INTRODUCTION

5–01   "Manchester United, of England's Premier league, has confirmed its status as one of the world's leading sporting brands with the announcement of pre-tax profits of £27.4 million . . . Nearly half the £87.9 million generated by the club in the financial year 1996/97 came from merchandise sales and TV revenue".[1]

Manchester United is not the only football club to recognise the opportunity to generate income off the pitch from dedicated supporters, but it is significantly ahead of its rivals. As a result of its licensing programme, whereby third parties are authorised to apply the club name and badge to various kinds of approved merchandise, it is arguable that the name has developed into more of a brand (as defined in Chapter 1) than just the name of a football club. Certainly the issues concerning whether to permit use of the Manchester United name and logo on new products are the same as those faced by any other brand owning business, as are the concerns as to how the name should be protected from unauthorised exploitation.

5–02   Whether the name is actually a brand is something of a moot point but is one of significance when considering the level of legal protection that will be granted to the club by the courts. If, as we shall see below, the club name is regarded as simply a name and its use on merchandise is a mere decoration and not an indication of origin then protection is weakened and the courts will be reluctant to prevent unauthorised use of the name by third parties in the absence of confusion. If, however, it can be shown that the name functions as an indication of origin or trade connection, then the courts are more likely to grant protection against unauthorised use.

5–03   In this chapter we will be looking in particular at the protection of brand names and logos when used outside the core business. First we will look at the marketing considerations relating to stretching the use of a brand name, from line extensions to brand extensions. One form of brand extension that has attracted attention from the courts is character merchandising. We will therefore look briefly at character merchandising and some of the risks associated with it. We will then consider the advantages of brand stretching and also the dangers to the original brand. This will lead to a discussion as to whether use of a brand name or image on a wide range of goods or services is merely decorative or whether there is more substance to it.

---

[1] "English Football Discovers It's All in the Brand" *Managing Intellectual Property*, October 1997, p. 6.

5–04   In light of the marketing considerations we will consider the legal protection available to branded products, addressing in particular the situation where the brand name is used outside the original core business or product, looking in detail at the position under the Trade Marks Act 1994 and the law of passing off. We will see that protection in the United Kingdom is limited particularly if the use is regarded as decorative, unless it can be shown that the brand has a wide reputation although even then the risk of confusion must still be a real possibility.

5–05   The English law has not developed as much to protect licensing or merchandising as it might, or more particularly as brand owners might like it to. We therefore consider the legal position in Australia relating to merchandising where the law has developed away from the traditional United Kingdom position (with its insistence upon a likelihood of confusion) by extending the law of passing off to include misappropriation as illustrated in three recent cases.

5–06   Finally, suggestions will be made as to how brand owners might consider marketing their products so as to minimise the current shortcomings in the English legal system and thus maximise the protection offered by the courts to brand owners in the absence of a change in either the law or the approach by the judiciary.

MARKETING CONSIDERATIONS

5–07   Like Manchester United, Budweiser decided to stretch the use of its brand name in the United Kingdom beyond its core business. Originally a producer of premium packaged lager, Budweiser has begun manufacturing a range of high quality jeans. As one marketer noted, consumers are "now able to wear their Budweiser jeans with their Marlboro jackets and Camel boots".[2] Unlike Manchester United, however, which licenses the use of its name and logo to a range of third parties, Budweiser is not intending to license its brand name but is intending to move into the manufacturing business itself. For the owner of the Budweiser brand this is the first time that it has used the Budweiser brand name on a product other than beer. If the move proves successful it could provide significant benefits for the brand as a whole from a marketing perspective since use of the name on premium clothing (that is jeans with a retail value of about £60) aimed at 18–28 year old men will add a youthful dimension to the brand's existing image in addition to reinforcing the brand's positioning as a premium priced quality product. Similar strategies have already been adopted by the owners of the Marlboro and Camel brands of cigarettes whose brands names are already used on a wide range of goods (albeit that their incentive for such a move is different[3]). If, however, Budweiser's move into clothing fails, it may possibly affect sales of Budweiser lager but because the two product areas are not closely related it should not have a serious adverse effect on sales unless the core personality of the brand is considered by consumers to be incompatible with a jeans brand and therefore the brand as a whole is lowered in the estimation of the consumer.

5–08   For many companies the decision whether to use an existing brand name on a new line of products or services or seek a new brand name is a difficult one and one that may depend more upon financial considerations than upon marketing

---

[2] *Marketing Week,* February 2, 1997, p. 19.
[3] Restrictions on the advertising of tobacco products mean that owners of tobacco brands need to find other ways of raising the profile of their brands and so maintain brand awareness. Licensing the use of the brand name on unrelated goods is just one way of keeping the brand visible.

ones. There are, of course, risks as well as rewards associated with the use of an established brand name on a new range of products. If successful, the venture can offer the opportunity not only to break into new markets more quickly but also to increase awareness of the original brand name.

(a) What is brand stretching?

5–09   It is because of the goodwill associated with an established brand name (and the attributes associated with it) to consumers that businesses consider extending the use of the name outside the original product area. According to Aaker "the use of a brand name established in one product class to enter another product class' is referred to as a "brand extension" (or brand stretching)."[4] The use of the brand names Mars on ice creams or Fairy on washing powder[5] are both examples of brand extensions. The original product areas were confectionery and washing up liquid respectively.

5–10   Brand extensions can be distinguished from "line extensions" which "occur when a company introduces additional items in a given product category under the same brand name, such as new flavours, forms, colours, ingredients and package sizes."[6] Examples of line extensions are Diet Cola and Caffeine Free Cola.

5–11   The majority of new products developed in grocery stores consist of line extensions. Indeed according to one survey of 6125 new products accepted by grocery stores in the first five months of 1991, only five per cent bore new brand names, six per cent were brand extensions, and 89 per cent were line extensions.[7] The decision to introduce a line extension may be made for a variety of reasons, perhaps because a company wishes to match a successful line extension of a competitor, to gain increased shelf space at the supermarket or to meet a perceived demand amongst consumers for a variant of an existing product. Whatever the reason for considering stretching the brand name, the brand owner needs to consider carefully whether the decision to extend the brand name either in the same product category or into a new area is in the best interests of the original brand.

5–12   Marketing textbooks use a variety of terms to cover the situation where an existing brand name is used on a new product including "brand extension", "line extension", "brand stretching", and "brand franchising". Lawyers, on the other hand, tend to refer to "licensing" or "merchandising" when referring to the use of a brand name, logo or image on products in a variety of different product categories, particularly if the owner of the original brand does not own or control the manufacture of the new product category but authorises a third party to apply the brand name, etc., in accordance with the terms of a licence or merchandising agreement. Whilst the term "franchising" is more commonly associated with the licensed use of a mark in connection with a business format (as for example the use of the name Burger King in connection with restaurant services or Kall Kwik in connection with copying and printing services) there is no reason to limit the term to these particular instances which might equally be described as examples of brand licensing albeit that the product area is the same as that associated with the original brand name, *i.e.* all licensees are effectively acting in the same product area. For the sake of simplicity, however, in this chapter the term "merchandise" will be used to

---

[4] Aaker, *Managing Brand Equity* (Free Press, 1991), p. 208.
[5] Both manufactured by Proctor & Gamble see Kotler *et al.*, p. 581.
[6] *ibid.* Kotler, p. 580.
[7] *ibid.*

refer to the actual products upon which the brand name, device, image (including the image of a personality), graphic representation (including an illustration of a character), or mark[8] is placed, the term "brand owner" or "merchandiser" will be used to refer to the person using the mark outside the original core business area.

5–13   One of the first companies to be involved in the business of character merchandising was Disney when in 1934 it created the cartoon character Mickey Mouse and subsequently began to licence the use of representations of its cartoon characters on, for example, clothing and also the manufacture of toys representing cartoon characters.[9] Merchandising, that is the business of placing a mark on a range of merchandise, is now a significant part of Disney's business; each new feature film is accompanied by an array of licensed merchandise ranging from traditional clothing and toys to meals at McDonalds.[10] Similar to character merchandising is the practice of personality merchandising where, instead of a character being the featured on merchandise, the subject is a personality or celebrity, using either the personality's name, image or identifying characteristics to evoke an association with the celebrity. The range of products to which a representation of the character or personality may be applied appears to be endless, limited only by the imagination of the brand owner and consumer's willingness to purchase the goods.

(b) The advantages and disadvantages of brand stretching

5–14   "In a competitive market there is pressure to innovate. But new product development is risky and most launches fail."[11]

In some consumer markets it has been estimated that the cost of introducing a completely new brand can be as much as $100 million.[12] Given that most launches fail it is understandable that businesses have been in search of ways to increase the likelihood of a product's success and simultaneously reduce the financial investment needed to establish a new brand. Use of an existing brand name with which consumers are familiar and with attributes that are already known facilitates the task of introducing the new product to consumers and encouraging them to try it. As two authors observed:

"Brand extensions . . . are attractive to firms that face the reality of high product failure rates because they provide a way to take advantage of brand name recognition and image to enter new markets. The leverage of a strong brand name can substantially reduce the risk of introducing a product in a new market by providing consumers the familiarity of and knowledge about an established brand".[13]

---

[8] To avoid cumbersome repetition the term "mark" will be used to refer equally to a brand name, image, device or graphic representation unless specifically indicated otherwise for example by reference to an image or character etc.
[9] For a more in depth consideration of character merchandising see Adams, *Character Merchandising* (London 2nd ed. Butterworths, 1996) and Jeremiah, *Merchandising Intellectual Property Rights* (Wiley, 1997).
[10] In 1974 a Disney Productions' Annual Report indicated royalty revenues in excess of $15,000,000.
[11] *Marketing Week,* April 29, 1994, p. 43.
[12] Brown "New? Improved?" *Business Week,* October 21, 1985, p. 108 A reasonable advertising and marketing launch alone will cost between £5–£7 million on top of the cost of research and development and the costs of bringing the product to market. *Marketing Week,* October 11, 1996, p. 39.
[13] Aaker & Keller "Consumer Evaluations of Brand Extensions" (1990) 54 *Journal of Marketing, p.* 27.

5-15 Extending use of the brand name into an area inconsistent with the image of the original brand can have serious consequences, as the Miller Brewing Company found out when in the early 1980s it extended the use of its successful Miller brand name from Miller High Life bottled beer to Miller Lite beer. Sales of Miller Lite increased from a 9.5 per cent share of the United States beer market in 1978 to 19 per cent in 1986. During the same period, however, the market share held by Miller High Life fell from 21 per cent to 12 per cent.[14] One explanation of the fall in market share of the original brand is that, whereas Miller High Life had a reputation as the "champagne of bottled beer", a lite beer was associated with a low calorie, watery product. According to Aaker, these associations could well have had a negative impact on consumers of the High Life brand thus accounting for the fall in market share. An alternative explanation might be that drinkers of the High Life brand switched to the Miller Lite brand, this is sometimes referred to as "cannibalisation" of the existing brand. The ideal outcome when stretching a brand is for the original brand to grow at the same time as the line extension with the result that the overall brand image is enhanced by the associations introduced by the extension. An acceptable outcome is for the new product to grow in sales whilst the original brand remains stable. The worst outcome is where the extension fails and sales of the original brand are also affected.[15]

5-16 Research has shown that consumer evaluations of brand extensions depend on the perceived fit of the new product with the existing brand, and that this fit is dependant on two factors in particular, product feature similarity and brand concept consistency.[16] Thus in order to maximise the benefits of using an existing brand name and the attributes associated with it and avoid the cannibalisation of the original brand it is important that the extension is consistent with the existing brand concept.

5-17 In the United Kingdom, the brand name Marks & Spencer, originally associated with the retail sale of clothing, has been successfully extended over the years to encompass not only the retail sale of food and furniture but also financial services including the provision of pensions, units trusts and life insurance. The company has been able to stretch the brand name successfully into these different areas by relying upon the consumers' perception of the brand as a mark of high quality, value for money and a name that can be trusted. Financial services now account for 18 per cent of the group's total operating profit.[16a] According to Marks & Spencer's Media Relations Manager:

> "Research shows that more and more people like to come to a name that is trusted, offers value for money and gives high quality service . . .".

In stretching its brand name to financial services Marks & Spencer recognises the importance of stressing the brand name:

> "The retail brand is widely known and highly regarded. We need to use that to demonstrate to our personal finance customers that the same brand means there is a link between the two—they'll get the same quality and value for money"[17]

---

[14] *ibid.* n.4, p. 222.
[15] *ibid.* n.5, p. 582.
[16] Park, Milberg & Lawson "Evaluation of Brand Extensions: The Role of Product Feature Similarity and Brand Concept Consistency (1991) 18 *Journal of Consumer Research* 185 at 192.
[16a] Marks & Spencer plc, 1998–99 Annual Report.
[17] "Easy money" *Design Week* Retail Supplement, May 1997.

An example of a company that was unsuccessful in its attempt to extend the use of its brand name into a new product area is Levi Strauss & Co. In 1979 the company decided to maintain business growth by expanding its market into a new sector by launching a range of classic tailored men's clothes under the brand name "David Hunter—Levi Tailored Classics".[18] The range consisted of men's tailored wool suits. The suits were of good quality and were comparable to those of competitors in terms of style, material, fashion and workmanship The brand proved to be a disaster despite costly professional development and promotional support and the product was withdrawn within a year. One of the reasons for the product failure was said to be the fact that the new range of tailored classic clothes did not "fit" (in terms of consumer perception) with the use of the Levi brand name which was associated with denim, hard wearing, working men and good value leisure or casual wear. Consumers of tailored clothing felt that the Levi name was inconsistent with top quality men's suits and they were not therefore persuaded to buy the suits.

5–18   The use of an established brand name can therefore be both a hindrance and a help to the introduction of a new product or service. When considering extending the use of a brand name the brand owner needs to consider carefully what associations are attached to the existing brand and ensure that the new product is consistent with those associations.

5–19   Research has indicated that concept consistency might have a greater significance in relation to a premium brand than a functional brand which suggests that consumers are more willing to accept the stretching of premium brands across products sectors.[19] This is borne out by the fact that many premium brands such as Dunhill, Gucci and Harley Davidson are used successfully across a broad spectre of products whereas functional names such as Timex, Ford or Dunlop are not.

5–20   A brand name already established as a mark of quality can, when used on a new product, give the new product a perception of quality from the moment of its launch as in the case of Marks & Spencer financial services. The extension should however seek to enhance and reinforce the attributes of the original brand name: use of a brand name associated with quality on a new product of poor quality will simply devalue the original brand name. If the new product is sufficiently removed from the original product certain attributes such as taste will not transfer to the new product:

> "Thus where Coca-Cola Orange Juice would not work, Coca Cola sweatshirts are acceptable".[20]

Hankinson and Cowking[21] have summarised the benefits of brand stretching:

- It enables a new product to take advantage of already established functional attributes and symbolic values associated with the original brand;

- it speeds up the process of establishing product awareness, because consumers are already familiar with the brand name and only need to be made aware of the new product;

---

[18] *ibid.* n.4, p. 206. This is a brand extension and not a line extension because tailored clothes are regarded as a different product category to casual clothes such as jeans.
[19] *ibid.* n.16, p. 192.
[20] *ibid.* n.4, p. 218.
[21] *Branding in Action* (McGraw Hill, 1993), p. 77.

- it can help consumer recognition and reduce communication costs by capitalising on the heavy advertising and promotional expenditure on the original brand. When promoting the original brand name the brand owner is also indirectly promoting the new product;

- it reduces the risk of purchase for a first time buyer in that the first time buyer can rely on the reputation of an established brand name, especially in relation to quality;

- it is easier to obtain distribution and shelf space from a retailer because the brand name itself has an established reputation and consumer following.

5–21   Not all marketers, however, are in favour of brand stretching. Ries and Trout, who are regarded by some[22] as the most ardent opponents of brand stretching, argue that the aim of a strong brand is to become, from the consumer's point of view:

"a surrogate or substitute for the generic name [of the product]".[23]

If the brand name becomes synonymous with or a shorthand for the product, the consumer need only refer to the brand name to indicate the product desired thus a shopping list might refer simply to "Pepsi, Lemsip, and Hellman's" rather than "Pepsi cola, Lemsip cold relief and Hellman's Mayonnaise". Ries and Trout go on to argue that line and indeed brand extensions work against this by destroying the unique association between brand name and product in the consumer's mind, thus diluting the distinctiveness of the brand name. Thus, if the consumer asks for Pepsi he is asked whether he wants Diet Pepsi, Pepsi Max, Original Pepsi. Whilst in a self-service environment such as a supermarket this may be only a limited disadvantage, the damage becomes greater the wider the spectrum of products/services upon which the same brand name is used and the greater the diversity of the packaging and labelling associated with each variant.

5–22   Dilution of the distinctiveness of a mark is certainly a concern both from a marketing and a legal perspective. Indeed, as Arnold notes[24]:

"The biggest single danger with a brand extension programme is that of diluting the original personality of the brand".

Dilution of the brand name can occur if there is undisciplined use or overexposure of the brand name as in the case of the Gucci brand name where at one point there were 14,000 licensed Gucci products.[25] The effect of this undisciplined use is that the brand itself can become devalued in the mind of the consumer. The consumer may no longer regard the brand as being exclusive or a status symbol but may instead regard it as commonplace if the use of the mark is unregulated. More recently this was experienced by the English pop group The Spice Girls, who licensed the use of their name and endorsed a wide range of products including Pepsi cola, Walker crisps, Elida Faberge, Channel 5, Polaroid and Chuppa Chups

---

[22] See n.21, p. 76, Hankinson & Cowking.
[23] Ries & Trout *Positioning: The Battle for your Mind* (McGraw Hill, 1st ed. revised, 1986), p. 102.
[24] Arnold, *The Handbook of Brand Management* (FT Pitman Publishing, London, 1993), p. 143.
[25] See n.4, p. 224.

lollipops, all within a relatively short time. This has arguably led to over exposure of the "brand" name and a consequent reduction in popularity. Careful handling of the brand can retrieve the name from the effects of dilution, but only by reducing the number of products available under or by reference to the mark and by carefully rebuilding the personality of the core brand, ensuring that the mark is only used on those products that fit with the original brand concept.

(c) Is a mark on merchandise a brand?

5–23   Can it be said that the Manchester United name is a brand simply because the mark is applied to a myriad of products? Is Thomas the Tank Engine, the train featured in The Railway Series of books written by the Rev. Awdry and subsequent star of the "Thomas the Tank Engine and Friends" television series, a brand because the mark is used on a wide range of products (from trains to umbrellas, clothes, plates, balls, etc.) all with similar packaging get-up and all bearing the image of the engine and the name of Britt Allcroft?[26] These questions are not easy to answer. We saw in Chapter 1 that a brand is more than just a product name or its packaging, that it includes both tangible and intangible values as perceived by the consumer. A brand is created through careful use of advertising and marketing in association with a particular brand name. Indiscriminate use of the brand name on a range of products is really a very crude form of branding which primarily serves to indicate a connection of some kind between the products and the owner of the mark.

5–24   Whether the use of a particular brand name or logo on a range of merchandise amounts to a brand will very much depend upon whether or not there is related marketing and advertising activity that seeks to create and sustain a recognisable brand personality or identity. It is suggested that, if the only common thread between the products marked is the brand name itself and consumers are unable to identify the brand personality, then it is suggested that the use of the mark is merely decorative and does not constitute a brand per se.

5–25   We have also seen that, from a marketing point of view, there may be a number of reasons for using one brand name on a range of different products, including the ability to facilitate the introduction of a new product range or to expand into new market sectors. Where the brand owner applies its trade mark to related (or even unrelated goods) of its own manufacture, as in the case of the Budweiser jeans referred to at the beginning of this chapter, there is usually no doubt that the trade mark functions as a brand. Where, however, the mark is licensed to a third party the position is not as clear cut.

5–26   It is possible that a brand owner may wish to use its mark on related goods for the purposes of advertising or promotion, that is, to apply the mark to items such as T-shirts, key fobs, cocktail stirrers, hats and bags in such a way as to increase consumer awareness of the brand name. In such a situation the brand owner's primary concern may not be with the quality of the promotional item, nor the recognition of the brand owner as the source of the products but rather the ability of the promotional item to advertise and promote the brand name. It is true that, as with all forms of advertising, the medium of the advertisement can affect the associations established in connection with the brand name in the mind of the consumer and for this reason the brand owner may not wish to use low quality materials. The fact that the brand owner's primary objective is that of advertising/

---

[26] The copyright owner.

promoting the brand can sometimes be inferred from the fact that such items are often given away by the brand owner free. In situations such as this the use of the brand name in relation to the promotional items does not from a marketing perspective seek to build the mark as a brand in relation to those promotional items *per se* but rather to reinforce the original brand and its brand personality. Choice of the type of promotional item may therefore be dictated by the nature of the primary brand but its function remains the same.

5–27   By way of contrast, the use of the name "Smirnoff" or "Dunhill" on a sweatshirt, from a legal perspective, raises a number of questions concerning the nature and function of the trade mark, the nature of the relationship between the owner of the brand name and the manufacturer of the garment; whether consumers are likely to be misled concerning this relationship; the existence, if any, of an endorsement of the garment by the brand owner; or whether the mark is a form of advertising only. Whether consumers purchase merchandise bearing such marks believing that there is a connection between the manufacturer of the product and the owner of the trade mark and whether they would still buy the product regardless of whether the product is "genuine" or "authorised" are questions at the heart of what is a complex legal debate regarding the legal status of the use of trade marks on merchandise. At the centre of this debate is the question of whether or not the mark functions as an indicator of origin. Traditionally the courts have assumed that consumers would not believe that a connection exists between two manufacturers using the same brand name in connection with unrelated goods, but recent developments suggest that the position may be about to change. It is certainly arguable that any use of a mark in connection with products outside the original core business is nowadays perceived as being connected with or authorised by the owner of the original mark as the phenomenon of brand stretching and merchandising is now so widespread. Equally it can be argued that purchasers of products bearing for example, the Manchester United mark, buy the goods because of the connection with the club and the attributes associated with the club name. It would be interesting to see whether a survey of consumers would confirm the view that to a significant proportion of consumers it does matter whether the goods are "genuine". If it can be shown that consumers are misled as to the origin of the new product line then the court is likely to grant relief.

5–28   There is much conjecture by the courts that the consumer buying a garment bearing a particular mark or image is buying it because of the decorative mark irrespective of the origin of the garment and any associations that may attach to the mark decorating it.[26a] A different approach may well be taken if the mark in question is the same as the name on the garment label (*i.e.* the name indicates the origin of the product) rather than simply decorative use, which is regarded as inferior use of the mark. Thus although licensed decorative use of the mark can help to increase brand awareness, the risk is that the court will not regard unauthorised use of the mark in this way as amounting to passing off or trade mark infringement which can have significant consequences for the brand owner, as will be seen below.

BRAND STRETCHING AND THE LAW

5–29   Having considered the various marketing reasons for choosing to extend the use of a brand name or mark outside the core business we will now turn to

---

[26a] See, for example, the comments of Laddie J. in *Elvis Presley Enterprises Inc. v. Sid Shaw Elvisly Yours* [1999] R.P.C. 543. His views were endorsed by Walker L.J. on appeal [1999] R.P.C. 567 at 577.

consider the question of legal protection of brand stretching. As with other aspects of brand protection (discussed in previous chapters) we will examine the different forms of legal protection offered by the laws of copyright, trade marks and passing off. Unless the mark in question is a device, image or character we will see that trade mark law potentially offers greater scope for protection against unauthorised imitation or use than copyright. Although, even for devices, images and characters trade mark registration offers a number of advantages. As a trade mark registration is a pre-requisite to obtaining protection under the TMA 1994 we will also look at the practical aspects of filing multiple trade mark applications and briefly consider whether licensing registered trade marks can affect their validity. We will see that passing off can only be relied upon by brand owner's to provide a remedy where the use of the mark concerned by a third party gives rise to a likelihood on the part of the public that the goods offered by third party are connected in some way with the brand owner. If consumers are indifferent to the source of the goods, or if the third party uses a disclaimer of any kind then the brand owner is unlikely to be in a position to succeed.

(a) Copyright infringement

5–30   Copyright can not be relied upon to protect single words,[27] personal names[28] or slogans from unauthorised reproduction by third parties although it can be relied on to prevent unauthorised reproduction of a logo or signature (assuming that the signature is more than just the printed letters of the name) on the basis that they are artistic works. This point has been emphasised in a number of decisions stemming back as far as 1867[29] and has been restated periodically:

> ". . . in this country we do not recognise the absolute right of a person to a particular name to the extent of entitling him to prevent the assumption of that name by a stranger . . . the mere assumption of a name, which is the patronymic of a family, by a stranger who had never before been called by that name, whatever cause of annoyance it may be to the family, is a grievance for which our law affords no redress."[30]

As Laddie J. commented in the *Elvis Presley* case[31]:

> ". . . if Elvis Presley was still alive, he would not be entitled to stop a fan from naming his son, his dog or gold fish, his car or house 'Elvis' or 'Elvis Presley' simply by reason of the fact that it was the name given to him at birth by his parents. To stop the use of the whole or part of his name by another he would need to show that as a result of such use, the other person is invading some legally recognised right."

Thus, unless the name in question is a registered trade mark or the use of the name by the third party amounts to passing off, the original owner of the name is powerless to prevent its adoption and use by another.

---

[27] See for example *Exxon v. Exxon Insurance* [1982] R.P.C. 69, CA and *Re Anne Frank Trade Mark* [1998] R.P.C. 379 where the owner of the copyright in the signature of Anne Frank tried to remove from the Register the registration of the Anne Frank trade mark on the basis of copyright in the signature.
[28] *Elvis Presley Enterprises Inc v. Sid Shaw Elvisly Yours* [1999] R.P.C. 567, CA.
[29] *Du Boulay v. Du Boulay* (1869) L.R. 2 P.C. 430.
[30] *ibid.* at p. 442.
[31] See n.53, p. 2.

Whilst on the one hand this may seem an entirely sensible approach for the courts to adopt it does cause difficulties for brand owners, particularly those involved in merchandising clothing in conjunction with marks consisting of personal names (be they designer names such as Ralph Lauren or characters such as Thomas the Tank Engine) which are not, or can not, be registered as trade marks. If such marks are copied or imitated by third parties brand owners can find themselves unable to do anything about it.

5–31 As we saw in Chapter 2, copyright arises automatically in relation to *inter alia* an original literary work or an artistic work.[32] In addition to other rights, the copyright owner (usually the author) has the exclusive right to copy the work and to issue copies of the work to the public.[33] Thus, the owner of a copyright work that is used in connection with a licensing programme, for example an illustration of a character (such as Thomas the Tank Engine) or a device mark such as a logo, signature or lettering style, can take action against a third party that reproduces its mark, or a substantial part of it, in a material form[34] (which includes making a copy in three dimensional form of a work originally in two dimensions[35]) without the copyright owner's consent.[36-37]

5–32 The difficulty for the brand owner frequently lies in the fact that the competitor does not copy the original mark either exactly or substantially. Indeed, it is much more likely that a competitor will seek to copy the "idea" rather than the "expression" *per se*. For example, a competitor of Britt Allcroft (the owner of the copyright in Thomas the Tank Engine character) may well reproduce illustrations of a train with a face on articles of merchandise but will this constitute a substantial reproduction? Although it is often said that the test of substantiality is a qualitative rather than a quantitative one[38] it is by no means certain that such a reproduction would be considered substantial. It would depend on a number of factors, not least what the style of the train was and whether overall it still looked liked the original. It could be argued that a train with a face on it is really an idea and all that Britt Allcroft owns is the exclusive right to use a particular expression, that is one particular image of a train bearing a face. If this is true, Britt Allcroft will be restricted in terms of the scope of its copyright and the types of representation that it might object to.

5–33 In *King Features Syndicate Inc v. Kleeman*,[39] the plaintiff was the owner of copyright in various cartoon strips (artistic works) of the character "Popeye". The defendant imported a range of dolls and brooches of "Popeye". Although the defendant had not copied one particular drawing exactly, there was a sufficient "family resemblance" for the House of Lords to find that there was infringement of copyright. As Lord Parker noted[40] "The salient features [were] practically identical". Although the law has changed since that case as regards dimensional shift copying (that is copying from a two dimensional drawing to create a three dimensional product) the principle still holds goods that reproduction of the salient features of the work will amount to infringement.

---

[32] s.1 CDPA 1988.
[33] *ibid.* s.16 CDPA 1988.
[34] s.17(2) CDPA 1988.
[35] Subject to s.52 CDPA 1988 discussed in detail in Chap. 3.
[36-37] Assuming that the copyright owner can demonstrate its title to copyright.
[38] *per* Lord Reid, *Ladbroke v. William Hill* [1964] 1 W.L.R. 273 at 276.
[39] [1941] A.C. 417, HL (the "*Popeye*" case) and the more recent case of *BBC Worldwide v. Pally Screen Printing* [1998] F.S.R. 665.
[40] *Popeye* case at 448.
[41] *Mirage Studios v. Counter-Feat Clothing Co. Ltd* [1991] F.S.R. 145 (the "*Ninja Turtles*" case).

5-34   In the *Ninja Turtles* case,[41] the defendant went one step further than the defendant in the *Popeye* case and produced its own version of the four humanoid turtle cartoon characters that formed the basis of the plaintiff's extremely successful character merchandising campaign. The defendant subsequently licensed its illustrations to third parties. Although the defendant's characters were not direct copies of the plaintiffs' characters it had clearly sought to imitate them. At the hearing of the application for interlocutory relief Browne-Wilkinson V.C. acknowledged his reluctance to determine whether or not the defendant's characters infringed the plaintiff's copyright[42]:

> ". . . although there are similarities in the graphic reproductions of the defendant's product to those of the plaintiffs' product, they are mainly reproductions of a concept, of the humanoid turtle of an aggressive nature. But whether that permits a claim in copyright or not seems to me to be a very open question; there is certainly an arguable case in copyright. I would not like to say what the final outcome of any case based in copyright would be."

In order to obtain interlocutory relief, the plaintiff in the *Ninja Turtles* case only had to show an arguable case and that the balance of convenience was in its favour. This it was able to do not just based on copyright but also on the basis of passing off. As is often the case with applications for interlocutory relief, the case did not progress to a full trial and so the question of whether or not copyright was infringed remains unclear. The case does, however, illustrate the difficulties faced by copyright owners where the defendant creates its own drawings that are different from those of the original copyright work, albeit inspired by it. The question of whether or not the defendant's work is an infringement is thus one of fact and depends on whether a substantial part of the plaintiff's work remains.[42a] It is not simply a question of how much skill, effort and judgment the defendant has employed.[42b] As Cornish observes[43]:

> "Where the defendant has reworked the plaintiff's material there comes a point beyond which the plaintiff has no claim. . . . the fact that the defendant has himself added enough by way of skill, labour and judgment to secure copyright for his effort does not, under the present law, settle the question whether he has infringed; rather the issue is whether a substantial part of the plaintiff's work survives in the defendant's so as to appear to be a copy of it." *(omitting references)*

5-35   Given the difficulties inherent in an action for copyright infringement where the defendant has altered the original work or has created its own version of it, it is appropriate, from the copyright owner's perspective, to base an action for redress not just on copyright infringement but also on passing off or trade mark infringement, if at all possible. Although the evidence needed in support of an action for infringement of a registered trade mark may be hard to obtain, and it may be difficult to establish the necessary misrepresentation to succeed in an action for passing off, it may be that the copyright owner can still meet these criterion even though a substantial part of the copyright work has not been reproduced.

---

[42] *ibid.* at p. 154.
[42a] *Redwood Music v. Chappell* [1982] R.P.C. 109; *Schweppes v. Wellington* [1984] F.S.R. 210; *Williamson Music v. Peasson Partnership* [1987] F.S.R. 97.
[42b] *Joy Music v. Sunday Pictorial* [1960] 2 Q.B. 60.
[43] *ibid.* at p. 363.

5–36 Licensing itself does not weaken the copyright protection available to the brand owner although the manner in which the work is licensed can affect the owner's ability to prevent unauthorised use of the mark based on copyright infringement. Before entering into a licensing arrangement, it is important that the copyright owner considers carefully issues such as the volume of merchandise to be produced, the return of stock bearing the mark after the termination of the licence arrangement, and the question of ownership of copyright in artwork and promotional materials developed by the licensee during the term of the licence. If the licence agreement does not address these issues, the copyright owner may find that it is unable to stop the sale and/or distribution of such items and that its only form of redress is breach of licence. Artwork created or developed during the course of a license agreement will not belong to the licensor unless there are provisions in the agreement transferring ownership of future copyright. Equally, reproductions of the copyright work made during the continuance of the licence will not automatically become infringements after the termination of the agreement since the reproduction was made with consent. Unless the licence agreement provides for the return of stocks to the copyright holder on termination the licensee will be free to sell stocks of products bearing the mark. To the extent that these sales are outside the terms of the licence agreement the copyright owner must base any action against the licensee on breach of contract not copyright infringement.

(b) Trade mark protection

5–37 For the brand owner considering stretching the use of the brand names, or other mark trade mark protection has a number of attractions, not least the fact that it lasts considerably longer than copyright protection in relation to commercial items. However, before considering the benefits of trade mark protection over copyright in the context of infringement we first need to consider the practical aspects involved in registering a mark in more than one class of the Register.

(i) Multiple trade mark applications

5–38 If a brand owner is considering extending the use of a brand name or mark to a different product or service in the foreseeable future then it is important that careful thought is given to the need for additional trade mark protection. Three different levels of protection are granted to the owners of registered trade marks under the TMA 1994.[44] Protection is automatic where an identical mark is used on identical goods (section 10(1)). Under section 10(2), a likelihood of confusion is an essential requirement when the mark is identical or similar and the goods/services are identical or similar and finally, under section 10(3) the proprietor must show that some advantage has been taken or some detriment suffered before protection will be granted. In view of the fact that protection is granted in decreasing measure from identical goods to dissimilar goods it is preferable that a mark is registered for all the goods in relation to which it is used. Whilst too broad a specification may be challenged by the Registry[45] either when the application is filed or at the examination of the application, it is more economical to reduce the

---

[44] The same observation was made by the Advocate General in relation to the structure of the Directive in *General Motors Corporation v. Yplon SA* [1999] E.T.M.R. 122 at 129.
[45] Under s.3(6) a broad specification may also be challenged at other times by third parties, *e.g.* during the opposition phase or in the context of an action for infringement—*Mercury Communications Ltd v. Mercury Interactive (UK) Ltd* [1995] F.S.R. 850 at 863 or in relation to revocation for non-use—s.46(1) TMA.

coverage of goods during the prosecution of the application than to file applications for additional goods at a later date.

5–39 Under the TMA 1994,[46] it is possible to file a single trade mark application covering a number of classes. This has the advantage of making the application process more cost effective as additional classes can be added at marginal cost. Simultaneous multi-class filings may not always be practical given the time taken to develop and establish a new brand before extending it into new product categories. At the time of filing the application the applicant must declare that it is either using the trade mark or has a bona fide intention[47] to do so in relation to all the goods covered by the application.

5–40 Ideally the application should cover all the goods on which it is intended that the mark will be used. This can however cause difficulties during the examination phase of the application as the Examiner may request evidence that the applicant does indeed intend to use the mark on all the goods listed in the specification. Where it is intended that the goods will be manufactured by a licensee and, at the time of applying for registration, no licensee has been identified, or if the intention is to license the use of the mark at some unspecified future date, then it is unlikely that the applicant will have suitable evidence to hand to overcome the objections raised by the Trade Marks Registry.

5–41 Under section 46(1)(a) of the TMA 1994 a trade mark can be cancelled on the grounds that it has not been used by the proprietor, or with his consent, for a continuous period of five years from the date of completion of the registration procedure or any subsequent five year period. This means that if a brand owner applies to register a mark, perhaps with the intention of licensing the mark at a future date, then the brand owner needs to be aware that if the licensing programme does not begin within the five year period with the consequence that no use is actually made of the trade mark on all or any of the goods for which the mark is registered then the registrations will become vulnerable to cancellation in respect of those goods for which there has been no use, at the instance of any third party. Only genuine use[48] of the mark on the goods listed in the specification and goods of the same description will be safe from the challenge. Unless the proprietor can show that there are "proper reasons" for non-use of the mark, or a reason for the Registrar to exercise his discretion, it will be removed from the Register. It has been held that the fact that it takes a long time to develop a brand is not a "proper reason" for non-use within the meaning of the Act.[49]

5–42 The brand owner can therefore be faced with a dilemma as to whether to register widely at the outset and risk revocation of the mark if licensing does not begin within five years, whether to refile the application before the end of the five year period to extend protection[50] or alternatively wait until a licensee is found before filing the application and risk a third party filing an application for the same

---

[46] s.32(4).

[47] s.32(3) is a procedural version of the substantive requirement set out in s.3(6) TMA 1994 which states that a trade mark shall not be registered if the application is made in bad faith. Knowing that the mark applied for is someone else's trade mark or if the registration is made with a view to blocking a competitor are acts that have in the past been regarded as "bad faith". See *Imperial Group Ltd v. Philip Morris & Co. Ltd* [1982] F.S.R. 72 and *Rawhide Trade Mark* [1962] R.P.C. 133. To satisfy s.32(3) the applicant merely needs to show that it has an honest belief that it had a good claim to be registered as proprietor of the mark. See *Al Bassam Trade Mark* [1995] R.P.C. 511.

[48] The meaning of "genuine" is the same as "bonafide" under the TMA 1938. *Re Academy Trade Mark Revocation* (November 27, 1998) (unreported) following the application of *Bon Martin* [1989] R.P.C. 53/7.

[49] *Re Invermont Trade Mark* [1997] R.P.C. 125.

[50] *Cussons v. Unilever* [1998] R.P.C. 369.

or a similar mark in the interim. It is suggested that it is preferable to file an application at the outset and risk revocation (particularly if the mark is in use, albeit in a limited field) than to wait and find that a third party has pre-empted the registration and the brand owner is not in a position either to challenge the registration or bring an action under passing off. The number of applications for revocation filed each year are relatively small compared to the number of applications for registration filed (although the number is increasing) and most are settled without a final determination by the Registrar.[51]

5–43   Under the TMA 1938, if a number of applications were filed in a variety of classes[52] there was a risk that the applications might be challenged under section 28(6) on the grounds of "trafficking" in the trade mark (especially if the applications were accompanied with registered user applications). Trafficking was prohibited under section 28(6) of the TMA 1938. Section 28(6) provided that:

> "The Registrar shall refuse an application if it appears to him that the grant thereof would tend to facilitate trafficking in a trade mark."

In the *Holly Hobbie*[53] case the House of Lords refused to allow the registration of the name Holly Hobbie as a trade mark in respect of a wide range of goods (in 12 classes) on the basis that the applicant was "trafficking" in the trade mark. Whilst the court could not agree on exactly what was meant by the term "trafficking" the general consensus was that it conveyed the notion of dealing in a trade mark as a commodity in its own right and not primarily to indicate or promote merchandise in which the proprietor was interested. Thus, in *Hollie Hobbie* the fact that the applicant had applied to register the mark in a wide range of classes in connection with goods which it did not currently make or intend to sell, and had provided registered user agreements indicating its intention to authorise third parties to apply the mark, led the court to believe that the applicant was dealing in the mark as a commodity in its own right. Although the registered user agreements contained provisions relating to quality control of the goods to which the mark was to be applied they were not considered sufficient to overcome the courts objection to the fact that the applicant was trafficking in the mark.

5–44   Although the TMA 1994 does not include provisions relating to trafficking, there is still a degree of judicial scepticism towards the idea that the use of trade marks in such circumstances function as indications of origin rather than decoration and are thus worthy of trade mark protection.[54]

(ii) Trade mark licensing

5–45   Having obtained a trade mark registration for its mark outside its core business a brand owner may decide, for various reasons, to permit a third party to use the trade mark or brand name rather than begin manufacturing the new product itself. Assuming that the mark is registered for the goods of interest the brand owner may license the use of its trade mark to the third party.

---

[51] Between 1994 and 1998, an average 483 revocation applications were filed each year, of which an average 67 per cent were subsequently withdrawn before a final decision had been made by the registrar. These figures are based on information supplied by the Trade Marks Office.
[52] Multi-class applications were not possible under TMA 1938.
[53] [1984] R.P.C. 329.
[54] See by way of example *Elvis Presley Enterprises Inc v. Sid Shaw Elvisly Yours* [1999] R.P.C. 567, CA.

A licence is the grant of permission or consent by the owner of an exclusive right to a third party to do acts that would otherwise amount to infringement. In the patent case, *Allen & Hanbury v. Generics*[55] it was said that:

> "a licence passes no proprietary interest in anything; it only makes an action lawful that would otherwise have been unlawful."

In the context of brand stretching, it is possible to license the use of the brand name, the use of a device mark or logo, the trade dress or any other form of mark in which the owner holds an exclusive right. Although the mark does not need to be registered in order to be licensed it is preferable as it makes it easier to identify the rights being granted in the agreement and is easier for the licensor to demonstrate ownership of the rights claimed.[56] From the licensees perspective, the registration of trade marks provides some reassurance that it will have the exclusive right to use the mark which justifies the royalty being paid. As not all aspects of a brand will necessarily be registered as trade marks we will also consider (below, at paras 5–97 to 5–119) the protection available to unregistered marks at common law.

5–46   Trade marks today are recognised as fulfilling a number of functions but, as we saw in Chapter 2, this has not always been the case. The oldest recognised function of a trade mark was that of indicating a single, identifiable source of manufacture. Initially the licensed use of a registered trade mark was considered incompatible with the nature of a trade mark as an indication of origin.[57] Indeed it was even regarded by the courts as deceptive. In 1914 in *Bowden Wire v. Bowden Brake*,[58] one of the earliest cases concerning trade mark licensing to be considered by the courts, the House of Lords refused to grant relief to a trade mark proprietor in an action for infringement against a former licensee, on the basis that the trade mark could no longer be said to indicate the source of the goods and thus was calculated to deceive the public. As a consequence the registration was removed from the Register.

5–47   As the function of trade marks evolved, however, so too did the attitude of the judiciary. The courts began to recognise that a trade mark could not only indicate an identifiable source of goods but also an anonymous source of supply. With the recognition that one function of a trade mark was to indicate consistent quality came acceptance of the notion that trade marks could be licensed without causing deception provided that the licensor ensured that real and effective means of quality control were exercised over the licensee.[59] It was not, however, until the passing of the TMA 1938 that licensing was formally permitted and even then only in certain limited circumstances.[60]

5–48   Under section 28 of the TMA 1938 it was necessary to record the existence of a licence agreement at the Trade Marks Registry in the form of a registered user agreement. The licensee was then regarded as a "permitted user" of the trade mark whose use of the mark was deemed use by the proprietor under

---

[55] [1986] R.P.C. 203 at 246.

[56] The proprietor of a registered trade mark is granted certain exclusive rights in the mark as a consequence of registration (s.9 TMA 1994). In contrast, the owner of an unregistered mark is not in a position to demonstrate his exclusive right without bringing an action for passing off.

[57] Wilkof *Trade Mark Licensing* (Sweet & Maxwell, London, 1995), p. 20 (hereafter "Wilkof").

[58] (1914) 21 R.P.C. 385.

[59] Wilkof p. 29.

[60] s.28(4) TMA 1938.

section 28(2) of the TMA 1938. The registration requirement enabled the Registrar to check whether or not effective means of quality control existed within the licence agreement. The Registrar had the power to refuse registration if he felt that the licence might work against the public interest, as in the *Hollie Hobbie* case.

5–49 Under the TMA 1994 it is no longer necessary to record a licence agreement at the Trade Marks Registry. Although in the interests of legal transparency licensors are encouraged to record licence agreements[61] the Registrar no longer has the same power or responsibility as regards monitoring their contents and in particular the provisions regarding quality control. As the White Paper, *Reform of Trade Marks Law*[62] observed:

> "The strongest guarantee that a proprietor will maintain control over the way in which his trade mark is used is that it is in his own interest to do so. A trade mark is a valuable piece of property, in terms both of its power to attract customers and of the royalties which can be demanded from licensees. Its value is however ultimately dependent on its reputation with the public. If the proprietor tolerates uncontrolled use of his trade mark the value of his property will be diminished. In an extreme case the registration of the mark may become liable to be revoked if it has become deceptive or generic through such use. It is however the responsibility of the proprietor, not the registrar, to prevent the devaluation of his own property."

Even though the Registrar is no longer in a position to monitor the content of licence agreements, quality control provisions remain an essential part of any trade mark licence agreement if the integrity of the trade mark registration is to be maintained. As Whitford J. noted in the *McGregor* case[63] (discussed below, at para. 5–51) a "bare licence under a trade mark has never been countenanced" because of the mark's function as an indicator of consistent quality.

5–50 The concept of licensing trade marks was only considered acceptable following the recognition of the function of trade marks as indicators of consistent quality. If the requirement to maintain quality control is removed the licensed use of trade marks could lead to the deception of the consumer as to the source of the goods and perhaps more importantly, the quality of the goods. This in turn can leave the registration vulnerable to revocation under section 46(1)(d) of the TMA 1994. Two cases demonstrate the risks that licensors face when they licence use of their marks but do not maintain adequate control over the quality of the goods produced. Although both cases were decided under the TMA 1938 in my view the same principles will be applied by a court under the TMA 1994 because although the law has changed the function of a trade mark as a mark of consistent quality has not.

5–51 The first case concerns the *McGregor* trade mark.[64] The McGregor trade mark was registered in connection with articles of clothing including dressing gowns. The proprietors of the mark agreed to the licensed use of the trade mark by Stirling Rubber Co. Ltd ("Stirling") in connection with dressing gowns. A registered user agreement was entered into which, amongst other things, required that the dressing gowns be manufactured in accordance with directions as to

---

[61] It is still possible to record the existence of licence agreements on the Register and indeed from the licensee's point of view there are certain advantages in doing so s.25(4) TMA 1994.
[62] Cmnd 1203 [1990] para 4.36 (hereafter "the White Paper").
[63] [1979] R.P.C. 37 at 53.
[64] *ibid.*

materials and methods of manufacture given from time to time by the registered proprietor, who also had a right to inspect and to take samples of the goods. During the period that the trade mark was licensed to Stirling the proprietor did not use the mark. After seven years in addition to manufacturing dressing gowns Stirling began to manufacture and sell other clothing under the McGregor trade mark including rain wear for men and women, outside the terms of the licence agreement (this was technically an infringement of the trade mark registration). At the same time, Stirling applied to cancel the registration on the grounds that the McGregor mark had not been in use for a continuous period of five years.[65]

5–52   Stirling argued that because it had used the trade mark outside the scope of the licence agreement, in that it had not made the dressing gowns in accordance with directions from the proprietor since the proprietor had given none, nor had it taken any steps to control the quality of the goods manufactured by Stirling and sold under the mark. Accordingly, Stirling argued that its use of the mark did not accrue to the benefit of the proprietor under section 28(2) and accordingly the mark had not been used within the relevant period as required under section 26(1)(b). Despite the fact that the court did not approve of Stirling's actions in that it had deliberately sought to infringe the trade mark, it was not persuaded to exercise its discretion in favour of the intervenor[66] on the basis that the intervenor had "gone into this with their eyes open as a commercial speculation". The Registrar agreed to the rectification of the mark on the basis that Stirling had established rights at common law in connection with the use of the McGregor trade mark which would enable it to take action against the intervenor, should it introduce clothing under the McGregor name into the United Kingdom. The Registrar therefore concluded that he should exercise his discretion in favour of revocation, thus enabling Stirling to file its own application for registration.

5–53   This case is significant in that it highlights the danger to the trade mark owner of licensing a mark but not maintaining effective quality control. Although the application for cancellation was based upon the fact that the trade mark had not been used for five years the High Court made it clear that in its view the mark was deceptive in that it was owned by one entity and used by another without any quality control. It is therefore possible, that had the cancellation action been based on the premise that the mark was liable to mislead the public,[67] it would have been successful.[67a]

5–54   The second case illustrating the risks of trade mark licensing that we shall consider is the *Job* case.[68] A French company registered the Job trade mark in the United Kingdom in connection with cigarette papers. In 1958 it entered into a licence agreement and registered user agreement in connection with the Job mark with a sister company ("the English company"). The agreement was for a term of 50 years and there was a fixed royalty payable. The registered user agreement provided that the French company should have access for inspection of goods and/

---

[65] s.26(1)(b) TMA 1938.

[66] After Stirling had began using the mark on rainwear the proprietor of the mark assigned its interest in the mark to an American company which used the name McGregor mark in the USA and wished to enter the U.K. market. The American company was aware of Stirlings use of the mark. As the assignment was not recorded at the time of the revocation action it applied to intervene on behalf of the proprietor.

[67] Under the provision equivalent to s.46(1)(d) TMA 1994.

[67a] The terms of s.46(1)(d) TMA 1994 are different from those under the TMA 1938 such that the deception must now be as to the nature, quality or geographical origin of the goods or relate to some other aspect of the goods. For this reason had an application for revocation been filed in this case under the TMA 1994 it is possible that it would have been successful.

[68] [1993] R.P.C. 118.

or methods of manufacture and be provided with samples, if requested. The English company began to use the trade mark but, although the French company helped to provide contacts and to get things started, the contact between the two companies became virtually non-existent. In 1969 the English company transferred its business, including the benefit of the contract, to Rizla Ltd, a related company. Rizla began to pay royalties to the French company. Rizla then applied to register the Job trade mark in its own name. It applied to cancel the mark in the name of the French company on the basis of non-use of the mark, that the French company's use of the mark would be deceptive, the fact that it, Rizla, had established common law rights, and that use of the mark by the French company would amount to passing off.

5–55   The Trade Mark Office rejected Rizla's application for a number of reasons, including estoppel. It held that in 1958 the French company had a significant reputation in the Job mark in the United Kingdom and it had sought to retain ownership of the mark by licensing its use to the English company. The English company, and Rizla, recognised the marks validity and reputation by entering into the 1958 agreement and paying royalties to the French company. Rizla was therefore estopped from arguing that the mark did not belong to the French company or was not registrable. Although the Registrar accepted that the French company had collected samples of the English company's goods, had analysed them and written reports, these activities were irrelevant if not communicated to the user. The Registrar therefore felt that insufficient quality control had been exercised by the French company. He also acknowledged that, all other things being equal, Rizla would have succeeded on the ground that the reputation in the mark had accrued to Rizla and thus the registration would lead to deception. However, he chose to exercise his discretion in favour of the French company.

5–56   This case again stresses the importance of exercising quality control if the proprietor of the mark is to maintain the integrity of the registration and so avoid a challenge to the mark's validity, either on the basis of non-use or because it may be regarded as deceptive. Although both cases that we have considered were determined under the TMA 1938, it is my view this same approach could be adopted under the new law.[69]

(iii) Trade Mark Use

5–57   The question of whether or not the allegedly infringing use of a trade mark is use "in a trade mark sense" was one that was particularly pertinent under the TMA 1938, which required "use as a trade mark" before a finding of infringement could be made. Although the TMA 1994 does not expressly state the need to show "use as a trade mark" a number of commentators[70] have suggested that it remains an essential pre-requisite to infringement. The crucial question for brand owners and one to which, at present there is no clear cut answer is whether the use of a mark (licensed or otherwise) on, for example, the front of a T-shirt or a watch, a mug or some other item, amounts to a trade mark use, that is as an indication of origin of the article in question and, if not, whether it affects the level of protection available to the brand owner.

During the past 10 years there have been only a few cases where this question has been considered in any detail. In *Unidoor Ltd v. Marks & Spencer plc*,[71] which

---

[69] See Annand & Norman, p. 133 and 201.
[70] Annand, p. 151; Kitchin & Mellor *The Trade Marks Act 1994* (Sweet & Maxwell, 1995), pp. 26–41.
[71] [1988] R.P.C. 275.

concerned the use of the slogan "Coast to Coast" on the front of T-shirts, Whitford J. said that:

> ". . . if I just had to decide [whether the use of the slogan in this way amounted to use as a trade mark] on a sight of the garment in question I have the gravest doubts as to whether it would ever be possible . . . to persuade me that this was in fact trade mark usage . . ."[72]

In Whitford J.'s opinion the traditional function of a trade mark is to indicate the source of the product. Given that the defendant had labels in the clothing bearing its usual trade mark St Michael, and that the plaintiff's use of the mark was in the same form (*i.e.* on the front of T-shirts and on the outside of clothing generally) and that no effort had been made by the plaintiff to draw consumer attention to the use of the slogan as a trade mark, the judge had grave doubts as to whether the use of the slogan amounted to use as a trade mark. Although the judge refused to grant interlocutory relief on the balance of convenience, his comments clearly indicate that the courts will not regard all uses of trade marks as necessarily being "trade mark use".

5-58   As noted above the TMA 1994 does not specify that use of a mark must be in a trade mark sense in order to be actionable by the brand owner. Section 9(1) states that the proprietor of a registered trade mark has exclusive rights in the trade mark which are infringed by "use" of the trade mark in the United Kingdom without consent. However, the infringement provisions set out in section 10(1), (2), and (3) of the TMA 1994 all require "use [of the sign] in the course of trade" in order to be enforceable. Some commentators have suggested that section 9 shows that there is no need for trade mark use, that all uses of the mark without consent are caught and that section 9(1) is no more than a "chatty introduction"[72a] to the details set out in section 10, and that section 10 merely introduces a requirement that the defendant be in business. Whereas others argue that section 10 requires use as a trademark.

5-59   The first case to address this point, *Bravado Merchandising v. Mainstream Publishing Ltd*,[73] favoured the former approach whilst more recent cases have supported the latter. *Bravado Merchandising v. Mainstream Publishing Ltd* concerned the publication of a book entitled *A Sweet Little Mystery—Wet Wet Wet—The Inside Story*. The plaintiff, the well known pop group, was the owner of the trade mark WET WET WET which had been registered in connection with books, printed matter and book covers. The plaintiff issued proceedings based on section 10(1) of the Trade Marks Act 1994, which states that "a person infringes a registered trade mark if he uses in the course of trade a sign which is identical with the trade mark in relation to goods or services which are identical with those for which it is registered". The defendant argued that the mark was not identical because the typeface used was different to that registered and, secondly, that the reference to Wet Wet Wet in the title of the book was to indicate the subject matter of the book, which was the pop group, rather than to suggest that the book was either published by the band or endorsed by it.

5-60   The case was heard in Scotland by Lord McCluskey, who refused the application for an injunction. Lord McCluskey held that use of the mark Wet Wet

---

[72] *ibid.* at p. 280.
[72a] *per* Jacob J. in *British Sugar plc v. James Robertson & Sons Ltd* [1996] R.P.C. 281 at 291.
[73] [1996] F.S.R. 205.

Wet as part of the title of the book was "use in a trade mark sense," but he went on to hold that use of the mark by the defendant fell within section 11(2)(b) in that it described the character of the product, *i.e.* the subject matter of the book. It is suggested that, although his decision was correct his reasoning is questionable. According to Jacob J. in the *Treat* case[74] Lord McCluskey could have reached the same conclusion by simply finding that the use of the words Wet Wet Wet in the title of the book did not amount to "use" in relation to the goods covered by the registration, that is books and book covers. In his view this would have been the correct approach. Indeed, Jacob J. went on to say that he saw no reason to limit the application of section 10 to instances where the infringing mark is used as a trade mark. All uses of the mark in the course of trade are, he suggests, caught by the provision unless the use falls within one of the exceptions set out in section 11. If this is so, then use of a mark on the front of a T-shirt or sweatshirt, even by way of ornamentation, would be actionable under section 10 unless it could be argued that the mark was not used "in relation to the goods", which would effectively bring us back to the requirement to show use the mark in a trade mark sense.

5–61 In *Trebor Bassett Ltd v. The Football Association*[75] where Rattee J. refused to grant relief to the Football Association for trade mark infringement on the grounds that its trade mark was reproduced by the plaintiff on cigarette cards depicting England players wearing their England shirts. In his view the mark was not being used in relation to the goods. In fact it was not being reproduced by the plaintiff at all, except as incidental to their reproduction of pictures of football players. Although Rattee J. refused to express a view as to whether "trade mark use" was necessary under section 10(1) he did say that Trebor Bassett was plainly not using the trade mark in respect of cards.

> "The logo appears on the cards only because it is worn by the players whose photograph appears on the card as part of that players England team football strip, to show that the player himself is an England team player . . . Trebor Bassett is not even arguably using the logo, as such, in any real sense of the word 'user', and is certainly not using it as a sign in respect of cards".

In the *One in a Million* case,[76] Deputy Judge Sumption Q.C. confirmed the view that use "in the course of trade" means use by way of business and "does not mean use as a trade mark". In the same case Aldous L.J. in the Court of Appeal left the question open when he said[77]:

> "I am not satisfied that section 10(3) does require the use to be trade mark use . . . but I am prepared to assume that it does."

By leaving the question open, uncertainty remains as to whether all uses of a registered mark by persons other than the registered proprietor will *prima facie* be regarded as infringements or whether, before a trade mark proprietor can succeed in a claim for infringement it is first necessary to establish that the offending mark has been used "as a trade mark".

---

[74] *British Sugar plc v. James Robertson & Sons Ltd* [1996] R.P.C. 281 (hereafter the "*Treat*" case).
[75] [1997] F.S.R. 211.
[76] *Marks & Spencer plc v. One in a Million* [1998] F.S.R. 265.
[77] *Marks & Spencer plc v. One in a Million* [1999] E.T.M.R. 61, CA.

(iv) Trade mark infringement

5–62 It is axiomatic that if a brand is successful it is likely that the brand name at least will be copied or imitated. If the imitation of copying takes place on or in relation to goods other than those identical to the goods on which the proprietor or merchandiser uses the mark, what can the brand owner do to stop it?

5–63 We have seen in previous chapters that it is only possible to bring an action for trade mark infringement if the trade mark concerned is registered.[78] If the mark is not registered the proprietor must rely on the law of passing off (discussed below at para. 5–97). If the offending sign is identical and is used on the same type of goods as the original mark, action can be taken under section 10(1) of the TMA. If, however, the mark is not identical, or if the goods are not identical, but similar then the trade mark owner can seek redress under section 10(2) of the TMA 1994 provided that there exists a likelihood of confusion.[79] If, however, an identical or similar mark is used by a third party, without consent, in relation to dissimilar goods then the proprietor must rely on section 10(3) of the TMA 1994.

5–64 Section 10(3) provides that:

> "A person infringes a registered trade mark if he uses in the course of trade a sign which—
>
> (a) is identical with or similar to the trade mark and,
> (b) is used in relation to goods or services which are not similar to those for which the trade mark is registered,
>
> where the trade mark has a reputation in the United Kingdom and the use of the sign, being without due cause, takes unfair advantage of, or is detrimental to the distinctive character or repute of the trade mark."

The wording of section 10(3) follows Article 5(2) of the Directive.[80] Although it has been said that this subsection of Article 5 was based upon Article 13A(2) of the Uniform Benelux Trade Mark Law 1971 there has been considerable debate as to the truth of this assertion and whether or not it can be relied upon when interpreting the Directive (in other words should the principles established in the Benelux in connection with the use of a similar mark in relation to dissimilar goods have application here).[81] A similar debate took place in relation to the meaning of section 10(2) and its derivation from Benelux law.[82] With regard to the latter, the position was resolved in the United Kingdom in the *Wagamama*[83] decision by Laddie J. and was subsequently confirmed by the European Court of Justice ("ECJ") in *Sabel BV v. Puma AG*.[84] Laddie J. considered the approach adopted by the Benelux court in cases such as that concerning Claeryn gin and Klarein

---

[78] Unless the mark is a well known mark, in which case it is possible to take action against the use of an identical or similar mark in relation to identical or similar goods under s.56 TMA 1994 without the benefit of an existing registration.

[79] The application and scope of s.10(2) was discussed in detail in Chap. 4.

[80] 89/104/EEC (the "Directive").

[81] The provenance of the subsection was acknowledged to be Art. 13A(2) of the former Uniform Benelux law by the Advocate General in *General Motors Corporation v. Yplon SA* [1999] E.T.M.R. 122 at 130.

[82] See Chap. 4 for a discussion of the arguments put forward.

[83] *Wagamama Ltd v. City Centre Restaurants plc* [1995] F.S.R. 713 ("*Wagamama*').

[84] C-251/95 November 11, 1997.

disinfectant[85] but rejected the notion that the court should look to the Benelux court for assistance in the interpretation of Article 5(1)(b) of the Directive section 10(2) TMA. Instead, Laddie J. sought to interpret the Directive by relying on the courts' traditional understanding of trade mark infringement.

5–65 Laddie J.'s comments, and those of the ECJ, are not only relevant to the interpretation of section 10(2) but may also extend to section 10(3) in so far as they relate to the relevance of Benelux law to the interpretation and application of this provision.[85a] As the Advocate General noted in *General Motors Corporation v. Yplon SA*,[86] although Article 5(2) of the Directive is clearly based on Article 13A(2) of the former Benelux law there are nonetheless important differences. First, protection is limited to marks with a reputation. Secondly, protection is provided only in relation to goods or services that are not similar and thirdly, the nature of the harm against which protection is provided is specified.

To succeed under this subsection the proprietor must show that:

- the registered mark and the offending sign are identical or similar;

- the respective goods or services are not similar;

- the registered mark has a reputation in the United Kingdom, and

- the use of the sign, being without the cause, takes "unfair advantage of" or is "detrimental to the distinctive character" or repute of the registered mark.

In view of the importance of this section we will consider each requirement in turn.

(c) Identical or similar marks

5–66 The first requirement under section 10(3) is that the registered mark and the offending sign must either be identical or similar. As noted in Chapter 4, the comparison is mark for sign[87] disregarding added matter.[88]

In most cases there will be no difficulty in identifying the mark but it is possible for it to be hidden or swamped although he did not give any examples. The effect of this approach is that the proprietor of a mark such as the word "Comfort" could potentially prevent all uses of the word (assuming that it was used on identical goods) whether the word is used on its own, or in combination with other words such as "Comfort and Joy" or in the form of a device mark or logo.[89]

5–67 Whilst the identification of an identical mark following this approach may generally produce acceptable results in the context of word marks, it can lead to unacceptable results in relation to graphic marks, for example would a registration

---

[85] Benelux Court of Justice, March 1, 1975, N.J. 1975, 472.
[85a] That said, Jacob J. noted, albeit obiter, that section 10(3) might cater for the sort of circumstances of the Claeryn/Klarein case, although he did not analyse the position further—*British Sugar plc v. James Robertson & Sons Ltd* [1997] E.T.M.R. 118 at 126. Neuberger J. observed that assistance may be available to English courts from jurisprudence developed elsewhere in the community because although section 10(3) is a significant extension of the rights of a trade mark owner in the United Kingdom it is not such a significant extension in other Member States—*Premier Brands U.K. Ltd v. Typhoon Europe Ltd, The Times*, February 22, 2000.
[86] [1999] E.T.M.R. 122 at 130.
[87] *Original Natural Resources v. Origin Clothing* [1995] F.S.R. 280.
[88] *British Sugar plc v. James Robertson & Sons Ltd* [1996] R.P.C. 281.
[89] For an interesting article comparing the scope of the marks "Comfort" and "Comfort and Joy" see James, "Only a Trade Mark Registration Brings Comfort (and Joy) in the U.K." *Trade Mark World*, January 1998, p. 22.

of a device comprising three stripes be regarded as identical to a sign comprising four stripes (on the basis that the fourth stripe should be disregarded as added matter)? If the registered mark is a composite mark it may be preferable to register the various components separately (if possible) rather than together on the basis that this may offer greater scope for challenging third party signs that incorporate any single element as opposed to only those marks that incorporate all elements.

5–68   The danger of the court's approach to identifying the sign is that it does not take into account how the sign is actually used by the defendant but inevitably assumes that the offending element of the mark is used on its own. Although factors such as the context of the defendant's use are taken into account when assessing the likelihood of confusion under section 10(2) they are not taken into account under section 10(1), thus even though a defendant incorporates other distinctive features as part of his sign these will not enable him to avoid a finding of identity.

5–69   To date, the ECJ has provided no guidance to indicate whether this approach is appropriate.

5–70   If the marks are not considered to be identical, then the question arises, are the mark and the sign similar? As we saw in Chapter 4, the test of similarity was set out by the ECJ[90] where it was held that the mark and the sign must be considered aurally, visually and conceptually and, where appropriate, the court must evaluate the importance to be attached to the different elements of a mark (*e.g.* the importance of words as against logos). The assessment of similarity is not, however, objective but should also take into account the context of the use (*i.e.* the goods/services on which the respective marks are used and the circumstances of use).[91–96] The assessment of similarity is thus a complex process designed to elicit whether use of the offending sign is likely to lead to confusion of the average reasonably informal, circumspect consumer, with an imperfect recollection of the mark.

5–71   Applying this approach marks that have been found to be similar include *inter alia* Wagamama and Rajamama,[97] and Viagra and Viagrene.[98–99]

5–72   In the case of *The Baywatch Production Company v. The Home Video Channel Limited*[1] which concerned the alleged infringement of the registered trade mark Baywatch (covering *inter alia* video tapes) by use of the mark Babewatch (in connection with the broadcast of pornographic television programmes, said to be a parody of the plaintiff's programme), Deputy Judge Crystal Q.C. held that the two marks Baywatch and Babewatch were not similar on the basis that there was no evidence of confusion. His finding was based upon the premise that the concept of "similarity" imported into section 10(3) the concept of a "likelihood of confusion". Such a view would mean that if the offending sign and the mark were identical it would not be necessary to show confusion whereas the use of a similar sign would require evidence of confusion. It is suggested that although the deputy judge was correct in looking to the surrounding circumstances it was wrong to say that the plaintiff was required to show a likelihood of confusion in order to succeed. This understanding has since been confirmed by the ECJ first in *Sabel v. Puma*, subsequently and more explicitly by the Advocate General (and the ECJ) in

[90] *Sabel BV v. Puma AG* [1998] E.T.M.R. 1; *Canon Kabushiki Kaishau v. Metro-Goldwyn Mayer Inc.* [1999] E.T.M.R. 1; *Windsurfing Chiemsee v. Huber and Altenberger* [1999] E.T.M.R. 585; *Lloyd Schuhfabrik Meyer & Co. v. Klijsen Handel BV* [1999] E.T.M.R. 690.
[91–96] *Lloyd Schuhfabrik Meyer v. Klijsen Handel BV* [1999] E.T.M.R. 690 at 698.
[97] See n.83, para. 5–64 above.
[98–99] *Pfizer Ltd v. Eurofood Link (UK) Ltd* December 13, 1999 (unreported).
[1] [1997] F.S.R. 22.

General Motors Corporation v. Yplon SA,[2] and more directly in *Premier Brands U.K. Ltd v. Typhoon Europe Ltd.*[2a]

5–73   One of the difficulties in assessing the similarity of the marks by reference to the goods on which they are used, as suggested by the ECJ in *Sabel v. Puma* is that marks that may be regarded as similar in the context of section 10(2) might not be regarded as similar under section 10(3). For example, Wagamama and Rajamama were held to be similar when both were applied to restaurants but would the marks still be regarded as similar if the sign Rajamama was applied to say noodles or rice? Whilst this problem does not arise in relation to the use of identical marks on different goods (since they will always be regarded as identical) the concept of similarity is less consistent. Indeed in *Canon Kabushiki Kaisha v. Metro-Goldwyn Mayer Inc*[3] the ECJ held that:

"A global assessment of a likelihood of confusion implies some interdependence between the relevant factors, and in particular a similarity between the trade marks and between these goods or services. Accordingly, a lesser degree of similarity between these goods or services may be offset by a greater degree of similarity between the marks, and vice versa."

5–74   Although these comments were made in the context of considering the application of the equivalent of section 10(2) rather than section 10(3) they will still apply to a consideration of similarity under section 10(3) albeit in relation to the need to show that an unfair advantage has been taken or a detriment suffered.

(d) Dissimilar goods

5–75   Having determined that the marks are identical or exhibit the necessary degree of similarity, the next issue to address is whether the goods are dissimilar. To determine whether the goods are dissimilar, one first has to look back at the registration certificate to identify the scope of the goods covered by the plaintiff's mark. The specification should be compared to the defendant's goods to see if they can be regarded as identical or similar. The test of whether or not the goods may be regarded as similar was set out by the High Court, in the *Treat* case by Jacob J.[4] This case concerned the use of the mark Treat on a desert syrup that could be poured over ice cream and Robertson's Toffee Treat which was a spread for use on bread. The Judge referred to a test that had previously been developed under the TMA 1938 in the *Jellinenk* case[5] (and had subsequently been applied by the House of Lords in the *Daiquiri Rum* case[6]) to determine whether or not goods could be considered as "goods of the same description" for the purposes of determining a conflict with a prior registration. Whether the goods could be regarded as similar depended, according to Jacob J., on a number of factors including:

- the respective uses of the respective products;
- the respective users of the products;

---

[2] [1999] E.T.M.R. 122 (the *"Chevy"* case) at 129.
[2a] *The Times*, February 22, 2000 (the *"Typhoo* cases").
[3] [1999] E.T.M.R. 1 at 7.
[4] *British Sugar Plc v. James Robertson & Sons Ltd* [1996] R.P.C. 281 at 296/7.
[5] [1946] 63 R.P.C. 59.
[6] [1969] R.P.C. 600 at 620.

- the physical nature of the products;

- the respective trade channels through which the products were distributed and sold;

- in the case of self service consumer items—whether they were likely to be found on the same shelf; and

- the extent to which the goods are competitive—whether the goods were considered by the trade to be the same or different.

5–76   In the *Treat* case, having considered each of these factors, the court held that the goods were not similar. This was in spite of the fact that the label on the jar of Robertson's Toffee Treat stated that it could be used as a topping for ice cream. Jacob J. found, however, that the products would be located in different areas of the supermarket and that the trade view was that the goods were considered to be part of different market sectors. As a consequence, the concept of similarity was interpreted particularly narrowly in this case. It thus highlights the difficulty that the courts have in trying to introduce external criteria to draw the line between similar and dissimilar goods which itself is too crude a distinction for achieving justice in the individual case.

5–77   The crudeness of the test in the *Treat* case is emphasised by the acknowledgment in the *Canon* case that a lesser degree of similarity between the respective goods or services can be offset by a greater degree of similarity between the marks. Thus one would have expected, in the *Treat* case that the goods would have been considered similar since the marks were identical. One explanation for the narrowness of the term in that case is the descriptive nature of the mark, a factor which, according to *Canon*, should be taken into account. Had *Treat* been heard after the *Canon* case this might well have been the outcome.

5–78   The application of the test of similarity in relation to goods can thus be unpredictable especially if more weight is given to one factor than to another. If the brand owner's mark is particularly distinctive or well known then it may be granted protection over a broader spectrum of goods than if the mark was not very distinctive and not widely known. Equally, if the sign closely resembles the mark, the range of goods covered may be wider still. For the brand owner involved in brand stretching there is some comfort in the fact that the more widely the brand name is known the greater the degree of protection granted. Equally, it is reassuring for the brand owner to know that the court will taken into account such commercial factors as the nature of the products, the distribution channels used and whether or not the products are regarded as competitive since this should mean that products that potentially end up side by side on a shelf will be regarded as similar even if, from a practical point of view, they are quite different.

5–79   If as a result of the application of the *Canon* test the goods are regarded as not similar, then to succeed under section 10(3) the proprietor must go on to show that the mark in question has a reputation in the United Kingdom.

(e) Reputation in the United Kingdom

5–80   It is unclear exactly what is meant by the phrase a "mark with a reputation in the United Kingdom". Does it mean, for example, that the mark must be well-known or famous, or simply that the mark must be one that has been used in the United Kingdom, or does it require a degree of notoriety somewhere in between these extremes? In paragraph 3.17 of the White Paper, the precursor to the TMA 1994, reference was made to the ability of owners of marks with a "wide reputation" to use their existing registrations to prevent the unauthorised use of identical or similar marks in relation to dissimilar goods. Neither the White Paper, nor the Act or the Directive, however, stated that the mark must be well known or famous. In the *Chevy* case, the Advocate General considered this provision and, having compared it to the provision relating to well known marks in the Paris Convention (Article *6bis*) concluded that a mark with a reputation "need not be as well known as a "well known mark".[7] Although the Advocate General refused to say whether a "mark with a reputation" was a qualitative or a quantitative concept he did indicate that it must be known to a significant proportion of the relevant sector of the public, although he stressed that it was not appropriate to specify a particular threshold percentage. In assessing the extent of a mark's reputation regard should be had to a variety of factors including (but not limited to) the market share held by the trade mark, the intensity, geographical extent and duration of its use and the size of the investment made in promoting the mark.[8] Territorially, it is sufficient if the mark has a reputation in a substantial part of the territory concerned; it does not have to have a reputation throughout the territory.[9] To ensure that the mark does not unduly benefit from too broad a scope of protection, however, both the Advocate General and the ECJ itself were at pains to stress that the national court must go on to consider whether an unfair advantage had been taken or a detriment suffered.

5–81   When the provision first appeared, commentators[10] speculated that the reference to "reputation" *per se* rather than to goodwill would have the effect of allowing a foreign plaintiff to bring action in the United Kingdom based upon the reputation of a mark in the United Kingdom even though the mark might not have been used in the United Kingdom. This would be of obvious benefit to those marks that have an international reputation but whose proprietors would not ordinarily be in a position to bring an action for passing off due to the lack of a trading presence in the United Kingdom. Whilst on the basis of the statute alone that may appear to be true, the criteria that the ECJ has indicated should be taken into account in assessing whether or not the mark has obtained the threshold reputation required suggests that factors relating to both actual use and promotion will be relevant. Unless more weight is given to promotional activity than to market share it is hard to see how a mark that is well known but not sold in the United Kingdom can attain the threshold required.

(f) Without due cause

5–81/1   It is for the defendant to show that the use of the offending sign is "without due cause".[10a] In the *Typhoo* case Neuberger J. rejected the suggestion that "without due cause" meant "bona fide" since this would mean that brand owners would be unable to stop use of the sign by an ignorant third party simply because the mark was innocently adopted. An assessment of the knowledge or subjective intentions of the defendant was therefore rejected. Instead, applying a purposive construction to the phase Neuberger J. held that it meant that the defendant had to show not only that the use of the sign was with due cause but also

---

[7] At p. 132.
[8] These factors were identified by the ECJ in the *Chevy* case [1999] E.T.M.R. 950 at 957.
[9] *ibid.*
[10] See Michaels, p. 47 and Annand and Norman, p. 157.
[10a] *Typhoo* case.

that the advantage or detriment suffered were not "without due cause". This interpretation was said to be based on the approach followed by the Benelux court in the Claeryn/Klaerin case.[10b]

(g) Unfair advantage or detrimental use

5–82   Some commentators[11] have suggested that this final clause of section 10(3) introduced into English law concepts of dilution (discussed below) and unfair competition hitherto unknown. As it is, the interpretation and subsequent application of this section in cases such as *BASF*[12] and *Baywatch*[13] has virtually dispelled such suggestions.

5–83   In the *BASF* case the High Court judge, Knox J., rejected an application for relief under this section on the basis that the plaintiff had not shown that an unfair advantage had been taken since no evidence of confusion had been submitted to the court. The plaintiff had registered the trade mark Opus in connection with agricultural and horticultural products in Class 5 and was seeking to restrain the defendant's use of the sign Farming Opus in relation to a farming directory. The mark Opus had been used by the defendant for a number of years in connection with different publications relating to buildings and property and it wished to expand into publications relating to farming property. The plaintiffs argued that use of the mark in this field by the defendant would take unfair advantage of its mark and would reduce the distinctive character of the plaintiff's mark.

5–84   It was held that in the absence of evidence of confusion it could not be said that an unfair advantage had been taken or that the plaintiff had suffered any detriment to its mark in terms of its character or repute. Accordingly the application was rejected. Thus, the requirement to show confusion, which has long been an essential part of classic trade mark infringement actions in the United Kingdom, emerged as an essential ingredient of section 10(3) even though the word "confusion" is not mentioned in the section at all. Although Knox J. did not explain exactly what he meant by confusion, it is likely that he was referring to consumer confusion as to the source of the defendant's goods. A requirement to show this type of confusion would clearly reduce the potency of the whole section. This would mean that no additional protection would be granted to marks with a reputation than that ordinarily available under the law of passing off. Given that the aim of the provision was to grant additional and more extensive protection to marks with a wide reputation, it would fail to achieve its aim if a likelihood of confusion is regarded as a pre-requisite. As the ECJ noted in the *Chevy* case[14] the harm that the provision is seeking to prevent is based on association rather than confusion *per se*. Consequently, what the plaintiff should be required to show is not confusion as to origin but rather an association of some kind. Whilst it is possible that consumers will be confused as to the association or connection between the producers of the two products it is unlikely that consumers will confuse the origin of the goods themselves bearing in mind the fact that the goods are quite different.

5–85   The danger of expanding the law without a sufficient explanation as to the intention of the legislators or the meaning of key terms leaves courts open to apply familiar concepts rather than developing new tools to assess, in this case,

---

[10b] *Lucas Bols* [1976] I.T.C. 420.
[11] See for example Annand and Norman, p. 156–157.
[12] *BASF PLC v. CEP (U.K.) Ltd* [1996] E.T.M.R. 51.
[13] [1997] F.S.R. 22.
[14] At p. 957.

whether an unfair advantage has been taken or a detriment suffered. A likelihood of confusion is not the only measure available to the court to assess damage. As outlined below there are other ways of determining what advantage, if any, has been taken.

5–86 Although the ECJ has confirmed[15] that it is not necessary to show confusion in order to succeed under Article 5(2) of the Directive, it has not gone as far as to indicate what is needed to show that an unfair advantage has been taken or a detriment suffered. It is suggested that Knox J. was correct in saying that in order to succeed under section 10(3) the brand owner must do more than simply point to a third party using an identical or similar mark on different goods.[16] However, in my view, Knox J. was wrong to import the requirement of a likelihood of confusion into a subsection which otherwise makes no reference to it. The section aims to prevent third parties from gaining a benefit at the expense of the trade mark owner. There is no reason why such a benefit should be limited to instances of mistaken identity.

5–87 In my view a proper construction of section 10(3) requires a brand owner to show that the third party has by his actions sought to draw to himself something of the goodwill or reputation associated with the original brand owner. This may for example, be by referring directly (or indirectly) to the brand owner in its advertising as in the *Baywatch* case where the defendant had placed an advertisement for its programme in a television scheduling magazine using a depiction of a woman with long blond hair wearing a red swimsuit (not dissimilar to Pamela Anderson, the star of the plaintiff's television programme). The caption on the advertisement read "The version that everyone wants to see". Alternatively, the defendant may adopt a similar lettering style, logo or trading colours, etc.[16a] If the brand owner's mark is so well known that any reference to the mark, irrespective of the context, will be taken to refer to the brand owner, as might be the case if the mark Marks & Spencer or Coca-Cola was used by a third party, then no additional reference direct or indirect should be necessary.[17] If the mark is not so well known, the brand owner should demonstrate a link or connection between his own mark and the use of the mark made by the third party in order to show that an advantage has been taken. It does not, in my view, mean that the brand owner must go as far as showing a likelihood of confusion as suggested by Knox J.[18]; an association between the two, or a reference by one manufacturer/supplier to the other should be sufficient.[19]

5–88 Evidentially it will no doubt be hard for brand owners to show that an unfair advantage has been taken of their registered trade marks. Unless the courts are willing to infer that it is inevitable that a benefit has been obtained by the defendant (as a result of direct or indirect reference to the original brand) as happened in the *One in a Million* case,[20] it will no doubt be difficult to establish the advantage gained especially if the marks themselves are not identical. It is suggested

---

[15] See *Sabel BV v. Puma AG* C-251/95, November 11, 1997 (See n.94, para. 20).
[16] See Carty "Dilution and Passing Off: Cause for Concern" (1996) 11 L.Q.R. 632 at 666. Carty agrees that in situations of "pure dilution" the courts should be wary of assuming dilution based on use of an identical or similar mark on dissimilar goods in the absence of evidence of damage.
[16a] In the *Typhoo* case, use of a very similar mark using the same combination of colours was not sufficient to show that a detriment had been suffered—it was not argued that an unfair advantage had been taken.
[17] *British Telecommunications plc & Othrs v. One in a Million Ltd* [1999] E.T.M.R. 61, CA.
[18] Supported by commentators such as Cornish, *Intellectual Property* (Sweet & Maxwell, 3rd ed., 1996) p. 624 (hereafter "Cornish") and Michaels, p. 47.
[19] See Prescott "Think Before You Waga Finger" [1996] 6 E.I.P.R. 317 at 319.
[20] *British Telecommunications plc & Othrs v. One in a Million Ltd* [1999] E.T.M.R. 61, CA.

that the stronger the mark the more likely it is that an advantage will have been taken.

5–89   Supporters of the Knox J. view argue that confusion is a necessary pre-requisite for protection under section 10(3) for two reasons, (a) because it is a requirement in relation to similar goods under section 10(2) and it would be illogical to provide greater protection in relation to dissimilar goods than that provided in relation to similar goods,[21] and (b) because otherwise it makes a nonsense of the classification system (that is, registration in one class would effectively grant protection in relation to dissimilar goods in the remaining 41 classes). As the Hearing Officer in the *Oasis* case (discussed below at para. 5–93) noted, this latter argument has some force.[22] Protagonists of the contrary view, however, emphasise that section 10(3) was intended to have wider application; it is not a progression of the protection available under section 10(2). Section 10(3) is, they argue *sui generis*. As Prescott explains,[23] section 10(3) is not mandated by the European Community, Article 5(2) of the Directive indicates that adoption of Article 5(2) is optional whereas Article 5(1) (the equivalent of section 10(2)) is mandatory. It is erroneous therefore to conclude that it is necessary to read into section 10(3) a requirement of likelihood of confusion merely because it appears in section 10(2).[24] Whilst Prescott concedes that a "likelihood of confusion" is one way of measuring the unfair advantage taken of the original mark he accepts that it is possible that the two manufacturer/suppliers will be "associated" by consumers even in the absence of confusion as to the origin of the goods.

5–90   If the brand owner can not show that an unfair advantage has been taken of its mark it may be in a position to show that the use of the offending sign by the defendant is detrimental to the distinctive character or repute of the brand owner's mark. As noted above, at the time of the adoption of this provision in the TMA 1994 it had been thought that this phrase introduced the concept of dilution into United Kingdom law. Dilution is a doctrine that originally developed in Germany[25] as part of the law of unfair competition but it is more generally associated with the American lawyer and academic Frank Schechter, although he did not actually use the term dilution. In Schechter's seminal article *The Rational Basis of Trademark Protection*[26] he argued that the only rational basis for trade mark protection was to preserve the uniqueness of a distinctive trade mark. Accordingly, he said, that such marks should be protected against "the gradual whittling away or dispersion of the identity and hold upon the public mind of the mark[27] as a result of its use on dissimilar goods". Schechter's concept of dilution was limited to distinctive marks and did not require the presence of either competition or confusion. His ideas were not, however, universally accepted although support for his views has grown.

5–91   Although no dilution statute was introduced during Schechter's lifetime a number of states did eventually introduce anti-dilution provisions leading finally to the adoption of a federal statute in 1995.[28] Under the Federal Trademark Dilution Act, only distinctive and famous marks are entitled to relief. In order to determine what amounts to distinctive and famous the statute set out a number of factors that the court may consider including:

---

[21] See Cornish, p. 624.
[22] *Oasis Stores Ltd's Trade Mark Application* [1998] R.P.C. 631 at, p. 647.
[23] See "Has the Benelux Trade Mark Law been Written into the Directive?" [1997] E.I.P.R. 99.
[24] This was mentioned specifically by Neuberger J. in the *Typhoo* case.
[25] Schechter "The Rational Basis of Trademark Protection" (1927) 40 *Harvard Law Review* 813 (1927) at 831.
[26] *ibid.*
[27] *ibid.* at 825.
[28] Federal Trademark Dilution Act.

- the degree of distinctiveness (acquired or inherent) of the mark;

- the duration and extent of use of the mark in connection with goods or services on which the mark is used;

- the duration and extent of advertising and publicity of the mark;

- the geographical area in which the mark is used;

- the channels of trade for the goods/services;

- the degree of recognition of the mark in the trading areas and channels of trade used by the trade mark owner;

- the nature and extent of use of the same or similar marks by third parties; and

- whether the mark is registered.

5–92   The trade mark owner seeking to rely on this section does not need to show a likelihood of confusion, mistake or deception as required under trade mark law, or competition between the owner of the famous mark and the third party as required under the law of Unfair Competition. Thus, the dilution statute provides a useful means of preventing the unauthorised use of a famous mark on dissimilar products. The point to note for the brand owner is that if he can not show that his mark is distinctive and famous then no relief from dilution will be available. Statutory exceptions regarding use of the famous mark do exist in relation to fair use for comparative commercial advertising or promotion, non commercial use of the mark and all forms of news reporting and commentary.

5–93   In the United Kingdom there have been a only few cases[29] that have so far sought to rely on this aspect of section 10(3) or the corresponding provision relating to opposition proceedings.[30] In the *Oasis* case the applicant's sign was identical to the opponent's Ever Ready mark originally used on batteries. The defendant was seeking to register the sign in connection with contraceptives including condoms. It was held that use of the mark on condoms would not in itself be sufficient to detrimentally affect the opponent's mark in the absence of any other evidence. In contrast, in the *One in a Million* case, the court was prepared to accept that the registration of the plaintiff's mark as a domain name by the defendant was in itself sufficient to detrimentally affect the distinctive character or repute of the mark. Although each case turned on its own facts it does highlight the difficulties for the brand owner who can not assume that merely because the defendant has used an identical mark that it will be held to be detrimental to the distinctiveness of the plaintiff's mark. That said, in the *Chevy* case the ECJ accepted that "the stronger the earlier mark's distinctive character and reputation the easier it will be to accept that detriment has been caused to it".[31] Bearing in mind the assessment that would already have been made by the court in relation to the mark's reputation, it is suggested that in order to assess whether a detriment has been suffered in relation to the earlier mark's distinctiveness the court should have regard to:

---

[29] Notably *British Telecommunications plc v. One in a Million Ltd* [1999] E.T.M.R. 61, CA; *Re Audi-Med Trade Mark* [1998] R.P.C. 863; *Oasis Stores Ltd's Trade Mark Application* [1998] R.P.C. 631; *Premier Brands U.K. Ltd v. Typhoon Europe Ltd, The Times*, February 22, 2000.
[30] s.5(3) TMA 1994.
[31] [1999] E.T.M.R. 950 at 958.

- the inherent distinctiveness of the earlier mark;

- the nature and extent of use of the same or similar marks by third parties; and

- the range of goods for which the earlier mark enjoys a reputation.

To these, the Hearing Officer in the *Oasis* case added[32]:

- whether the respective goods though dissimilar are related or sold through the same outlets; and

- whether the earlier mark will be any less distinctive for the goods/services for which it has a reputation than it was before.

5–94   In my view, these additional questions are unnecessary and are likely to result in too narrow an interpretation of the section. As a result, protection will be denied in all but the most exceptional cases where there is what might be described as a common field of activity or a degree of nexus in business areas thus limiting protection to those instances where the defendant's goods are closely related to those of the plaintiff. If, as has been said above, the intention of the provision is to grant protection against dilution, a loss of distinctiveness, then there does not need to be a relationship between the plaintiff's goods and those of the defendant. Equally, it is not always possible to assess the full impact of the defendant's actions at the time of the plaintiff's action. As noted in Chapter 4 in relation to Sainsbury's Classic Cola, the adoption of a similar mark (or in that case trade dress) by one competitor can lead to a number of other competitors following suit which can make it hard to assess the ultimate impact of the defendant's actions.[32a] As Schechter himself noted, the harm is the gradual whittling away of the mark's distinctiveness. Consequently it should be sufficient for the court that the original mark is both inherently distinctive and distinctive in the market place, and grant protection accordingly. To do otherwise would be to refuse protection in all situations except where the sign is used on dissimilar but related goods which can not have been the original intention of the Act, or the Directive.

5–95   In the *Oasis* case the hearing officer rejected the idea that the mere use of an identical mark would be detrimental to the distinctiveness of the earlier mark saying that[33]:

"Any use of the same or similar mark for dissimilar goods or services is liable to some extent, to dilute the distinctiveness of the earlier mark the provision is clearly not intended to have the sweeping effect of preventing the registration of any mark which is the same as, or similar to, a trade mark with a reputation. It is therefore a matter of degree."

In the slightly later case of *Audi–Med*[34] the same Hearing Officer held that the proprietor of an earlier mark could only oppose the registration of an identical

---

[32] *Oasis Stores Ltd's Trade Mark Application* [1998] R.P.C. 631 at 649.
[32a] See Appendix C, photograph 15 which illustrates the trade dress of a number of colas including Coca Cola and Sainsbury's Classic Cola. Virgin Cola and Marks & Spencer's Cola both adopted their red trade dress after the dispute between Sainsbury's and the Coca Cola Company.
[33] *ibid.* at p. 649.
[34] *Re Audi-Med Trade Mark* [1998] R.P.C. 863.

mark for dissimilar goods if the detriment suffered was more than *de minimis*.[35] Again, although it may be true that the individual registration concerned would only have a *de minimis* effect on the existence of the earlier mark the existence of the later registration would no doubt make it easier for others using similar marks to obtain registration thus further diluting the distinctiveness of the original mark. The question then becomes—at what point can it be said that the effect is more than *de minimis*?

5–95/1 In the *Typhoo* case, having considered the marks (Typhoo and Typhoon), the nature of the respective goods (tea and kitchen utensils), the extensive reputation of the plaintiff's mark and the fact that there was no evidence of confusion or dilution, relief was refused. Whilst the judge acknowledged that the absence of any of these factors were not, on their own, fatal, taken together and bearing in mind that there is no other detriment to the plaintiff as a result, the judge could not accept that the mark had been infringed. Such an outcome is disappointing for brand owners and reinforces the view that protection will only be available under section 10(3) where a clear link can be shown between the respective parties' use of the marks.

5–96 For owners of licensed trade marks, section 10(3) offers the possibility of obtaining protection against the unauthorised use of an identical or similar mark across the full range of goods and services available without the need to register the mark in each class. If the courts interpret section 10(3) widely, such that use of an offending sign does not have to be "trade mark use" and no evidence of confusion is required, licensing will not adversely affect the level of protection obtained but may, on the contrary, enhance it as a result of the increased awareness of the brand name and its increased association with a broad range of goods. If, however, the courts insist upon "trade mark use", this could severely reduce the ability of brand owners to take action under section 10(3) since it could be argued by potential defendant's that their use of the plaintiff's mark (developed in relation to a different product category) on say a sweatshirt was not trade mark use and so avoid liability. This is a particular risk for marks used on or in relation to clothing. Equally, if brand owners are obliged to provide evidence of confusion as to origin in relation to the use of offending signs on dissimilar goods, it is likely that they will be unsuccessful since consumers may associate marks without stopping to consider whether there is an economic link between two enterprises. In such a situation it would be true to say, as Wilkof has suggested[36] that trade mark licensing has come full circle in that it is "at odds with the legal framework that governs trade mark use", in which case it is time that further consideration is given to the function of trade marks today, and in particular whether they have now developed into assets in their own right and thus are worthy of more appropriate protection.[37]

(i) Passing off

5–97 A number of cases relating to the use of an identical or similar mark in relation to dissimilar goods have reached the courts during the past 50 years or so but, in general terms, the courts have been reluctant to grant extensive protection to plaintiff's outside the plaintiff's usual field of business activity. Some of the cases highlight the court's belief that consumers will not be misled into thinking that there is a connection between the parties because of the diversity of business

---

[35] *ibid.* at p. 873.
[36] Wilkof, p. 35.
[37] This point will be discussed further in Chap. 8.

interests *i.e.* that there was no "common field of activity". The absence of a common field of activity has, in many cases, been sufficient to avoid a finding of misrepresentation or a likelihood of confusion, with the consequence that the action has failed.

5–98   Thus in general terms, (in the absence of fraud) the law of passing off has not protected businesses as well as it might from the unauthorised use of brand names or marks associated with one producer or product category when used on another. For example, as in the case of the name "Stringfellows", which was originally associated with a night-club and was subsequently used in relation to potato chips an injunction was denied.[38] Only in exceptional cases such as *Walter v. Ashton*,[39] *Harrods v. Harrods Bank*,[40] *Dunhill v. Sunoptic*[41] and *Lego*,[42] and merchandising cases such as *Judge Dredd*[43] and *Ninja Turtles*[44] have the courts been willing to recognise the potential of the original brand owner to diversify (or stretch the use of its brand name through licensing) and have granted injunctions to protect brand owners against third party use of the same or similar mark in relation to dissimilar goods. Such protection is based on the fact that consumers will believe that there is a connection between the plaintiff and the defendant despite their diversity of interest. This belief requires that the mark itself be distinctive (as opposed to descriptive) and widely recognised. Where the mark or brand name concerned is descriptive or not widely known the courts have shown that they are reluctant to assume that consumers will make the necessary connection and that damage will be suffered as a consequence.[45]

5–99   The increasing recognition that a brand is a valuable asset in its own right has led to calls for protection against dilution but, as demonstrated in decision of the Court of Appeal in the *Harrods*[46] case, the courts are divided as to whether protection should be granted in the absence of confusion or a likelihood of confusion. To understand the reasons for the current approach adopted by the courts it is helpful to look back at some of the more significant cases relating to dissimilar goods and in the light of these, insight may be gained into the likely approach of the court in future.

5–100   The principles on which actions for passing off are founded were identified by Parker L.J. in *Spalding v. Gamage*[47] where it was said that nobody has the right to pass off their goods as the goods of someone else. Thus the tort seeks to protect the business or goodwill of the plaintiff which is likely to be injured by the misrepresentation of the defendant. Quoting an earlier case,[48] Parker L.J. described the concept of goodwill as:

". . . the benefit and advantage of the good name, reputation and connection of a business. It is the attractive force which brings in custom."

Passing off thus protects goodwill or customer connection; it does not protect the mark *per se*. In *Star Industrial Co. Ltd v. Yap Kwee Kor*[49] it was said that:

---

[38] *Stringfellow v. McCain Foods (GB) Ltd* [1984] R.P.C. 501, CA.
[39] (1902) 2 Ch. 282.
[40] (1924) 41 R.P.C. 74, CA.
[41] [1979] F.S.R. 337, CA.
[42] *Lego System A/S v. Lego M Lemelstrich Ltd* [1983] F.S.R. 155.
[43] *IPC Magazines Ltd v. Black & White Music Corp* [1983] F.S.R. 348.
[44] *Mirage Studios v. Counter-feat Clothing Company Ltd* [1991] F.S.R. 145.
[45] *Newsweek Inc v. The British Broadcasting Corporation* [1979] R.P.C. 441, CA.
[46] [1996] F.S.R. 697.
[47] (1915) 32 R.P.C. 273.
[48] *CIR v. Muller* [1901] A.C. 217 at 223.
[49] [1976] F.S.R. 256, PC.

"a passing off action is a remedy for the invasion of a right of property not in the mark, name or get-up improperly used, but in the business or goodwill likely to be injured by the misrepresentation made by passing off one person's goods as those of another."

Thus, in order to succeed in an action for passing off the plaintiff must show that it has a business or goodwill to protect and that the defendant has made a misrepresentation causing damage to the plaintiff's business. Although these three elements are inextricably linked (indeed it is often difficult to separate each element in decisions of the court) it is helpful to consider them separately.

(h) Goodwill

5–101   One question raised by the emphasis of the court on the need to show damage to goodwill is the extent of the plaintiff's goodwill. Although passing off is principally concerned with the protection of goodwill as a form of legal property, reputation (which is a matter of fact) is relevant in determining the scope of the plaintiff's protectable interest, in that the misrepresentation often turns on the reputation associated with the plaintiff's mark.[50] If the defendant starts to use a mark identical to that of the plaintiff but in a different area of business, will there be a misrepresentation and will the plaintiff's goodwill be damaged as a consequence? As Whitford J. noted in *Alfred Dunhill Ltd v. Sunoptic SA*,[51] at first instance, the plaintiff must show that it has a reputation in the goods on which the defendant is using, or proposes to use, the mark:

"if not the precise goods which they are endeavouring to stop these defendants using, of such a kind that the reputation could be said to spill over and extend sufficiently far to lead the public purchasing the goods in question to believe, . . . that there must be some trade connection with the plaintiff".

Although at first instance Dunhill was unable to show that its reputation extended beyond tobacco and smoker's requisites, it was able to establish on appeal (after submitting further evidence of its business activities) that as a result of its extensive licensing programme its reputation extended to luxury goods generally. It was therefore able to prevent the defendant from selling sunglasses and spectacles under the name Christopher Dunhill even though it had not itself sold such goods under the Dunhill name in the United Kingdom.

5–102   Whitford J.'s explanation of what the plaintiff must show to succeed in passing off (set out above) is a concise summary of the current position, albeit that the plaintiff does not have to prove a spill over reputation as such but rather a sufficient reputation such that there is a real risk that a substantial number of persons amongst the relevant section of the public would believe that there is a business connection between the plaintiff and the defendant.[52]

5–103   Where the plaintiff has used the particular mark only in relation to one type of product it can be hard to demonstrate that purchasers will assume that there is a trade connection in relation to dissimilar products or services unless the mark is particularly distinctive and widely known. In the *Lego* case the mark was

[50] Wadlow, p. 50.
[51] [1979] F.S.R. 337 at 341.
[52] *Lego System A/S v. Lego Lemelstrich Ltd* [1983] F.S.R. 155.

shown to be both distinctive and a household word.[53] The evidence submitted to the court indicated that a significant proportion of the public would associate any use of the mark LEGO with the plaintiff. As we will see, this is a particularly high threshold that few brand owners have been in a position to establish. Indeed, many of the cases relating to character merchandising have foundered because of this requirement even though the marks themselves were widely known.[54]

(i) Misrepresentation

5-104   The plaintiff must show that there has been a misrepresentation as a result of the use of the mark or the get up by the defendant and that this has led consumers to believe that the goods in question originate from the plaintiff or are in some other way connected with the plaintiff. The issue of misrepresentation is dependant on the extent of the plaintiff's goodwill since if the plaintiff can not show that its reputation extends to a particular field then no use of the offending sign in that field can amount to a misrepresentation.

5-105   Whether or not the acts of the defendant complained of amount to a misrepresentation is a question of fact. It is not necessary for the plaintiff to show that consumers believe that the plaintiff is the source of the goods; it is sufficient if the consumer believes that there is a connection between the plaintiff and the defendant as a consequence of the defendant's use of the mark.[55] Prior to the *Lego* case, the court attempted to address the issue of the scope of the plaintiff's goodwill and the existence of a misrepresentation by insisting that there be a "common field of activity" between the parties.[56] In the *Uncle Mac* case, the court denied an injunction to an entertainer who broadcast a well known children's programme under the name "Uncle Mac" when he sought relief against a cereal manufacturer who began marketing a breakfast cereal under then name "Uncle Mac's Puffed Wheat" with the slogan "Uncle Mac loves children and children love Uncle Mac". The court held that, in the absence of fraud, there could only be confusion if there was a "common field of activity" between the plaintiff and the defendant. The court took the view that consumers would not connect the entertainer with the defendant's cereal product due to the diversity of their respective fields of business. Because their business interests were considered to be so different, there was held to be no misrepresentation or damage to the plaintiff.

5-106   In the *Lego* case, however, Falconer J. interpreted the requirement to show a "common field of activity" as a shorthand reference to the need to show a real possibility of confusion. Thus an injunction was granted to Lego, even though the defendant operated in an entirely separate and distinct area of business. Two of the key factors in reaching this decision were the widespread recognition of the Lego name and its unique association with the plaintiff. Falconer J. concluded that:

> "if . . . the plaintiff's mark has become part of the English language in the sense that everybody associates LEGO with a particular company, namely the manufacturers of LEGO toy construction sets and building bricks, then the misrepresentation by the defendant's use of the mark is easier to assume and to prove; on the other hand, if the mark or name concerned has only a

---

[53] *ibid.*
[54] See for example *Tavener Rutledge Ltd v. Trexapalm* [1975] F.S.R. 479.
[55] *Ewing (trading as Buttercup Dairy Company) v. Buttercup Margarine Company Ltd* (1917) 34 R.P.C. 105 and *Bulmer (HP) Ltd & Anr v. J Bollinger SA & Anr* [1978] R.P.C. 79.
[56] *McCulloch v. Lewis A May (Produce Distributors) Ltd* [1947] 2 All E.R. 845 (the "*Uncle Mac*" case).

limited field of recognition it is obviously more difficult to establish its understanding as denoting the plaintiff's goods in a field which is not directly comparable with the field of that plaintiff's goods."[57]

Although Falconer J. is credited with the demise of the requirement to show a common field of activity in the United Kingdom, in truth he simply restated the need to show a real possibility of confusion, which is dependent upon the likelihood of consumers believing that the new product or business is in some way connected with the original product or business.

5–107   In Australia the requirement to show a common field of activity was laid to rest much earlier in the case of *Henderson v. Radio Corporation Pty Ltd.*[58] In this case the court formally rejected the common field of activity concept, taking the view that the defendant's activities were a misappropriation of the plaintiff's goodwill rather than a misrepresentation. The case signalled what was to be a change in approach of the Australian Court of Appeal to instances of both character merchandising and the use of established brand names or marks on dissimilar goods compared to its English counterpart. Although the Australian case was referred to by Falconer J. in his judgment, it did not influence his reasoning as regards the meaning of the "common field of activity". Instead, his decision was said to be based on *obiter dicta* of Lord Diplock in *Erven Warnink BV v. J. Townend & Sons (Hull) Ltd*[59] which indicated that a cause of action may lie in passing off even though the plaintiff and defendant are not competing traders in the same line of business.

5–108   The test of a likelihood of confusion referred to by Falconer J. could be said to correspond to the marketing concept of the "perceived fit" of the third party product within the brand personality of the original brand. If the product "fits" with the original brand, in a marketing sense, then it is likely that consumers will believe that there is a connection between the original brand owner and the third party brand. Such an approach is supported by the findings in the *Stringfellow*,[60] *Dunhill*[61] and *Marigold*[62] cases although not by the *Wombles* case[63] where although use of the mark on rubbish skips could be said to "fit" within the concept of the brand the court found that there was no likelihood of confusion. It, could however, be said that this case forms an exception simply because it relates to character merchandising rather than to a brand *per se*.

5–109   The exact nature of the misrepresentation that must be shown by the plaintiff remains, however, in some doubt. For example, in the *Harrods* case[64] it was said that a connection by way of sponsorship would not be sufficient, rather the plaintiff must be considered by the consumer as in some way responsible for the quality of the allegedly infringing goods. This can present a problem for the owner of the original mark as in the case of a mark like the Manchester United badge or Smirnoff logo, where the mark is applied to, for example, the front of a pullover or sweatshirt that is known by the consumer to be manufactured by a particular third party such as Umbro or Fruit of the Loom. In such cases, do consumers assume that

---

[57] *Lego System A/S v. Lego Lemelstrich Ltd* [1983] F.S.R. 155 at 187.
[58] [1969] R.P.C. 218, CA.
[59] [1980] R.P.C. 31, HL at 93.
[60] [1984] R.P.C. 501, CA.
[61] [1979] F.S.R. 337, CA.
[62] *LRC International Ltd v. Lilla Edets Sales Co. Ltd* [1973] R.P.C. 560.
[63] *Wombles Ltd v. Wombles Skips Ltd* [1975] F.S.R. 488.
[64] At 713.

there is a connection between the brand owner and the marker of the garment, and if so what sort of connection? Does the consumer believe that the brand owner is responsible for the quality of the garment, even if the third party manufacturer has a stronger reputation in the field in question than the brand owner? If not, what is the function of the brand name or mark in such a situation?[65] If the garment is made by a recognised third party the consumer may well believe that there is a connection but not necessarily one involving quality control in respect of the garment. In such a situation, according to Millett L.J. in *Harrods*, the plaintiff would not be entitled to relief as against an unauthorised third party using the mark in a similar situation as no misrepresentation has been made by the third party as to quality control. This is a problem commonly experienced in relation to character merchandising and personality merchandising where it is said that consumers seek to acquire the representation of the mark itself rather than the thing marked. In other words, the function of the mark is purely decorative. In such circumstances it is argued that the mark does not serve to indicate origin and accordingly its use can not be protected by means of passing off. Laddie J. emphasised this point in his forthright comments (albeit *obiter*) in the *Elvis Presley* case[66]:

> "When people buy a toy of a well known character because it depicts that character, I have no reason to believe that they care one way or the other who made, sold or licensed it. When a fan buys a poster or a cup bearing an image of his star, he is buying a likeness, not a product from a particular source. Similarly the purchaser of any one of the myriad of cheap souvenirs of the royal wedding bearing pictures of prince Charles and Diana Princess of Wales, want momentoes with likenesses. He is likely to be indifferent as to the source."

Although Laddie J. was addressing the question of trade mark use in the context of opposition proceedings his comments (which were endorsed by the Court of Appeal) are indicative of the judicial attitude towards to the use of marks in a decorative manner rather than to indicate a trade connection.

5–111   If, however, the plaintiff can show that the consumer is aware of the existence of licensing arrangements and believes that he/she is purchasing "genuine goods" because of the use of the mark then it may be possible to prevent unauthorised use on the basis that consumers are misled into believing that the goods are genuine when they are not.[67] The difficulty with this approach is that it assumes that consumers care whether or not the goods are genuine. This argument was raised by Laddie J. in the *Elvis Presley* case which concerned the registration of three Elvis Presley trade marks and an opposition by the proprietor of the earlier registration, Elvisly Yours. Laddie J. questioned the use of representations of the singer Elvis Presley on a range of merchandise and in particular whether the marks indicated source or were simply decorative. Although the facts of the case are quite different to a situation of passing off his question is equally relevant to situations involving designer clothes or sportswear prominently displaying the name or mark

---

[65] For further discussion of this particular point see Isaac "Merchandising or Fundraising?: Trade Marks and the Diana, Princess of Wales Memorial Fund" [1998] E.I.P.R. 441 where it is suggested that in such circumstances the mark may act as a certification mark. See also Belson "Brand Protection in the Age of the Internet" [1999] E.I.P.R. 481, for a discussion of the changing role of trade marks from indications or source to certifications marks as a result of extensive licensing.
[66] *Re Elvis Presley* trade marks [1997] R.P.C. 543 (hereafter the "*Elvis Presley*" case).
[67] This was an argument that found favour in the *Ninja Turtles* case.

of, say, Nike or Calvin Klein. If it can be shown that consumers are indifferent as to whether the goods are genuine (or not) this could defeat the argument.

(j) Damage

5–112   In addition to a misrepresentation and goodwill, the plaintiff must also show that it will suffer damage as a consequence of the defendant's actions. If there is a possibility of confusion but no damage the action will fail.[68] The damage may take the form of an inability to diversify or extend the plaintiff's business as in the *Marigold* case[69] where an injunction was granted by the High Court against a defendant who had launched a brand of toilet paper under the name Marigold. The plaintiff already used the name Marigold in respect of rubber gloves and babies pants and was considering extending the use of the brand to other articles including nappy liners and disposable nappies. In view of the plaintiff's existing reputation and its intention to expand into what was regarded as a "similar" area to the defendant's, there was said to be a real risk of confusion and accordingly an injunction was granted.

5–113   When considering the question of the damage suffered by the plaintiff Lego, Falconer J. took into account the fact that:

> "licensing or franchising another trader to use LEGO in the gardening equipment area would be lost if the defendants are allowed to continue using LEGO . . . in relation to their products".[70]

He went on to find that loss of this licensing opportunity would constitute damage to the goodwill of the LEGO name. Thus the loss of a licensing opportunity was regarded as sufficient damage upon which to succeed in an action for passing off. However, damage to merchandising potential generally is not considered to be a sufficient basis upon which to grant relief.[71]

5–114   In *Newsweek Inc v. The British Broadcasting Corporation*[72] interlocutory relief was refused by the Court of Appeal because *inter alia* the proposed extension of the plaintiff's business activities into the field of broadcasting was considered to be too speculative to be taken into account. The plaintiff had sought to prevent the defendant adopting the descriptive name "Newsweek" as the title of a news related television programme on the basis of its prior use of the mark in connection with a current affairs magazine. In addition to finding that the mark was largely descriptive and not widely known the Court of Appeal held that there was very little likelihood of confusion.

5–115   The loss of licensing opportunity is not the only form of damage that is recognised by the court. The courts have, in exceptional circumstances, also granted relief against tarnishment and dilution. For example, in *Annabel's (Berkeley Square) Ltd v. G Schock*[73] the damage to the goodwill of the plaintiff's night-club, known as Annabel's, took the form of the lowering of its reputation in the estimation of the public as a consequence of the subsequent use of the same name in connection with the defendant's escort agency. This was one of the first cases

---

[68] See *Stringfellow*.
[69] *LRC International Ltd v. Lilla Edets Sales Co. Ltd* [1973] R.P.C. 560.
[70] *ibid.* p. 194.
[71] *Stringfellow* case.
[72] [1979] R.P.C. 441, CA.
[73] [1972] R.P.C. 838.

where "tarnishment" that is, use that is detrimental to the character or repute of the plaintiff's mark by lowering its reputation, was accepted by the court as a valid head of damage.

5–116 The *Elderflower Champagne* case[74] was the first case in which the Court of Appeal acknowledged that dilution was an acceptable head of damage in a claim for passing off. Dilution in this case took the form of blurring or erosion of the uniqueness of the mark champagne such that the reputation is debased.

5–117 In the *Harrods*[75] case, however, a differently constituted Court of Appeal held by a majority (Millett and Beldam L.JJ.) that dilution, without evidence of confusion, was not sufficient to succeed in a passing off action. Thus reinforcing the view that a misrepresentation is still an essential element of the tort. In that case the plaintiff, the famous retail store, sought an injunction to stop the defendant's use of the name "The Harrodian School" on the basis of passing off. The defendant argued that the name was not intended to have any reference to the plaintiff but was chosen because the site on which the school was built was known locally by that name because the plaintiff had previously owned a club on the site. Relief was refused at first instance and on appeal the decision was affirmed, based principally on the fact that there was no evidence of confusion. According to Millett L.J., it was not sufficient for the plaintiff merely to show that the public would make a connection between the plaintiff's and defendant's businesses. Rather, the plaintiff had to show that the public considered that it was responsible for the quality of the defendant's goods/services. Millett L.J. acknowledged that the requirement to show a common field of activity referred to in the *Uncle Mac* case had been discredited on the basis that it was "contrary to numerous previous authorities" however, he stressed that whilst the lack of a common field of activity was not fatal it was not irrelevant either. Quoting Slade L.J. in the *Stringfellow* case,[76] he emphasised that the further removed from one another the respective fields of activities, the less likely it was that any member of the public could reasonably be confused into thinking that the one business was connected with the other.

5–118 Commenting on the question of whether dilution was a sufficient form of damage to justify relief, Millett L.J. said that:

> "Erosion of the distinctiveness of a brand name has been recognised as a form of damage to the goodwill of the business with which the name is connected in a number of cases, particularly in Australia and New Zealand; but unless care is taken this could mark an unacceptable extension to the tort of passing off. To date the law has not sought to protect the value of the brand name as such, but the value of the good will which it generates; and insists on proof of confusion to justify its intervention. But the erosion of the distinctiveness of a brand name which occurs by reason of its degeneration into common use as a generic term is not necessarily dependent on confusion at all . . . I have an intellectual difficulty in accepting the concept that the law insists upon the presence of both confusion and damage and yet recognises as sufficient a head of damage which does not require confusion."

In contrast, in a dissenting judgment, Sir Michael Kerr said that in his view both the misrepresentation and the likelihood of confusion were self evident. The public

---

[74] *Taittinger SA v. Allbev Ltd* [1993] F.S.R. 641.
[75] *Harrods Ltd v. Harrodian School Ltd* [1996] R.P.C. 697, CA.
[76] *Stringfellow Ltd v. McCain Foods GB Ltd* [1984] R.P.C. 501, CA at 535.

would, he said, be confused into thinking that the plaintiff was somehow "mixed up with" the defendant's school, that this amounted to misappropriation and the damage suffered was the dilution and loss of control of the plaintiff's reputation as a result of the mistaken belief that the two businesses were connected. As Carty observes, the language used by Sir Michael Kerr is much more in keeping with a claim for unfair competition or misappropriation rather than passing off and for this reason his comments can not be said to fall squarely within existing jurisprudence.[77]

5–119   Whilst the *Harrods* case may be criticised as being weak authority for the proposition that passing off can be relied upon to protect a mark against dilution, it is indicative of the problems associated with the concept of dilution generally and the struggle to fit the concept within the existing framework of legal protection. Whilst dilution of itself does not require confusion it continues to be confined to situations where it is a necessary pre-requisite. If the courts were to accept that dilution is actionable in the absence of confusion, then passing off could well develop into something akin to a law of unfair competition, albeit that such a development would be at odds with the roots of the tort. As it is, although dilution has been recognised to some degree it remains limited to a head of damage and a likelihood of confusion remains an essential requirement of the tort

CONCLUSION

5–120   At the beginning of this chapter the question was raised as to whether stretching the use of a brand name across a wide range of goods/services can strengthen or weaken the protection afforded to a brand owner. We have seen that, from a marketing point of view, there is a danger in over exposing or over stretching the brand (*i.e.* using the brand name on too many or too diverse a range of products) such that the personality and distinctiveness of the brand itself is lost or diluted. Equally, licensing the use of a mark in connection with a broad range of goods/services can cause the mark to be viewed as purely decorative and not as an indication of origin. This in turn can result in a lower level of protection being granted by the courts in respect of trade mark infringement because the courts will only enjoin use which gives rise to confusion as to origin and arguably if the use of the mark is purely decorative there can be no confusion. Thus licensing can weaken the protection available in the United Kingdom.

5–121   On the other hand, use of the brand name by the proprietor across a wide range of goods may not suffer the same fate if it can be said that the mark is actually indicative of source. If, however, the mark itself is descriptive or is a graphic representation and is not used on labels, etc., but only used decoratively then it may still be vulnerable to challenge on the basis that it is not used as a mark and similar unauthorised use by third parties may be difficult to prevent.

5–122   Comparing the protection afforded under section 10(3) (as interpreted by Knox J. and Deputy Judge Crystal Q.C.) with that available at common law, it can be seen that there is little difference between them. Both require the plaintiff's mark to be distinctive and to have a reputation amongst a significant proportion of the relevant public (although passing off requires goodwill, rather than a mere reputation). Although passing off requires a likelihood of confusion and, on the face of it section 10(3) of the TMA 1994 does not, in reality, in view of the way in

---

[77] See "Passing Off at the Crossroads" [1996] E.I.P.R. 629 at 631.

which the section has been interpreted to date and the criteria needed to establish that an unfair advantage has been taken, or a detriment suffered, the plaintiff must at least show a likelihood of association which is not that far removed from the position under passing off. Whilst section 10(3) is arguably broader because of the comparison "mark for sign" which disregards extraneous matter (such as any disclaimer as to authorisation) passing off takes into account all the circumstances.

5–123 In Australia the law of passing off has been extended by the courts to provide relief in situations where there has been misappropriation of reputation (notably in the field of character merchandising[78]) based on the defendant's use of the plaintiff's mark or other indicia associated with the plaintiff. Protection is granted on the basis that the use of indicia (such as the name or likeness of a character or personality) recognised as being associated with the plaintiff misleads the consumer into believing that there is a connection between the plaintiff and defendant which causes damage to the plaintiff. It is not, however, necessary to show confusion, it is sufficient to show that the defendant has sought to reap where he has not sown, or to take advantage of the plaintiff's goodwill. It has been suggested by Carty[79] that the extension of the law of passing off in this way to provide protection in the absence of consumer confusion is at odds with the root of the tort in protecting goodwill, rather than the mark *per se*.

5–124 Greater protection may be available in the United Kingdom under the tort of passing off than under trade mark infringement, if it can be shown that consumers are misled into believing that a connection exists between the plaintiff's and the defendant's goods. However, the risk of confusion remains an essential ingredient. A brand owner is more likely to be successful under passing off if the brand name or mark is inherently distinctive and is widely known as in the *Lego* case.

5–125 It is unlikely that passing off will be extended in the United Kingdom as far as it has been in Australia since, despite the comments of Sir Michael Kerr in *Harrods*, the majority view remains that the primary function of trade marks is to indicate origin, they are not assets protectable in their own right.

5–126 Although section 10(3) of the TMA 1994 has the potential to provide greater protection to brand owners when their marks are used by a third party on dissimilar goods, the current restricted interpretation of this section with its emphasis on the need to show a connection between the plaintiff's goods and those of the defendant has seriously reduced the effectiveness of the section such that it now adds little to the existing law of passing off. Unless and until the courts find a more appropriate means of assessing whether, in the absence of confusion, an unfair advantage has been taken, or a detriment suffered, it is feared that protection under section 10(3) will remain limited and reliance on the law of passing off will remain the brand owner's main recourse.

5–127 In Australia it has been recognised that:

> "[t]he rejection of a general tort of unfair competition or unfair trading does not involve a denial of the desirability of adopting a flexible approach to traditional forms of action when such an approach is necessary to adapt them to meet new situations and circumstances".[80]

---

[78] See *Hogan v. Pacific Dunlop Ltd* (1988) 83 A.L.R. 403 and *Hogan v. Koala Dundee* (1988) 83 A.L.R. 187.
[79] "Dilution and Passing off: Cause for Concern" [1996] 112 L.Q.R. 632.
[80] Deane J. *Moorgate Tobacco Co. Ltd v. Philip Morris Ltd (No. 2)* 56 A.L.R. 193 at 214.

It is suggested that the Australian court has indeed adopted a more flexible approach in extending the tort of passing off to provide protection against the unauthorised appropriation of a person's reputation or goodwill.

5–128 Although, as Sir Michael Kerr observes in the *Harrods* case, there is growing recognition that a mark is a valuable asset in its own right and unauthorised use of that asset by a third party can take unfair advantage of the investment made by its owner and cause damage to the distinctiveness or reputation of the mark. The courts have so far shown themselves to be reluctant to increase the scope of protection available to brand owners on the basis that "monopolies should not be so readily created".[81] But such a view misconstrues the nature of the monopoly. Granting a brand owner the exclusive right to use a particular name or mark on products/services does not create a monopoly in products/services *per se,* others remain free to compete with the brand owner albeit under another name or mark. All that the brand owner obtains is exclusivity in relation to a particular word or mark with which it has established a reputation and brand image or personality through substantial investment in advertising and marketing promotion. In my view, the brand owner should be free to use such a mark himself or to license a third party to do so. He should not have to hope that no third party will pre-empt him by adopting the mark for use in an unrelated product area. Nor should the brand owner be concerned to show that the licensed mark is being used to indicate source—it should be sufficient that his mark adorns a product. To allow a third party to exploit the unauthorised use of another's mark, whether disclaimers are used or not, should not, in my view, be encouraged as the third party is simply free riding on the back of the goodwill/reputation engendered in the mark by the brand owner.

5–129 Stretching the use of a brand name or mark from one product area to another is an indication of the strength of the intangible aspects of a brand. Whilst some brands are more elastic than others there should be no reason to deny the brand owner protection against those who would seek to obtain a commercial advantage at their expense.[82]

---

[81] *per* Simon Brown L.J. in the *Elvis Presley* case.
[82] This is discussed further in Chap. 8.

CHAPTER 6

Advertising and Promotion

INTRODUCTION

6–01 So far we have considered the commercial importance of the physical aspects of a brand—product appearance, product packaging and associated merchandising—and we have also looked at the legal protection available to these different facets of a brand. We will now turn to consider what is traditionally regarded as a separate area of marketing namely, advertising, promotion and sponsorship (together referred to as "brand promotion"). Whilst all three aspects of brand promotion play an important part in the way that a brand is developed, the main focus of this chapter will be on the role played by advertising since advertising is usually the main form of brand promotion used. The aim of this chapter is to show that the different aspects of brand promotion contribute to the overall "gestalt" of a brand by associating the brand with particular imagery, positive associations and emotional values.[1] We will see that brand promotion is an essential part of building and maintaining a brand and helps to inform the consumer about the product and in the process helps to reduce the time spent by the consumer in making purchasing decisions.

6–02 Whilst economists recognise the importance of informative brand promotion, on the basis that a perfect market demands perfect enlightenment of those who buy and sell, criticism is often levelled against persuasive advertising because it does not increase demand as a whole, it only increases wants and it uses up resources in the process.[2] Does this mean that persuasive advertising is ineffective? Not at all, but as we shall see the effectiveness of advertising in increasing markets is open to debate.[3]

6–03 As we consider the legal protection of brand promotion, we will see that the level of protection currently available is limited. Indeed, the technical nature of the law of copyright and the limitations in the application of the tort of passing off to situations involving confusion or deception, very often result in the denial of protection to the advertiser in spite of the defendant's intention to trade off the benefit of the plaintiff's brand promotion. Those, like Brown,[4] that believe that persuasive advertising is wasteful of resources and of dubious social utility, also argue that the courts should not protect interests deriving from it. In other words, opponents of persuasive advertising argue that the advertising function of trade names, trade symbols and advertising generally should be denied legal protection in the interests of free competition provided that any use of these elements by competitors does not confuse or deceive consumers.

---

[1] See Chap. 1, paras 1–11 and 1–55 for further discussion concerning the meaning of "gestalt".
[2] Brown "Advertising and the Public Interest: Legal Protection of Trade Symbols" (1948) 57 Yale L.J. 1165 ("Brown") at 1168.
[3] See Kyle "The Impact of Advertising on Markets",(1982) *Journal of Advertising*, 345 ("Kyle").
[4] Brown, p. 1190.

6–04 These arguments are similar to those expressed by the Privy Council in the *Pub Squash*[5] case (discussed below at paragraph 6–49) where Lord Scarman emphasised the need to balance the competing interests of the protection of the plaintiff's investment in his product and his advertising and the protection of free competition. The balance is, without doubt, a fine one—but have we currently got the balance right? As we look at the process of brand promotion, its role in the creation of successful brands, and at the legal protection available, we need to ask ourselves this question again and again.

ADVERTISING—A MEANS OF COMMUNICATION

6–05 The Report of the EEC Committee on the Environment, Public Health and Consumer Protection[6] defined advertising as:

> ". . . the process of persuasion, using the paid media, in which purchasers of goods, services or ideas are sought. Its primary aim is to convince the consumer to obtain the advertiser's product/service and/or his specific brand. Advertising is thus a commercial message designed to influence consumer behaviour".

Advertising is the process of communication between the brand owner/manufacturer and the consumer. Without advertising, the consumer would not be aware of technical advances, the development of new brands or improvements in existing brands. The consumer might be unaware of how a particular product worked, how it might meet the consumer's needs or the context in which it could be used. Advertising is therefore part of a dialogue with consumers about the brand, introducing the consumer to the brand and explaining the brand to them in terms of product benefits and attributes. Market research enables the brand owner to obtain feedback from the consumer and to complete the dialogue. Advertising is communication. It seeks to convey information to the consumer about aspects of a particular brand. It can take many and various forms and may involve a variety of media. Although virtually any communication between brand owners and consumers could be regarded as an advertisement, for the purposes of this chapter we will limit ourselves to radio and television commercials, posters and print media (*e.g.* newspapers, magazines, etc.).

6–06 The importance of advertising is underlined by the commitment of brand owners to spending vast sums of money on the promotion of their brands. It is not only manufacturers who are spending significant sum of money in advertising, indeed, in 1996 the top 10 brands ranked in terms of media spend, were all retailers or service providers.[7] The number one brand was BT, which spent £54.73 million in connection with its "call stimulation" campaign. Cocoa Cola, the leading consumer goods brand, was ranked 28th with a media spend of £15.17 million.

ADVERTISING EFFECTIVENESS

6–07 Whilst the ability of advertising to convey information is welcomed by consumer groups and economists, its role in persuading customers to purchase

---

[5] *Cadbury Schweppes Pty Limited v. Pub Squash Pty Ltd* [1981] R.P.C. 429 ("*Pub Squash*").
[6] Cm (1991) 0147 final — C30337/91 — SYN343 PE154.377/fin, p. 15.
[7] Campaign Report April 25, 1997.

products is open to continued criticism and debate. The effectiveness of advertising is a very contentious subject and is one that has received renewed attention in recent years, particularly from financial directors in large organisations looking to save money by reducing what appear to be inflated advertising budgets. In defence of advertising effectiveness, the IPA has sought to argue that advertising should be regarded as investment in a brand and on this basis is seeking to gain recognition for the premise that advertising spend should be entered on the balance sheet as an indicator of the value of a brand.[8] Such a proposal does not, however, address the question of effectiveness as such, but rather assumes that it is. In his paper, *The Impact of Advertising on Markets*,[9] Kyle identified a two horned dilemma which researchers in the advertising industry face and from which they have not yet established a means of extracting themselves[10]:

> "The dilemma is this: if advertising is effective in increasing (for example) sales of alcoholic drink, it can quite easily be accused of being nothing more than an anti-social tool, the properties of which range from those of a propaganda device of Orwelliam proportions, an uncontrolled, insidious, persuasive activity capable of changing consumers' 'desires', to the more academic ideas . . . that it is a means by which large capitalist corporations (often multi-national) control demands. . .
>
> To deny such results appears to raise the other dilemma—that if advertising has no effect in raising sales of brand product categories or in moulding consumers' tastes . . . then it must be wasteful."

6–08 In his analysis Kyle distinguishes between the effect of advertising at a macro level, that is the level of consumption of a market generally, and sales of a particular product or brand, at the micro level. The difficulty of analysing the effectiveness of advertising at the micro level is that so many different variables can affect the consumer's ultimate decision to purchase the brand that it is difficult, he says, to obtain any meaningful results. Although, as Kyle observes, a large proportion of continuous market research is devoted to the collection of measures such as awareness, intentions to buy, penetration and usage surveyors (all part of the model of the consumer buying process).

6–09 At the macro level, the aggregation of existing brands of the same product, such as tea (which may be regarded as part of the hot drinks market or part of a wider non-alcoholic drinks market), leads to difficulties because it is not clear at what stage different components of the market (*e.g.* milk and tea) become competitors. Research carried out in respect of aggregate consumption in the United States has shown that there is little support for the hypothesis that total advertising has any effect upon total consumption.[11] This has been confirmed by similar studies in the United Kingdom.[12]

6–10 One answer to this problem is perhaps to consider the effectiveness of advertising on the market sector as a whole and then disaggregate the different

---

[8] Butterfield and Haigh, "Understanding the Financial Value of Brands" *IPA Report* 1998.
[9] See n.3 above.
[10] (1982) *Journal of Advertising*, 345 at 345
[11] Kyle, p. 348 quoting from research conducted by Ashley, Granger & Schmalensee, "Advertising and Aggregate Consumption: An Analysis of Causality" (1980) *Econometrica* 48 (July).
[12] Kyle, p. 348 quoting from Sturgess, "Dispelling the Myth: The Effects of Total Advertising Expenditure on Aggregate Consumption" 1(3) *Journal of Advertising: The Quarterly Review of Marketing Communications* 201.

parts of the market and consider these areas separately. The effectiveness of advertising on a market at a slightly less aggregated level in relation to cigarettes (originally part of the tobacco market) confirmed that advertising did not have an effect on the level of consumption of cigarettes as a whole leaving Kyle to conclude that further disaggregation was necessary.[13] Where a market is disaggregated to the level of substitutability he suggests that advertising will have an effect.

6–11 Whether it is possible to disaggregate the market to a level that is not distorted by consumer behaviour is open to debate. Certainly, brand owners try to analyse the effectiveness of their own advertising campaigns (although the criteria chosen as the basis for the analysis are often strongly criticised). The strongest evidence for the effectiveness of advertising is a brand with a significant market share where the differences between competing brands are small and the product itself is low risk, or low involvement, in that it does not require detailed analysis or understanding by the consumer prior to purchase. One such product is the Andrex brand of toilet tissue. Andrex is by far the biggest brand in this market and has been since the early 1960's when soft toilet tissue became the norm.[14] Further, Andrex is not only the biggest brand in the toilet tissue market, it is also the most expensive and the fastest selling brand in the mark.[15] Research has shown that Andrex is significantly preferred by consumers. Not only does it perform well in blind tests but it is marketable preferred when branded as Andrex rather than as an unnamed product. As Baker notes:

"This branded over blind preference effectively shows Andrex 'added value'— that is the value attributed to a brand over and above its functional attributes. Bearing in mind the nature of the product, the size of this 'added value' is exceptional".

6–12 The explanation for the popularity of the Andrex brand as against competing brands of toilet tissue is said to be the advertising campaign used by Andrex involving a Labrador puppy. The advertising is exceptionally well remembered by consumers and has been effective in communicating the essential features of the product, namely its softness, strength and length. The puppy first appeared in the advertising for Andrex in 1972 and has been a consistent feature in advertisements ever since. As a result of the advertising campaign the puppy is now inextricably linked with the Andrex brand, although it does not feature at all on the product packaging. Despite frequent attempts by competitors to launch competing products it has continued to maintain its lead both in terms of price and market share. This cannot be accounted for on the basis of the quality of the product alone but must at least in part be due to the positive associations that consumers have of the brand as a result of the advertising.

"Econometric modelling has shown [the Andrex] advertising to have had a strong positive influence on Andrex's sales. Over the last 10 years, OHAL estimate that TV advertising has accounted for 20-25 million cases which at current prices is in excess of £300m for a MEAL listed expenditure of £54m".[16]

---

[13] Sinnot, Gillian and Kyle, *The Relationship Between Total Cigarette Advertising and Total Cigarette Consumption in the UK* (Metra Limited, London, 1979). See also Boddewyn, "Cigarette Advertising Bans and Smoking: The Flawed Policy Connection" (1994) 13 *International Journal of Advertising* 311.
[14] Advertising works number 7, IPA Advertising Effectiveness Awards 1992 ed. Chris Baker, (NTC Publications Limited, 1993), p. 53.
[15] *ibid.* p. 55.
[16] *ibid.* p. 53.

Thus it seems, that whilst it is difficult to prove that advertising is effective at the macro level, advertising can be very effective at the micro level, but what makes an advertisement effective?

THE DECISION MAKING PROCESS

6–13 The classical model of consumer decision making divides the process into six steps of buyer readiness from brand awareness, to knowledge, liking, preference, conviction and finally to purchase.[17] Consumers are said to ascend through these stages of readiness from first hearing of a brand to actual purchase of the brand. The steps are not necessarily equidistant. Some products will be approached by consumers with more caution than others depending upon the risk factor (*e.g.* the economic commitment or greater psychological commitment). Products that are "low risk" are not likely to involve a great amount of conscious decision making. Once brand loyalty has been established less time will be spent on the decision making process. Branding thus assists in establishing simple decision rules and so helps to reduce the time spent consciously making a decision for frequently used products.[18] Although this hierarchical approach to decision making may be criticised as being inadequate, the model offers a useful framework within which to consider how advertising works.[19]

6–14 Depending upon the nature of the brand in question and how long it has been established, the corresponding advertising may focus upon one or more particular facets of the decision making process. Typically, advertising for a new brand will focus, at least initially, on the provision of information (*i.e.* brand awareness and knowledge) with prominent and frequent references to the brand name and with an emphasis on the novel aspects of the particular product. Once a degree of awareness has been established, the advertiser will change the emphasis in advertisements with a view to developing more persuasive advertising, emphasising product characteristics, notably the intangible aspects of the brand, to enable the consumer to understand the brand and to be able to differentiate it from competing products and so develop a preference for the product. Once the brand has become established, the objective in the advertising will usually be to remind consumers of the product and to address consumer perceptions of the brand, as Arnold notes[20]:

> "As it becomes harder to find any other differentiator than 'image', 'reputation' or 'personality', promotion becomes ever more important. The added values of a brand start and end with consumer perception. As it is communication which feeds perception, promotion is necessarily the heart of branding".

6–15 Brands such as Cocoa-Cola and Andrex, that have been on the market for a considerable length of time and for which there is already a high level of brand awareness, need to place particular emphasis on the brand image, that is how consumers perceive the brand, in order to differentiate themselves from competing products which the consumer might otherwise perceive as being the same.

---

[17] Kotler *et al*, p. 687.
[18] Chisnall, *Consumer Behaviour* (McGraw Hill, London, 3rd ed., 1994) p. 294, ("Chisnall").
[19] For further discussion of the criticisms of hierarchical models of advertising see Chisnall at 294 and 295.
[20] *The Handbook of Brand Management* (*Financial Times*, Pitman Publishing, London, 1993), p. 158.

THE FORM AND CONTENT OF ADVERTISING

6–16 Lord Leverhume, the founder of the Anglo-Dutch corporation Unilever, is famously quoted as saying that half of his advertising was ineffective but the problem was knowing which half. Research conducted into the effectiveness of advertising has confirmed that only 46 per cent of advertising campaigns for established brands showed a positive impact on sales although the percentage is slightly higher at 59 per cent for new products.[21]

6–17 Why is advertising so hit and miss? Human communication is a complex process. Society does not respond uniformly to the same stimuli because of the loyalties, prejudices, desire for self interest and experience of past incidents innate in each of its members. It is therefore impossible for advertising to generate a uniform effect. For example, one of the slogans used in the United Kingdom by the mobile telephone company Orange was "The future is bright. The future is Orange". Use of this slogan in Northern Ireland might have a serious detrimental affect on consumer perception because of the political associations of the colour orange. This interference with the message communicated through advertising is known as "noise" and leads to distortions of the message communicated.

6–18 In order to build an advertising campaign the advertiser or sender of the communication needs to define the objective of the advertisement, whether it be to raise awareness, build comprehension of the brand or maintain its profile. Once the objective has been defined (the message content) the message needs to be encoded into symbolic form *i.e.* into words and illustrations that will be used for the advertisement (message format).

In order to succeed in its objective the message must gain attention, hold interest in the brand, create desire for the brand and result in action, *e.g.* actual purchase of the brand and all this must be achieved within 30 seconds! This process is sometimes referred to by the acronym AIDA.[22] To achieve this the sender may use rational, emotional or moral appeals.

6–19 Different forms of advertising may be employed by advertisers to convey the message to the relevant target market. As the first task of any advertisement is to gain attention some advertisers choose to use striking or shocking subject-matter. Benetton, for example, has used this technique on a number of occasions using contentious images that have included human foetuses, a blood spattered army uniform and German Olympians giving the Nazi salute.[23] The various forms of advertising used by manufacturers include:

- conventional advertising—focusing upon the brand and its characteristics

- shock tactics—*e.g.* Calvin Klein and Benetton—using particular settings that offend public morals;

- comparative advertising—comparing one brand directly or indirectly with those of a competitor;

- tandem advertising—advertising one product on the back of another;

- product sponsorship—endorsing an event or programme to raise awareness and build brand associations;

---

[21] See Abraham & Lodish, p. 521 and Mercer "Marketing".
[22] Kotler *et al*, p. 691.
[23] *The Independent on Sunday,* July 30, 1995.

- ambush marketing—particularly in the context of sports sponsorship— using advertisements that use associations with an event so as to suggest a connection;

- product placement—endorsement through contextual use in say a film or TV programme;

- celebrity endorsement—associating a particular celebrity with a particular product.

ADVERTISING REGULATION

6–20   Advertising in the United Kingdom is regulated through a matrix of civil, criminal and trade mark laws. In the main, the contents of advertisements are governed by various industry codes which form an extensive regulatory framework. The regulatory framework is run by various trade and professional bodies that make up the advertising business. The Committee of Advertising Practice ("CAP") lays down industry standard codes of conduct, the British Code of Advertising Practice ("BCAP"). The Advertising Standards of Authority jointly administers the BCAP code with the BCAP. Special codes apply to television and radio advertising.[24] In addition the Control of Misleading Advertising Regulations 1988[25] administered by the Director General of the Office of Fair Trading, sets out the statutory framework governing advertising contents and forms the backbone of the BCAP Code.

6–21   The CAP code establishes three general rules regarding all advertisements namely:

- all advertisements should be legal, decent, honest and truthful;

- all advertisements should be prepared with a sense of responsibility to consumers and to society; and

- all advertisements should respect the principles of fair competition generally accepted in business.

If the ASA considers that an advertisement is in breach of the BCAP code it can require the advertiser to withdraw or amend it. If however, the advertiser fails to remove or amend the advertisement the ASA has to rely upon other media organisations who are informed of the breach to refuse to publish the advertisement in question. Legal sanctions are only available under the control of misleading advertising regulations not under the BCAP code.[26] For this reason the ASA can be said to lack teeth. One example of a company that persistently ignored the ASA is French Connection Ltd whose advertising campaign involving the letters "FCUK" was the subject of several complaints. French Connection then registered the letters as a trade mark and as a result the ASA felt unable to condemn use of the trade mark.[26a] In addition to the BCAP Code advertisers need to beware actions for

---

[24] The ITC Code of Advertising Standards and Practice Autumn 1995 (ITC code) and the RA Advertising and Sponsorship Code of August 1996 (RA Code).
[25] S.I. 1988 No. 915.
[26] For further discussion of self regulation of the advertising industry see Fitzgerald, "Self Regulation of Comparative Advertising in the UK" [1997] ENT.L.R. 250.
[26a] *French Connection Ltd v. Antony Todseerom Sutton* I.P.D. February 2000.

infringement of copyright, trade mark infringement, passing off or malicious falsehood if the advertisement in any way emulates or refers to a competitor's brand or advertising.

THE LEGAL PROTECTION OF ADVERTISING

6–22   One of the risks faced by owners of an effective advertising campaign is that the campaign, or elements of it, may be copied, or emulated, by a competitor. Or, instead of imitating a brand owner's advertising, a competitor may choose to make references in its advertisements to the brand owner's products or advertising. Such references can be direct, as in the case of a comparative advertising that mentions or depicts a competitor's brand, or indirect by means or a "reply advertisement" which seeks to respond to or poke fun at a competitor's advertisement, or may take the form of a parody of it. What action, if any, can a brand owner can take to protect its advertising from such treatment?

6–23   As we have seen before, there are a matrix of different laws that regulate advertising some of which may be relied upon by a brand owner if his advertising is the subject of plagiarism. We will focus primarily on copyright, trade mark and common law protection in the form of passing off since these are the primary intellectual property rights relevant to this field. If, in addition to infringing the intellectual property rights the advertising is misleading it may well fall foul of the Control of Misleading Advertising Regulations 1988[27] causing the Director General of Fair Trading to take action and/or a complaint might also be made to the body responsible for regulating the relevant media concerned (e.g. the ASA, if it involves print media). For the purposes of this discussion, however, we will focus only on the causes of action founded on intellectual property rights since these provide brand owners with the opportunity of obtaining injunctive relief and damages.[28]

(a) Copyright infringement

6–24   As we saw in Chapter 2, copyright may be relied upon to protect *inter alia* a literary, musical or artistic work from substantial reproduction in a material form without the copyright holder's consent, during the copyright period.[29] At the risk of stating the obvious, before a brand owner can consider bringing an action for copyright infringement it is important to establish that the brand owner holds the relevant copyright. Most advertising campaigns are created by advertising agencies on behalf of the brand owner and unless there is a written assignment transferring ownership copyright will remain with the person or agency responsible for creating the work.[30]

6–25   An advertisement can include literary, musical or artistic works since, in addition to any graphical representations, there may be text, a voice over or even a soundtrack depending on whether the advertisement is in print or a radio or television commercial. For the purposes of this chapter the focus will primarily be on literary and artistic works rather than musical works since it is rare for

---

[27] S.I. 1988 No. 915.
[28] For a more detailed account of advertising law generally see Crown, *Advertising Law and Regulation* (Butterworths, London, 1998) and Campbell & Yaqub, *European Handbook on Advertising Law* (Cavendish Publishing, London, 1999). Although the latter work does not address the issue of the infringement of intellectual property rights it does consider advertising law in various jurisdictions.
[29] s.17 Copyright Designs and Patents Act 1988 ("CDPA").
[30] *Hutchison Personal Communications Ltd v. Hook Advertising Agency Ltd* [1996] F.S.R. 549.

allegations of infringement to be made in relation to the music accompanying an advertisement except in connection with claims as to authorship of the original work.

6–26 It is unusual, though not unheard of, for an advertisement to be reproduced in its entirety. In *AGL Sydney Ltd v. Shortland County Council*[31] a television commercial promoting gas as a form of domestic heating was reproduced in its entirety by the defendant who was promoting the use of electricity as a form of domestic heating. The defendant had taken sufficient of the claimant's commercial to remind viewers of it (in attempt to avoid infringement of copyright) and had added a short epilogue to the plaintiff's commercial drawing attention to the advantages of an electrical heating and hot water system over the gas system featured in the original commercial. Although the defendant argued that the plaintiff's commercial had not been reproduced since it had filmed its own commercial albeit using the same set and the same actors it was none the less held to infringe the plaintiff's copyright.

6–27 In general terms therefore, brand owners can only rely on copyright for protection where there has been an unauthorised reproduction of a copyright work such as an advertisement or a representation of the brand owner's product as for example in situations of comparative advertising.[32] In *IPC Magazines Limited v. MGN Limited*,[33] the plaintiff was the publisher of a woman's magazine called "Woman". The defendant was the publisher of The Sunday Mirror newspaper and was responsible for a television advertisement which featured a womens' magazine supplement and compared it to the plaintiff's magazine, the front cover of which appeared in the commercial. The plaintiff successfully alleged copyright infringement primarily because the whole cover of the plaintiff's magazine was depicted in the defendant's advertisement. Although the defendant tried to argue that the inclusion of the copyright work was "incidental" within the meaning of section 31 of the CDPA and therefore did not amount to infringement, the court rejected this contention and held that the inclusion of Woman magazine was an essential and important feature of the advertisement.

6–28 This case highlights a curious anomaly in the current law in that whilst it is possible to refer to a competitor's registered trade mark in comparative advertising (as detailed in Chapter 7) it is not, it seems, possible to reproduce the product's appearance. It is possible that in future situations of comparative advertising, the courts will be reluctant to enforce copyright protection in this way because of this anomaly.

6–29 The inconsistency was recognised by the European Court of Justice ("ECJ") in *Parfums Christian Dior SA v. Evora BV*[34] (discussed below at para. 6–42). It is, however, ironic that it was the submissions of the United Kingdom Government that drew the court's attention to the inconsistency stating that[35]:

". . . where enforcement by the trade mark proprietor of a parallel copyright would have the same effect as that which is objectionable in relation to a trade mark *such enforcement cannot be permitted* even if in carrying out legitimate advertising and promotion of goods a parallel trade reproduces a trade mark proprietor's copyright works." *(emphasis added)*

---

[31] [1991] E.I.P.R. D–6.
[32] The subject of comparative advertising is discussed at in Chap. 7.
[33] [1998] F.S.R. 431.
[34] [1998] E.T.M.R. 26 (the "*Dior*" case).
[35] [1997] E.T.M.R. 323 at 343.

In the *Dior* case, the ECJ restricted the protection afforded to copyright owners in relation to the reproduction of protected works in advertising, on the grounds that their rights should not be broader than the right conferred on a trade mark owner in the same circumstances.[36] Although in a practical sense this is a logical limitation[37] it is curious since the functions of and the philosophical justifications for protection under copyright and trade mark law are quite different.[38]

6–30 The consequence of the *Dior* decision for brand owners is that whilst they can seek to restrict the form and content of advertisements featuring their products prepared by authorised distributors and retailers as a matter of contract, they are not ordinarily able to prevent/restrict the form or content of advertisements prepared by independent third parties. Given the importance of advertising in building and maintaining a brand's image and market this is a significant loss of control of the communication process from the brand owner's perspective unless it is limited to representations of the product and its packaging on their own. If third parties are permitted to develop advertisement using, for example, celebrities holding or using the product, this might well interfere with the brand owner's own advertising message which could have serious repercussions for the brand image and yet, on the face of it, the brand owner would be powerless to stop it.

6–31 So far, we have considered the position relating to the reproduction of a copyright work in its entirety, however, in reality it is more likely that a competitor will seek to copy a particular image, format, idea or theme than the exact execution of the idea (although the boundary between the idea and the expression can be a very blurred one).[39] In order for there to be infringement the defendant must have copied a substantial part of the copyright work.[40] The test is qualitative rather than quantitative[41] and, according to Cornish at least, is "a major tool for giving expression to the court's sense of fair play".[42] Whilst it is clear that copyright infringement is not limited to cases of exact reproduction, there is no simple test by which to evaluate whether what has been taken (in terms of quantity and quality) is unacceptable.[43] Ultimately it is for the court to decide based on the facts of the particular case and its own sense of fairness. This can, however, lead to harsh results as in the *Norowzian* case discussed below.

6–32 *Norowzian v. Arks Limited (No. 1)*[44] concerned an advertisement for Guinness stout entitled "Anticipation". Norowzian, who was a film director, had made a short film entitled "Joy" that pioneered a new technique called "jump cut" editing or "jump cutting". The film Joy featured a man dancing to music in what was said to be a very quirky fashion. The process of "jump cut" editing involved the excising of sections of the original film within a sequence of movements by the actor such that the apparently consecutive movements undertaken by the man in the film could not actually have been undertaken. The result was the very quirky

---

[36] *ibid.* at p. 42.
[37] The Advocate General described the application of the principle of exhaustion of rights in relation to goods to the advertisement of those goods as a "common sense approach". *Parfums Christian Dior SA v. Evora BV* [1997] E.T.M.R. 323 at 334.
[38] For a more detailed consideration of the justification for protection see Chap. 8, para. 8–09 *et seq.*
[39] As discussed in Chap. 2 the distinction between idea and expression has given rise to much debate and has been the basis of much litigation over the years although the usefulness of the distinction has been questioned. See Laddie, Prescott & Vitoria, *The Modern Law of Copyright & Designs* (Butterworths, London, 2nd ed., 1995), p. 2.
[40] s.16(3) CDPA.
[41] *per* Lord Reid, *Ladbroke v. William Hill* [1964] 1 W.L.R. 273 at 276.
[42] Cornish, p. 362.
[43] *ibid.* at p. 363.
[44] [1999] E.M.L.R. 69 ("*Norowzian*").

dance. The film was not strictly speaking an advertisement but was intended to be a show reel for the purpose of eliciting business from advertising agents. One agency that was shown the film, Arks, subsequently prepared an advertisement for Guinness stout which featured a man doing a quirky dance whilst waiting for his pint to settle. The advertisement used the jump cutting technique. Although the defendant had approached the plaintiff to make the commercial the plaintiff had refused. The defendant had therefore arranged for a third party to make the film.

6–33   Despite the fact that the defendant admitted that the plaintiff's film "Joy" was the source of its original idea and that the director of the commercial "Anticipation" was given a copy of the Joy film as an instructional model from which to work, the plaintiff's copyright was held not to have been infringed. This somewhat surprising result is accounted for by the technical nature of the law of copyright. Although the overall look of the two finished films was similar, the exact movements of the two dancers were different, as was the setting. As one of the witnesses noted[45]:

> "Any similarities which do exist between 'Joy' and 'Anticipation' lie prin-cipally in the visual impact of the two works; an impact which is achieved by camera positions, and filming, cutting and editing techniques."

6–34   The plaintiff based his claim on copyright in the choreography as a dramatic work,[46] but the judge, Rattee J., concluded that the film Joy did not incorporate a dramatic work since, as a result of the jump cutting, the dance portrayed in the film could not possibly have been performed. Consequently, there could be no infringement of the dramatic work. Although the original film (*i.e.* before the editing process had been undertaken) would have had copyright protection, the plaintiff's claim that the film itself had been copied was struck out on the ground that it was "hopeless" since infringement required copying of the actual film and there had been no copying of the actual frames of the film. Despite the plaintiff's plea that this left him without protection at all the judge was unmoved. Rattee J. was of the view that Norowzian was seeking to protect the originality of his finished film (that is, the idea of the "quirky" dance) rather than the dramatic work itself and in any event it was not for him to fill any lacuna resulting from his determination of what amounted to a dramatic work.

6–35   Although *Norowzian* is an unusual case, it does highlight the problems presented by the technical nature of copyright law. Copyright law only provides a remedy where there has been a reproduction. Where the defendant reproduces the plaintiff's work unaltered then it is a question of whether the proportion taken is significant. If, however, the defendant alters or adapts the work then the issue becomes more complex depending on the degree of the alteration/adaptation. The question is whether anything substantial remains of the plaintiff's original work so as to appear to be a copy of it.[47]

6–36   Where the defendant's advertisement is a "reply" advertisement, that is, it is responding to a competitor's advertisement[48] rather than reproducing any aspect of it, there can be no risk of copyright infringement. If, on the other hand, the defendant seeks to parody the advertisement then, as far as copyright law is

---

[45] *ibid. at p. 74.*
[46] s.3(1) CDPA.
[47] *Redwood Music v. Chappell* [1982] R.P.C. 109.
[48] For example the advertisement for Kaliber beer with the text "Hello Girls" which responded to the Wonderbra advertisement "Hello Boys".

concerned, the question remains—is a substantial part of the claimant's work reproduced?[48a] Whilst it may still be possible for the author of the copyright work to object to the parody on the basis of the author's moral right there is no case law in the United Kingdom on this point to indicate whether or not such a claim might prove successful. Cornish suggests that the provisions should be interpreted in a "creative" way to allow parodies on the basis that they are a healthy source of social criticism.[49]

6-37 Whilst this may be true a parody can seriously undermine the positive associations engendered by a brand's advertising and significantly damage the brand's reputation. A careful balance therefore needs to be established.

6-38 If a defendant adopts only some elements of a plaintiff's commercial there is not only a risk that it may not be sufficient to be regarded as a substantial reproduction but also, if the defendant uses a slight variation or a different setting then it is possible that there will be no infringement. In relation to infringement of literary works such as novels or plays, it has been held that copying the plot with or without minor modifications for the purposes of reproduction in a film or a stage play[50] will constitute an infringement, even if the actual words used to work out the plot are not copied. A similar approach has been adopted in relation to non-literal copying of computer programs.[51] In relation to artistic works the court has relied upon the "look and feel" of the plaintiff's work[52] as the basis of its assessment as to whether there has been substantial copying.[53]

6-39 In the United States the "look and feel" approach has also been applied, according to Zaichkowsky,[54] to advertising cases:

> "Courts have recently begun deciding advertising copyright infringement cases by comparing the 'look and feel' of the commercial instead of single elements. The idea behind using the whole advertisement is that one would have had to see the original in order to create the infringing advertisement. This is certainly a step forward but, unfortunately, sometimes this 'look and feel' is taken apart by focusing on the different individual elements."

As Zaichkowsky notes, however, the application of the "look and feel" approach has its limitations particularly if the court undertakes a detailed scrutiny of the individual elements of an advertisement in the same way that textual copying is usually assessed.[55]

6-40 Although copyright law can in some respects appear flexible (as in the case of what amounts to a substantial reproduction) it can also be very inflexible (as in the *Norowzian* case) which can lead to harsh results. What is needed is a truly flexible framework within which courts can assess the extent to which a defendant has based his advertisement (or product packaging) on an advertisement (and product packaging) of a competitor and so decide, having regard to the overall look

---

[48a] *Williamson Music v. Pearson Partnership* [1987] F.S.R. 97.
[49] Cornish, p. 394.
[50] *Kelly v. Cinema Houses* [1928–1935] Mac. C C 362.
[51] By way of example see *John Richardson Computers Ltd v. Flanders Ltd* [1993] F.S.R. 497, *Ibcos Computers Ltd v. Barclays Finance Ltd* [1994] F.S.R. 659. See also Cornish, p. 446–450.
[52] *Bauman v. Fussell* (1953) [1978] R.P.C. 485 at 487.
[53] Again, a similar approach has been adopted in relation to computer screen displays. See Cornish, p. 454–456.
[54] *Defending Your Brand Against Imitation* (Quorum Books, Westwood, 1995), p. 79.
[55] *National Hockey League v. Pepsi-Cola Canada Ltd* Supreme Court of British Columbia No. C902104 (June 2, 1992).

of both aspects of the plaintiff's brand, whether the defendant has obtained an unfair advantage as a result of "copying" the work undertaken by the plaintiff. We will explore further in Chapter 8 the form that such a new approach might take.

(b) Trade mark infringement

6–41   As we have seen in earlier chapters it is not only possible for brand names to be registered but also for packaging and, in certain circumstances, product shapes to be registered as trade marks if they meet the criteria set out in sections 1 and 5 of the TMA and are not excluded by section 3. Equally, slogans or catch phrases used in advertisements can be registered if they meet the same criteria.[56] The difficulty for many slogans, however, is that they are primarily descriptive, or are exhortations to buy, and when first used they lack the necessary degree of distinctiveness to be accepted as trade marks. It is only after the advertisement has been used, perhaps for a number of years, that the brand owner is in a position to demonstrate secondary meaning sufficient to enable the mark to be accepted for registration.[57] As a consequence, the slogan is vulnerable to use by a third party during this time and unless the owner can make out a case of passing off there is little that the brand owner can do to prevent the slogan from being usurped (either in an identical or a modified form) by a third party.[58]

6–42   Apart from instances of comparative advertising (which are discussed in detail in the next chapter) there are few reported cases that involve the use of third party trade marks in advertising. One notable exception is *Parfums Christian Dior SA v. Evora BV*,[59] where the plaintiff initiated legal action following the defendant's use of representations of the plaintiff's fragrance products Eau Savage, Poison, Fahrenheit and Dune. Both the appearance of the respective products and the associated names were registered as trade marks and both were used in advertising by the defendant in connection with its chain of chemist shops, without the plaintiff's consent. The defendant was not part of the plaintiff's exclusive distribution network and had purchased the products on the parallel market. The plaintiff argued that the use of its trade marks in advertising, without its consent, amounted to infringement of its exclusive rights under Article 7(2) of the Trade Marks Directive[60] on the basis that the condition (that is, the prestigious nature) of the goods was impaired as a consequence of the poor quality of the advertising. The ECJ rejected this argument, however, and held that where trade-marked goods were put on the market in the Community with the consent of the trade mark owner, a reseller, besides being free to resell those goods, was also entitled to use the trade mark in order to bring the goods to the public's attention for the further commercialisation of those goods. Only if the advertising can be shown to seriously damage the reputation of the goods can the brand owner object to it by relying upon its trade mark rights.

6–43   Whilst recognising the importance of advertising in creating a market for goods and the possible damage to the reputation of a brand as a result of poor quality advertising, the decision fails to take into account the need for consistency

---

[56] *I Can't Believe it's Yogurt* [1992] R.P.C. 533. The position under the TMA is more relaxed than under the previous law where even well known slogans such as "Have a Break . . . Have a Kit Kat" were refused registration because they lacked the necessary distinctiveness and were not considered to be trade marks *i.e.* used to indicate the origin of goods (see *Have a Break Trade Mark* [1993] R.P.C. 217.
[57] *I Can't Believe it's Yogurt* [1992] R.P.C. 533 at 537.
[58] *RHM Foods Limited v. Bovril Limited* [1983] R.P.C. 275.
[59] [1998] E.T.M.R. 26.
[60] Directive 89/104 of December 21, 1988 ("Trade Marks Directive").

in advertising if the brand image is to be maintained and enhanced. Whilst on the one hand it is acceptable for a supermarket, say, to advertise that it stocks Heinz Baked Beans (a product that one would expect to be sold in a supermarket) it is right or appropriate for it to advertise the sale of Compaq computers or Rolex watches? The ECJ, in its decision, limited the right to advertise to those resellers that habitually market articles of the same description, but not necessarily the same quality, as the goods protected by the relevant trade mark. Thus in theory, supermarkets such as Tesco and Asda would not be able to advertise such goods unless they habitually sell these goods. The question that inevitably arises, however, is what "habitually" means. Does it mean that the reseller must have sold these type of goods for a particular period of time before the advertisement can be allowed? Is it sufficient that the trader only sells the goods when it can get hold of them or must they be in stock permanently? Given the court's acknowledgment of the vulnerability of the image associated with a mark it is suggested that the reseller should be in a position to show that the relevant goods are stocked regularly and not sporadically otherwise this would undermine the limitation entirely.

6–44   As regards the level of damage that needs to be shown before a trade mark proprietor would be entitled to take action, the court held that[61]:

> ". . . damage could occur if, in an advertising leaflet distributed by him, the reseller did not take care to avoid putting the trade mark in a context which might seriously detract from the image which the trade mark owner has succeeded in creating around his trade mark."

The level of damage must be "serious" before it will be actionable although no indication is given by the ECJ as to what would be regarded as serious damage.[62] However, the Advocate General indicated that, as a general rule, trade mark owners should not[63]:

> ". . . be entitled to object to respectable advertising by respectable trades, even if it can be shown that there is some damage to the product's luxurious image by virtue of the fact that such advertising is inferior to that of selected distributors."

The Advocate General went on to say that trade mark owners could not expect resellers to comply with the same conditions as selected distributors. Whilst indicating that there might be exceptional circumstances to which a trade mark owner could object, for example, where a certain form of advertising positively degraded the product's image, as opposed to simply being of a lesser standard, he admitted that it was not easy to establish "where the line should be drawn" concluding that it was a question of fact in each case.[64] Factors which the Advocate General suggested might be taken into account when assessing whether there might be a risk of damage include (i) whether authorised distributors have carried out advertising in a similar fashion without complaint from the trade mark owner; (ii) whether the trade mark owner had set up a water tight distribution system, and (iii) whether the selective distribution system was open to objection on competition grounds.[65]

---

[61] At p. 39–40.
[62] At p. 40.
[63] [1997] E.T.M.R. 323 at 341.
[64] ibid. at p. 341.
[65] ibid. at p. 340.

6–45   From the Advocate General's comments it is clear that the onus is on the trade mark owner to ensure consistency amongst its authorised distributors if it wishes to maintain a high standard overall. However, in reality, whatever its standard of advertising, it is likely to be exceptional that the trade mark owner will succeed in being able to object to the quality of a third party's advertising. As has been noted before, this loss of control over the advertising of branded products is potentially a serious loss of control for brand owners particularly where luxury or prestigious goods are concerned since here maintaining the image of the brand is crucial to its continued success.

6–46   One final example of the use of third party registered trade marks in advertising is in connection with the assertion that the advertiser's goods are compatible with those of the trade mark owner or, in relation to services, that the advertiser is able to offer his services in relation to the trade mark owner's goods. Although this situation is discussed at length in Chapter 7 it is worth highlighting here how such use of a registered trade mark can affect the image of the brand.

6–47   In *BMW v. Deenik*[66] a garage owner advertised the fact that he had expertise in repairing and servicing BMW cars by using the phrases "BMW Specialist", "Specialised in BMWs" and "Repairs and Maintenance of BMWs". BMW objected to the use of its registered trade mark in this way and issued proceedings, which were ultimately referred to the ECJ, basing its claim on Article 5 of the Directive. The court held that the use of BMW's registered trade mark in these circumstances was justified on the basis that otherwise the garage owner would not be able to promote his services and further, that it fell within the scope of Article 7 of the Directive in that the defendant was referring to genuine BMW cars which had been put on the market with BMWs consent. Article 7 states that[67]:

> "1. The trade mark shall not entitle the proprietor to prohibit its use in relation to goods which have been put on the market in the Community under that trade mark by the proprietor or with his consent.
> 2. Paragraph 1 shall not apply where there exist legitimate reasons to oppose further commercialisation of the goods, especially where the conditions of the goods is changed or impaired after they have been put on the market."

6–48   Although the decision at first appears very sensible it does mean that it is much harder for the brand owner to distinguish between those garages that are authorised dealers and those that are not. Where the brand (and more particularly the brand image) is associated with a particular quality of after sales service that the consumer will receive, the loss of control in terms of who may use the trade mark can have an impact on the brand image especially if the quality of the service provided by the non-authorised garage is significantly below that provided by an authorised garage and consumers perceive that non-authorised garages are authorised because they use the trade mark, or that there is no difference between authorised and non-authorised garages. In the case of the former in the United Kingdom it may be possible for the plaintiff to rely on the proviso in section 10(6) of the TMA) but, as with the *Dior* case, it is likely that the plaintiff will need to

---

[66] *Bayerische Motorenwerke AG v. Deenik* [1999] E.T.M.R. 339 ("*BMW v. Deenik*").
[67] Advocate General's decision [1998] E.T.M.R. 348 at 364.

show a risk of serious damage.[67a] Alternatively, it may be possible, in the United Kingdom at least, to bring an action for passing off on the basis that consumers are deceived into believing that the garage is authorised but this relies on consumers caring about the distinction which they may not, if they do not appreciate the difference in the level of service actually being provided.

(c) Passing off

6–49   By far the most common civil action resulting from the alleged copying of advertisements is that of passing off.[68] As Wadlow notes,[69] it is possible to initiate an action for passing off if a third party copies an advertising theme or style provided that that theme or style is sufficiently distinctive of the plaintiff and is calculated to mislead and cause damage. For most potential plaintiffs the first hurdle is demonstrating that the advertising theme is in fact distinctive of it and it alone, such that its use by the defendant constitutes a misrepresentation. Merely showing that the defendant has emulated the plaintiff's advertising is not enough. The plaintiff needs to show that consumers seeing the defendant's advertisement believe that the goods either emanate from or are in some way connected with the plaintiff. As Lord Scarman noted in the *Pub Squash* case[70] (discussed below):

> "The width of the principle now authoritatively recognised by the High Court of Australia and the House of Lords is, therefore, such that the tort is no longer anchored, as in its early nineteenth century formulation, to the name or trade mark of a product or business. It is wide enough to encompass other descriptive material, such as slogans or visual images, which radio, television or newspaper advertising campaigns can lead the market to associate with a plaintiff's product, provided always that such descriptive material has become part of the goodwill of the product. And the test is whether the product has derived from the advertising a distinctive character which the market recognises."[71]

6–50   Whether or not the particular advertisement or slogan is distinctive is a question of fact in each case. If the advertisement or slogan is not distinctive then in spite of the defendant's behaviour, the plaintiff's claim will prove unsuccessful. In *Standard Ideal Company v. Standard Sanitary Manufacturing Company*[72] the plaintiff complained that the defendant had traded off its goodwill as a result of its adoption of the name Standard in connection with the sale of sanitary equipment. The application was dismissed by the House of Lords on the basis that the word "standard" was an ordinary English word and that no secondary meaning had been established despite the plaintiff's use of the mark. As Lord Macnaghten observed[73]:

> ". . . although the defendant company has availed itself unscrupulously, if not unfairly, of the labour, ingenuity, and expenditure of the plaintiff company in preparing the ground and educating the public on sanitary questions and

---

[67a] *Akiebolaget Volvo v. Heritage (Leicester) Ltd* (Rattee J., May 7, 1999) (unreported) is an example of a reference to a "Volvo Specialist" which was held to infringe the registered trade mark. See Martino Robinson "Car Wars: The Volvo Empire Strikes Back" [1999] E.I.P.R. 630.
[68] For a detailed discussion of this area see Wadlow, p. 464–469.
[69] *ibid.* at p. 464.
[70] *Cadbury Schweppes Pty Ltd v. The Pub Squash Co. Ltd* [1981] R.P.C. 429 (the "*Pub Squash*" case).
[71] *ibid.* at 490.
[72] [1911] A.C. 78, HL.
[73] *ibid.* at p. 86.

bringing into notice the most fashionable and up-to-date articles of toilet use, it is impossible to come to the conclusion that the trade designation adopted by the defendant is calculated to deceive or lead customers to believe that in buying its goods they are buying the goods of the plaintiff company."

The same problem was encountered in the South African case of *Hoechst Pharmaceuticals (Pty) Ltd v. The Beauty Box (Pty) Ltd (in liquidation)*[74] where the defendant had allegedly copied elements of the plaintiff's advertising and packaging for use on its competing product. The plaintiff argued that its slimming product, Fibre Trim, and its associated packaging and advertising were distinctive and widely recognised as being indicative of the source of the product. However, the Appellate court rejected this argument, holding that many of the symbols that Hoechst claimed to be distinctive of it namely, a yellow tape measure and a slim blond woman wearing a swimming costume were common to slimming commercials generally and thus were not indicative of source and so when used by the defendant did not amount to a misrepresentation in any way.

6–51   It is therefore in the interests of brand owners to ensure that distinctive advertising themes are chosen wherever possible to ensure the maximum chance of being able to protect them in the event that they are emulated by a competitor.

6–52   In *RHM Foods Limited v. Bovril Limited*[75] the plaintiff objected to a television commercial produced by the defendant on the basis that it had deliberately copied its theme of featuring the wives of celebrities using Bisto to make gravy and had used the expression "browns, seasons and thickens" which the plaintiff claimed was associated by members of the public with Bisto. The Court of Appeal, *obiter*, accepted that such similarities could, *prima facie*, form the basis of a successful action although on that occasion the court was considering a different issue.

6–53   *Elida Gibbs Limited v. Colgate-Palmolive Limited*[76] is another case concerning the theme of an advertising campaign. In this case the plaintiff intended to launch a new advertising campaign based upon a "tree" theme in which a comparison was made between a tree with its roots embedded in and growing in the earth and a tooth with its roots embedded in and nourished by the gum. The plaintiff claimed to have used a similar theme approximately 30 years previously although the evidence in support of this claim was very thin. Shortly before the launch of the campaign to the public, but after the plaintiff's trade and press launch, the defendant placed advertisements for its toothpaste using a tree theme in national newspapers in an attempt to pre-empt the plaintiff's campaign. Although the defendant had previously used a tree theme in connection with its advertisements for toothpaste in France and Belgium it had not previously used the theme in the United Kingdom. The plaintiff sought an injunction *quia timet*, to stop the defendant from using the tree theme. The action was based on passing off rather than copyright because the drawings used in the respective advertisements were not in any way identical. The court acknowledged that to allow both parties to use the tree theme for toothpaste would inevitably result in confusion. As the plaintiff had mounted an extensive advertising campaign at considerable expense and the defendant was aware of the plaintiff's intended campaign when it began its own campaign, it was held that in accordance with principles of equity an injunction should be granted.

---

[74] [1987] (2) SA 600 (Appellate Division).
[75] [1983] R.P.C. 275, CA.
[76] [1983] F.S.R. 95.

6–54   In the *Elida Gibbs* case although the plaintiff could not show at the date the writ was issued that its advertising campaign was distinctive of it, the court was prepared to accept that a substantial reputation connecting the plaintiff with the tree theme would be likely to be established very quickly once a large course of television advertising had taken place.[77] On the face of it the court was far more sympathetic towards the plaintiff in this case than in the slightly earlier case of *Pub Squash*.

6–55   The Australian *Pub Squash* case is a good example of a new product and advertising theme having been developed by the plaintiff and then imitated by the defendant. The plaintiff's new product was a slightly aerated, lemon drink called Solo. It was sold in a yellow can[78a] and was subject to intense television and radio advertising using slogans like "those great old squashes the pubs used to make". The target market was adult men and the television advertising emphasised this featuring in one commercial action shots of a rugged lone canoeist shooting rapids. At the end of the advertisement the canoeist gulped down a can of Solo and wiped his chin with the back of his hand. Other executions were also developed which maintained the "macho" theme. A limited product launch took place in 1973 and was followed in September 1974, with a national launch that was very successful. The advertising was, to use Judge Powell's words "quite remarkable" in that it was widely remembered by consumers.[78]

6–56   In April 1975 the defendant launched its competing lemon drink called "Pub Squash". The drink, which was sold in a can of the same shade of yellow as the Solo, was supported by television advertising on a smaller scale than that of the plaintiff's and included certain features or effects that were similar to the Solo commercial and also invoked a theme of nostalgia. In particular the hero of the Pub Squash commercial was depicted engaged in vigorous physical pursuits and included the hero ripping open a can of the drink. In one commercial the final scene was reminiscent of the Solo advertisement with the actor wiping his chin with the back of his hand although this was cut from the final version of the commercial. The plaintiff issued proceedings alleging passing off and unfair trading. Powell J. dismissed the application on the grounds that the defendant had not misrepresented its goods as those of the plaintiff even though the defendant had chosen a product name and packing for its product that derived from and was intended to gain the benefit of the plaintiff's past and anticipated advertising campaign, and the plaintiff's package for its product. The plaintiff appealed to the Privy Council who upheld the decision of the trial judge. Lord Scarman acknowledged the defendant's intention to take advantage of the market developed by the advertising campaign for Solo, but nonetheless held that it could not be shown that the defendant had infringed the "intangible intellectual property rights" in the goodwill attaching to the plaintiff's product. The issue, he said, was simply one of fact. The judge was reluctant to infer a likelihood of deception merely because the defendant had imitated the plaintiff's product. As Lahore noted in his comment on the case,[79] the conduct of the defendant was "nothing less than theft of the plaintiff's advertising effort" and yet the plaintiff found itself without a remedy and powerless to prevent others from following suit.

6–57   Advertisements that refer directly to a competitor, such as comparative advertisements, and cause confusion in the process may be actionable under passing

---

[77] *ibid.* at p. 98.
[78] *Pub Squash* at 446.
[78a] See Appendix C, photograph 16.
[79] "The Pub Squash Case Legal Theft or Free Competition" [1981] E.I.P.R. 54.

off.[80] If, however, the reference is indirect such that neither the plaintiff nor the plaintiff's product are actually identified in the advertisement then there can be no basis for a claim of passing off.[81]

CONCLUSION

6–58   In this chapter we have seen that advertising plays a significant part in the creation of a brand's gestalt. It not only informs purchasers of the brand's existence, how to use the product, its unique features, etc., it also illustrates the physical and social context in which the advertiser wishes the product to be used, and so helps to establish the brand image. When consumers subsequently choose to purchase the brand they are often influenced by the image created by the advertising. This is particularly true of premium brands where the actual differences between competing brands are said to be minimal, as in the case of Andrex, and where blind tests show that consumers can not distinguish between competing brands.

6–59   To be effective an advertisement must not only inform a consumer of a brand's existence it must also persuade the customer to buy the product. If the advertisement is confusing, that is, it is not clear which brand is being advertised, then it will fail to be effective—it will not increase sales. As Wadlow notes,[82] in the context of passing off actions:

"... the defendant's advertisements are useless if they do not attract customers to him specifically, and if they do that successfully then they can hardly be mistaken for advertisements issued by the plaintiff."

If the defendant's advertisements are not mistaken for the plaintiff's then there can be misrepresentation and so no passing off. As we saw in the Norowzian case, if there is no actual copying then there can be no copyright infringement either. Although it is possible to rely on trade mark law even that requires the registered trade mark (usually the brand name) to be reproduced or one very similar to it, and, in certain circumstances evidence of a likelihood of confusion before infringement will be found. Only passing off provides a remedy for the brand owner whose style of advertising is copied and then only if the theme copied is so distinctive that its use by the defendant will amount to a misrepresentation. For this reason it is unusual for cases to be brought alleging the copying of advertisements in isolation, although the Bisto case is one such example. It is more common for the defendant to use aspects of a competitor's advertising either on the packaging of his product, as in the Hoechst case, or in advertising promoting a similar looking product as was the case in Pub Squash. But if those features do not appear on the claimant's product packaging then it will be much harder to show passing off as the brands may well look different on a side by side comparison.

6–60   In all of these cases what we see is that despite the weight of advertisement used by brand owners (both in terms of volume and cost) on advertising the courts are reluctant to grant brand owners exclusive rights to features of their advertising campaigns either because they are not considered to be distinctive (in a

---

[80] See for example McDonald's Hamburgers Ltd v. Burgerking (UK) Ltd [1986] F.S.R. 45 discussed in Chap. 7.
[81] Schulke & Mayr U.K. Ltd v. Alkapharm U.K. Ltd [1999] F.S.R. 161.
[82] Wadlow, p. 465.

legal sense) or because no evidence of actual confusion could be produced to the court. Given the complexity of the consumer decision making process, the circumstances in which buying decisions are made and the speed at which they take place, it is hard to see how a judge in a court room can realistically assess the likelihood of consumer confusion. Current survey techniques with their artificial decision making environment are not designed for the scrutiny of the courtroom and consequently very often do not stand up to legal scrutiny. Some new means therefore needs to be found either of demonstrating consumer confusion or of forming the basis for granting legal protection.

6–61   In the *Hoechst* case referred to above the plaintiff specifically sought to rely on the "gestalt impression" of the brand which it described as being "a composite memory image derived from the recollection of visual perceptions received at different times from the . . . [product] pack and from advertising sources".[83] Unfortunately, however, when pressed by the judge to provide authority for the proposition that consumers perceived brands in this way and the brand at issue in particular, the plaintiff failed to produce any evidence and as a consequence abandoned its reliance on this concept. Thus it seems that the concept of a brand as comprising more than just the physical aspects of a product, its packaging and trade mark, and the process by which consumers are influenced by advertising remain as alien concepts to the court.

6–62   When advertising form or content is copied from a competitor the copier obtains a free ride on the back of the original advertiser who has not only invested significantly in the creation of the advertisement and has input his labour, skill and judgment to create the advertisement, but he also taken the commercial risk in using the advertisement. Is it right that a third party should be free to take advantage of his efforts provided only that he does not confuse or mislead consumers? Surely the balance between free and fair competition on the one hand and the protection of the interests of brand owners on the other has leant too far in favour of free competition? This issue will be explored further in Chapter 8.

[83] *ibid.* at p. 614.

CHAPTER 7

Comparative Advertising

INTRODUCTION

7-01   Prior to 1994, comparative advertising was relatively uncommon in the United Kingdom. In part this was due to the fact that such campaigns were fraught with legal difficulties since a reference to a competitor's trade mark brought with it the risk of an action for trade mark infringement (if the mark was registered), malicious falsehood and/or passing off. (Even reference to a visual representation of a competitor's product was not free from risk as Dell Computer Corporation discovered to its cost.[1]) Although there were ways around the problem, for example by referring to a company's full corporate name instead of its trade mark,[2] they were cumbersome and unpopular.

7-02   Since the implementation of the Trade Marks Act 1994 ("TMA") which permits the use of a third party's registered trade mark subject to certain conditions, comparative advertising has become more widespread, particularly in fiercely competitive markets such as the mobile telephone market and indeed the telecom industry generally.

7-03   The aim of this chapter is to consider the practice of comparative advertising, the assumption that it benefits the consumer and the risks for the brand owner, or rather the comparison brand (that is, the brand with which the comparison is made). New, or unknown brands, benefit most from comparative advertising[3] because of the potential for transfer of the intangible values associated with the comparison brand[4] with, or to, the new brand (discussed below). By looking at the nature of the comparisons in question, and the effects of some forms of comparative advertising, it is hoped that the commercial scene will be set so that an examination of the legal position regarding such advertisements can take place, in context.

7-04   Our legal examination will start with a brief look at the position under the old law (that is, pre 1994) and will then focus on section 10(6) of the TMA, the section permitting to the use of registered trade marks by third parties. We will consider in detail the interpretation of this provision in the light of recent cases with a view to determining what is, and what is not, permissible. As the TMA is not the only means by which brand owners can seek redress we will also consider briefly the basis for bringing an action to restrain comparative advertising on other grounds.

---

[1] *Compaq Computer Corporation v. Dell Computer Corporation Ltd* [1992] F.S.R. 93.
[2] *Pompadour Laboratories Limited v. Stanley Frazer* [1966] R.P.C. 7 and *Duracell International Limited v. Ever Ready Limited* [1989] F.S.R. 87.
[3] Barry "Twenty Years of Comparative Advertising in the United States" (1993) 12 *International Journal of Advertising* ("Barry").
[4] Discussed in Chap. 1.

7-05 In view of the forthcoming deadline for implementation of the harmonising directive on comparative advertising[5] in April 2000, we will consider what impact, if any, the Comparative Advertising Directive ("CAD") will have on the current United Kingdom position and the proposed statutory instrument that will implement its terms.

7-06 Having considered the practice of comparative advertising and the current legal constraints, it is hoped that an appreciation will be gained of the extent to which new or unknown brands can obtain an unfair advantage at the expense of established brands. In conclusion attention will be drawn to the gaps that currently exist with regard to the protection of branded products in the context of comparative advertising.

WHAT IS MEANT BY COMPARATIVE ADVERTISING?

7-07 The meaning of the term "comparative advertising" may, at first, appear self evident, but for reasons that will become clear later, it is important to specify, at this stage, what is meant by the term in the context of this discussion.

7-08 A survey of advertisements reveals that there are three categories into which all advertisements fall[6]:

1. advertisements that refer only to one brand of product and make no reference to competing products either directly or indirectly—"non-comparative" advertisements (NCA);

2. advertisements that refer only to attributes of one brand of product but that refer indirectly to the attributes of rival or competing products—"indirectly comparative" advertisements (ICA); and

3. advertisements that directly compare attributes of one product with attributes of a specifically named or recognisably presented, competing brand—"directly comparative" advertisements (DCA).

Although it is common for both ICAs and DCAs to be referred to as comparative advertisements it is important to distinguish between these different categories as, in some countries, neither ICAs nor DCAs are allowed, whereas in others one or both are permitted. The United Kingdom is an example of a European country that allows both (within limits) whereas Germany is an example of one that allows neither ICAs nor DCAs. Accordingly, the well known tag line used in the United Kingdom in advertisements for Carlsberg lager—"Probably the best lager in the world"—is not one that is heard in Germany where it would lead to the advertisement being regarded as an ICA since it implies that all other lagers are inferior to Carlsberg lager.

7-09 Although comparisons can be made between non-competing goods, as in the case of the series of advertisements used by British Telecom in the United Kingdom to stress the low cost of charges for telephone calls by comparing the cost

---

[5] Directive 97/55/E.C. of October 6, 1997 (O.J. L290/18) amending Directive 84/450/EEC concerning misleading advertising so as to include comparative advertising (hereafter referred to as the "Comparative Advertising Directive").

[6] A recent content analysis of television advertisements in America found that about 60 per cent contained indirect comparative claims, 20 per cent contained direct comparative claims, and 20 per cent contained no comparative claims—Pechmann & Stewart "The Development of a Contingency Model of Comparative Advertising" Working Paper No 90–108, Marketing Science Institute, Cambridge, MA.

with the low price of everyday items such as sausages, a pint of beer or a Kit Kat bar, for the purposes of this discussion consideration will only be given to advertisements that seek to compare attributes of products or services within the same class or category of goods/services. Comments made later in this chapter concerning the advantages of comparative advertising through product association will, however, apply equally to this type of advertisement.

7–10 Comparisons made in comparative advertisements can be either positive or negative and may seek either to associate or differentiate two (or more) brands. "Associative comparative advertisements largely emphasise brand similarities whereas differentiative ones focus on brand differences."[7] In many cases, an advertisement will have both an associative and a differentiating dimension. For example, an advertisement that refers to computer A in terms that it is as good as, or equivalent to, computer B but half the price—seeks to associate the two products in terms of quality but to differentiate them in terms of price. These two functions (association and differentiation) need to be considered carefully if comparative advertisements are to be used effectively since the impact that they have on consumers may be different.

WHY USE COMPARATIVE ADVERTISING?

7–11 In their classic article on comparative advertising,[8] Wilkie and Farris explain that:

> "[t]he primary basis for marketers' interest in this phenomenon is its potential for increasing profits through market share gains."

Although marketers are attracted to comparative advertising because of its supposed persuasive influence upon consumers, there is little published data available to substantiate the claim that it is more persuasive that NCAs. As we shall see in a moment, on those occasions when DCAs have been known to have an effect on market share (as in the DCAs featuring the products of Unilever and Proctor & Gamble discussed below) a legal battle often ensues which undermines the reliability of the results. For example, when Schick Inc. used a successful comparison campaign in connection with its Fleximatic shaver that resulted in its market share growing rapidly from 8 per cent to 24 per cent—a gain worth some $28 million in terms of sales[9]—it was followed by a legal battle. As a result, the advertisement was withdrawn on the grounds that the campaign was "false in some details and misleading in its overall implications".[10] To draw direct conclusions on the effectiveness of such advertising campaigns is therefore extremely difficult.

7–12 Both the Federal Trade Commission ("FTC") in the United States and the Commission of the E.U. have expressly promoted comparative advertising on the basis that it enables consumers to reach more informed and rational purchasing decisions, increasing consumer information and comprehension of the brand in the process. This is to some extent surprising given that advertising itself is not regarded as being objective and consumers do not always make rational purchasing

---

[7] Randall, Miniard, Barone, Manning & Till "When Persuasion Goes Undetected: The Case of Comparative Advertising" (1993) Vol. XXX *Journal of Marketing Research*, 315.
[8] Wilkie & Farris "Comparison Advertising: Problems and Potential" (1975) 39 *Journal of Marketing*, 7.
[9] "Schick Inc Teeters on the Razor's Edge", *Business Week,* May 5, 1975, p. 38.
[10] "Competitors Hail NARB for Schick Shaver Ruling", *Advertising Age,* January 7, 1974, p. 1.

decisions. Indeed the Report of the E.C. Committee on the Environment, Public Health and Consumer Protection ("the E.C. Report") on the proposal for a directive on comparative advertising defines advertising as[11-12]:

"... the process of persuasion, using the paid media, in which purchasers of goods, services or ideas are sought. Its primary aim is to convince the consumer to obtain the advertiser's product/service and/or his specific brand. Advertising is thus a commercial message designed to influence consumer behaviour. ... The commercial involves both information and promotion, always with the aim of enhancing the message which the advertiser wishes to put across to the consumer in order to influence the latter in favour of the particular product/service. *The objective information value of the commercial is thus secondary*, as the information is used solely if, and in so far as, it can act as a persuasive element in the advertisement." *(emphasis added)*

Furthermore, in the context of comparative advertising, the E.C. Report draws attention to the fact that no in depth research had been carried out either inside or outside the Community to demonstrate whether such advertisements do actually increase the information available to consumers or indeed whether comparative advertisements affect the decision making process at all. Nonetheless, there appears to be an underlying assumption that comparative advertising is in the interests of the consumer despite the absence of any real evidence.

7–13   Among those calling for the relaxation of the laws concerning comparative advertising are consumer lobby groups. They do so in the belief that these advertisements enable consumers to compare competing products objectively, much like the consumer reports featured in Which? magazine or What Computer? magazine. However, there is no evidence to suggest that comparative advertisements are more informative than non-comparative advertisements.[13] As noted in the E.C. report, in the advertising world, the presentation of objective information in advertisements is not of primary concern. Indeed, the E.C. Report specifically states that the advertiser should not be required to restrict the content of advertisements to purely objective information as that "runs counter to the very spirit of advertising".[14] Instead, it is said that the consumer should be assumed to be a purchaser who is a responsible person who should be allowed to assess the information independently in the light of his/her own particular preferences and needs.

7–14   Whilst a certain amount of information may indeed be helpful as part of the process of evaluation, too much information can result in consumer confusion as consumers try to evaluate what might appear to be irreconcilable claims to superiority (even if they can be substantiated by the advertisers).[15] This in turn may result in consumers "switching off" to comparative advertisements as a result of information overload![16] To avoid such a situation by restricting advertisements to the presentation of objective information may be unduly restrictive for advertisers and may not actually assist the consumer in reaching his/her purchasing decision.

[11-12] COM(91) 0147 final—C30337/91—SYN343; PE154.377/fin, p. 15.
[13] Barry at 339 referring to the findings of seven different research teams.
[14] *ibid.*
[15] Dworkin, " 'Knocking Copy' Comparative Advertising—A Survey of United Kingdom Practice" [1979] E.I.P.R. 41 *summarising the findings of Boddewyn & Morton Comparison Advertising: A Worldwide Study* (Hastings House, New York, 1978).
[16] *ibid.*

Whilst it is accepted that the information included in advertisements should be factually correct, honest, truthful and not misleading, should it go beyond this to draw attention to what may be perceived as negative attributes or should these be for the consumer to discover—does *"caveat emptor"* still apply?

7–15 So, is comparative advertising effective? It depends, as Barry notes,[17] on what type of comparison you consider and at what stage of the decision making process. Because of the range of variables involved (from different types of comparative advertisement, *i.e.* DCAs or ICAs, involving established brands or new/unknown brands, and the range of consumer knowledge, *i.e.* whether the consumer is already aware of the brand and is positive or negative towards it) and the different stages of the decision making process at which they can have an effect there is very little consensus as a result of research already undertaken regarding its overall effectiveness.[18]

7–16 Although it has been suggested by some[19] that there is a lack of evidence to substantiate the claim that comparative advertisements are effective in terms of their persuasive value (*i.e.* to persuade more consumers to buy the product), others argue that this is due in part to the inadequacies of the system by which such preference swings are measured.[20] The net result is that there remains no clear evidence that comparative advertisements actually result in changed purchasing decisions.

7–17 Pechmann and Ratneshwar[21] conducted various experiments to assess the effectiveness of comparative advertisements in relation to the second stage of the decision making process,[22] brand positioning, and found that by far the most effective use of DCAs was in the area of associating new brands with established brands.

7–18 For the producers of a new brand this can provide an effective marketing "short cut" in conveying brand values and attributes to consumers thereby imparting much more information than would be the case if an equivalent NCA was used. For example, a new brand of soft drink need only be referred to as "the same as Coca-Cola" and a whole host of information and attributes are conveyed to the consumer including a description of its taste, function, target market and image as well as other emotional values. If the advertisement includes a claim that it is cheaper than the leading brand, then it is clear that this new brand has obtained a significant commercial advantage by being able to describe itself as "the same as" rather than having to describe the actual taste and market for the brand as if starting from scratch. All this is obtained merely by referring to the leading brand Coca-Cola! It is for this reason that the manufacturers of leading brands wish to prevent use of their valuable trade marks by third parties (particularly the owners of new or unknown brands) in DCAs to stop them taking unfair advantage of (or "free riding" on the back of) the established brand owner's investment and success in communicating product values to consumers. This concern was shared by the Economic and Social Committee of the European Parliament in its Opinion[23] on the proposed Comparative Advertising Directive, which stated that:

---

[17] At p. 330.

[18] See Barry at p. 345.

[19] Notably Wilkes & Farris in their article referred to in n.8.

[20] See n.6.

[21] "The Use of Comparative Advertising for Brand Positioning: Association versus Differentiation" (1991) 18 *Journal of Consumer Research* 145.

[22] Described in detail in Chap. 6.

[23] Opinion on the proposal for a Council Directive concerning comparative advertising and amending Directive 84/450/EEC concerning misleading advertising O.J. No. C49 February 24, 1992, p. 35 at para 3.4.

". . . the Committee considers the presentation of a product . . . as an imitation or replica of another is simply an unfair enticement to the consumer which seeks to exploit the reputation of another product while recognising the inferior nature of the product being advertised. Such presentation should be banned, as it does not respect the principles of consumer protection (the consumer would be misled) nor of the protection of the product being compared."

The response of the European Council to these concerns is discussed in further detail below.

7–19 Pechmann and Ratneshwar also found that, in contrast to the above, the use of DCAs to promote established brands, had a tendency simply to reinforce consumers' stereotypic beliefs that the advertised and comparison brands were much the same.[24] If that occurs, the advertisements will tend to associate the products rather than differentiate them. Since this is unlikely to be the aim of such an advertisement it is perhaps a warning to owners of established brands that a NCA might perhaps be a more effective alternative when trying to communicate product differences.

7–20 In their article entitled *When Persuasion Goes Undetected: The Case of Comparative Advertising*[25] the authors point out that of more persuasive weight than comparative advertisements, are juxtaposed advertisements by different brand owners, or separate advertisements in close proximity, where the features advertised by both brands are roughly comparable such that consumers can read both advertisements and come to their own independent conclusions regarding the relative merits of both products.

Case Study

7–21 The launch in the United Kingdom in May 1994 of the new Unilever brand, Persil Power, was supported with a budget of £12.5 million for promotion and marketing.[26] Following the launch, Proctor & Gamble ("P&G"), its main competitor, immediately began a series of advertisements attacking the new "manganese accelerator" ingredient of Persil Power warning consumers that Unilever's new brand might be successful in removing stubborn stains as it claimed, but that it rotted clothing in the process. At the time of the launch Persil had a market share of 27.9 per cent compared to P&G's Ariel which had 28.6 per cent. By June 1994 these figures had changed, with Persil having increased its market share to 28.2 per cent (Ariel down to 26.4 per cent) despite the negative publicity brought about by P&G's advertising. The importance of the battle can be appreciated when it is realised that every market share point across Europe is estimated to be worth £60 million!

7–22 The fact that Persil's market share rose, despite P&G's, prima facie, very damaging campaign, would suggest that consumers were not influenced by advertisements of this kind. Indeed, according to a survey conducted in August 1994 (when the battle was perhaps at its hottest) only 54 per cent of those questioned realised that there was a dispute and of these 51 per cent had seen press advertisements either condemning or defending the manganese accelerator. Only

---

[24] "The Use of Comparative Advertising for Brand Positioning: Association versus Differentiation" (1991) 18 *Journal of Consumer Research* 145.
[25] Randall *et al*, (1993) Vol. XXX *Journal of Marketing Research* 315.
[26] All figures taken from *Marketing Week*, August 26, 1994.

12 per cent of housewives believed P&G's claim and 16 per cent believed its denial by Unilever. A startling 42 per cent, however, did not believe either company! Was the advertising therefore a waste of time and money?

7–23   P&G defended its advertisements on the basis that it was providing information to the consumer, indicating that the consumer needed to know which brands included the damaging ingredient and which did not. Ironically, Ariel Ultra (P&G's brand) which was launched after Persil Power, was believed to include the controversial "manganese accelerator" ingredient although no mention is made of this in P&G's own promotions.

7–24   Although legal proceedings were commenced as part of the battle they did not reach the courts. The negative publicity eventually forced Unilever to announce, in February 1995, the withdrawal of Persil Power in the face of evidence that it damaged clothing. As a consequence of the withdrawal consumer confidence in the Persil brand[27] as a whole suffered and its market share dropped to less than 21 per cent.[28] Thus although Unilever won the first round of the battle in terms of increasing precious market share and convincing consumers of the benefits of its brand (through NCA principally), P&G won the day, despite the lack of consumer credibility in its advertising.

7–25   Consumer confidence in innovation across the sector has been affected by the above episode[29] and Unilever has been forced to rebuild the image and credibility of its Persil brand as a consequence. It has sought to achieve this in part by reintroducing the old (1968) style of packaging design. The child depicted on the old packaging became a symbol for Unilever of the caring and trusted image that it sought to epitomise. Consumers were familiar with the old packaging design and, in an effort to regain consumer confidence and to convince consumers that the brand was as reliable as before, Unilever deliberately chose to reintroduce the trusted symbol. The relaunch was backed by a £25 million investment in brand rebuilding through advertising and marketing, an indication perhaps of the struggle that Unilever would face in reversing its fortunes. Only time will tell whether Persil can indeed rebuild its trusted image in the meantime P&G's market share has grown as has that held by the own-label market.[30]

7–26   As the above case study illustrates, consumers are not always taken in by the claims of advertisers and are likely to be particularly sceptical about comparative advertising.[31-32] This can be because the comparison is laughable, in that the advertiser has sought perhaps to differentiate two brands on the basis of features that the consumer had not associated with the brand advertised (e.g. the price, where the consumer knows that the advertised brand is considerably cheaper, as in the case of a Metro car advertised as cheaper than a Mercedes car). In such cases the consumer quickly realises the incongruity of the comparison. Alternatively, it may be that consumers are wary of the truthfulness of an advertisement extolling the virtues of one product at the expense of another. Consumers realise that the

---

[27] The Persil name was used on a range of products including several different types of washing powder. Although the "accelerator" ingredient was not present in all Persil products the debacle affected the whole brand. According to figures published in *Marketing Week* February 12, 1998, p. 5, the brand had still not recovered its former position.
[28] Figures taken from the *The Financial Times*, April 30, 1996.
[29] *Marketing Week*, February 12, 1998 at p. 30.
[30] According to figures published in *Marketing Week* February 12, 1998 at p. 29, P&G's total market share (including the brands Ariel, Bold and Daz) amounts to 52 per cent whilst that held by Unilever (with brands Persil, Surf and Radion) is around 24 per cent, just slightly ahead of the own label brands.
[31-32] Boddewyn & Marton "Comparison Advertising and Consumers" 7 *Journal of Contemporary Business* 135.

advertiser's comments are less than objective. As Barry notes in the conclusion to his survey of comparative advertising in the United States over the past 20 years[33]:

> "The only area of consensus appears to be in comparative advertising's lack of credibility. All the empirical work reviewed [in his article] indicates that the comparative format is suspect and less believable than non-comparative advertising."

7-27 References to the results of clinical or laboratory tests or statistical data of one form or another if compiled by an independent body are one way of increasing the credibility of the comparison in question. Indeed, as Barry observes,[34]:

> "The important exception to this credibility finding is when comparative claims are substantiated, especially when those substantiations are 'produced' by independent testing organisations."

7-28 In light of this, it is surprising to see that the restriction placed on references to test data in comparative advertisements set out in the first draft of the Comparative Advertising Directive (discussed below), so that they would only be permitted if the accuracy of the advertising message could be readily verified, have been omitted from the final version of the Directive.

WHAT IS THE LEGAL POSITION?

7-29 In the United Kingdom the legal position concerning comparative advertising is complex: it is regulated by a matrix of statutory legislation, torts, regulations and codes of practice. For example, the Consumer Protection Act 1987 sets out the constraints for using price comparisons, the Trade Marks Act 1994 regulates the use of registered trade marks by third parties, the Trades Descriptions Act 1968 prohibits false trade descriptions and the Control of Misleading Advertising Regulations 1988 is principally concerned with the accuracy of statements used in advertising. The accuracy of information presented in advertisements and its interpretation by consumers can also give rise to actions under the torts of trade libel (malicious falsehood) and/or passing off. As we saw in Chapter 6 (paragraph 6–20 and following.) The Committee of Advertising Practice ("CAP") lays down industry standards in the form of the BCAP Code, which concerns the content of advertisements generally, and this is enforced by, amongst others, the Advertising Standards Authority ("ASA"). If the advertisement is to be broadcast on television or radio then further codes are also applicable. There is therefore no single reference point for determining what is or is not acceptable as a comparative advertisement in the United Kingdom.

7-30 For the purposes of this discussion, which will address the rights granted to brand owners and their ability to challenge comparative advertisements, our analysis will focus on the position under the Trade Marks Act and the common law actions of passing off and trade libel, as these are the principle causes of action available to brand owners. Although it is possible to rely on copyright as a basis for challenging a comparative advertisement (as discussed in paragraphs 6–27 to 6–29) such cases are rare in practice.

---

[33] At p. 346.
[34] Barry, p. 346.

(a) The use of registered trade marks in advertisements

7–31   Historically, the courts have been reluctant to enjoin a defendant from comparing its products with those of a competitor unless the brand name of the competitor's product was a registered trade mark. This restriction was first introduced on the statute book in the form of section 4(1)(b) of the TMA 1938 and was relied upon by brand owners for over 50 years to prevent third parties from using registered trade marks in advertisements without their consent.[35] Examples of the "use" of a registered trade mark caught by section 4(1)(b) include advertisements featuring direct comparisons between competing products[36] as well as charts comparing branded products with "smell alike" equivalents.[37] The relevance of these cases now is principally in the demonstration of the creativity of those involved in developing DCAs without actually mentioning the competitor's registered mark.

7–32   Some companies rose to the challenge and devised ICAs and/or DCAs that were held not to infringe registered trade marks. One example is the case of *Duracell International Ltd v. Ever Ready Ltd*[38] where Ever Ready used a DCA stating that its batteries lasted longer than those produced by its rival, Duracell. The advertisement referred to the corporate name, Duracell Batteries Limited, not the trade mark Duracell and depicted (in black and white) the appearance of the distinctive Duracell battery (without mentioning the brand name). It was held that Ever Ready had not infringed the trade mark registration for Duracell because it had used the corporate name and not the registered trade mark. Furthermore, although Duracell had registered the appearance of its battery as a trade mark, the registration was limited to the colours copper and black and since the representation used by Ever Ready was black and white, Ever Ready was held not to have infringed this registration either. Other companies, like Triton Packaging in the *Chanel*[39] case, fell foul of the provision. In that case Triton Packaging, the defendant, included in its distributor's manual a comparison chart which incorporated references to various registered trade marks belonging to Chanel for the purpose of identifying the equivalent "smell alike" fragrance. Although not in the form of an advertisement to the public in the traditional sense, the use of Chanel's registered trade marks in this way was still held to be an infringement.

7–33   The wording of section 4(1)(b) was strongly criticised on a number of occasions for being unclear[40] but, in any event, it has now been replaced by section 10(6) of the TMA 1994 which operates as a form of defence to permit reference to a registered trade mark by a third party in certain limited circumstances.

7–34   As we have seen in earlier chapters, section 10 of the TMA 1994 sets out the scope of the trade mark owner's rights and identifies what constitutes infringement of a registered trade mark. By virtue of section 10(1), use of an identical trade mark in relation to identical goods will amount to infringement. Thus, the use of a competitor's registered trade mark will *prima facie* amount to infringement. section 10(6), however, states that:

---

[35] For a more detailed account of the history of this provision in relation to comparative advertising see Dworkin "'Knocking Copy' Comparative Advertising—A survey of United Kingdom Practice" [1979] E.I.P.R. 41 and also Mills "Comparative Advertising—Should it be Allowed?" [1985] E.I.P.R. 417.
[36] *Compaq Computer Corporation v. Dell Computer Corporation Ltd* [1992] F.S.R. 93.
[37] *Chanel v. Triton Packaging Ltd* [1993] R.P.C. 32.
[38] [1989] F.S.R. 87.
[39] See n.37.
[40] See for example the comments made by Sir Wilfred Greene M.R. in *Bismag Ltd v. Amblins (Chemists) Limited* (1940) R.P.C. 209, CA.

"Nothing in the preceding provisions of this section shall be construed as preventing the use of a registered trade mark by any person for the purpose of identifying goods or services as those of the proprietor or licensee.

But any such use otherwise than in accordance with honest practices in industrial or commercial matters shall be treated as infringing the registered trade mark if the use without due cause takes undue advantage of, or is detrimental to, the distinctive character or repute of the trade mark".

As a consequence of this change in the law, comparative advertising is now much more common in the United Kingdom although not perhaps as commonplace or as aggressive as that practised in the United States.[41]

(b) The Effect of section 10(6) of the Trade Marks Act 1994

7-35 The Government first expressed its intention to permit the use of a competitor's trade mark in comparative advertising in 1990 in its White Paper on the *Reform of Trade Marks*.[42] Whilst recognising that the practice of comparative advertising was more acceptable than it used to be, the Government indicated that advertisers should still not be free to ride on the back of a competitor's trade mark.

7-36 When the Trade Marks Bill first introduced in the House of Lords, the clause received a mixed reception with opponents arguing that it was inappropriate for the Government to introduce legislation on this subject at that stage given the discussions at E.C. level to introduce a directive on the subject. Lord Strathclyde, the minister responsible for introducing the legislation, defended the Government's position stating that:

"The government has been persuaded that there is no harm in comparative advertising . . . provided that it makes fair use of a registered mark for the purpose of informing the public. As foreshadowed in the White Paper, the Bill seeks to chart a middle course; allowing comparative advertising but providing safeguards for the owner of a registered trade mark".[43]

The wording of section 10(6) does not, however, reflect the wording used in the Comparative Advertising Directive (or any of its earlier drafts) and this has given rise to concern that the provision will now need to be revised in light of the Directive (discussed further below).

7-37 The exact origin of the wording in section 10(6) is not clear and, unfortunately, neither is its meaning. Annand and Norman suggest[44] that the wording is a combination of Articles 5(5) and 6(1) of the Trade Marks Directive.[45] The first of these clauses, they say, was included in the Trade Marks Directive in order to allow Benelux to retain the infringement criterion of Article 13A(2) Uniform Benelux Trademark Law 1971. The Benelux law regards use of a registered trade mark without the proprietor's consent as trade mark infringement. Article 5(5) does not specifically refer to comparative advertising but states that Article 5 (the rights conferred by registration):

---

[41] Willimsky "Comparative Advertising: An Overview" [1996] E.I.P.R. 649.
[42] Cm 1203 clause 3.28.
[43] *Hansard*, January 18, 1994 House of Lords Public Bill Committee col 42.
[44] Annand and Norman, p. 159.
[45] 89/104/EEC (hereafter the "Trade Marks Directive").

"shall not affect provisions in any Member State relating to the protection against the use of a sign other than for the purposes of distinguishing goods or services, where use of that sign without due cause takes unfair advantage of, or is detrimental to, the distinctive character or repute of the trade mark."

Annand and Norman suggest that the United Kingdom Government took this to mean that it was free to legislate on the subject of comparative advertising. Article 6(1) sets out the limitations on the effect of a registered trade mark in terms of use "in accordance with honest practices in industrial or commercial matters". By combining these two clauses the Government has, they say, effectively permitted not only comparative advertising but any reference to a registered trade mark by a third party, provided that the qualifications set out in the second half of section 10(6) are met.

7–38   The application of section 10(6) to situations of comparative advertising was confirmed by Laddie J. in *Barclays Bank Plc v. RBS Advanta*[46] and his analysis has helped to clarify the meaning of this subsection. However, his account of the provenance of the wording is different to that put forward by Annand and Norman. He suggested that the first part was "home grown" but that the first half of the proviso could be traced back to Article 10 of the Paris Convention dealing with Unfair Competition. This explanation was echoed by Jacob J.[47] although neither judge sought to suggest that the provision had any bearing on how the subsection should be interpreted. Whatever the correct explanation is, Laddie J. agreed that the subsection was "a mess".[48]

7–39   Laddie J. acknowledged that the meaning of the first half of the subsection was clear in that it permits comparative advertising.[49] However, the second half, was far from clear. In the *Barclays Bank* case, the defendant, RBS Advanta, had used as part of its promotion of a new Visa card the trade mark Barclaycard (with other trade marks belonging to third parties) in a leaflet comparing *inter alia* the annual fee, the monthly interest rate and other interest charges of each of the service providers. Barclays Bank objected to this use of its registered trade mark alleging trade mark infringement.

7–40   Laddie J. stated that to succeed under this section the onus was on Barclays Bank to show that the use complained of was:

(a) not in accordance with honest practices; and

(b) without due cause took unfair advantage of, or was detrimental to, the distinctive character or repute of the trade mark.

The test of honesty is, he said, an objective one. As Jacob J. expressed it in a later case "[w]ould a reasonable reader be likely to say, upon being given the full facts, that the advertisement is not honest?".[50] Or to put it another way, could a "reasonable trader . . . honestly have made the statements he made based upon the information that he had".[51] In assessing whether the advertisement was honest Laddie J. ignored the fact that the advertisement did not draw attention to all of

---

[46] [1996] F.S.R. (hereafter "*Barclays Bank*").
[47] *Cable & Wireless plc v. British Telecommunications plc* [1998] F.S.R. 383 at 391.
[48] *Barclays Bank* at 313.
[49] *ibid.*
[50] *per* Jacob J. *Vodafone Group PLC & Anr v. Orange Personal Communications Services Ltd* [1997] F.S.R. 34 ("hereafter '*Vodafone v. Orange*' ").
[51] *per* Jacob J. in *Cable & Wireless plc v. British Telecommunications plc* [1998] F.S.R. 383 at 391.

the features of the plaintiff's product or service, that it might poke fun at the plaintiff's goods whilst emphasising the benefits of the advertiser's product. Mere puffery was not dishonest; consumers were, he said, accustomed to advertising hyperbole.

7–41 Continuing his analysis of the subsection Laddie J. said that the final clause of section 10(6) added "nothing of significance" to the first part of the proviso thus, if the use (*i.e.* the advertisement) is misleading, there will be infringement provided that it is above the level of *de minimis*. In the slightly later case of *Vodafone Group v. Orange*[52] Jacob J. went further stating that if the use complained of was not honest it went without saying that it "takes unfair advantage of" or is "detrimental to" the distinctive character or repute of the mark.

7–42 Prior to the *Barclays Bank* case commentators on the Act[53] had suggested that the reference to "honest practices in industrial and commercial matters" might be interpreted with reference to particular practices or codes of conduct developed in different commercial sectors, as in the motor industry[54] and the computer industry where a rather more robust view of comparisons were taken compared to other commercial sectors. Laddie J., however, rejected this approach on the basis that it would prove harder to avoid infringement in heavily regulated trades than in others thus leading to a disparity in standards. Instead, he said that the test of honesty should be an objective one "gauged against what is reasonably to be expected by the relevant public of advertisements for the goods or services at issue".[55] Whilst acknowledging that this could vary depending upon the nature of the goods or services he ruled out the possibility of relying purely upon industry agreed codes of conduct or regulations.

7–43 To this analysis of section 10(6) Deputy Judge Michael Crystal added, in *British Telecommunications plc v. AT & T communications (U.K.) Ltd,*[56] that the advertisement (or relevant publication) should be viewed as a whole and should not be subject to minute textual analysis as this was not something upon which the reasonable reader would embark. The deputy judge also went on to say that in cases like this for an interlocutory injunction, the court should not hold that the words used are seriously misleading unless:

"on a fair reading of them in their context and against a background of the advertisement as a whole they can really be said to justify that description".

Whilst these cases have helped to clarify the meaning of this subsection, as one commentator observed[57] following the *Barclays Bank* case:

"In weighing the respective interests of the consumer and the trade mark owner, rather than striving for an equal balance, the balance appears to have come down in favour of the consumer, with the result that advertisers have now been given more scope to be confrontational in their advertising."

---

[52] *ibid.*
[53] Such as Annand & Newman, *The Trade Marks Act 1994* (Butterworths, London, 1994).
[54] In *Vodafone v. Orange* (p. 39) Jacob J. referred to a virtual moratorium in the motor industry on the enforcement of claims under s.4(1)(b) Trade Marks Act 1938.
[55] *Barclays Bank* at, p. 316.
[56] [1997] ENT. L.R. E-96 and referred to in *Cable & Wireless plc v. British Telecommunications plc* [1998] F.S.R. 383 at 389.
[57] J. Radcliffe "Comparative Advertising after Barclays Bank v. RBS Advanta" [1996] 4 ENT. L.R. 164

7–44   Whether use of a competitor's trade mark in a comparison chart, such as that in issue in the *Chanel* case, would still amount to infringement will depend upon whether the chart is considered to be in accordance with "honest practices" or as Jacob J. put it, would a reasonable reader on being given the full facts regard the advertisement as honest? This will very much depend on what the standard of honesty is. In the *Barclays Bank* case Laddie J. acknowledged that an advertisement that took unfair advantage of the distinctive character or repute of a trade mark would not be honest[58] but would this be the reaction of the reasonable reader? If it would not be the response of the reasonable reader, then the trade mark owner could not, according to existing jurisprudence, prevent the use of its mark in such a situation despite the Government's expressed intention that it should be able to do so.[59]

7–45   If brand owners are able to show that the advertisement is misleading they will be able to take action to prevent use of their marks.[60] If, however, the advertisement does not mislead the public they will no longer be able to stop them. This position may change following the implementation of the Comparative Advertising Directive[61] (see below, para. 7–60).

(c) Use of unregistered trade marks

7–46   Whether or not a competitor's trade mark is registered, its use by a third party in a comparative advertisement may result in an action for malicious falsehood or passing off by the trade mark owner, if it can be shown that the words complained of were false or caused confusion to the public. We will consider each of these causes of action separately.

(i) Malicious falsehood

7–47   To succeed in an action for malicious falsehood (also known as injurious falsehood or trade libel) the plaintiff must show[62] that:

(a) the words complained of were false;

(b) they were published maliciously; and

(c) they were calculated to cause the plaintiff pecuniary damage.

Before determining the first question, the court must decide upon the natural and ordinary meaning of the phrase or wording in question. Unlike trade mark infringement, the tort of malicious falsehood has a "one meaning rule" under which the phrase complained of is deemed to have only one meaning. This curiosity is due to the origin of the tort as a form of libel where juries had to agree on a single meaning as being "right" in order to award damages dependant upon the defamatory meaning they attributed to the words.[63] Although Jacob J. in the

---

[58] *Barclays Bank* at 316.
[59] How the Chanel case would be decided under the present law is very much a moot point. Michaels notes that Morcom ("A Guide to the Trade Marks Act 1994" at, 40) Annand and Norman suggest that it would still be an infringement although the Current Law Statutes annotation suggests that it would not. Michaels is doubtful that it would be considered an infringement: see Michaels, *A Practical Guide to Trade Mark Law* (Sweet & Maxwell, London, 2nd ed., 1996) p. 103.
[60] *Emaco Ltd & Aktiebolaget Electrolux v. Dyson Appliances Ltd*, *The Times* February 8, 1999.
[61] Directive 97/55/EC (hereafter "the CAD").
[62] *Vodafone Group v. Orange* at 36.
[63] See *Charleston v. News Group* [1995] 2 All E.R. 313, *per* Lord Bridge at 316 for further discussion of this point.

Vodafone v. Orange case questioned the need for the one meaning rule in the context of an action for malicious falsehood, given that there is no jury and the award of damages is compensatory, he did not, however, challenge the rule or reinterpret it.

7–48   To identify the one meaning, the court must consider what the meaning of the statement would be to the ordinary, reasonable, fair-minded reader. Once the single meaning has been distilled the test is whether a jury could reasonably conclude that the statements made were true.[64] It is not sufficient to show that a proportion of the public would consider the meaning to be false, as is the case in passing off.

7–49   The damaging untruth may arise by implication as in the *Compaq* case[65] where the "statements" consisted of two advertisements in which the defendant compared pictures of its products with pictures of the plaintiff's products stating that the products were "basically the same as" the plaintiff's products. On the facts, it was held that there were significant differences between the products illustrated, accordingly the statements were held to be false. In *De Beers Abrasive Products Ltd v. International General Electric Co. of New York Ltd*[66] the statements in dispute were made in a pamphlet which purported to be a report of laboratory experiments comparing the performance of the respective companies' products. Although the defendant argued that the statements were merely advertising puffs and should not be taken seriously it was held that the test to be applied was whether a reasonable man would take the claim being made as being a serious claim or not. Since the defendant had presented what purported to be a proper scientific test it must have been intended that it would be taken seriously.

7–50   In the *Vodafone v. Orange* case the statement at issue was "On average, Orange users save £20 every month". The saving was stated to be in comparison with Vodafone or Cellnet's equivalent tariffs. Jacob J. said that he had little doubt that the statement would be understood to mean that "on average, if Orange users had been on Vodafone or Cellnet, they would have had to pay £20 more per month".[67] On the facts it was held that the statement was true.

7–51   In the *Vodafone v. Orange* case the plaintiff argued that the statement was so obviously false that malice should be inferred. Although Jacob J. accepted that it was possible in some cases to infer malice where a person makes a statement that is so self-evidently false that if he says he believes it one does not believe him, he did not accept that that could be said of the defendant. In general terms, if the person who makes the statement knows that it is untrue then it will be regarded as made with malice whether or not the defendant intended to benefit himself rather than injure the plaintiff. If, on the other hand the defendant believes the statement to be true but he makes it in order to injure the plaintiff this too will suffice.[68]

7–52   The need to show that the single meaning of the statement at issue is false, coupled with the need to show that it was published maliciously makes this action a hard one for plaintiffs to establish. In the *McDonald v. BurgerKing*[69] case discussed below, McDonald based its claim on both malicious falsehood and passing off. Although unsuccessful on the former because it could not show that the words themselves were false or that they were published maliciously or recklessly, it

---

[64] *per* Glidewell L.J. in *Kaye v. Robertson* [1991] F.S.R. 63 at 68.
[65] See n.18.
[66] [1975] 2 All E.R. 599.
[67] *Vodafone v. Orange* at 41.
[68] *Wilts United Dairy v. Robinson* [1957] R.P.C. 220 at 237.
[69] [1986] F.S.R. 45.

was successful in relation to passing off. For this reason the actions are often, but not always, brought in tandem.

7–53   To avoid an action for malicious falsehood the creator of a comparative advertisement should take all reasonable steps to verify the accuracy of the material that is to be published and ensure that products that are identified as "equivalent" or "basically the same" are for all practical purposes equivalent or else to specify the distinctions. A useful check is to ask someone unconnected with the preparation of the advertisement what they believe the advertisement to be saying, if this meaning is false or misleading the advertisement should be modified accordingly.

(ii) Passing off

7–54   If a potential plaintiff is unable to make out a case of malicious falsehood because it cannot show that the words have a single meaning that is false and that the statement has been maliciously or recklessly published it may be able to show that there is a misrepresentation, i.e. that customers are deceived into believing that the defendant's product is that of the plaintiff. For example, two brands are compared in an advertisement and the consumer/reader believes as a consequence of the advertisement that both brands emanate from the same manufacturer. It is sufficient if a substantial proportion of the public holds this view albeit that it is not the only meaning of the advertisement.

7–55   The example given above is what actually happened in the case of *McDonald's Hamburgers Ltd v. BurgerKing (U.K.) Ltd*[70] following Burger King's use of the phrase "Not just Big, Mac. . . . You know when you've got a Whopper" in an advertisement for its Whopper burger. Although not a DCA in the strict sense, the advertisement did include a reference to the competing brand, albeit in the form of a pun. Burger King was seeking to associate its brand of burger, Whopper, with the Big Mac burger, sold by McDonald's, which at that stage was more widely known. The Whopper burger was differentiated from the Big Mac burger in terms of product content. The court found that there was a risk of deception in that it was unclear to readers of the advertisement whether Whopper was a variation of a Big Mac and whether it was available at Burger King or McDonald restaurants. Although Burger King argued that it was clear from the text of the advertisement that a Whopper burger was obtained only from Burger King establishments, the court held that consumers were unlikely to read the small print of the advertisement (given the positioning of the advertisement inside underground trains), and the remainder of the text was unclear.

7–56   This risk of consumer confusion was also identified by Wilkie and Farris as being inherent in DCAs either in terms of which brand is actually sponsoring the advertisement or in terms of which brand has the attributes being promoted. Clarity in DCAs is therefore particularly important.

7–57   *Ciba Geigy v. Parke Davis*[70a] is another passing off case where confusion as to the business responsible for the advertisement was alleged. Parke Davis successfully defended the action resulting from the promotion of its pharmaceutical brand Diclomax Retard in an ICA. When stressing the equivalent quality of its product and its price advantage over that of its rival, Parke Davis avoided a potential claim for passing off and trade mark infringement by referring to Ciba

---

[70] [1986] F.S.R. 45. It should be noted that at the time of the legal action neither Big Mac nor Whopper were registered trade marks. If Big Mac had been registered McDonald's could possibly have brought an action for trade mark infringement instead.
[70a] [1994] F.S.R. 8.

Geigy's trade mark in an indirect manner. Ciba Geigy had for many years used a picture of an apple in connection with its branded prescription drug Voltarol. Unlike the word Voltarol, the apple device was not registered as a trade mark. In an advertisement directed at doctors who prescribed drugs, the defendant used a picture of an apple with a bite taken out of it with the caption:

> "Diclomax Retard takes a chunk out of your prescribing costs. Diclomax Retard offers everything you'd expect from Diclofenac Retard [the generic name of the drug] with one crucial difference. The price."

7–58 The association with the brand leader was made through use of the apple although there was no specific reference to the brand name Voltarol. Ciba Geigy was unable to initiate legal action based upon trade mark infringement because its apple mark was not registered. Although it initiated proceedings based on passing off and injurious falsehood (concerning allegedly false information in the advertisement) it was unsuccessful.[71] Ciba Geigy was unable to show that there was an actionable misrepresentation on the part of Parke Davis such that consumers were misled or confused as to the origin of the brand Diclomax Retard. Parke Davis had made it clear in its advertisement that Diclomax Retard originated from Parke Davis and not from Ciba Geigy. Despite filing a substantial volume of evidence in the form of affidavits from doctors claiming that they were confused as to the source of Diclomax Retard, the court concluded that since there was no direct reference to either Ciba Geigy or its product in the advertisement there was no actionable misrepresentation. Whilst it was clear that Parke Davis' drug was being associated with that of Ciba Geigy's, Parke Davis was not seeking to suggest that its product emanated from the plaintiff. In short, the advertisement successfully both associated the brands and differentiated between them.

7–59 The lesson to learn from this case is that any comparison of competing brands using unregistered trade marks should leave the consumer in no doubt as to the origin of each product or an action for passing off may follow. It also indicates the court's reluctance to prevent ICAs in the absence of confusion as this would significantly increase the scope of passing off.

E.C. DIRECTIVE ON COMPARATIVE ADVERTISING

7–60 The Directive concerning misleading advertisements[72] was the precursor to the Comparative Advertising Directive ("CAD")[73] which is referred to as the second stage of implementation of a policy aimed at increasing the information available to consumers and preventing the exploitation of unfair advertising. Although proposals relating to comparative advertising were originally included in the proposal for the Misleading Advertising Directive they proved too contentious and had to be removed before the directive was adopted along with provisions relating to unfair advertising.[74]

7–61 The first draft of the CAD was published in June 1991 and took the form of an amendment to the Misleading Advertising Directive. In April 1994 a second

---

[71] *Ciba Geigy Plc v. Parke Davis & Co. Ltd* [1994] F.S.R. 8.
[72] 84/450/EEC of September 10, 1984 (1991 O.J. C180/14) (hereafter the "Misleading Advertising Directive").
[73] Directive 97/55/EC 1997 O.J. L290/18.
[74] Opinion of the Economic and Social Committee O.J. C49, para. 1.2, February 24, 1992 (hereafter the "Opinion").

draft was published incorporating the comments of both the Economic & Social Committee and the European Parliament. A Common Position statement was published in July 1996. The final version of the CAD was adopted by the European Parliament on October 6, 1997 and its provisions must be implemented by Member States before April 23, 2000.

7–62   Although the text of the Directive is substantially the same as that originally put forward, a number of significant amendments were made during the adoption process, which taken together with the fact that it took over six years to reach an agreement on the terms of the directive gives an indication of the strength of feeling (and diversity of views) that exist within the E.U. on this subject. As McCormick notes[75]:

> "The progress of the Directive from conception to publication has been slow and the subject of significant debate, taking almost 20 years to come to fruition. The amount of debate is indicative of the differing approaches which have been adopted to date throughout member states, and the significant culture shock for many in allowing the practice of comparative advertising."

The Commission's justification for addressing the subject of comparative advertising is based on the fact that currently comparative advertising is permitted in some member states but not in others. This not only creates barriers to trade it also puts consumers and advertisers in certain Member States at a disadvantage and can lead to distortions in competition particularly in situations of cross border advertising.[76]

7–63   The CAD therefore aims to harmonise the laws throughout the EU.[77] The Commission has also expressed the belief that harmonisation of comparative advertising will stimulate competition between suppliers to the advantage of consumers.[78] Presumably this is expected to happen as a result of drawing the consumer's attention to the advantages of one product as against competing products. This, of course, presupposes that consumers are rational and are swayed by the advertising.

7–64   Under the terms of the CAD, comparative advertising must be permitted in each member state under certain very stringent conditions.[79] The recitals to the CAD set out the background to the Directive and, as with all directives, are important when it comes to interpreting its scope. As the Economic and Social Committee observed in its Opinion[80] on the first draft of the CAD:

> "Comparative advertising is a sales promotion device that compares products or services. It can be a useful source of information, provided that it is strictly regulated. However, it must be specified at the outset that the *main aim of the proposal should extend beyond consumer protection; the rights of the manufacturer whose product is being compared must be respected in equal terms with those of the consumer.* . . . Accordingly, comparative advertising should only

---

[75] "The Future of Comparative Advertising" [1998] E.I.P.R. 41.
[76] Amended proposal for a Directive concerning comparative advertising and amending Directive 84/450/EEC concerning misleading advertising, Explanatory memorandum, p. 2. See also recital (3) CAD.
[77] Recital (2) CAD.
[78] CAD recital (2).
[79] It is interesting to note that the first draft omitted any reference to stringent conditions, its inclusion is an indication of the substantial opposition encountered by the Commission to its proposals.
[80] 92/C49/10.

be permitted insofar as it meets these two priority requirements."[81] (*emphasis added*).

7-65 Two recitals (numbers (9) and (19)) introduced as a result of the discussions on the second draft of the directive echo this concern, acknowledging that comparative advertising can be abused to the extent that it is anti-competitive and that it can take unfair advantage of an existing brand's goodwill. Recital (9) seeks to limit the potential for abuse by restricting comparisons to those between "competing goods and services meeting the same needs or intended for the same purpose". Thus it will not be possible under the CAD to compare for example, the sound quality of a Compaq multimedia computer with say a Sony hi-fi system as the two machines are not intended for the same purpose even though it may be possible to listen to a compact disc on both. Recital (19) seeks to address the issue of "free riding" and we will return to this in a moment.

7-66 Recital 13 of the CAD specifically states that use of a competitor's registered trade mark in a comparative advertisement for the purpose of identifying origin will not amount to trade mark infringement. Indeed the Minutes to the Community Trade Mark Regulation make it clear that in the context of use of a registered trade mark by a third party, "use in advertising" does not include use in comparative advertising (Article 9(2) of the Regulation—the equivalent of Article 5(3) of the Trade Marks Directive).

7-67 Comparative advertising is defined in Article 1(3) of the CAD as:

"any advertising which explicitly or by implication identifies a competitor or goods or services offered by a competitor".

Comparative advertising is only permitted when certain conditions are met. The conditions are set out in Article 1(4) and can be summarised as being an objective comparison between:

- goods or services meeting the same needs or intended for the same purpose;
- one or more material, relevant, verifiable and representative features (which may include price); and
- products with the same designation of origin (where applicable).

It must not:

- mislead;
- create confusion;
- discredit or denigrate the goods/services, trade marks or trade name of a competitor;
- take unfair advantage of the reputation of a trade mark, or of the designation of origin of competing products; or
- present goods or services as imitations or replicas of goods/services bearing a protected trade mark.

---

[81] It is interesting to note that the Opinion also indicates that the Committee "hopes that the rules on advertising will soon form part of a broader regulatory framework covering unfair competition".

On the whole the conditions are self evident although it will no doubt be some time before the full meaning of terms like "confusion" are fully understood, does it, for example refer to confusion as to origin in the trade mark sense or is it a lower threshold?

7–68 The area that is likely to generate the most debate is the area concerning the use of "imitation" or "replica" goods and the issue of "unfair advantage". It is not clear what will be considered a "replica" or an "imitation" for the purposes of the CAD, whether, for example, the offending product/service must have exactly the same appearance as the branded product (*i.e.* effectively a counterfeit product), or whether a substitute brand such as the "smell-alike" fragrances the subject of the *Chanel* case in the United Kingdom will be sufficient. Although the directive itself does not provide any answer to these questions the Opinion[82] of the Economic and Social Committee on the draft proposals may provide a clue to the purpose of the provision. The Opinion states that[83]:

". . . the presentation of a product as an imitation or replica of another is simply an unfair enticement to the consumer which seeks to exploit the reputation of another product while recognising the inferior nature of the product being advertised."

This provision suggests that ICAs and DCAs that compare established brands with new or unknown brands will be caught by the provision and therefore disallowed. If this is the case how will it affect lookalike products such as own label products? Will use of the house mark (in most cases, the store name) as part of the brand name overcome this exception, on the basis that the store name will be well known? If it will not save the own label product then the CAD will undoubtedly prove an effective means of preventing new brands from positioning themselves as equivalents to existing brands? Much will depend on how the CAD is interpreted and applied, initially by national courts, but ultimately by the European Court of Justice.

7–69 It is unlikely, based upon previous experience of the implementation of the Trade Marks Directive,[84] that implementation of the CAD by the United Kingdom legislature will throw any light on the meaning of the text of the CAD. It is more likely that amendments to United Kingdom legislation will incorporate identical phraseology to that used in the CAD.

7–70 Article 1(9) of the CAD allows Member States to introduce more stringent provisions to ensure greater protection against misleading advertisements but it specifically excludes the introduction of more stringent criteria concerning the nature of the comparison itself. It is hard to imagine exactly what the Commission had in mind here except perhaps ensuring higher standards in relation to advertising of services since it specifically refers to providing more extensive protection for "persons carrying on a trade, business, craft or profession".

7–71 Article 1(9) also provides member states with the opportunity of introducing bans or limitations on the use of comparative advertising in relation to advertising for professional services. One example may be the legal profession where the United Kingdom Law Society *inter alia* has been lobbying to ensure that the provisions will not apply in this field.

---

[82] 1992 O.J. C49/35.
[83] See n.82 at para 3.4.
[84] See n.24.

7-72 Where advertising has already been banned within a Member State for certain goods or services the CAD will not oblige a member state to permit comparative advertising. Thus, in France, for example, where advertising tobacco or alcohol products is not permitted there will be no obligation to permit comparative advertising.

7-73 Once the CAD has been implemented therefore, all member countries must permit ICAs and DCAs. The fact that the information must be objective and verifiable presumably means that we have seen the last of advertisements such as those commonly used to promote pet food which suggest that "eight out of ten cats prefer brand X". Unless the advertiser can prove this preference it will fall foul of the limitations expressed in Article 4 of the CAD.

7-74 The CAD will be implemented in the United Kingdom by means of secondary legislation rather than by means of a specific Act of Parliament, in much the same way as the Misleading Advertising Directive[85] was implemented. A Consultation paper on the proposals for implementation was circulated in September 1999 and the draft statutory instrument was expected to be laid before the relevant Minister early in March 2000. The Government has taken the view that section 10(6) of the TMA 1994 will not need to be amended on the basis that its terms are broader than the proposed statutory instrument in the sense that it is not limited to situations of comparative advertising. Accordingly, brand owners will have a new cause of complaint to consider in situations of comparative advertising, namely breach of the Control of Misleading Advertisement (Comparative Advertisements) (Amendments) Regulations 2000, as it will be known (or Comparative Advertising Regulation), in addition to existing causes of action for trade mark infringement, passing off and malicious falsehood.

7-75 In practical terms the new comparative advertising regulation should be reflected in changes to the CAP Code. At present, in addition to its general rules that "[a]ll advertisements should be legal, decent, honest and truthful" and that "[a]ll advertisements should respect the principles of fair competition generally accepted in business", the Code specifically states that comparisons can be made between the advertiser's product and that of a competitor provided that it is clear and fair and that no element of the advertisement gives the advertiser an artificial advantage.[86] The Code is, however, silent on the question of comparisons between established and new brands. Whether it will be amended to take into account the CAD or whether it will rely on its existing rules regarding the principles of fair competition remain to be seen. Although, as Fitzgerald points out,[87] the standard of the Codes are in theory more rigorous than the common law being concerned as they are with general "fairness", in practice they have been interpreted liberally, with particular reliance being placed on the ability of consumers to critically asses claims in advertisements and to complain accordingly.

7-76 As we saw in the previous chapter, if the ASA considers that an advertiser is in breach of the BCAP Code it will be asked to withdraw or amend it. Although a complaint to the ASA is cheaper than taking legal action the response is not as quick as an interlocutory application can be and there is no award of damages.

---

[85] See n.37.
[86] Rule 19 BCAP Code.
[87] Fitzgerald, "Self Regulation of Comparative Advertising in the United Kingdom" [1997] ENT. L.R. 250 at 252.

CONCLUSION

7–77 Those in favour of comparative advertising advocate its use in the interests of providing more information for consumers and promoting competition. Willimsky[88] argues that:

"Competition, by its very nature, is 'unfair' and leaves no room for sentimental paternalism. The very reason competitors enter a market is to 'eliminate' as many competitors as possible and to acquire the largest possible market share. All competitive advertising does is to verbalise commercial activity . . . Comparative advertising mirrors free market activity and any restrictions other than the condition of truth are unjustifiable and therefore not to be imposed."

As attractive as this argument may at first seem, it fails to take into account the fact that "free market activity" is not entirely "free" but is regulated to avoid its worst excesses.[89] In the same way, it is submitted, comparative advertising should be restricted. The difficult question is where should the balance lie?

7–78 As Pickering notes:

"There is an assumption underlying the arguments of those in favour of comparative advertising that it necessarily has much in common with the reports produced by consumers' organisations such as the Consumers' Association and will consequently contain factual and almost impartial observations aimed at facilitating the consumer's decision, but not influencing it".[90]

As we have seen, although there is no factual basis for the assumption that comparative advertising will increase the level of information available to consumers it clearly underlies both the United Kingdom Government's decision to permit comparative advertising and the Commission's proposal for the CAD. If, despite this lack of evidence, we are prepared to accept the assumption, does it mean that all forms of comparative advertising should be permitted? By no means. Even the Government and the Commission accept that not all comparisons should be allowed and that some restraint is needed to curb the potential for abuse. In particular, the Commission recognised that the use of established brands in comparison with imitation or replica products was "unfair". Although the current wording of section 10(6) of the TMA is unclear as to whether such comparisons will fall foul of its provisions, implementation of the CAD in the United Kingdom should ensure that this type of advertisement is restrained. To achieve this goal, however, the United Kingdom needs to implement not just the letter of the CAD but also the spirit.

7–79 Without the framework of a law of unfair competition, the United Kingdom has neither statutory nor common law principles that require it to implement a policy of "fairness" in the commercial realm. Although BCAP applies a general principal of fairness as regards the content of advertisements, it does not provide a means of redress for aggrieved businesses. In the absence of such a policy, the CAD could provide an effective means of controlling the balance between the interests of brand owners and the competing demands of a market economy.

---

[88] "Comparative Advertising: An Overview" [1996] E.I.P.R. 649.
[89] As in the case of, for example, Art. 85 EEC (formerly Article 86 of the Treaty).
[90] Trade Marks in Theory and Practice (Hart, Oxford), p. 129.

7–80   If the spirit of the CAD (that is, the spirit of fairness) is not evident when it comes to enforcing the terms of the CAD then, there is a risk that a gap in the legal protection of branded products will emerge. In particular, comparative advertisements that are primarily used to exploit the reputation attributed to an established brand if not caught by the provisions regarding "replicas" will undermine the market position of established brands. The result will be that the swing in favour of consumer interests that began with the introduction of section 10(6) will increase at the expense of brand owners whose rights in the exclusivity of their brands (and their associated imagery) will be eroded. Although it might appear advantageous to move the boundary in the direction of fewer restrictions (*e.g.* by allowing all associative advertisements), to do so would undermine the position of brand owners who would be powerless to prevent competitors from using representations of their brands as a spring board from which to launch their own brands.

CHAPTER 8

A Proposal For Change

INTRODUCTION

8–01 "The protection of trade-marks is the laws recognition of the psychological function of symbols. If it is true that we live by symbols, it is no less true that we purchase goods by them. A trade-mark is a merchandising short cut which induces a purchaser to select what he wants, or what he has been led to believe he wants. The owner of a mark exploits this human propensity by making every effort to impregnate the atmosphere of the market with the drawing power of a congenial symbol. Whatever the means employed, the aim is the same—to convey through the mark, in the mind of potential customers, the desirability of the commodity upon which it appears. Once this is attained, the trade mark owner has something of value."[1-3]

In this analysis of the functions of trade marks and their ability to communicate to the consumer, Frankfurter J. focuses on the value of established trade marks to their owners and the attractiveness of using such a trade mark to a third party as a means of obtaining a short cut in the communication process. In 1941 when these comments were made, brands had not developed in the way that we know them today. As a consequence Franfurter J. attributes to the trade mark qualities associated with the brand (as opposed to a trade mark *per se*). However, as we have seen in previous chapters, the essential function of a trade mark is to indicate the origin as interpreted by European courts. A disparity thus exists between the protection afforded to trade marks as indicators of origin and the attributes of a brand. As we saw in Chapter 1 brands have developed significantly during the course of last fifty years since these comments were made. Changes in the manner in which products are marketed (from local suppliers to national or even international suppliers); and sold, especially the growth of self service stores (which have shifted the burden of decision making onto the consumer rather than relying upon the recommendations of the shopkeeper), have resulted in changes in the environment in which consumers make their purchasing decisions as well as changes in the role of trade marks and branding *per se*. At the same time, continuing advances in technology, both in terms of media advertising, through the development of commercial radio and television and now over the internet and developments in product sophistication[4] have not only made it easier for brand owners to communicate with their customers on a global basis but have made it essential to do so. However, technology has also made it much easier for others to poach upon both the commercial magnetism of the mark and other aspects of the

---

[1-3] *per* Frankfurter J. *Mishawaka Rubber & Woollen Manufacturing Co. v. SS Kresge Co.* 316 U.S. 203 (1941) (U.S. Supreme Court).
[4] Such that everyday products include increasingly complex technology causing consumers to rely more heavily on branding as a means of product differentiation and risk reduction.

brand either by replicating the appearance of successful products, or by relying upon the consumers awareness of one brand to sell another or by trying to emulate those aspects of a competitor's marketing strategy that are particularly successful (such as advertising themes and emotional attributes). The English law reports bear witness to the fact that brand owners are often successful in seeking to stop such conduct.[5] In part this is because elements of their brands are not recognised by the courts and partly because of gaps in the legal protection that does exist.

SHORTFALLS IN PROTECTION

8-02   We have seen from the discussions in earlier chapters the various ways in which brands play an important role in commerce today as symbols of quality, value, attitude and experience established through brand advertising and sponsorship. We have considered the various elements that together comprise a brand. We have looked at the commercial importance and the legal protection of the appearance of the product itself, its label, packaging, advertising and merchandising. From a detailed examination of these elements we have seen that there is something of a shortfall between what the marketer regards as a brand and those aspects of a brand that the law will recognise as worthy of protection under existing intellectual property laws. This has meant that there are a number of gaps or lacunae where little or no protection is available to the brand owner, despite the investment in research, development, creation, marketing and sustained advertising of the brand. Whilst it is accepted that investment alone does not justify legal protection, it is suggested that the efforts of brand owners to create and market something of value to consumers, distinctive in appearance and frequently innovative in itself, warrants protection of some form from third parties who would otherwise seek to take unfair advantage of the brand owner's creative labour, skill and investment. Before considering whether such protection can be justified on the basis of legal theory, and what form it might take, we need first to crystallise exactly where it is thought that protection is lacking and what kind of protection is needed to fill the lacunae previously identified.

8-03   Given the current interpretation of section 10 of the TMA 1994[6] and the present scope of the tort of passing off, protection can be said to be lacking in relation to:

- product simulation (with particular reference to the shape of an article[7]);

- the use of an identical or similar mark in connection with similar goods where there is no confusion as to origin (in the classic sense) although there maybe confusion in a broader sense in terms of an association, affiliation, sponsorship or commercial connection[8];

- the use of an identical or similar mark in connection with dissimilar goods in the absence of confusion (in the classic sense)[9] sometimes referred to as dilution; or

---

[5] See, for example, the *Pub Squash* case; the *Puffin v. Penguin* case, the *Baywatch* case, the *European*, to name but a few. *Athletes Foot Marketing Associates Limited v. Cobra Sports Limited* [1980] R.P.C. 343; *Dalgety Spillers Foods v. Food Brokers("Pot Noodles")* [1994] F.S.R. 504. *United Biscuits (UK) v. Burton's Biscuits* [1992] F.S.R. 14, *Wombles v. Womble Skips* [1975] F.S.R. 488.
[6] Discussed in detail in Chaps 4 and 5.
[7] As discussed in Chap. 3, paras 3–105—3–113.
[8] As discussed in Chap. 4, paras 4–70—4–73.
[9] As discussed in Chap. 5, paras 5–120—5–129.

- image appropriation and the use of advertising images and marketing strategies.[10]

(a) Product simulation

8–04   The actual appearance of a branded product tends to receive limited protection under the laws of copyright, designs, trade marks or passing off, particularly if the appearance is either regarded as non distinctive (in terms of indicating the source of the product as in the *Roho* case[11]) or functional, as in the recent case involving the *Philips* rotary shaver.[12–14] The defendant's intention to take advantage of the commercial efforts of the plaintiff in situations such as these is not in any doubt and yet it seems that no protection is available to the brand owner despite recognition in the Trade Marks Directive itself that a trade mark can consist of the shape of goods or their packaging.[15] That particular features of shape can come to be associated by consumers with particular manufacturers is not a fact that courts willingly accept especially if the owner of the mark in question has also had the benefit of patent or registered design protection.[16] Such reluctance stems from the courts expressed unwillingness to perpetrate a monopoly granted under a patent by means of trademark protection should be accepted and not be denied merely to avoid conferring a monopoly. It is possible to register as designs novel product configurations that have aesthetic appeal this can prove expensive if every article produced by a company is to be registered. Further, not all articles will qualify for protection. The UDR can assist by providing a measure of protection but it is not available to all businesses, only those falling within the qualification criteria or first marked (exclusively) in a qualifying country.[17]

(b) Confusion as to origin

8–05   We saw in Chapter 4 that, as a result of the interpretation of section 10(2) of the TMA 1994 in *Wagamama*[18] it is not an infringement of a registered trade mark to use an identical or similar sign in relation to identical or similar goods in the absence of confusion even if consumers associate the offending sign with the owner of the registered trade mark. It is as a consequence of this need to demonstrate confusion that brand owners have been unable to challenge successfully the "lookalike" packaging used by some supermarkets. It has, until recently, been difficult for brand owners to show that consumers "confuse" in the strict sense a lookalike product with that of the branded product it imitates. Whilst

---

[10] As discussed in Chap. 6.

[11] *Hodgkinson & Corby Ltd v. Wards Mobility Services Ltd* [1995] F.S.R. 169.

[12–14] *Philips Electronics NV v. Remington Consumer Products* [1998] E.T.M.R. 124 (the "*Philips* case"). According to the White Paper "Reform of Trade Marks Law" (Cmnd 1203 para 2.20) the aim of s.3 is "to prevent the trade marks system being used to obtain an automatic and indefinite extension of the monopoly conferred by a patent, design or copyright". An argument put forward in the *Philips* case but not determined.

[15] Art. 2 Trade Marks Directive 89/104/EEC December 21, 1988 ("the Directive"). Whilst it is true to say that the s.3 TMA 1994 is based on Art. 3(1)(e) of the Directive, the manner in which the section has been interpreted and applied, particularly in the *Philips* case, is arguably more in keeping with the position under the TMA 1938 than that intended under the Directive. In any event, until the case is considered by the ECJ and the meaning of the Article is made clear, it is unlikely that owners of three dimensional shape trade marks will be able to rely on their registrations with confidence especially if the mark in question is an integral part of the product.

[16] See *Philips* case and *Canadian Shredded Wheat* case.

[17] s.217 CDPA 1988.

[18] *Wagamama Ltd v. City Centre Restaurants plc* [1995] F.S.R. 713 ("Wagamama") and confirmed in *Sabel v. Puma AG* [1998] E.T.M.R. 1.

consumers often assume that a lookalike product is manufactured by the brand owner this has not been treated as sufficient to amount to confusion. Thus there is a gap in the protection afforded to brand owners in that they are unable to take steps to prevent third parties from imitating their brands (their products or packaging) in the absence of confusion as to origin.[19]

(c) Dissimilar goods

8–06 As we saw in Chapter 5, the use of an identical or similar mark on dissimilar goods by an unauthorised third party, can cause difficulties for a brand owner especially if the consumer is not confused as to the origin of the goods (either because of the prominence of the defendant's house mark on packaging, or because of a disclaimer as to whether the goods are "official") or if there is no obvious unfair advantage taken or detriment suffered.[20] In such a situation, a brand owner is unlikely to obtain relief based either on the law of passing off or under section 10(3) of the TMA 1994 (according to its current interpretation). Indeed, even if consumers do believe that a connection exists (in the broad sense) with the original brand owner (perhaps as a result of the packaging style, colour scheme or imagery used), protection will be denied unless it can also be shown that the use is "without due cause" and either an "unfair advantage" has been taken or that the use was "detrimental to distinctive character or repute of the trade mark".[21] As this causes the scope of the subsection to be interpreted narrowly a gap in protection exists for owners of brands with a reputation where the brand name and/or trade dress are used in an identical or similar form in relation to dissimilar goods.

(d) Image appropriation and the use of advertising and marketing strategies

8–07 A further gap in protection exists in relation to image appropriation, that is, where one trader has established a particular image in the context of a promotional campaign for a product, and a second trader seeks to use the same image or series of images in order to promote its goods. Examples of this include the *Pub Squash* case[22] referred to in Chapter 6 where the defendant copied the imagery used in the plaintiff's advertising and promotional activities, and the *Elida Gibbs* case[23] in which the defendant tried to pre-empt the plaintiff's advertising campaign. In the former case particularly, the court refused to grant relief to the plaintiff on the basis that there had been no infringement of copyright and that there was no general law of unfair competition. There is therefore a shortfall in protection as regards the misappropriation of images, advertising and marketing strategies in the absence of a substantial reproduction sufficient to sustain an action for copyright infringement.

---

[19] A recent survey conducted by Taylor Nelson AGB plc dated March 1998 in connection with lookalike products found that 34 per cent of those involved in the survey thought that a commercial agreement existed between the parties where two products looked similar compared to 23 per cent when the products looked different and were packaged distinctively. A report by the Consumer Association also supports the view that a significant number of consumers (almost three out of ten) buy or select the wrong products in supermarkets, many (63 per cent) as a result of similarities in packaging, especially in relation to colour (59 per cent)—see *The Times* April 25, 1998.
[20] See the *Baywatch* case discussed in Chap. 5, para. 5–72 and *Premier Brands U.K. Ltd v. Typhoon Europe Ltd*, *The Times*, February 22, 2000.
[21] See Chap. 5, para. 5–82 *et seq.* for a detailed discussion of these terms.
[22] *Cadbury Schweppes Pty Ltd v. The Pub Squash Co. Ltd* [1981] R.P.C. 429 ("Pub Squash").
[23] *Elida Gibbs Ltd v. Colgate Palmolive Ltd* [1983] F.S.R. 95. Discussed in Chap 6. Para. 6–53—6–54.

8–08   Having identified these various lacunae in the law,[24] the next question to determine is whether the law should be changed in order to rectify these apparent shortcomings or whether competitors should be permitted to copy aspects of product design, get-up, packaging, advertising, etc., that are not the subject of patent, copyright, registered designs or trade marks as is currently the case.

JUSTIFYING INTELLECTUAL PROPERTY RIGHTS

8–09   In order to determine whether there should be additional protection for certain aspects of brands and branded products it is helpful to consider first, the basis upon which legal protection is ordinarily granted to objects of intellectual property, before addressing the question of whether there is sufficient justification to increase protection as regards brands.

8–10   A number of theories have been advanced to justify the grant of intellectual property rights. Each seeks to explain why protection should be granted, although none are universally accepted.[25] The importance of formulating an acceptable justification as to why intellectual property rights might be recognised is not purely an academic question but is one that may be relevant when determining the application of legal principles in novel situations.[26] We shall consider here three of the principal theories put forward, namely an economic theory, a moral rights theory based on notions of "desert" and finally a moral rights theory based on natural rights principles.

8–11   We shall consider each theory in turn, in order to explore whether additional protection can be justified under any or all of them. In so doing, we will see that not all intellectual property rights can be justified on the basis of the same theories. More specifically, different theories have been advanced to justify copyright and patent protection compared to those for trade mark protection. We will therefore need to consider whether the additional protection sought for brands can be justified on either basis or whether a separate justification is needed.

(a) An economic theory

8–12   Perhaps the most widely accepted theory for justifying the grant of property rights in intellectual property in the current "free market" climate is that based on

---

[24] Ricketson in arguing for the introduction of a law of unfair competition based on the principle of "reaping without sowing" also identified shortfalls in legal protection in relation to product simulation, image stealing and importing a reference. Although intellectual property laws have changed somewhat since his article was published most of these shortfalls in protection remain. See "Reaping Without Sowing"; Unfair Competition and Intellectual Property Rights in Anglo-Australian Law [1984] U.N.S.W.L.J. 1.
[25] Although those advocating the grant of new intellectual property rights are frequently expected to justify their grant, as we saw in Chap. 2, neither the patent nor the copyright systems of protection were justified on philosophical grounds prior to their establishment. On the contrary, both were rationalised over a period of years once their existence had been accepted. See Rose, *Authors and Owners* (Harvard University Press, London, 1994) ("Rose") p. 4 where he notes that the Statute of Anne in 1709 was, at least in part, a legislative extension of an existing regulatory practice and it was not until the issue of common law copyright was considered in, for example, *Millar v. Taylor* (1796) that the question of legal theory was considered. See MacLeod *Inventing the Industrial Revolution* (Cambridge University Press, Cambridge, 1988) ("MacLeod") Chap. 1 for a similar analysis of the patent system.
[26] As Abrams points out in his article "The Historic Foundation of American Copyright Law: Exploring the Myth of Common Law Copyright" (1983) 29 *Wayne Law Review* 1126, the difference in the reasoning of the U.S. Supreme Court from that of the Court of Appeal in the case of *Sony Corp of America v. Universal Studios Inc* (1984) 464 U.S. 417, 78 and *Universal Studios Inc v. Sony Corp of America* (1981) 659 F. 2d. 963 respectively, can be explained on the basis of the different copyright philosophies applied. The case concerned the use of video equipment for home recording and the liability of the manufacturer of the recording equipment for copyright infringement. Although the Court of Appeal found the manufacturer liable the Supreme Court held that it was not.

economic principles. The grant of a proprietary right has, according to Landes & Posner,[27] both a "static" and a "dynamic" benefit; "static" in that the owner has a positive benefit as a result of ownership of the property right, and a dynamic benefit in that it acts as an incentive to invest in the creation or improvement of the subject of the property right knowing that it cannot be taken by third parties.

8–13   In economic terms, granting exclusive rights[28] to the creator of original works (in the form of copyright) or novel inventions (in the case of patents) is justified because it encourages the creation or disclosure of ideas by providing an incentive to the author or inventor. The incentive is in the form of a limited period of exclusive exploitation (in relation to the patent) or protection from copying (in the case of copyright), which imposes costs on society in terms of (i) the monopoly price charged for the work which will limit the number of people gaining access to the work, and (ii) the cost of producing future works because borrowing from previous works is not possible thus making it harder for future authors.

"The optimal degree of copyright protection is that which maximises the difference between the benefits of induced creativity and the costs of increased author's rights."[29]

The period for patent protection is shorter than that for copyright and this may be explained on the basis that the scope of the right granted is greater.[30–31]

8–14   The grant of a patent right protects the investment of the inventor in research and development and also gives the inventor the benefit of knowing that the end product is protected against copying or even independent manufacture—thus encouraging further investment in research and development thereby ultimately encouraging the advancement of science.[32] Whilst patent protection can be justified on this ground, and copyright protection can similarly be justified as an economic incentive to create, *inter alia*, literary works,[33] it is hard to justify trade mark protection solely on this basis because trade marks are not seen as being creative works in themselves[34] and are not considered to be novel inventions of the calibre protected by patents.[35] Instead, trade marks have tended to be viewed as a

---

[27] "Trademark Law: An Economic Perspective" (1987) 30 *Journal of Law & Economics* 265 at 265 ("Landes & Posner").
[28] Some would say "monopoly rights", although in a strict sense a monopoly as such is not granted since "a monopoly takes way from the public the enjoyment of something which the public possessed" and the public did not own the object of the intellectual property before the inventor or author created it, it only owned the raw materials as it were, not the finished product. See Tyerman "The Economic Rationale for Copyright Protection for Published Books: A Reply to Professor Breyer" (1971) 18 *UCLA Law Review* 1100 at 1101.
[29] Yen "Restoring the Natural Law" (1990) 51 *Ohio State Law Journal* 517 ("Yen").
[30–31] Patent protection provides absolute monopoly protection so that an independent inventor of the same subject matter would be held to have infringed a valid patent whereas with respect to copyright infringement, the monopoly right granted is limited to copying. Thus independent creation would not infringe. Copyright protection is thus more limited in scope. Where this is truly the case, however, it may be possible for the patentee to obtain an extension of the patent period by means of the grant of a Supplementary Protection Certificate (reg. 5 Patents (Supplementary Protection Certificates for Medicinal Products) Regulation 1992). The term of a U.K. patent is 20 years (s.25 Patents Act 1977), but the time taken to prepare a product for market after the patent application has been filed, means that the period of actual exclusive use is often less than the statutory term.
[32] This justification for patent protection was recognised by Laddie J. in *Wagamama*.
[33] Yen argues that copyright protection is not based on economic considerations alone. Relying upon judicial precedent and basic copyright doctrines of originality and the idea/expression dichotomy he argues that the true justification of copyright law is Locke's theory of property, that is natural law.
[34] See *Exxon v. Exxon Insurance* [1982] R.P.C. 69, CA.
[35] To the extent that they are creative (*e.g.* device marks) they also attract copyright protection as regards their creative components.

means of communicating information to consumers, regarding the source, the quality and the identity of the manufacturer.[36] The protection of trade marks thus operates to protect a trader's goodwill, to protect consumers against confusion as to the source of products and to protect the function of trade marks as consistent and reliable indicators of quality[37] and so provide a marketing short cut for consumers who can rely on the sign or symbol to communicate product quality, trustworthiness, etc. The reliability of trade marks as ciphers of product dependability and consistent quality reduces consumer search costs by enabling a purchaser to select a tried and tested product rather than having to re-evaluate or reassess a purchasing decision each time a product is purchased.[38]

8–15   As the Attorney General observed in *Hag II*[39]:

> "Whereas patents reward the creativity of the inventor and thus stimulate scientific progress, trade marks reward the manufacturer who consistently produces high-quality goods and they thus stimulate economic progress. Without trade mark protection there would be little incentive for manufacturers to develop new products or to maintain the quality of existing ones. Trade marks are able to achieve that effect because they act as a guarantee, to the consumer, that all goods bearing a particular mark have been produced by or under the control of, the same manufacturer and are therefore likely to be of similar quality. The guarantee of quality offered by a trade mark is not of course absolute, for the manufacturer is at liberty to vary the quality; however, he does so at his own risk and he—not his competitors- will suffer the consequences if he allows the quality to decline . . .
>
> A trade mark can only fulfil that role if it is exclusive. Once the proprietor is forced to share the mark with a competitor, he loses control over the goodwill associated with the mark. The reputation of his own goods will be harmed if the competitor sells inferior goods. From the consumer's point of view, equally undesirable consequences will ensue, because the clarity of the signal transmitted by the trade mark will be impaired. The consumer will be confused and misled."

Thus the protection of those aspects of trade marks which indicate source, quality and/or identity can be justified on the basis of the promotion of economic efficiency.[40] Whereas trade marks and reputations for consistency and quality take time to establish and require investment in the development of the product and communication of the product attributes through advertising, they are relatively cheap and easy to copy. The stronger the trade mark the greater the incentive is to copy.[41] However, to perform its economic function trade marks must not be duplicated.[42] If a third party "free rider" is able to copy the established mark and capture some of the established trade mark owner's profit (because consumers confuse the trade mark with the original) it will be able to undercut the original

---

[36] See Cornish and Phillips "The Economic Function of Trade Marks: An Analysis with Special Reference to Developing Countries" (1982) 13 I.I.C. 41.

[37] Trade marks thus encourage investment in quality and consistency. .

[38] "What a [trade mark] does is to enable the purchaser to link goods or services to a range of personal expectations about quality which derive from previous dealings, recommendations of others, attractive advertising and so on" Cornish, *Intellectual Property* (Sweet & Maxwell, London, 1st ed., 1981) p. 469.

[39] *SA CNL-Sucal NV v. Hag GF AG* [1990] 3 C.M.L.R. 571 at 583 ("Hag II").

[40] Landes & Posner at p. 266.

[41] *ibid.*, p. 270.

[42] *ibid.*, p. 269 and AG in Hag II quoted above at para. 8–15.

brand and, if not checked by law, free riding will eventually destroy the value of the original trade mark and thus eliminate the incentive to develop the trade mark.[43]

8-16   Similar principles apply to computer software (in that they are expensive to create[44] but relatively easy to copy). In the seminal article entitled *A Manifesto Concerning the Legal Protection of Computer Programs* by Samuelson and others,[45] the authors explain how, if copying of computer software is allowed, it can lead to asymmetrical market failure. Market failure occurs when competitors in the market face different entry costs (where for example the second comer is able to reduce his costs by copying the first comer); the market failure is asymmetrical because it is only suffered by the first comer in the market, that is the one responsible for the initial research and development costs.

8-17   As with computer programs, failing to adequately protect the trade mark created by an organisation may lead to a reduction in investment in the trade mark as a means of communication since the organisation will know that the trade mark can be copied with impunity by a third party as soon as the product is launched. This, in turn, will mean that there is no incentive for the first company to improve product quality or to innovate because it cannot hope to recover the cost of such investment through lead time in the market alone. The fact that the second comer has not invested in research and development means that it can afford to undercut the first company. Furthermore, if the consumer cannot rely on the trade mark as a short cut symbol of assurance of quality control and reliability then the trade mark will not reduce the consumer's search costs which means that the consumer will be left re-evaluating the options available each time a purchasing decision needs to be taken. As Gordon notes[46]:

"... allowing free copying generates short-term economic benefits for the consumer but is likely, because of disincentive effects, to fail to serve consumers' long run interests. Given this tension between short- and long-term economic effects of both creation and copying, it is no easy matter to determine what balance would achieve the highest net value."

Although the authors of *Manifesto* advocate a market orientated approach to the protection of computer software concluding that protection should be limited to a relatively short period to protect "market lead time" this would be inappropriate in relation to trade marks or indeed brands. Whereas patent protection is limited because only a short term is thought to be necessary to provide an appropriate incentive, if the protection of trade marks was equally limited their use by third parties (beyond the period of exclusivity) would result in the loss of distinctiveness of the original trade mark and accordingly the trade mark would lose its value both to the consumer (as a unique identifier, an assurance of quality and indication of source) and to the trade mark owner.

8-18   A further important distinction between software protection and trade mark protection concerns the nature of the subject being protected. Computer software protection focuses upon the creation of a product (software) whereas trade mark protection centres on the creation of a reputation. Accordingly, it is appropriate that trade mark protection be maintained for as long as the reputation

---

[43] *ibid.*, p. 270.
[44] The notion of "creation" in this context refers to the actual writing of the computer program.
[45] (1994) 94 *Colum L.Rev* 2308 (hereafter "Manifesto").
[46] "Assertive Modesty: An Economics of Intangibles" (1994) 94 *Colum. L.Rev.* 2579 at 2587 ("Assertive Modesty").

continues. Furthermore, as there is not a shortage of trade marks or elements from which to develop a trade mark, there is no reason to limit the extent of their use by brand owners provided that protection does not extend beyond the actual use of the trade mark (that is, once the mark ceases to be used) and that the mark in question is distinctive and not descriptive (since others would be deprived of the ability to describe their products).[47] Thus continued protection of a trade mark for the life of its use in relation to the product makes economic sense.[48]

8–19   Thus we can see that in economic terms protection of a trade mark can be justified as long as the mark is in use, if it reduces consumer search costs and if the trade mark can be relied upon as a symbol of origin or quality assurance. Failure to provide protection can lead to asymmetrical market failure, as "free riders" seek to trade off the investment and creative effort of the original brand owner. Too great a level of protection, however, would restrict competition and increase the search costs for manufacturer's seeking to adopt new trade marks.

8–20   Economic theory cannot, however, be relied upon to justify extending protection beyond trade marks to other aspects of a brand unless the imitation of these additional aspects also creates consumer confusion and increases consumer search costs. If there is no confusion as to source then it could be argued that additional protection would restrict competition and increase manufacturers' search costs without providing additional benefits to the consumer.[49]

8–21   Neither can additional protection be justified, in economic terms, on the basis of the rationale applied to patents and copyright (that is as an incentive), if it is felt that the aspects of brands that require additional protection will be developed in any event without any further incentive in the form of increased protection. Unlike copyright and patents, where the inventor/author may need encouragement to disclose an invention/creation which he might otherwise keep to himself, brand owners need no such encouragement to disclose their brands for the simple reason that there would be no brand without disclosure. In other words it is only as a result of disclosure that a brand actually evolves and this, in turn, is as a result of the need for the brand owner to differentiate his goods from those of competitors. Whilst it is possible to argue on economic grounds, that brand owners need an incentive to create brands, it is suggested that an alternative justification to that of economic theory is needed if brand owners' rights are to be extended (in the absence of classic confusion) beyond the scope of existing intellectual property institutions.[50]

(b) A moral theory

(i) A moral theory based on "desert"

8–22   Becker, who has written extensively on the subject of desert theory, explains[51] that the desert theory is a moral theory which seeks to justify the grant of

---

[47] Landes & Posner at p. 288.
[48] *ibid.* at p. 287.
[49] This does, of course, depend on how such additional benefits are assessed and quantified. Additional benefits could be in the form of consumer confidence in the reliability or functionality of a technical product. For example, in the case of mobile telephones, a consumer unfamiliar with the technical nature of the product may rely upon the strength of a brand name alone on the basis that the brand in question has established a particular reputation for providing value for money.
[50] Kamperman Sanders argues that economic theory provides compelling reasons for protecting intellectual creations but notes that property rule based systems give rise to monopoly situations. He therefore advocates a liability based system of protection. See Kamperman Sanders, *Unfair Competition Law* (Clarendon Press, Oxford, 1997) 120 ("Unfair Competition").
[51] "Deserving to Own Intellectual Property" [1993] 68 *Chicago-Kent Law Review* 609. See more generally, Becker, "Property Rights: Philosophical Foundations" (Routledge Kegan Paul, Boston, 1980).

a proprietary right to the creator of intellectual property on the basis that the "effort" in creating the thing "deserves" to be recognised and rewarded such that the creator can prevent imitation of his work.[52]

8–23   The difficulty with the desert theory is in determining what efforts are deserving of protection and the measure of protection to be granted. As Spence points out,[53] assessing effort as a means of determining whether to grant a reward can produce mixed results:

> "Many of the best valuable intangibles are the result of moments of inspiration that involve little or no apparent effort on the part of the person claiming the intangible. The work of the perspiring, but not the inspired, 'creator' would be protected by law."

Hettinger also argues[54] that a property right is not an appropriate reward if it is disproportional to the effort expended by the creator. Hettinger defines "effort" as including not how hard someone worked to achieve a result but the amount of risk assumed and the degree to which moral considerations were integral in choosing the result intended. He goes on to say that "desert" should not necessarily be proportional to the effort, but to the social value of the thing produced. The reason for this narrow interpretation of "desert" is presumably to encourage creative effort to be directed towards those works with a social value rather than works of no social value. He acknowledges, however, that such an assessment would be extremely difficult to apply in practice.

8–24   Becker, on the other hand, argues that the desert principle can be justified on the basis that the "creator" has produced something of benefit to society which entitles him to receive in turn, a benefit from society and that property rights are the most fitting and proportional return for that benefit.[55] Once again, however, there is the thorny question of proportionality since some would argue that the benefit to the author of a property right outweighs that received by society. Whether the effort in writing a comic (a work of copyright) is proportional in value to that of the copyright granted (that is the life of the author plus 70 years) and whether it is right that authors of complex computer programs and great works of literature deserve the same benefits as authors of comics, etc., are questions that are not easily answered by the desert theory. Given these shortcomings, it is difficult to rely upon a moral theory (based on the principal of "desert") to justify an increase in the protection of branded products identified as necessary above.

(ii) A moral theory based on principles of natural law

8–25   One exponent of the natural rights theory of laws is John Locke. His theories concerning property acquisition as a result of labour expended are set out in his book entitled *Two Treatises of Government* published in 1698. Locke sought to explain the theory of property acquisition and the duties of persons' towards each other based on the idea that a person's body belongs to that person and the product of his labour is his also. His labour theory of property (his first main thesis) states that:

---

[52] Luke 10 v. 7 "For the labourer is worth his hire".
[53] See his criticism of calls for the introduction of a general law against misappropriation of what he calls "valuable intangibles" based upon the moral theory of desert. "Passing Off and the Misappropriation of Valuable Intangibles" (1996) 112 L.Q.R. 472 at 487 ("Spence").
[54] "Justifying Intellectual Property" (1989) 18 *Philosophy & Public Affairs* 31 at 41.
[55] p. 625.

"Though the earth, and all inferior creatures be common to all men, yet every man has a property in his own person. This nobody has any right to but himself. The labour of his body, and the work of his hands, we may say, are properly his."[56]

Locke's second main thesis was that the appropriation of an unowned object arises out of the application of human labour towards that object, subject to the proviso that there is "enough and as good left over"[57]:

"For this labour being the unquestionable property of the labourer, no man but he can have a right to what that is once joined to, at least where there is enough and as good left in common for others."

Thus, in an unowned orchard, if a labourer picks apples for himself, according to the Lockean principle the labourer will own the apples he picks provided that Locke's caveat applies, that there is sufficient left in the common orchard for others. This proviso is meant to ensure that there is no basis for complaint by others since the labourer has not impaired the position for anyone else. Locke also stated that a person should not take more than he has need of since this would create spoilage and would needlessly deprive others.[58]

8–26   The Lockean theory of property rights can be applied (and indeed has been applied[59]) not only to physical property but also to intellectual property, such that a person can be said to own as property the intellectual objects of his labour, namely the articles that he invents or creates, designs or writes. The Lockean proviso that there must be "enough and as good left over" ensures that there is a public domain from which future creators or inventors can draw.

8–27   Professor Gordon,[60] however, warns against the continued expansion of intellectual property rights based on natural law theory because of the perceived danger that such rights will harm the rights of others to take from the common pool of resources. Gordon's concern is that if the product of all intellectual effort or labour resulted in the grant of a property right there would not be "enough and as good left over" for future creators/inventors and this would in turn cause the system to breakdown. If, however, the proviso can be shown to be satisfied, Gordon accepts that the labourer will receive a reward for his labour at no cost to others.[61]

8–28   Thus Locke's theory can be employed to support an argument for the expansion of intellectual property rights to provide a property right[62] to a labourer (in our case a brand owner) who has expended labour in the creation of a brand, provided that it can be shown that there remains a sufficient public domain from

---

[56] The Second Treatise, Chap. 5 "Of Property" s.27 in *Locke Political Writings* (Penguin, London, 1993) p. 274 ("Locke").

[57] *ibid.*, p. 274.

[58] *ibid.*, s.31, p. 276.

[59] See for example Libling "The Concept of Property: Property in Intangibles" (1978) 94 L.Q.R. 103, whilst not referring to Lockean theory directly the arguments put forward are the same. See also Rose, pp. 5–8, *Millar v. Taylor* at 2335 and (Lord Hardwicke) at 2308. Locke himself considered the question of literary property and, in particular, the term of protection of copyright works in his letters, see Letter to Edward Clarke dated January 2, 1683, and his Memorandum, both referred to in Rose at p. 33.

[60] "A Property Right in Self Expression Equality and Individualism in the Natural Law of Intellectual Property" (1993) 102 Yale L.J. 1533 ("Self Expression").

[61] *ibid*, at p. 1565.

[62] That is, an exclusive right in the property to the owner of the property, to assign the property, to sell it and/or to exclude others from using it or taking it.

which the elements of the brand have been taken to enable third parties to create brands of their own. Such an approach is accepted by Spence[63] as "justify[ing] the right to prevent misappropriation by imitation" and is said to have "strong intuitive appeal". Since there is an infinite number of permutations of names, lettering styles, colouring, graphic illustrations, etc., from which to build a new brand,[64] it is suggested that Locke's proviso can be satisfied and thus Locke's theory can be used as a basis to justify the grant of additional protection to brand owners as a result of their labour. If, however, Gordon is correct and the grant of additional property rights does adversely affect the rights of others to create brands from the common pool because of insufficient resources remaining in the pool, then the further grant of rights can not be justified. It is accepted that if brand owners are granted wide ranging absolute rights particularly in respect of limited resources (such as say single colours in respect of all product packaging), then there is a risk that competitors will soon run out of available materials (in this case colours) from which to choose. If, however, the right is limited to say colour combinations, or combinations of colour and graphics as applied to particular objects such as product packaging, then the number of possibilities from which competitors can choose increases, as indeed it does when the resources are not absolute as in the case of graphics generally.[65] Lockean theory does therefore support an argument for increasing the rights of brand owners but one which would not support brand rights over certain limited resources.

8–29 As Gordon points out,[66] ordinarily, the person seeking to claim a property right is expected to justify why the law should enable him to exclude others from his property. However, if the "common pool" of resources is not diminished as a result of the grant of the property right then it should be for the would-be appropriator to bear the burden of explaining why the labourer's property claim should not prevent him from using that which would otherwise belong to the labourer. The responsibility for bearing the burden of proof is not, however, a simple issue[67]; in practice, the question of whether or not a particular right will be acknowledged or granted is often determined by policy (as a result of lobbying) or politics rather than a matter of establishing the requisite burden of proof.[68]

8–30 One of the weaknesses of Locke's theory of property is its requirement of exclusive possession which, of necessity, deprives others of the benefit of the product of the labour.[69] Thus in the case of the apples picked in the orchard, the

---

[63] Spence at pp. 491–492.

[64] "Our analysis suggests that the universe from which trademarks are picked is very large" Landes & Posner at p. 273. Although these comments were made in relation to trade marks it is suggested they can equally be applied to brands since the building blocks from which brands are created are the same, as those of trade marks.

[65] Of course, there is the objection that to allow ownership of one combination restricts what is left for others such that there is not as much and as good left over. Whilst it is accepted that in theory there may be at least one less option available, in practice the range of alternatives available to others is such that there is "enough and as good left over".

[66] Self Expression at p. 1566.

[67] It is a common theme in writings on legal theory for the exponent to state that the burden of proving the justification for the grant (or refusal to grant a right) should be on the one opposing the view put forward. See for example Gordon, Hettinger (referred to above at nn.60 and 54 respectively) and Paine "Trade Secrets and the Justification of Intellectual Property: A Comment on Hettinger" *Philosophy & Public Affairs* 19:247.

[68] See Strowel, *Of Authors and Origins* (Clarendon Press, Oxford, 1994) at p. 236 ("Strowel") where he explains that in France the acceptance of the *droit d'auteur* as a property right based on natural law principles can be traced back to the French Revolution, and in particular the value ascribed to property rights by the Revolutionary legislators resulting in a broad interpretation of the rights of an author.

[69] For other criticisms of Locke see Nozick, "Anarchy, State and Utopia" (Basil Blackwell, Oxford, 1974) at p. 175 and Harris, *Property & Justice* (Clarendon Press, Oxford, 1996) at pp. 202–203.

labourer, of necessity, must have exclusive possession of the apples in order to enjoy them. Hettinger argues, however, that because the creator of intellectual property does not need exclusive possession in order to enjoy the fruit of his labour there is a weakness in applying the Lockean approach to intellectual property. As more than one labourer can "enjoy" the fruit of the intellectual labour the grant of exclusive possession (*i.e.* a property right) is unnecessary. Thus for example, if the product of the labourer's intellectual labour is the invention of a wheelbarrow, it does not deprive the labourer of his enjoyment of the wheelbarrow if a second labourer seeing how the first barrow is made goes off and makes his own.[70]

8–31   In spite of this weakness, Hettinger recognises that the moral argument that one has a right to possess and personally use what one has developed does have some merit but he goes on to question whether the labourer should have the right to trade his right (in our example, his right in the invention of the wheelbarrow) and receive the full market value for it. Thus Hettinger distinguishes between the recognition of the labour and the labourer's ability to receive the market value for the resulting product. Hettinger's concern is that the labourer did nothing to create the market value for his product (which may be significant) and which may be disproportionate to the amount of effort expended by him. Spence[71] too is concerned that the labourer does not exert enough effort and questions Locke's assumption that it is to a large extent the labour that gives rise to the value of a product. The point at issue for both Hettinger and Spence is how to measure the contribution of the labourer's effort. Locke sought to rely on his experiences of real property to explain that:

> ". . . 'tis labour indeed that puts the difference of value on everything; and let anyone consider what the difference is between an acre of land planted with tobacco or sugar, sown with wheat or barley; and an acre of the same land lying in common, without and husbandry upon it, and he will find that the improvement of labour makes the far greater part of the value"[72]

8–32   Whilst Spence rejects out of hand the application of Locke's words to intellectual property,[73] it is suggested that Locke was correct in that there is a close association between the labourer and the product of his labour. In relation to intangible aspects of a brand, as with tangible property, however, a subjective assessment of the quality of the labour does not assist in determining the application of Locke's theory. If the level of effort is perceived to be a significant factor then this might be overcome by introducing a threshold below which a property right would not be granted, *i.e.* *de minimis* effort would not create a property right. The difficulty would be in determining such a threshold[74] and we

---

[70] In the debate over literary property, the proponents of literary property argued that Locke's theory did not justify common law rights in invention because the quality of labour was less.

[71] Spence at p. 493.

[72] Locke at p. 281 (s.40).

[73] His rejection is based on Locke's assumption that mixing labour with raw materials gives rise to an association between the labourer and his "creation" sufficient to establish a property right. In Spence's view, the proportion of labour to raw materials is insufficient (in the context of intellectual property) to form the basis of a property right. In other words, Spence regards the degree of creativity involved as being too small to justify the grant of a property right in relation to aspects of intellectual property. (Spence at pp. 492–493).

[74] Similar thresholds have already been established in other areas of intellectual property law for example single words and titles under copyright law, and descriptive words under trade mark law. See for example *Exxon Corp v. Exxon Insurance Consultants* [1982] R.P.C. 69, CA and *British Sugar plc v. James Robertson & Sons Ltd* [1996] R.P.C. 281.

shall return to this question later. Thus we have seen that Locke's theory of property can plausibly justify the proposition that a labourer is entitled to the fruits of his labour.

8–33   In Gordon's critical analysis of the extension of property rights to aspects of intangible intellectual property,[75] she recognises that "it is unjust to appropriate the fruit's of another's labour".[76] Gordon thus steps beyond the justification of protection based on natural rights to justify protection of those rights against misappropriation using the expression made famous in the United States case of *International News Service v. Associated Press*[77] where it was said that a copyist was "reap[ing] where it ha[d] not sown"[78] and where accordingly the Supreme Court granted the plaintiff protection against what the court regarded as "unfair" competition. The recognition that it is unjust to appropriate the fruits of another persons labour might, she suggests, be regarded as restitutionary in that[79]:

> ". . . it reflects a belief that some unspecified rewards are due to those whose labour produces benefits and that when third parties intercept these rewards, the law should intervene to effect their restoration."

Whereas Ricketson advocates the introduction of a general law against misappropriation based upon the reap/sow principle,[80] Gordon warns that the restitutionary principle (which, as she describes it, seems to conflate the principle of natural law with desert theory) cannot be applied to all situations of "unjust enrichment" (*i.e.* where reap/sow applies):

> ". . . when taken literally, as a stand alone prohibition on free riding, the restitutionary claim is drastically overloaded. A culture could not exist if all free riding were prohibited within it . . .".[81]

8–34   Gordon sets out a number of pre-conditions that the plaintiff should be required to satisfy in order to establish a valid reap/sow claim. Meeting these criteria does not *ipso facto* entitle a plaintiff to relief, the preconditions merely define the category of cases where recovery is possible. Thus Gordon's proposal cannot be described as an action for misappropriation alone since not all misappropriations are considered to be actionable. Instead, Gordon describes her proposal as an action for "unfair competition" or more accurately "malcompetitive copying". The preconditions for an action for malcompetitive copying are:

(i)   that the defendant knowingly copied an "eligible intangible";

(ii)   in a context of asymmetrical market failure;

---

[75] "Intellectual Property and the Restitutionary Impulse" [1992] 78 *Virginia Law Review* 149 ("Restitutionary").
[76] Gordon herself does not justify the initial grant of a property right on the basis of Lockean labour theory but by tracing the restitutionary notion to its roots in "corrective justice" a concept originally described by Aristotle (Aristotle, *The Nicomacean Ethics* 84–86 (Hippocrates G. Apostle tran. 1975)), or more particularly a variation on this concept referred to as "status quo—corrective justice".
[77] 248 U.S. 215 (1918 Supreme Court).
[78] Hereafter the "reap/sow principle".
[79] Restitutionary at p. 167.
[80] Ricketson " 'Reaping without Sowing': Unfair Competition and Intellectual Property Rights in Anglo-Australian Law" [1994] U.N.S.W. Law Journal 1 ("Ricketson").
[81] Restitutionary at p. 167.

(iii) where a competitive nexus exists between the plaintiff and the defendant; and

(iv) there is a situation of non-reciprocity between the parties.

Taking each element in turn, Gordon explains that to satisfy the first requirement the plaintiff must show that the defendant's act of copying was deliberate in that he knew that the material copied was the property of another. Innocent infringement is therefore beyond the scope of Gordon's actionable reap/sow claim. There must be a situation of asymmetrical market failure, which, as we have already seen, means that one party must face a barrier to entry into a market which subsequent entrants do not face thus making it economically more attractive to copy than to create. Gordon's third requirement flows from the essence of the reap/sow principle. If the plaintiff and defendant do not operate in competition such that the defendant does not take sales away from the plaintiff, then the defendant cannot be said to be unjustly enriched at the plaintiff's expense. Accordingly Gordon suggests that the plaintiff is not entitled to relief. If, however, the plaintiff can show that the defendant is operating in an area into which the plaintiff is about to expand, then it should be possible to obtain relief.

8–35   Gordon's final requirement reflects her view that society does not develop without copying and that all creators copy, to a degree, pre-existing works. Accordingly, if the defendant can show that the plaintiff copied from another source, or that the plaintiff will in turn copy the defendant's work then the plaintiff's claim can be defeated. If, on the other hand, the plaintiff can demonstrate that the reproduction by the defendant is of no reciprocal value to the plaintiff, then the plaintiff should, in Gordon's view, be entitled to redress.

8–36   As a prerequisite to Gordon's action for "malcompetitive copying" the plaintiff must demonstrate that it owns an "eligible intangible" which the defendant has copied. A "eligible intangible" is described as consisting of something that was deliberately created (over and above any existing legal duty to create) with the expectation of reward or control; that the plaintiff must have clearly marked the intangible as being its own property (*i.e.* tagged it). Finally, the plaintiff must show that the intangible is suitable for the purposes of trading in a market. Gordon herself admits, that this final requirement is something of a "grey area" which needs to be "fleshed out by the courts on a case by case basis". She highlights the possible obstacles to protection under this final head as being policy considerations such as free speech which can act to deny protection to what would otherwise be regarded as an "eligible intangible" noting that the "tort of . . . malcompetitve copying will remain a highly dangerous judicial tool"[82] until such time as this grey area is clarified by means of judicial precedent.

8–37   Finally, Gordon argues against the recognition of a proprietary right for the creator advocating instead for the payment of damages by the defendant. Although Gordon does not identify what actions might constitute malcompetitive copying, she does provide a means of determining liability based on restitutionary principles, taking into account the conduct of the parties.

8–38   Kamperman Sanders, in his analysis of unfair competition laws, criticises Gordon's proposal on the grounds that her requirement for tagging, "presupposes that the plaintiff can exercise control on the basis of acquired rights".[83] This, he

---

[82] *ibid.* at p. 224.
[83] Unfair Competition at p. 152.

says, amounts to a property claim before the right is granted. Kamperman Sanders goes on to argue that although Gordon's criteria for liability are taken from the doctrine of unjust enrichment "they are displaced by the need for claims on protectable interests (tags)".[84-85] As a consequence, he argues that Gordon's action for malcompetitive copying becomes a property claim rather than a liability based action for unjust enrichment. This shift from liability for unjust enrichment to a property claim can, he suggests, be reversed if the acts of the defendant are predominant in the assessment of unjust enrichment, this in turn would place greater emphasis upon Gordon's requirement of competitive nexus. This modified interpretation of Gordon's criteria would bring her action for malcompetitive copying alongside Kamperman Sander's own proposal for a law of unfair competition—or as he calls it, an action for "malign competition" which is also based on principles of unfair competition and restitution.

8–39   Spence[86] also criticises Gordon's proposition because, in his view, her treatment of the reap/sow principle as the basis of an action for malcompetitive copying fails to address the question of "whether a plaintiff should be given rights of any kind, including property rights, in a valuable intangible". Instead, according to Spence, Gordon addresses the next question which is "how the law should respond when the property in a valuable intangible is used without consent."

8–40   If, however, the grant of property rights can be justified based on the application of Locke's theory (as discussed above[87]), then restitutionary principles (based on status quo-corrective justice criteria) could be used to justify legal intervention on behalf of an inventor/creator to obtain redress against an unauthorised user. In such a situation restitutionary principles would provide a suitable basis for extending protection and would satisfy the objections raised *inter alia* by Spence. Though liability for "unjust enrichment" may not equate with "property rights" the latter usually allow an "owner" to obtain injunctive relief etc and damages where these is no loss.

(iii) Moral theory as applied to brands

8–41   In the situation that we are concerned with here, namely the protection of brands, the moral theory would justify the brand owner's desire for additional protection without necessarily requiring the grant of a full monopoly right in the brand.

8–42   It does this first, by acknowledging that the exercise of labour, skill and investment by the brand owner (or more properly the brand creator) gives rise to a property right in the object of his creation namely the brand. Reproduction of the brand (or elements of it) by a defendant, in competition with a brand owner, would form the basis of an action for unjust enrichment provided that the defendant has benefited at the plaintiff's expense. It would also be necessary for the plaintiff to show that the market will fail because the defendant does not face the same barriers to entry as the plaintiff and, as a consequence, will seek to undercut the plaintiff. Although in this scenario the brand owner is not granted a full monopoly right in respect of his creation, the undesirable anti-competitive behaviour of the defendant would be restrained.

8–43   If we accept that additional protection can be justified on the basis of moral theory (a combination of natural rights and the principles of restitution)[88]

[84-85] Unfair Competition at p. 157.
[86] Spence at p. 491.
[87] pp. 14–18.
[88] Or even based on economic theory, as suggested by Kamperman Sanders (see n.43 above).

such that third parties should be prevented from seeking to trade off the labour, skill and investment of others and profit unjustly by so doing, then the next question to consider is how this increased protection should be formulated.

THE OPTIONS

8–44   It is suggested that the level of protection afforded to branded products falls short of that needed to maintain a "fair" market economy and that additional protection can be justified on the basis of moral theory, but how should such protection be achieved and how will it fit with current international obligations, in particular the Paris Convention, the Berne Convention, the Treaty of Rome and the GATT-TRIPS Agreement? A number of alternative means exist through which changes may be introduced including self regulation of codes of practice, modification of the common law, or the introduction of primary legislation aimed specifically at this area of commerce. We shall consider each possibility in turn before addressing the international dimension and existing treaty obligations.

(a) The means for introducing change

(i) Self-regulation

8–45   Rather than introduce a new statutory framework setting out the increased scope of protection for branded products it would be possible instead to introduce a system of codes of practice and, by means of secondary legislation, to appoint a particular body to regulate the application of the codes to the relevant business sectors involved. Such a system already operates in relation to the regulation of advertising material (as discussed below).

8–46   Administratively it may be more economical to employ a system of self-regulation rather than rely on the civil courts (or criminal courts). The costs to the parties themselves might also be lower if the codes could be enforced by means other than the civil court system. It would, of course, be necessary to determine whether an official "regulator" should be appointed and, if so, the scope of its powers. Should the regulator, for example, be permitted to initiate proceedings on its own behalf against offenders or should it only be permitted to act in response to a complaint of some kind. In either case, it is essential that the body responsible for enforcing the code is in a position to institute and enforce penalties for non-compliance otherwise there is a danger that businesses would ignore the body completely.

8–47   As noted in Chapter 6, the body responsible for administering the system of self-regulation within the advertising industry is the Committee of Advertising Practice ("CAP"), which is responsible for devising and enforcing the codes of practice (the "Codes"). The CAP acknowledges[89] that the strength of the system of self-regulation depends on the long term commitment of all those involved.

8–48   Whilst the Advertising Standards Authority ("ASA") has been responsible for enforcing the system of self regulation in the advertising industry for a number of years, the effectiveness of such self regulation remains open to question. Whilst self regulation enables a more flexible approach to be taken to enforcement, the regulatory organisation is frequently criticised for not being independent of the industry that it is regulating.[90] Furthermore, the ASA does not, itself, have the

---

[89] See para 68.2 of the British Codes of Advertising and Sales Promotion ("Advertising Codes").
[90] ". . . the ASA is an independent organisation representing the consumer, funded by the advertising industry . . . to enforce a code developed by the advertising industry. It has no government backing and only a quasi-legal status. It is hardly surprising that many within the industry are unclear where its first duty lies and may outside the industry doubt its independence". *Marketing* July 10, 1997.

necessary power to take action against offenders. Instead it must refer the matter to
the Office of Fair Trading ("OFT") which in turn will decide whether any formal
action should be taken against an offender. Whilst this ability to refer matters to the
OFT can prove effective it is still true to say that the ASA lacks the legal
wherewithall to ensure compliance with its decisions, at least initially. Thus, it is
possible for businesses to abuse the Codes (perhaps by publishing a controversial
advertisement) and ignore the ASA's ruling as in the case of French Connection
which ignored rulings of the ASA in connection with its use of the slogan FCUK in
advertising.[90a] The delay caused by the referral to the OFT means that an
injunction, if granted, may well be too late to prevent a controversial
advertisement.

8-49   Thus although it is possible for a new system of brand protection to be
enforced by means of self regulation, if it is to be effective it not only needs the
long term commitment of all those involved (which itself may prove difficult since
it is not necessarily in everyone's interests to comply with the codes[91]), but it also
needs sufficient powers to compel parties to comply with its decisions. Like the
ASA,[92] it would also have to be independent of the sector of industry in which it
operated.

8-50   Following the lobbying of the Brand Producers and Brand Owners Group
(BPBOG) against the increasing use of lookalikes in supermarkets, at the time of the
reading of the Trade Marks Bill (November 1995), the Institute of Grocery
Distribution[93] set up a dispute resolution procedure to tackle the problems
concerning packaging and trade dress. In the preamble to the statement setting out
the resolution procedure the IGD acknowledged the importance of distinctive and
innovative product appearance in creating goodwill and the risk of consumers
mistakenly believing that the own label product was made by the brand owner due
to similarities in packaging, stating that:

> ". . . in the interests of consumers and the legitimate promotion of goodwill
> and co-operation within industry, it is desirable to:
>
> - encourage competition but avoid commercial plagiarism in packag-
>   ing and trade dress;
> - minimise the risk of consumers either selecting products by mistake,
>   or assuming that different products have been made by the same
>   manufacturer; and
> - respect the unique identity of innovative new product packaging by
>   not adopting its distinctive and arbitrary features . . ."

The resolution procedure provides a channel for resolving disputes for those
organisations that are signatories to the procedure.[94] The first limitation of the
procedure therefore is the fact that it does not extend to all businesses involved in
grocery distribution not to mention those involved in the manufacture and retail
sale of branded or own label products.

[90a] *French Connection Ltd v. Antony Toolseeram Sutton* IPD 23013 (February 2000).
[91] This assumes that a code of conduct can actually be agreed by the various industry sectors involved.
This may not be a straightforward matter as the experience of the Institute of Grocery Distribution
discovered (see below at paras 8-50—8-52).
[92] At least half of the 12 member council appointed to govern the ASA is unconnected with advertising
business (Advertising Codes para. 68.12).
[93] A trade organisation of which most supermarkets are members ("IGD").
[94] At the time of writing retailers that have signed up to the dispute resolution procedure include Tesco
plc, J Sainsbury plc and the Argyll Group.

8–51   The first stage of the IGD procedure involves "urgent bilateral talks" at director level. If the dispute is not resolved it is then referred to the Centre for Dispute Resolution for mediation in accordance with its protocols. Subject to agreement by the parties, the mediator may be asked to give a recommendation as to the outcome of the dispute but it is not binding on the parties. This means that if the alleged offender is unwilling to change those aspects of its product that cause offence to the brand owner, the procedure for dispute resolution will not compel the offender to change its product. There is therefore little incentive to the brand owner to use this procedure.

8–52   As the dispute resolution procedure is entirely confidential and no public disclosures are made without the consent of both parties, it is extremely difficult to assess whether or not the procedure is at all effective. Clearly it has its limitations, notably, that:

(i)   the outcome of a case dealt with in accordance with the procedure remains secret unless both parties agree to disclosure;

(ii) members of the IGD are not obliged to use the procedure—it thus requires willingness on both sides to submit themselves to the procedure;

(iii) the outcome of the resolution process is not binding on the parties; and

(iv) it only applies to the grocery trade.

Whilst some of these shortcomings could be overcome by using secondary legislation to implement the code,[95] this does not overcome the fact that the process of mediation is inappropriate when dealing with situations of infringement. Mediation is generally speaking suited to situations where compromise arrangements can be reached. Infringements of intellectual property rights do not usually arise in situations that can be compromised in any meaningful way without undermining the rights of those involved. Further, in relation to dissimilar goods, the diversity of trade areas in which the parties operate could prevent difficulties. For these reasons, it is felt that introducing new codes, along the lines of those already introduced by the IGD, with a view to enforcement by means of self-regulation would not be an appropriate means of meeting all four shortfalls especially if the self-regulation took the form of mediation.

(ii) Common Law

8–53   Common law is the process by which each judicial determination adds to the existing body of reasoning for application to future cases for which no exact precedent exists. It is the incremental growth of decisions and judicial reasoning that enables the common law to be flexible, to adapt to new circumstances and be applied in new situations. As Callmann[96] observes:

"[i]nflexible though laws made by judicial decision may be . . . the process of formulation of such laws allows for a far greater variation to meet different circumstances. General rules derived from numerous specific situations are

---

[95] As in the case of the self-regulation of advertising which was established by the Control of Misleading Advertising Regulations 1988.
[96] "He who reaps where he has not sown: Unjust enrichment in the law of unfair competition" (1942) 55 *Harvard Law Review* 595 at p. 609 "Callmann".

more adaptable in their outline to other situations of the same nature, whatever their inadequacies when confronted by major social and economic changes".

Callmann argues in favour of the introduction of a general rule of law introduced by government and elaborated by the courts such that:

"one who has used his intellectual, physical, or financial powers to create a commercial product should be afforded judicial relief from a competitor who seeks to 'reap where he has not sown'".[97]

He believes that the courts are "the most desirable agency" to introduce and develop such a concept of law. In England, however, judges have been reluctant to develop new areas of law without the express mandate of Parliament, or in the case of E.C. legislation, the Council and Parliament.[98] Although I agree that the judiciary is best suited to develop such a body of law, without a clear mandate to do so it is extremely unlikely that it will.[98a] A legislative solution is therefore the only realistic solution, however inflexible it may be when compared to a common law or self-regulatory approach.[99]

(iii) Legislation

8–54   There are a number of disadvantages in introducing a change in the legal status quo by means of legislation. Callmann, referring to Savigny,[1] points out that codification by statute[2]:

"induces an interpretation of words instead of consideration of the nature of the question; it pretends to be complete and all-embracing when it never can be so; it demands a dangerously abstract formulation of rules; it is too static, too unchangeable."[3]

There are difficulties in relying upon statute to regulate commercial practice not least because of the difficulty in anticipating the circumstances in which the new law will have to operate, the difficulties of avoiding ambiguity and providing certainty of meaning. It is not possible for statutes to adapt quickly if written on the basis of technological assumptions without risks to the cohesion of the statute concerned.[4] Due to the procedural formalities involved in the introduction of new legislation it inevitably takes time for new statutes to be introduced or for existing ones to be amended. By comparison the common law develops and is able to adopt much more quickly. However, as noted above, if the judiciary is not willing to increase the scope of protection available to branded products through the common law it is essential that legislation be implemented to tackle the issue. Care will need

---

[97] Callmann, at p. 612.
[98] See for example the comments of Laddie J. in *Wagamama* at p. 731.
[98a] Members of the judiciary have expressed doubts in a number of cases as to the desirability of judge made law. See by way of example *Moorgate Tobacco v. Philip Morris* [1985] R.P.C. 219.
[99] Callmann agrees that if the courts will not act to introduce such principles of unfair competition the legislature must do so. See Callmann, at p. 611.
[1] Savigny, Vom Beruf Unsrer Zeit Fur Gesetzgebung und Rechtswissenshaft (3d. Ed 1892) 10.
[2] Callmann, p. 609.
[3] Although this can hardly be said of the civilian codes.
[4] As in the case of computer software which is regarded as a "literary work" even though it is quite different in nature from other material covered by that definition.

to be taken, however, to ensure that the purpose of the statute is clear and unequivocal so that the exercise of judicial discretion might be encouraged to support the expressed purpose of the Act.

(b) International obligations

8–55   Before turning to consider in detail the form that any additional legislation might take, we need first to ensure that its adoption would not be in conflict with existing international treaty obligations. The principle treaties of interest in this area are the Paris Convention, the Berne Convention, the Treaty of Rome and the GATT-TRIPS Agreement. If new legislation conflicts with the provisions of any of these agreements then implementation could be challenged at an international level (in a case of the breach of the Treaty of Rome at the European Court of Justice, and of the GATT-TRIPS Agreement at the World Trade Organisation[5]). It is therefore important to examine the provisions of these treaties at this stage to ensure compliance.

(i) Paris Convention

8–56   As we saw in Chapter 2 the Paris Convention provides for a minimum standard of protection in member countries of industrial property including *inter alia* trade marks and the repression of unfair competition.[6] Member countries are obliged to provide particular forms of protection and to ensure that there is no discrimination against those that are not nationals of the countries concerned. In other words there must be national treatment by member countries for nationals of all member countries. This therefore means that if the government introduces new legislation to provide greater protection for aspects of branded products, it must ensure that protection is available to nationals of all Paris Convention countries and not just to United Kingdom nationals or members of the E.U. unless it can be argued that the extended form of protection falls outside its scope as was the case of the unregistered design right.

8–57   The treaty is not exhaustive in that it is possible to provide forms of protection in addition to those specified in Article 1, albeit that such additional protection may fall within the general umbrella term of the "repression of unfair competition" specified in Article 1. Of particular interest in relation to the latter is Article 10bis which for example, places an obligation on members states to provide effective protection against unfair competition. If the new legislation proposed below can be regarded as a form of unfair competition law then, it is submitted, it will fall within the terms of the Paris Convention and will not be in conflict with it even though the rights that we are seeking to protect, in particular the intangible aspects of brands, are not specifically referred to in the treaty. Ricketson[8] concurs with this view and argues that although the misappropriation of valuable intangibles are not specifically covered, as a matter of principle, Article 10bis(2):

> "must . . . include misappropriation of intangible business values, as these are usually accepted as forming the most important part of the concept of unfair competition."

---

[5] Neither the Paris Convention nor the Berne Convention include provisions relating to enforcement of their terms.
[6–7] Art. 1 of the Paris Convention.
[8] Ricketson at p. 36.

If this is indeed the case then adoption of the proposals set out below would not be contrary to the Paris Convention. Alternatively, if the proposed new legislation could be said to protect the rights of author in their literary and artistic works then it would arguably fall outside the scope of the Paris Convention and would fall within the terms of the Berne Convention.

(ii) The Berne Convention

8–58 Like the Paris Convention, the Berne Convention seeks to establish a minimum standard of protection throughout members of the Union. Its sphere of application relates to the rights of authors in their literary and artistic works. Although the expression "literary and artistic works" is very wide and is said to encompass "every production in the literary, scientific and artistic domain, whatever may be the mode or form of its expression". If the elements of the brand that we are seeking to protect (in particular the intangible aspects of a brand) do not fall within this definition then the Berne Convention will be of no relevance to my proposed new legislation. It is suggested that those elements of a brand that we are concerned with do fall outside the Berne Convention because they have been denied protection under existing legislation including the Copyright, Designs and Patent Act, as discussed earlier in the book.

(iii) The Treaty of Rome

8–59 One of the principle tenets of the Treaty of Rome is the establishment of a Common Market which permits the free movement of goods. In order to achieve this aim the members of the Treaty agree to work towards an approximation (and to a harmonisation of laws) to eliminate all quantitative restrictions on imports and all other measures having equivalent effect.[9] Whilst acknowledging that the operation of intellectual property laws are not primarily concerned with placing restrictions on imports the Treaty accepts that the exercise of intellectual property rights can effectively restrict the importation of goods that are alleged to infringe those rights. In order to balance these competing interests the ECJ has endeavoured to draw a line between the existence of intellectual property rights and the exercise of these rights so that rights may not be exercised in such a way as to act as a barrier to the free movement of goods. Provided that the proposed new law does not indiscriminately act as a barrier to the free movement of goods it should not be in conflict with treaty obligations. Furthermore, it can be said that the introduction of new legislation in England constitutes a step towards harmonisation of laws with other E.U. members rather than a law to protect the interests of members of the United Kingdom, only then the new law is unlikely to be challenged at the European level. One consequence of this would be that the new right would need to be made available to all members of the E.U. and the United Kingdom, so as to avoid a challenge on the basis of discrimination. Provided that the new provisions comply with these requirements they should not be in conflict with the Treaty of Rome.

(iv) GATT-TRIPS Agreement

8–60 As we saw in Chapter 2, the expressed aim of the GATT-TRIPS Agreement[10] is:

---

[9] Art. 28 EU (formerly Art. 30, Treaty of Rome).
[10] For further information concerning the impact of the TRIPS Agreement see Kaufman "The Impact of the Trade Related Aspects of Intellectual Property Rights Agreement on Tradmark" *TMW* Sept 1997 at 30 and Blakeney *Trade Related Aspects of Intellectual Property* (Sweet & Maxwell, London, 1996) especially at 45–80.

"to reduce distortions and impediments to international trade and to promote effective and adequate protection of Intellectual Property rights and to ensure Intellectual Property rights do not become barriers to trade".

Under Article 1 of the TRIPs Agreement members are permitted, but not obliged, to implement more extensive protection than that specified under the Agreement provided that it does not contravene the terms of the Agreement. By virtue of Article 2, members must comply with Articles 1 to 12 and 19 of the Paris Convention. As we have already seen, if the proposal for new legislation was based on principles of unfair competition it would arguably be within the provisions of the Paris Convention (in particular Article 10bis) and would not be contrary to any other provision of the GATT-TRIPS Agreement. Accordingly, the government would be free to introduce such a new provision should it choose to do so without the risk of a challenge at international level.

8–61 If, on the other hand, new legislation was expressed in the form of the protection of the rights of authors then it would fall under the umbrella of the Berne Convention. Under Article 9 of the TRIPS Agreement members agree to comply with Articles 1 to 21 of the Berne Convention (1971) but excluding Article 6bis.

8–62 Although TRIPS also provides that member countries will adhere to the Berne Convention, for the reason stated above, this will have little impact in relation to my proposed legislation in the field of brands because it falls outside the scope of literary and artistic works covered by the Convention. We can now therefore turn to consider the question of what form such new legislation might take bearing in mind that the rights granted should not discriminate against either members of the E.U. or the Paris Convention (as widened by the TRIPS Agreement).

THE PROPOSAL—PROTECTION AGAINST "UNFAIR COPYING"

8–63 It is suggested that the shortfall in protection outlined above can best be remedied by introducing a new statutory framework for protection against acts of unfair competition.

(a) Unfair competition

8–64 I would advocate the introduction of a general law of unfair competition based on restitutionary principles along the lines of that proposed by Gordon[11] with the aim of introducing a standard of business ethics that would be applicable across the full spectrum of business dealings. Its basis would be that of unjust enrichment; its form might be such as that identified in the WIPO model law of unfair competition.[12] However, in view of the United Kingdom's traditional hostility towards the introduction of such a wide-ranging measure a more limited unauthorised copying right (based on principles of unjust enrichment) is proposed as an interim measure.

(b) Introducing protection against "unfair copying"

8–65 Recognising the reluctance of British Governments to introduce a general law of unfair competition, an alternative approach would be to introduce new "*sui*

---

[11] Restitutionary at p. 277.
[12] For further discussion regarding such a proposal see Kamperman Sanders *Unfair Competition Law* (Clarendon Press, Oxford, 1997).

generis" legislation targeted specifically at increasing the protection of branded products. Adopting a *sui generis* approach is a recognised way of addressing a legal problem that does not fall squarely within an existing statutory framework of intellectual property protection,[13] as in the case of, for example, semiconductor chip topographies, functional designs and more recently databases. Each of these areas suffers from the problem that traditional legal protection is regarded as inappropriate (either being too strong[14] or inadequate[15]) and therefore fails to provide the measure of protection commensurate with the work created. As a consequence, (in the absence of specific legislation) the article in question can be easily copied, and with impunity.[16] The result of such copying can be to discourage investment in the development of these types of product or work because of the risk that the creator will not be able to recover his investment. *Sui generis* legislation can help to redress this imbalance by granting the creator, designer, etc., an exclusive period of ownership of the thing created for a limited period of time sufficient to enable the creator to recover his investment (a "protected lead time"). In each case, the scope of the property right has been limited and includes a reproduction, or copying of a substantial part of the article/work. Setting out the protection in this way limits the scope of the right granted and enables independent creation without infringing the right. The legislation also has the effect of penalising "free riders" or those who would "reap where they have not sown", (the essence of the principle of unfair competition).

8–66   A general law of unfair competition based on the principle of unjust enrichment would perhaps obviate the need for all these stand alone legal hybrids to provide protection as new technologies emerge. Such a law would have the advantage of providing a more general safety net acting as a market regulator—avoiding market failure brought about as a result of unfair copying—and supplementing remedies for infringement of intellectual property rights.[17] If, however, the government prefers to introduce *sui generis* legislation in this piecemeal fashion (perhaps because in each case it is felt that the scope of each new law is narrow and therefore ostensibly non-contentious), then it may prefer to introduce a *sui generis* "brand right" along the lines suggested below.

(i) A brand right

8–67   A *sui generis* brand right should aim to protect a brand from unauthorised or "unfair" copying, that is to say it is the act of copying the brand (or a substantial part of it) that gives rise to liability. As such, the brand owner is not granted an "absolute monopoly" right but rather a "qualified monopoly" right.

---

[13] "One legislative approach to the problems posed by . . . market failures has been a haphazard series of *sui generis* schemes" Karjala "Misappropriation as a Third Intellectual Property Paradigm" (1994) Colum L.Rev. 2594 at 2598 ("Karjala") and Reichman "Legal Hybrids: Between the Patent and Copyright Paradigms" (1994) 94 Colum L.Rev. 2432.
[14] *British Leyland v. Armstrong Patents Co. Ltd* [1986] R.P.C. 279, H.L.
[15] *Magill RTE and ITP v. E.C. Commission* ("Magill") [1995] F.S.R. 530, ECJ.
[16] As noted in recital 7 of the Database Directive (96/9/EC of March 11, 1997) the creation of articles such as databases involve investment of considerable human, technical and financial resources but can be easily copied at a fraction of the cost needed to design them independently. Thus, as recital 40 makes clear, the *sui generis* right established under the Directive aims to protect this investment for the limited duration of the right.
[17] See Lahore "The Herschel Smith Lecture 1992: IP Rights and Unfair Copying" [1992] 12 E.I.P.R. p. 433 in which Lahore recognises that those calling for additional protection in relation to functional designs, computer software and circuit layouts really want protection from unfair copying and argue that such a law can develop effectively within a common law system. See also Karjala, p. 2958 where he suggests focusing on "unfair methods of copying" as an alternative to a *sui generis* approach.

8–68   What is a brand?   The brand right would recognise the brand owner's exclusive right in any aspect (in whole or in part) of the concept[18] of a brand (including it's advertising) and in the brand's overall look and feel. A brand itself would need to be defined as including a list of elements, which should not be exhaustive, but could include the brand name, its appearance, trade dress, packaging design, label, shape or configuration, advertising and promotional themes, and the emotional and intangible aspects of the brand.

8–69   A brand distinguished from a product   Given this wide interpretation of the term "brand" and its potential to include the appearance of a product, it is important to distinguish between a "brand", a "product" and a "trade mark".

8–70   If the brand right were to be established then a "trade mark" would be considered as the source identifier. Whatever aspect of the brand truly acts as an indication of source of the brand should be regarded as the trade mark. This may mean that the trade mark is just a word mark or a device mark, or in exceptional cases may be a three dimensional mark as in the case of the "flying lady" on a Rolls Royce motor car. There may indeed be a number of such signs used in connection with a single brand. The important point to bear in mind is that the source identifier should be evident to consumers from the moment that the brand is launched (*i.e.* it should not depend on marketing strategies, or advertising and promotional activity and it would not therefore include emotional or intangible attributes). The source identifier should be protected by means of trade mark registration.

8–71   The distinction between a brand and a product is, in some respects, similar to the distinction between idea and expression in copyright, in that it is hard to define and that the more general the distinction the more unhelpful it becomes. In order to distinguish a brand and a product it is necessary to consider three stages of the development of the brand. The first stage is the manufacturing process. What is it that is being manufactured? Is it a commodity item (such as toothpaste) or is it a unit (such as a razor or a garment)? It is suggested that for the purposes of the brand right, the product is the result of the manufacturing process, excluding any source identifier or packaging, etc.

8–72   The second stage to consider is the market in which the item is sold. Here the questions to consider are: what commodity is the consumer buying? What can be substituted for the product on offer? What is the generic equivalent of the product offered? These questions are designed to reveal exactly what the market description is for the product in issue. The final stage in the analysis is to consider the product as finally marketed. If all traces of the brand were removed at this stage (*e.g.* packaging, labelling, trade marks, distinctive colouring, non functional design attributes, etc.), what would be left?

8–73   The aim of this three stage analysis is simply to try to distil the product from the brand *per se*. The distinction is an important one since the brand right aims to grant protection in respect of the brand and not in relation to the product itself. Equally, the aim is not to grant additional protection to trade marks as such but rather to protect those elements of a brand that are not adequately protected under existing intellectual property regimes. Thus when assessing the question of infringement in relation to the new brand right, more emphasis should be given to

---

[18] This term is used in order to refer not just to the visual appearance of the brand, the product, its packaging etc but also to the marketing style, strategy and intangible aspects of the brand. It is not, however, intended to limit the brand to an "idea" as such.

those aspects of the brand not protected by trade mark registration than those that are. In so doing it is hoped that brand owners will be more realistic (as opposed to optimistic) about those features of a brand that operate as indications of source, registering them as trade marks but leaving the remainder to be protected by the brand right.[19]

8–74   As I have said, it is in recognition of the role of branding in the promotion and subsequent sale of products and services (as described in more detail in Chapter 1) that we are now considering the form that the additional protection identified should take. To provide additional protection to a product's shape, for example, formulation or method of manufacture would, on the face of it, be supplementing existing legislative frameworks in respect of patents and registered designs without introducing requirements of novelty of equal stringency. Whilst it may be argued that such tests as these are inappropriate when seeking to protect a brand owner against "free riding" care should still be exercised to ensure that legislation that is intended primarily to protect branded products is not used for anti-competitive purposes. Thus the new right does not seek to provide protection of products *per se*—this is beyond the scope of the proposed new law—instead it aims to protect the "brand" (*i.e.* that which is added to, or built around the product) rather than the product itself.

8–75   **Limitations/exclusions**   Thus the new brand right should not be used to extend patent or similar forms of protection unless it can be shown that the defendant has slavishly copied an element (or elements) of the brand in order to take advantage of the plaintiff's effort when various equally effective alternatives exist. Equally the brand right should not be used to protect single words or single colours from unauthorised reproduction by competitor unless, in the case of colours it can be shown that the colour played a particularly significant role in the overall appearance of the brand and its use by a third party is such that it seeks to take unfair advantage of the first brand because of its association with the colour in question. In the case of single words, protection by the means of brand right is denied because of a lack of creativity involved in the creation of single words.[20] The same will be true of descriptive words and other *de minimis* creations, although this does not mean that particular phrases made up of common words may not be protected, unless they are no more than clichés.

8–76   It may also be necessary to develop other limitations over a period of time on a case by case basis once it is seen how the right develops in practice and what elements of brands are commonly reproduced. Whilst, no doubt, some will suggest the need for a "free speech" exception and also perhaps an exception for parodies, I would not endorse such blanket exclusions at the outset.[21]

8–77   **Liability**   As has already been stated, the intention of this new brand right is to protect a brand against unauthorised copying. Defendants could always be assured that provided their work was independently created rather than copied

---

[19] This might also, arguably, have the added advantage of reducing the number of trade mark applications filed in respect of descriptive marks and non-distinctive marks, which are currently filed on the basis that trade mark registration currently offers the only means of protecting these elements of a brand.

[20] See the discussion on, p. 18 concerning the need to establish thresholds as a basis for granting protection.

[21] An example of this would be the use of a poster using Coca-Cola script but using the words "enjoy cocaine" — see *Coca-Cola Company Inc v. Alma Leo USA Inc. 719 F. Supp. 725 (NDILL 1989).*

from a competitor, they would not be liable for infringement. No doubt there will be some cases where the courts will be called upon to determine whether or not a particular defendant has copied a competing brand or simply taken his inspiration from the competing brand. Although it is not easy for the court to draw a line in such a situation, it would not be the first piece of legislation that called for a judicial assessment of such a distinction. A similar position exists in relation to an allegation[22] of copying in relation to copyright[22] and in relation to unregistered design right (as illustrated in the case of *Amoena v. Trulife*[23]). It is for the court to assess the degree of copying by the defendant and the degree of labour exercised by him and to balance this against the degree of similarity with the plaintiff's work and so assess whether any unfair advantage (or unjust enrichment) has been taken. Case law has shown that it is not beyond the ability of the court to look at all the circumstances of the case and to consider the two brands and so determine whether the defendant's action amounts to unfair copying in accordance with the principles of unjust enrichment.

8–78   Liability would therefore arise as a result of copying (or reproducing in any material form) a substantial part of any aspect of a brand (either directly or indirectly) for *commercial purposes*. Whilst it is anticipated that the brand right will most frequently be relied upon by brand owners against competitors, it would not be essential that the defendant be a competitor. Thus the brand right could be relied upon, for example, by the owner of the Pepsi Cola brand to prevent an unauthorised third party from producing a pencil case of the shape and appearance of a can of Pepsi Cola albeit that the third party cannot be said to be a competitor of Pepsi in the strict sense.

8–79   As the mischief that the new statute seeks to prevent is the unauthorised copying of the brand (or elements of the brand), confusion is not a pre-requisite in assessing whether or not there has been unauthorised (or unfair) copying. In determining what amounts to a "substantial" part of the brand, regard should be had not only to the elements of the brand that have been reproduced, but also to the number and proportion of the elements taken or imitated and the overall "look and feel" of the two products as compared to other products in the market.[24] Regard should also be had to those elements that are common to the trade when considering the proportion of elements reproduced.[25]

8–80   As with copyright protection the test of substantiality should primarily be a qualitative and not a purely quantitative test.[26] Unlike copyright though, the court should take into account not only the visual elements of the branded product (such as its packaging) but also the intangible aspects of the brand and the imagery used in the advertising and marketing as this can play a significant role in developing communicative values surrounding the brand in the mind of the consumer and associating particular imagery with the brand. For example, extensive use of a slogan such as "the mint with the hole", over a number of years not only creates a valuable link between the advertising and a feature of the brand, it can also become an asset in itself. The court should also bear in mind the fact that it is not necessary

---

[22] Where what has been "copied" is of primary concern. See for example *Krisarts v. Briarfine* [1980] R.P.C. 213, *Redwood Music v. Chappell* [1977] F.S.R. 537, *Elanco v. Mandops* [1982] R.P.C. 109.
[23] Unreported May 25, 1995 where what the defendant has "added" is of concern.
[24] This is similar to the existing regime in relation to infringement of computer software as applied in *Computer Associates International Inc v. Altai Inc* 982 F. 2d. 693 (2nd Cir. 1992).
[25] This is similar to the position under the law of passing off where elements of the plaintiff's get-up that are "common to the trade" are taken into account when assessing distinctiveness. See Wadlow, p. 432.
[26] *Ladbroke v. William Hill* [1964] 1 W.L.R. 273, HL at 276.

for the two products to be visually identical for the consumer to attribute aspects of one brand to another. It is sufficient if the newcomer's brand incorporates a number of features that might lead consumers to think that there is a connection between the two products as this would enable the consumer to benefit at the expense of the established brand.

8–81   Whereas it is intended that the brand right will be relied upon by brand owners to challenge in particular, lookalike products, no doubt some brand owners will seek to extend use of the right to prevent competitors from using a particular colour scheme or product description. Without wishing to rule out the possibility that copying one particular element of a brand may be significant in terms of unjustly enriching the would-be defendant, those responsible for enforcing the new right should consider carefully whether a defendant should be held liable when what has been copied is but a small part of the original brand and its effect is diluted because of the additional effort that the defendant has invested in to developing other aspects of his brand. It is difficult (as well as undesirable) to draw a rigid line and state that the defendant must copy at least 10 per cent of the plaintiff's brand, or three elements of that brand, before he will be held liable. Such details of application can really only be established on a case by case basis. In, for example, the Classic Cola/Coca-Cola dispute, the elements copied were (i) the red can (albeit it was a different shade of red), (ii) the word Cola in white script, and (iii) the position of the script (vertically). Of primary significance, however, was the prominence of the red colour can. Given the strength of the association between Coca-Cola and the red coloured can, the use of the same (or similar) colour by a competitor on a competing product would in my view amount to unfair copying and would therefore have been actionable under the brand right with or without the use of the white script.

8–82   However, that does not mean that the Coca-Cola Company is in a position to challenge any third party use of the colour red *per se*. The brand right would not be that broad. The adoption of the colour red, with white lettering on a non-competing, non-substitution product where there is no market overlap (*e.g.* in this case, cigarettes) would be unlikely to infringe unless the typescript or advertising used was such that a link might be established by consumers and so lead to a transference of brand values and thus benefit the cigarette manufacturers. The exclusive right granted to the brand owner would be in respect of "original brands". To qualify for protection the overall concept of the brand must be "new" (a concept akin to the unregistered design right test that is, not commonplace, trite, trivial, hackneyed or common-or-garden in appearance).[27] As Laddie J. noted in the *Ocular Sciences* case[28]:

> ". . . a design made up of features which, individually, are commonplace is [not] necessarily commonplace."

The question is whether the combination is commonplace. This concept is also analogous to the protection afforded to a compilation under the Copyright, Designs and Patents Act 1988. In determining whether or not the appearance of a brand is new, regard should be had to all the elements of a brand as defined above including lettering colour and style, the colour of the packaging, the position of any graphics on packaging and the overall shape and appearance of the brand, etc. Although

---

[27] *Ocular Sciences v. AVCL* [1997] R.P.C. 289 ("Ocular Sciences").
[28] *ibid.* at 429.

most brands have some elements that are "new" the level of protection granted to them under the terms of the brand right will vary depending upon the proportion of "new" elements. For example, Nescafé recently introduced a new pack design for its Gold Blend coffee. This would attract brand protection because the jar itself is unusual. If it had retained its old jar shape but changed only the label design, the protection would be narrower as other competing brands use similar jar shapes. Thus if a "new" brand is introduced and there is an existing competing brand that looks similar, an infringing brand would need to be very similar indeed in order to be actionable (assuming of course that the similarity resulted from unfair copying).

8–83   Defences   As has been said previously, and as is the case under copyright and design right laws, it would be a defence to any action for infringement to show that the defendant had not copied the brand but had arrived at the same result independently, without reference to the plaintiff's brand. As with copyright law the burden of proof should be on the defendant to show that he did not copy once access and opportunity have been shown by the plaintiff.[29] Although it may at first appear that this is an onerous burden on the defendant to prove a negative, in practice it should be much easier for the defendant to point to the source of his inspiration (or more particularly for the designer, the source of his instructions) and the various stages in his design process, than for the plaintiff to prove that the defendant copied. As with designs, the brand right would be infringed by possessing, selling, offering or exposing for sale in the course of business an infringing brand or importing the infringing brand into the United Kingdom for commercial purposes.

8–84   Duration   As a competitor involved in unfair copying is seeking to improve his position at the expense of his competitor without investing in research and development himself but by "free riding" on the success of another, the duration of the brand right should not be of fixed duration but should extend for as long as the particular concept of the brand continues in use (that is, use on a commercial scale). If, however, the appearance of the brand is changed, for example the product is remodelled,[29a] the brand right should disappear or lapse, three years after the date that the "old" brand (or label or packaging, etc.) was used by the proprietor. The period of three years has been suggested as this would provide sufficient time for the proprietor to establish and make known its remodelled appearance so as to avoid any risk of transference of values to any subsequent user. The aim is to protect the brand owner's use of his current investment; once he abandons (that is, ceases to use) any aspect of the brand concept it should fall into the public domain but only after the brand owner has had time to communicate the change to consumers and in so doing effectively transfer the investment (and goodwill) previously made in the "old" brand to the "new" brand. Allowing a third party to take up a packaging design based on one just cast aside by a competitor would enable the competitor to reap where he had

---

[29] See in relation to copyright principles *Francis Day & Hunter v. Bron* [1963] Ch. 587, CA ("Francis Day"); see also *Amoena v. Trulife* referred to below in connection with subconscious copying in relation to design right. As Wilberforce J. noted in *Francis Day* (at 614) proof of copying is dependant on a number of factors including: the defendant's degree of familiarity with the work; the character of the work; the objective similarity between the plaintiff's and the defendant's work; the probability that such similarities could be coincidental; and the existence of other influences on the defendant.
[29a] Repackaged, re-named, re-launched, or if a new label is used or the brand is no longer supplied or sold (on a commercial scale).

not sown, that is to take advantage of the competitor's reputation and investment in the "old" brand at the point in time when the change was effected and before the owner is able to transfer the value of his investment to the elements of his "new" brand.

8–85   Whilst those opposed to granting brand owners further protection might argue that the brand right is too long in duration, the brand right will only provide protection against copying for as long as the elements are in use. This means that given the current frequency with which packaging is redesigned, in some cases the brand right will limit protection to a period of just a few years—thus replenishing the public domain at frequent intervals.[30] In any event, the right will be no longer than the protection available under passing off which will continue to protect a residual good will.[31]

8–86   **Ownership**   Frequently a marketing company works with a new product development team to launch a new brand. The appearance of the brand and its packaging may well be developed in conjunction with a design consultancy and an advertising agency may well be engaged to develop marketing and promotional materials. The brand itself may be manufactured by a subsidiary company separate from the marketing organisation. In view of the fact that a number of different, and possibly unrelated, businesses may well be involved in the creation, design, marketing and promotion of a brand not to mention the financial investment in the brand, the question of ownership of the proposed brand right could prove to be a complex issue. Instead of seeking to allocate ownership based on notions of who the creator of the brand is (a question that may prove difficult to answer) I would suggest that ownership of the brand right be allocated to the business that took the initiative in developing the concept of the brand, was responsible for the financial investment in the brand and who assumed the risk in launching the brand. Whilst the answers to these questions may not all lead to the same business it is likely that one particular business was the driving force behind the development and launch of the brand and it is this business that should, in my view, receive the benefit of the brand right. The criterion are thus cumulative. Whilst the allocation of rights to the business responsible for investing in and assuming the financial risk connected with a new venture is not the usual basis for granting proprietary rights, it is not without legal precedent.

8–87   The new database right introduced as part of the implementation of the Database Directive[32] makes similar provision for the "person who takes the initiative in obtaining, verifying or presenting the contents of a database and assumes the risk".[33] Adopting an approach similar to the traditional copyright approach would give rise to the possibility of multiple owners of different aspects of the brand or a number of joint owners of the brand right which could prove unworkable. Allocating the right to the business responsible for the development and launch of the brand also has the added advantage of granting the right to the person or business likely to be in the best position to enforce the right.

---

[30] If an advertising image is used but subsequently replaced the term of protection comes to an end three years after the date the use ceased. If the business seek to reintroduce an "old" advertising theme or image it would be entitled to protection only if it was in a modified form and provided that it had not been "acquired" from the public domain by a third party in the interim.
[31] *Ad Lib v. Granville* [1972] R.P.C. 673 where a residual goodwill was protected even though the business had ceased five years earlier.
[32] Directive 96/9/EC dated March 11, 1997.
[33] s.14(1) Copyright and Rights in Databases Regulations 1997, S.I. 1997 No. 3032.

8–88 Protection is cumulative The brand right would be additional to any other right that the brand owner might have under copyright, patent, designs or trade mark law, or under passing off. The protection would be cumulative because the brand right seeks to fill an existing gap in protection. It is unlikely that the brand right would be used as a substitute for existing forms of protection such as trade mark registration as it would, in all probability, remain easier for example to show infringement under section 10(1) of the TMA 1994 than to show that the owner had a "new" brand and that the defendant had copied a substantial part of the brand. It is also more likely that plaintiffs would seek to rely on the brand right and trade mark infringement as alternatives, in much the same way as plaintiffs currently rely on trade mark infringement and passing off. Accordingly, I do not propose to limit the availability of the action, nor to draw any rigid boundary between what is protected and what is not. However, that does not mean that a plaintiff should be in a position to recover under more than one cause of action. Bringing an action under the new brand right would be particularly attractive to brand owners who are not in a position to bring proceedings under either passing off or under existing trade mark law, but unless the provisions are interpreted very widely indeed, it is unlikely that it will replace existing causes of action.

8–89 Remedies The successful brand owner should be entitled to an injunction, damages or an account of profits or otherwise, as indeed are available under, for example, the design right. Gordon[34] argues that a monetary payment only (*i.e.* no injunction) made by the defendant is an appropriate remedy. It is suggested that this would only be appropriate where the unjust enrichment has been in respect of a right that could be compulsorily licensed (such as a patent). It would be inappropriate, in my view, for certain aspects of a brand to be subject to a compulsory licence because of their need to be distinctive to avoid consumer confusion. Other aspects might be licensed depending on the circumstances. It is suggested, on balance, to confine the plaintiff to a remedy of damages would be inadequate since the damage to the distinctiveness of the plaintiff's brand would continue and damages alone would not redress the balance as between the plaintiff and the defendant.

8–90 It would obviously be necessary for the courts to develop a body of precedent before the new law could be said to be certain in the scope of its application.

If the courts interpret the new law appropriately, the effect will be to discourage copying, to encourage independent creation, and to raise standards in business. The result will be the creation of more distinctive brands which can be protected from imitation by competitors. If, however, the courts are seen to take a lenient view (that is, to adopt narrow interpretation) of what amounts to a substantial part of a brand or what may be considered "unfair" copying, then the statute may prove to be too weak to rectify the imbalances of the market place, with the result that the socially unacceptable behaviour of "reaping without sowing" will continue and may even increase.

8–91 It is hoped that the adoption of a statutory framework along the lines suggested above will provide the measure of protection needed to overcome the weaknesses in the existing forms of protection identified at the beginning of this chapter. To provide an indication as to how such a law might operate in practice,

---

[34] Restitutionary at 270 and 280.

we will now consider two practical examples, the first concerns a situation involving lookalikes, the second, two competing brands.

(ii) The Brand Right in Practice

Example 1—Gillette v. Blueprint

8–92   Two brands of deodorant body spray are depicted in photograph 18 in Appendix C. On the left is the Gillette brand, on the right the supermarket own brand, sold under the name Blueprint. From the photograph it can be seen that both cans incorporate clear plastic tops (this was previously a feature unique to the Gillette brand[35]); both brands use a similar typeface, in the same colour, against the same colour background, although the names themselves are different. The layout of both cans are similar in that they depict the brand name, the descriptor and the logo in that order looking down the can. Both cans use similar colours although these are reversed on the lookalike can; the can itself is, however, the same size and shape and style.

8–93   Under the existing laws of trade mark infringement and passing off it is unlikely that Gillette would be successful in obtaining an injunction (or any other remedy) to prevent the use of the lookalike brand without evidence of consumer confusion. Despite the obvious similarities in the appearance of the lookalike brand, a finding of confusion is unlikely given the use of a brand name that is both visually and phonetically very different to the Gillette brand name. As it is unlikely that the appearance of the can would be registrable without the words Gillette on it, it is unlikely that there would be a basis of a claim for infringement of the packaging (as a trade mark).

8–94   Under the terms of the brand right described above (paras 8–67—8–91), however, the test would be whether a substantial part of the whole or any aspect of the Gillette brand has been reproduced as a result of copying. Clearly a substantial part of the appearance of the brand has been reproduced. The overall look and feel of the lookalike brand is strikingly similar to that of the Gillette brand albeit that the actual words and colours are not reproduced. It would therefore be for the manufacturer of the lookalike brand to show that it had not copied the appearance of the Gillette brand when designing its brand. Given that no other brand of deodorant in this sector of the market has a similar appearance to the Gillette brand[35a] it is likely that Gillette would prove successful in its claim of unfair copying with the consequence that it would obtain an injunction against the producer of Blueprint deodorant.

Example 2—Solo v. Pub Squash

8–95   In Chapter 6 we considered the New Zealand case concerning the lemonade drink known as Solo and the competing brand Pub Squash.[36] In that case the court held that there was no passing off despite the facts that: the Pub Squash formula was as close to that of Solo as it could be, the can was the same size, shape and colour as the Solo brand and that the advertising used similar themes and mannerisms. Applying the brand right test, Cadbury-Schweppes would need to show that a substantial part of the brand, or aspects of the brand were reproduced. The question would be whether the size shape and colour of the can together with

---

[35] Compare with photograph 19 which illustrates a range of products that compete with Gillette.
[35a] See Appendix C, photograph 19.
[36] Pub Squash.

the imagery used in the advertising campaign and the intangible aspects of the brand amounted to a substantial part of the brand. Given the visual impact of the can compared to those of competing products and the distinctive theme of the advertisements it is submitted that a substantial part of the brand had been reproduced. Given that the defendant was aware of the plaintiff's brand and would have seen the plaintiff's advertisements it would be for the defendant to show that it did not copy the plaintiff's brand either in terms of its appearance or its advertising theme. As Powell J. noted in the court of first instance, the defendant:

> "set out in a deliberate and calculated fashion to take advantage of the plaintiffs' past and anticipated future efforts in developing a market for a product such as Solo, and that in particular, the defendant by its officers, sought to copy or to approximate the formula for Solo, and chose a product name and package for the defendant's proposed product derived from and intended to gain the benefit of the plaintiffs' past and anticipated advertising campaign, and the plaintiffs' package for their product."

8–96   As one commentator observed[37] "[s]uch conduct is nothing less than theft of the plaintiffs' advertising effort". Under the terms of the proposed brand right, Cadbury-Schweppes would have a cause of action and would be entitled to an injunction against further use of the offending brand and advertising, etc., costs and damages. The brand right would not enable the plaintiff to take action against all producers of lemon squash but only those that seek to take advantage of aspects of the plaintiff's brand's reputation, image or marketing/advertising strategy in other words the plaintiff's labour, investment and creative skill. The fact that the brand right provides a remedy against copying would mean that the plaintiff would not have to establish that its brand is distinctive (in the sense that it is recognised as being well known), only that it is distinctive compared to competing products. This is a tremendous advantage for new brands which can otherwise be copied before they have established the requisite level of distinctiveness on which to base an action for passing off.

CONCLUSION

8–97   The thesis that I have sought to present in this book is that, one who has used his intellectual, physical or financial powers to create a commercial product such as a brand, should be entitled to protect that brand from a third party that would seek to take unfair advantage of the labour, skill or investment of the brand's creator. Although the existing framework of patents, copyright, designs and trade mark laws provide a plethora of mechanisms for protection, lacunae still exist which if not filled will mean that courts will continue to deny brand owners' protection for certain aspects of their brands. These gaps are apparent, especially as regards intangible aspects such as brand image, marketing strategies and advertising formats. By introducing a statutory brand right of the kind outlined above, a measure of protection can be achieved to fill these lucarne until such time as a law of unfair competition of general application is introduced.

8–98   The introduction of a new brand right based on principles of misappropriation and limited by unjust enrichment principles would not necessarily be at

[37] Lahore "The Pub Squash Case: Legal Theft or Free Competition" [1981] E.I.P.R. 54.

odds with the United Kingdom's obligations *vis-à-vis* its European colleagues. Most E.U. Member States have laws of unfair competition which provide protection against misappropriation especially in circumstances of competition. Thus, in the absence of a harmonised law of unfair competition the introduction of a limited brand right based on comparable principles would be a useful interim measure until such time as unfair competition laws are harmonised.

8–99   Increasing the protection available to aspects of branded products would not be anti-competitive as some suggest, nor would it make it harder for businesses to develop new brands (except by preventing copying) since its emphasis is against copying and not against independent development.[38] As noted by Lord Islwyn in connection with lookalikes during the debate in the House of Lords[39]:

> "We should all recognise that brands are important in a free market economy. They are the basis on which a differentiation can be made between products and the basis on which there is competition. By comparison lookalikes distort competition by deceiving consumers and by reaping a financial reward from a competitor's ideas, investment, effort and risk. There would seem to be a weakness in the United Kingdom law which makes this country particularly vulnerable to lookalikes . . . I urge the Government to consider the issue seriously."

Lord Islwyn's comments concerning the dangers of lookalike brands apply equally to other aspects of brand imitation as does his observation that the United Kingdom law fails to provide adequate protection. It is time that this deficiency was addressed.

---

[38] Ricketson at 31.
[39] The debate concerned a proposed amendment to the Competition Bill to include the WIPO model law on unfair competition (February 23, 1998 *Hansard,* p. 522/3). The proposed amendment was ultimately withdrawn.

APPENDIX A

Trade Marks Act 1994

CHAPTER 26

A–01   An Act to make new provision for registered trade marks, implementing Council Directive No. 89/104/EEC of 21st December 1988 to approximate the laws of the Member States relating to trade marks; to make provisions in connection with Council Regulation (EC) No. 40/94 of 20th December 1993 on the Community trade mark; to give effect to the Madrid Protocol Relating to the International Registration of Marks of 27th June 1989, and to certain provisions of the Paris Convention for the Protection of Industrial Property of 20th March 1883, as revised and amended; and for connected purposes.   [21st July 1994]

Be it enacted by the Queen's most Excellent Majesty, by and with the advice and consent of the Lords Spiritual and Temporal, and Commons, in this present Parliament assembled, and by the authority of the same, as follows:-

PART I

REGISTERED TRADE MARKS

Introductory

Trade marks

1.—(1) In this Act a "trade mark" means any sign capable of being represented graphically which is capable of distinguishing goods or services of one undertaking from those of other undertakings.

A trade mark may, in particular, consist of words (including personal names), designs, letters, numerals or the shape of goods or their packaging.

(2) References in this Act to a trade mark include, unless the context otherwise requires, references to a collective mark (see section 49) or certification mark (see section 50).

Registered trade marks

2.—(1) A registered trade mark is a property right obtained by the registration of the trade mark under this Act and the proprietor of a registered trade mark has the rights and remedies provided by this Act.

(2) No proceedings lie to prevent or recover damages for the infringement of an unregistered trade mark as such; but nothing in this Act affects the law relating to passing off.

Grounds for refusal of registration

Absolute grounds for refusal of registration

3.—(1) The following shall not be registered —

(a) signs which do not satisfy the requirements of section 1(1),

(b) trade marks which are devoid of any distinctive character,

(c) trade marks which consist exclusively of signs or indications which may serve, in trade, to designate the kind, quality, quantity, intended purpose, value, geographical origin, the time of production of goods or of rendering of services, or other characteristics of goods or services,

(d) trade marks which consist exclusively of signs or indications which have become customary in the current language or in the *bona fide* and established practices of the trade:

Provided that, a trade mark shall not be refused registration by virtue of paragraph (b), (c) or (d) above if, before the date of application for registration, it has in fact acquired a distinctive character as a result of the use made of it.

(2) A sign shall not be registered as a trade mark if it consists exclusively of—

(a) the shape which results from the nature of the goods themselves,

(b) the shape of goods which is necessary to obtain a technical result, or

(c) the shape which gives substantial value to the goods.

(3) A trade mark shall not be registered if it is—

(a) contrary to public policy or to accepted principles of morality, or

(b) of such a nature as to deceive the public (for instance as to the nature, quality or geographical origin of the goods or service).

(4) A trade mark shall not be registered if or to the extent that its use is prohibited in the United Kingdom by any enactment or rule of law or by any provision of Community law.

(5) A trade mark shall not be registered in the cases specified, or referred to, in section 4 (specially protected emblems).

(6) A trade mark shall not be registered if or to the extent that the application is made in bad faith.

Specially protected emblems

4.—(1) A trade mark which consists of or contains —

(a) the Royal arms, or any of the principal armorial bearings of the Royal arms, or any insignia or device so nearly resembling the Royal arms or any such armorial bearing as to be likely to be mistaken for them, or it,

(b) a representation of the Royal crown or any of the Royal flags,

(c) a representation of Her Majesty or any member of the Royal family, or any colourable imitation thereof, or

(d) words, letters or devices likely to lead persons to think that the applicant either has or recently has had Royal patronage or authorisation,

shall not be registered unless it appears to the registrar that consent has been given by or on behalf of Her Majesty or, as the case may be, the relevant member of the Royal family.

(2) A trade mark which consists of or contains a representation of—

(a) the national flag of the United Kingdom (commonly known as the Union Jack), or

(b) the flag of England, Wales, Scotland, Northern Ireland or the Isle of Man,

shall not be registered if it appears to the registrar that the use of the trade mark would be misleading or grossly offensive.

Provision may be made by rules identifying the flags to which paragraph (b) applies.

(3) A trade mark shall not be registered in the cases specified in —

section 57 (national emblems, &c. of Convention countries), or
section 58 (emblems, &c. of certain international organisations).

(4) Provision may be made by rules prohibiting in such cases as may be prescribed the registration of a trade mark which consists of or contains—

    (a) arms to which a person is entitled by virtue of a grant of arms by the Crown, or

    (b) insignia so nearly resembling such arms as to be likely to be mistaken for them,

unless it appears to the registrar that consent has been given by or on behalf of that person.

Where such a mark is registered, nothing in this Act shall be construed as authorising its use in any way contrary to the laws of arms.

Relative grounds for refusal of registration

5.—(1) A trade mark shall not be registered if it is identical with an earlier trade mark and the goods or services for which the trade mark is applied for are identical with the goods or services for which the earlier trade mark is protected.

(2) A trade mark shall not be registered if because —

    (a) it is identical with an earlier trade mark and is to be registered for goods or services similar to those for which the earlier trade mark is protected, or

    (b) it is similar to an earlier trade mark and is to be registered for goods or services identical with or similar to those for which the earlier trade mark is protected,

there exists a likelihood of confusion on the part of the public, which includes the likelihood of association with the earlier trade mark.

(3) A trade mark which —

    (a) is identical with or similar to an earlier trade mark, and

    (b) is to be registered for goods or services which are not similar to those for which the earlier trade mark is protected,

shall not be registered if, or to the extent that, the earlier trade mark has a reputation in the United Kingdom (or, in the case of a Community trade mark, in the European Community) and the use of the later mark without due cause would take unfair advantage of, or be detrimental to, the distinctive character or the repute of the earlier trade mark.

(4) A trade mark shall not be registered if, or to the extent that, its use in the United Kingdom is liable to be prevented—

    (a) by virtue of any rule of law (in particular, the law of passing off) protecting an unregistered trade mark or other sign used in the course of trade, or

    (b) by virtue of an earlier right other than those referred to in subsections (1) to (3) or paragraph (a) above, in particular by virtue of the law of copyright, design right or registered designs.

A person thus entitled to prevent the use of a trade mark is referred to in this Act as the proprietor of an "earlier right" in relation to the trade mark.

(5) Nothing in this section prevents the registration of a trade mark where the proprietor of the earlier trade mark or other earlier right consents to the registration.

Meaning of "earlier trade mark"

6.—(1) In this Act an "earlier trade mark" means —

    (a) a registered trade mark, international trade mark (UK) or Community trade mark which has a date of application for registration earlier than that of the trade mark in question, taking account (where appropriate) of the priorities claimed in respect of the trade marks,

    (b) a Community trade mark which has a valid claim to seniority from an earlier registered trade mark or international trade mark (UK), or

(c) a trade mark which, at the date of application for registration of the trade mark in question or (where appropriate) of the priority claimed in respect of the application, was entitled to protection under the Paris Convention or the WTO agreement as a well known trade mark.

(2) References in this Act to an earlier trade mark include a trade mark in respect of which an application for registration has been made and which, if registered, would be an earlier trade mark by virtue of subsection (1)(a) or (b), subject to its being so registered.

(3) A trade mark within subsection (1)(a) or (b) whose registration expires shall continue to be taken into account in determining the registrability of a later mark for a period of one year after the expiry unless the registrar is satisfied that there was no *bona fide* use of the mark during the two years immediately preceding the expiry.

Raising of relative grounds in case of honest concurrent use

7.—(1) This section applies where on an application for the registration of a trade mark it appears to the registrar—

(a) that there is an earlier trade mark in relation to which the conditions set out in section 5(1), (2) or (3) obtain, or

(b) that there is an earlier right in relation to which the condition set out in section 5(4) is satisfied,

but the applicant shows to the satisfaction of the registrar that there has been honest concurrent use of the trade mark for which registration is sought.

(2) In that case the registrar shall not refuse the application by reason of the earlier trade mark or other earlier right unless objection on that ground is raised in opposition proceedings by the proprietor of that earlier trade mark or other earlier right.

(3) For the purposes of this section "honest concurrent use" means such use in the United Kingdom, by the applicant or with his consent, as would formerly have amounted to honest concurrent use for the purposes of section 12(2) of the Trade Marks Act 1938.

(4) Nothing in this section affects—

(a) the refusal of registration on the grounds mentioned in section 3 (absolute grounds for refusal), or

(b) the making of an application for a declaration of invalidity under section 47(2) (application on relative grounds, where no consent to registration).

(5) This section does not apply when there is an order in force under section 8 below.

Power to require that relative grounds be raised in opposition proceedings

8.—(1) The Secretary of State may by order provide that in any case a trade mark shall not be refused registration on a ground mentioned in section 5 (relative grounds for refusal) unless objection on that ground is raised in opposition proceedings by the proprietor of the earlier trade mark or other earlier right.

(2) The order may make such consequential provision as appears to the Secretary of State appropriate—

(a) with respect to the carrying out by the registrar of searches of earlier trade marks, and

(b) as to the persons by whom an application for a declaration of invalidity may be made on the grounds specified in section 47(2) (relative grounds).

(3) An order making such provision as is mentioned in subsection (2)(a) may direct that so much of section 37 (examination of application) as requires a search to be carried out shall cease to have effect.

(4) An order making such provisions as is mentioned in subsection (2)(b) may provide that so much of section 47(3) as provides that any person may make an application for a declaration of invalidity shall have effect subject to the provisions of the order.

(5) An order under this section shall be made by statutory instrument, and no order shall be made unless a draft of it has been laid before and approved by a resolution of each House of Parliament.

No such draft of an order making such provision as is mentioned in subsection (1) shall be laid before Parliament until after the end of the period of ten years beginning with the day on which applications for Community trade marks may first be filed in pursuance of the Community Trade Mark Regulation.

(6) An order under this section may contain such transitional provisions as appear to the Secretary of State to be appropriate.

Effects of registered trade mark

Rights conferred by registration trade mark

9.—(1) The proprietor of a registered trade mark has exclusive rights in the trade mark which are infringed by use of the trade mark in the United Kingdom without his consent.

The acts amounting to infringement, if done without the consent of the proprietor, are specified in section 10.

(2) References in this Act to the infringement of a registered trade mark are to any such infringement of the rights of the proprietor.

(3) The rights of the proprietor have effect from the date of registration (which in accordance with section 40(3) is the date of filing of the application for registration):

Provided that —

    (a) no infringement proceedings may be begun before the date on which the trade mark is in fact registered; and

    (b) no offence under section 92 (unauthorised use of trade mark, &c. in relation to goods) is committed by anything done before the date of publication of the registration.

Infringement of registered trade mark

10.—(1) A person infringes a registered trade mark if he uses in the course of trade a sign which is identical with the trade mark in relation to goods or services which are identical with those for which it is registered.

(2) A person infringes a registered trade mark if he uses in the course of trade a sign where because —

    (a) the sign is identical with the trade mark and is used in relation to goods or services similar to those for which the trade mark is registered, or

    (b) the sign is similar to the trade mark and is used in relation to goods or services identical with or similar to those for which the trade mark is registered,

there exists a likelihood of confusion on the part of the public, which includes the likelihood of association with the trade mark.

(3) A person infringes a registered trade mark if he uses in the course of trade a sign which—

    (a) is identical with or similar to the trade mark, and

    (b) is used in relation to goods or services which are not similar to those for which the trade mark is registered,

where the trade mark has a reputation in the United Kingdom and the use of the sign, being without due cause, takes unfair advantage of, or is detrimental to, the distinctive character or the repute of the trade mark.

(4) For the purposes of this section a person uses a sign if, in particular, he —

    (a) affixes it to goods or the packaging thereof;

    (b) offers or exposes goods for sale, puts them on the market or stocks them for those purposes under the sign, or offers or supplies services under the sign;

    (c) imports or exports goods under the sign; or

    (d) uses the sign on business papers or in advertising.

(5) A person who applies a registered trade mark to material intended to be used for labelling or packaging goods, as a business paper, or for advertising goods or services, shall be treated as a party to any use of the material which infringes the registered trade mark if when he applied the mark he knew or had reason to believe that the application of the mark was not duly authorised by the proprietor or a licensee.

(6) Nothing in the preceding provisions of this section shall be construed as preventing the use of a registered trade mark by any person for the purpose of identifying goods or services as those of the proprietor or a licensee.

But any such use otherwise than in accordance with honest practices in industrial or commercial matters shall be treated as infringing the registered trade mark if the use without due cause takes unfair advantage of, or is detrimental to, the distinctive character or repute of the trade mark.

Limits on effect of registered trade mark

11.—(1) A registered trade mark is not infringed by the use of another registered trade mark in relation to goods or services for which the latter is registered (but see section 47(6) (effect of declaration of invalidity of registration)).

(2) A registered trade mark is not infringed by —

    (a) the use by a person of his own name or address.

    (b) the use of indications concerning the kind, quality, quantity, intended purpose, value, geographical origin, the time of production of goods or of rendering of services, or other characteristics of goods or services, or

    (c) the use of the trade mark where it is necessary to indicate the intended purpose of a product or service (in particular, as accessories or spare parts),

provided the use is in accordance with honest practices in industrial or commercial matters.

(3) A registered trade mark is not infringed by the use in the course of trade in a particular locality of an earlier right which applies only in that locality.

For this purpose an "earlier right" means an unregistered trade mark or other sign continuously used in relation to goods or services by a person or a predecessor in title of his from a date prior to whichever is the earlier of—

    (a) the use of the first-mentioned trade mark in relation to those goods or services by the proprietor or a predecessor in title of his, or

    (b) the registration of the first-mentioned trade mark in respect of those goods or services in the name of the proprietor or a predecessor in title of his;

and an earlier right shall be regarded as applying in a locality if, or to the extent that, its use in that locality is protected by virtue of any rule of law (in particular, the law of passing off).

Exhaustion of rights conferred by registered trade mark

12.—(1) A registered trade mark is not infringed by the use of the trade mark in relation to goods which have been put on the market in the European Economic Area under that trade mark by the proprietor or with his consent.

(2) Subsection (1) does not apply where there exist legitimate reasons for the proprietor to oppose further dealings in the goods (in particular, where the condition of the goods has been changed or impaired after they have been put on the market).

Registration subject to disclaimer or limitation

13.—(1) An applicant for registration of a trade mark, or the proprietor of a registered trade mark, may —

    (a) disclaim any right to the exclusive use of any specified element of the trade mark, or

(b) agree that the rights conferred by the registration shall be subject to a specified territorial or other limitation;

and where the registration of a trade mark is subject to a disclaimer or limitation, the rights conferred by section 9 (rights conferred by registered trade mark) are restricted accordingly.

(2) Provision shall be made by rules as to the publication and entry in the register of a disclaimer or limitation.

Infringement proceedings

Action for infringement

14.—(1) An infringement of a registered trade mark is actionable by the proprietor of the trade mark.

(2) In an action for infringement all such relief by way of damages, injunctions, accounts or otherwise is available to him as is available in respect of the infringement of any other property right.

Order for erasure, &c., of offending sign

15.—(1) Where a person is found to have infringed a registered trade mark, the court may make an order requiring him —

(a) to cause the offending sign to be erased, removed or obliterated from any infringing goods, material or articles in his possession, custody or control, or

(b) if it is not reasonably practicable for the offending sign to be erased, removed or obliterated, to secure the destruction of the infringing goods, material or articles in question.

(2) If an order under subsection (1) is not complied with, or it appears to the court likely that such an order would not be complied with, the court may order that the infringing goods, material or articles be delivered to such person as the court may direct for erasure, removal or obliteration of the sign, or for destruction, as the case may be.

Order for delivery up of infringing goods, material or articles

16.—(1) The proprietor of a registered trademark may apply to the court for an order for the delivery up to him, or such other person as the court may direct, or any infringing goods, material or articles which a person has in his possession, custody or control in the course of a business.

(2) An application shall not be made after the end of the period specified in section 18 (period after which remedy of delivery up not available); and no order shall be made unless the court also makes, or it appears to the court that there are grounds for making, an order under section 19 (order as to disposal of infringing goods, &c.).

(3) A person to whom any infringing goods, material or articles are delivered up in pursuance of an order under this section shall, if an order under section 19 is not made, retain them pending the making of an order, or the decision not to make an order, under that section.

(4) Nothing in this section affects any other power of the court.

Meaning of "infringing goods, material or articles"

17.—(1) In this Act the expressions "infringing goods", "infringing material" and "infringing articles" shall be construed as follows.

(2) Goods are "infringing goods", in relation to a registered trade mark, if they or their packaging bear a sign identical or similar to that mark and—

(a) the application of the sign to the goods or their packaging was an infringement of the registered trade mark, or

(b) the goods are proposed to be imported into the United Kingdom and the application of the sign in the United Kingdom to them or their packaging would be an infringement of the registered trade mark, or

(c) the sign has otherwise been used in relation to the goods in such a way as to infringe the registered mark.

(3) Nothing in subsection (2) shall be construed as affecting the importation of goods which may lawfully be imported into the United Kingdom by virtue of an enforceable Community right.

(4) Material is "infringing material", in relation to a registered trade mark if it bears a sign identical or similar to that mark and either—

(a) it is used for labelling or packaging goods, as a business paper, or for advertising goods or services, in such a way as to infringe the registered trade mark, or

(b) it is intended to be so used and such use would infringe the registered trade mark.

(5) "Infringing articles", in relation to a registered trade mark, means articles—

(a) which are specifically designed or adapted for making copies of a sign identical or similar to that mark, and

(b) which a person has in his possession, custody or control, knowing or having reason to believe that they have been or are to be used to produce infringing goods or material.

Period after which remedy of delivery up not available

18.—(1) An application for an order under section 16 (order for delivery up of infringing goods, material or articles) may not be made after the end of the period of six years from—

(a) in the case of infringing goods, the date on which the trade mark was applied to the goods or their packaging,

(b) in the case of infringing material, the date on which the trade mark was applied to the material, or

(c) in the case of infringing articles, the date on which they were made,

except as mentioned in the following provisions.

(2) If during the whole or part of that period the proprietor of the registered trade mark—

(a) is under a disability, or

(b) is prevented by fraud or concealment from discovering the facts entitling him to apply for an order,

an application may be made at any time before the end of the period of six years from the date on which he ceased to be under a disability or, as the case may be, could with reasonable diligence have discovered those facts.

(3) In subsection (2) "disability"—

(a) in England and Wales, has the same meaning as in the Limitation Act 1980;

(b) in Scotland, means legal disability within the meaning of the Prescription and Limitation (Scotland) Act 1973;

(c) in Northern Ireland, has the same meaning as in the Limitation (Northern Ireland) Order 1989.

Order as to disposal of infringing goods, material or articles

19.—(1) Where infringing goods, material or articles have been delivered up in pursuance of an order under section 16, an application may be made to the court—

(a) for an order that they be destroyed or forfeited to such person as the court may think fit, or

(b) for a decision that no such order should be made.

(2) In considering what order (if any) should be made, the court shall consider whether other remedies available in an action for infringement of the registered trade mark would be adequate to compensate the proprietor and any licensee and protect their interests.

(3) Provision shall be made by rules of court as to the service of notice on persons having an interest in the goods, material or articles, and any such person is entitled—

(a) to appear in proceedings for an order under this section, whether or not he was served with notice, and

(b) to appeal against any order made, whether or not he appeared;

and an order shall not take effect until the end of the period within which notice of an appeal may be given or, if before the end of that period notice of appeal is duly given, until the final determination or abandonment of the proceedings on the appeal.

(4) Where there is more than one person interested in the goods, material or articles, the court shall make such order as it thinks just.

(5) If the court decides that no order should be made under this section, the person in whose possession, custody or control the goods, material or articles were before being delivered up is entitled to their return.

(6) References in this section to a person having an interest in goods, material or articles include any person in whose favour an order could be made under this section or under section 114, 204 or 231 of the Copyright, Designs and Patents Act 1988 (which make similar provision in relation to infringement of copyright, rights in performances and design right).

Jurisdiction of sheriff court or county court in Northern Ireland

20. Proceedings for an order under section 16 (order for delivery up of infringing goods, material or articles) or section 19 (order as to disposal of infringing goods, &c.) may be brought—

(a) in the sheriff court in Scotland, or

(b) in a county court in Northern Ireland.

This does not affect the jurisdiction of the Court of Session or the High Court in Northern Ireland.

Remedy for groundless threats of infringement proceedings

21.—(1) Where a person threatens another with proceedings for infringement of a registered trade mark other than—

(a) the application of the mark to goods or their packaging,

(b) the importation of goods to which, or to the packaging of which, the mark has been applied, or

(c) the supply of services under the mark,

any person aggrieved may bring proceedings for relief under this section.

(2) The relief which may be applied for is any of the following—

(a) a declaration that the threats are unjustifiable,

(b) an injunction against the continuance of the threats,

(c) damages in respect of any loss he has sustained by the threats;

and the plaintiff is entitled to such relief unless the defendant shows that the acts in respect of which proceedings were threatened constitute (or if done would constitute) an infringement of the registered trade mark concerned.

(3) If that is shown by the defendant, the plaintiff is nevertheless entitled to relief if he shows that the registration of the trade mark is invalid or liable to be revoked in a relevant respect.

(4) The mere notification that a trade mark is registered, or that an application for registration has been made, does not constitute a threat of proceedings for the purposes of this section.

Registered trade mark as object of property

Nature of registered trade mark

22. A registered trade mark is personal property (in Scotland, incorporeal moveable property).

Co-ownership of registered trade mark

23.—(1) Where a registered trade mark is granted to two or more persons jointly, each of them is entitled, subject to any agreement to the contrary, to an equal undivided share in the registered trade mark.

(2) The following provisions apply where two or more persons are co-proprietors of a registered trade mark, by virtue of subsection (1) or otherwise.

(3) Subject to any agreement to the contrary, each co-proprietor is entitled, by himself or his agents, to do for his own benefit and without the consent of or the need to account to the other or others, any act which would otherwise amount to an infringement of the registered trade mark.

(4) One co-proprietor may not without consent of the other or others—

  (a) grant a licence to use the registered trade mark, or

  (b) assign or charge his share in the registered trade mark (or, in Scotland, cause or permit security to be granted over it).

(5) Infringement proceedings may be brought by any co-proprietor, but he may not, without the leave of the court, proceed with the action unless the other, or each of the others, is either joined as a plaintiff or added as a defendant.

A co-proprietor who is thus added as a defendant shall not be made liable for any costs in the action unless he takes part in the proceedings.

Nothing in this subsection affects the granting of interlocutory relief on the application of a single co-proprietor.

(6) Nothing in this section affects the mutual rights and obligations of trustees or personal representatives, or their rights and obligations as such.

Assignment, &c. of registered trade mark

24.—(1) A registered trade mark is transmissible by assignment, testamentary disposition or operation of law in the same way as other personal or moveable property.

It is so transmissible either in connection with the goodwill of a business or independently.

(2) An assignment or other transmission of a registered trade mark may be partial, that is, limited so as to apply—

  (a) in relation to some but not all of the goods or services for which the trade mark is registered, or

  (b) in relation to use of the trade mark in a particular manner or a particular locality.

(3) An assignment of a registered trade mark, or an assent relating to a registered trade mark, is not effective unless it is in writing signed by or on behalf of the assignor or, as the case may be, a personal representative.

Except in Scotland, this requirement may be satisfied in a case where the assignor or personal representative is a body corporate by the affixing of its seal.

(4) The above provisions apply to assignment by way of security as in relation to any other assignment.

(5) A registered trade mark may be the subject of a charge (in Scotland, security) in the same way as other personal or moveable property.

(6) Nothing in this Act shall be construed as affecting the assignment or other transmission of an unregistered trade mark as part of the goodwill of a business.

Registration of transactions affecting registered trade mark

25.—(1) On application being made to the registrar by—

(a) a person claiming to be entitled to an interest in or under a registered trade mark by virtue of a registrable transaction, or

(b) any other person claiming to be affected by such a transaction,

the prescribed particulars of the transaction shall be entered in the register.

(2) The following are registrable transactions—

(a) an assignment of a registered trade mark or any right in it;

(b) the grant of a licence under a registered trade mark;

(c) the granting of any security interest (whether fixed or floating) over a registered trade mark or any right in or under it;

(d) the making by personal representatives of an assent in relation to a registered trade mark or any right in or under it;

(e) an order of a court or other competent authority transferring a registered trade mark or any right in or under it.

(3) Until an application has been made for registration of the prescribed particulars of a registrable transaction—

(a) the transaction is ineffective as against a person acquiring a conflicting interest in or under the registered trademark in ignorance of it, and

(b) a person claiming to be a licensee by virtue of the transaction does not have the protection of section 30 or 31 (rights and remedies of licensee in relation to infringement).

(4) Where a person becomes the proprietor or a licensee of a registered trade mark by virtue of a registrable transaction, then unless—

(a) an application for registration of the prescribed particulars of the transaction is made before the end of the period of six months beginning with its date, or

(b) the court is satisfied that it was not practicable for such an application to be made before the end of that period and that an application was made as soon as practicable thereafter,

he is not entitled to damages or an account of profits in respect of any infringement of the registered trade mark occurring after the date of the transaction and before the prescribed particulars of the transaction are registered.

(5) Provision may be made by rules as to—

(a) the amendment of registered particulars relating to a licence so as to reflect any alteration of the terms of the licence, and

(b) the removal of such particulars from the register—

(i) where it appears from the registered particulars that the licence was granted for a fixed period and that period has expired, or

(ii) where no such period is indicated and, after such period as may be prescribed, the registrar has notified the parties of his intention to remove the particulars from the register.

(6) Provision may also be made by rules as to the amendment or removal from the register of particulars relating to a security interest on the application of, or with the consent of, the person entitled to the benefit of that interest.

Trusts and equities

26.—(1) No notice of any trust (express, implied or constructive) shall be entered in the register; and the register shall not be affected by any such notice.

(2) Subject to the provisions of this Act, equities (in Scotland, rights) in respect of a registered trade mark may be enforced in like manner as in respect of other personal or moveable property.

Application for registration of trade mark as an object of property

27.—(1) The provisions of section 22 to 26 (which relate to a registered trade mark as an object of property) apply, with the necessary modifications, in relation to an application for the registration of a trade mark as in relation to a registered trade mark.

(2) In section 23 (co-ownership of registered trade mark) as it applies in relation to an application for registration the reference in subsection (1) to the granting of the registration shall be construed as a reference to the making of the application.

(3) In section 25 (registration of transactions affecting registered trade marks) as it applies in relation to a transaction affecting an application for the registration of a trade mark, the references to the entry of particulars in the register, and to the making of an application to register particulars, shall be construed as references to the giving of notice to the registrar of those particulars.

Licensing

Licensing of registered trade mark

28.—(1) A licence to use a registered trade mark may be general or limited.

A limited licence may, in particular, apply—

(a) in relation to some but not all of the goods or services for which the trade mark is registered, or

(b) in relation to use of the trade mark in a particular manner or a particular locality.

(2) A licence is not effective unless it is in writing signed by or on behalf of the grantor.

Except in Scotland, this requirement may be satisfied in a case where the grantor is a body corporate by the affixing of its seal.

(3) Unless the licence proves otherwise, it is binding on a successor in title to the grantor's interest.

References in this Act to doing anything with, or without, the consent of the proprietor of a registered trade mark shall be construed accordingly.

(4) Where the licence so provides, a sub-licence may be granted by the licensee; and references in this Act to a licence or licensee include a sub-licence or sub-licensee.

Exclusive licences

29.—(1) In this Act an "exclusive licence" means a licence (whether general or limited) authorising the licensee to the exclusion of all other persons, including the person granting the licence, to use a registered trade mark in the manner authorised by the licence.

The expression "exclusive licensee" shall be construed accordingly.

(2) An exclusive licensee has the same rights against a successor in title who is bound by the licence as he has against the person granting the licence.

General provisions as to rights of licensees in case of infringement

30.—(1) This section has effect with respect to the rights of a licensee in relation to infringement of a registered trade mark.

The provisions of this section do not apply where or to the extent that, by virtue of section 31(1) below (exclusive licensee having rights and remedies of assignee), the licensee has a right to bring proceedings in his own name.

(2) A licensee is entitled, unless his licence, or any licence through which his interest is derived, provides otherwise, to call on the proprietor of the registered trade mark to take infringement proceedings in respect of any matter which affects his interests.

(3) If the proprietor—

(a) refuses to do so, or

(b) fails to do so within two months after being called upon,

the licensee may bring the proceedings in his own name as if he were the proprietor.

(4) Where infringement proceedings are brought by a licensee by virtue of this section, the licensee may not, without the leave of the court, proceed with the action unless the proprietor is either joined as a plaintiff or added as a defendant.

This does not affect the granting of interlocutory relief on an application by a licensee alone.

(5) A proprietor who is added as a defendant as mentioned in subsection (4) shall not be made liable for any costs in the action unless he takes part in the proceedings.

(6) In infringement proceedings brought by the proprietor of a registered trade mark any loss suffered or likely to be suffered by licensees shall be taken into account; and the court may give such directions as it thinks fit as to the extent to which the plaintiff is to hold the proceeds of any pecuniary remedy on behalf of licensees.

(7) The provisions of this section apply in relation to an exclusive licensee if or to the extent that he has, by virtue of section 31(1), the rights and remedies of an assignee as if he were the proprietor of the registered trade mark.

Exclusive licensee having rights and remedies of assignee

31.—(1) An exclusive licence may provide that the licensee shall have, to such extent as may be provided by licence, the same rights and remedies in respect of matters occurring after the grant of the licence as if the licence had been an assignment.

Where or to the extent that such provision is made, the licensee is entitled, subject to the provisions of the licence and to the following provisions of this section, to bring infringement proceedings, against any person other than the proprietor, in his own name.

(2) Any such rights and remedies of an exclusive licensee are concurrent with those of the proprietor of the registered trade mark; and references to the proprietor of a registered trade mark in the provisions of this Act relating to infringement shall be construed accordingly.

(3) In an action brought by an exclusive licensee by virtue of this section a defendant may avail himself of any defence which would have been available to him if the action had been brought by the proprietor of the registered trade mark.

(4) Where proceedings for infringement of a registered trade mark brought by the proprietor or an exclusive licensee relate wholly or partly to an infringement in respect of which they have concurrent rights of action, the proprietor or, as the case may be, the exclusive licensee may not, without the leave of the court, proceed with the action unless the other is either joined as a plaintiff or added as a defendant.

This does not affect the granting of interlocutory relief on an application by a proprietor or exclusive licensee alone.

(5) A person who is added as a defendant as mentioned in subsection (4) shall not be made liable for any costs in the action unless he takes part in the proceedings.

(6) Where an action for infringement of a registered trade mark is brought which relates wholly or partly to an infringement in respect of which the proprietor and an exclusive licensee have or had concurrent rights of action—

(a) the court shall in assessing damages take into account—

    (i) the terms of the licence, and

    (ii) any pecuniary remedy already awarded or available to either of them in respect of the infringement;

(b) no account of profits shall be directed if an award of damages has been made, or an account of profits has been directed, in favour of the other of them in respect of the infringement; and

(c) the court shall if an account of profits is directed apportion the profits between them as the court considers just, subject to any agreement between them.

The provisions of this subsection apply whether or not the proprietor and the exclusive licensee are both parties to the action; and if they are not both parties the court may give such directions as it thinks fit as to the extent to which the party to the proceedings is to hold the proceeds of any pecuniary remedy on behalf of the other.

(7) The proprietor of a registered trade mark shall notify any exclusive licensee who has a concurrent right of action before applying for an order under section 16 (order for delivery up); and the court may on the application of the licensee make such order under that section as it thinks fit having regard to the terms of the licence.

(8) The provisions of subsections (4) to (7) above have effect subject to any agreement to the contrary between the exclusive licensee and the proprietor.

Application for registered trade mark

Application for registration

32.—(1) An application for registration of a trade mark shall be made to the registrar.
(2) The application shall contain—

(a) a request for registration of a trade mark,

(b) the name and address of the applicant,

(c) a statement of the goods or services in relation to which it is sought to register the trade mark, and

(d) a representation of the trade mark.

(3) The application shall state that the trade mark is being used, by the applicant or with his consent, in relation to those goods or services, or that he has a *bona fide* intention that it should be so used.

(4) The application shall be subject to the payment of the application fee and such class fees as may be appropriate.

Date of filing

33.—(1) The date of filing of an application for registration of a trade mark is the date on which documents containing everything required by section 32(2) are furnished to the registrar by the applicant.

If the documents are furnished on different days, the date of filing is the last of those days.

(2) References in this Act to the date of application for registration are to the date of filing of the application.

Classification of trade marks

34.—(1) Goods and services shall be classified for the purposes of the registration of trade marks according to a prescribed system of classification.

(2) Any questions arising as to the class within which any goods or services fall shall be determined by the registrar, whose decision shall be final.

Priority

Claim to priority of Convention application

35.—(1) A person who has duly filed an application for protection of a trade mark in a Convention country (a "Convention application"), or his successor in title, has a right to priority, for the purposes of registering the same trade mark under this Act for some or all of the same goods or services, for a period of six months from the date of filing of the first such application.

(2) If the application for registration under this Act is made within that six-month period—

(a) the relevant date for the purposes of establishing which rights take precedence shall be the date of filing of the first Convention application, and

(b) the registrability of the trade mark shall not be affected by any use of the mark in the United Kingdom in the period between that date and the date of the application under this Act.

(3) Any filing which in a Convention country is equivalent to a regular national filing, under its domestic legislation or an international agreement, shall be treated as giving rise to the right of priority.

A "regular national filing" means a filing which is adequate to establish the date on which the application was filed in that country, whatever may be the subsequent fate of the application.

(4) A subsequent application concerning the same subject as the first Convention application, filed in the same Convention country, shall be considered the first Convention application (of which the filing date is the starting date of the period of priority), if at the time of the subsequent application—

(a) the previous application has been withdrawn, abandoned or refused, without having been laid open to public inspection and without leaving any rights outstanding, and

(b) it has not yet served as a basis for claiming a right of priority.

The previous application may not thereafter serve as a basis for claiming a right of priority.

(5) Provision may be made by rules as to the manner of claiming a right to priority on the basis of a Convention application.

(6) A right to priority arising as a result of a Convention application may be assigned or otherwise transmitted, either with the application or independently.

The reference in subsection (1) to the applicant's "successor in title" shall be construed accordingly.

Claim to priority from other relevant overseas application

36.—(1) Her Majesty may by Order in Council make provision for conferring on a person who has duly filed an application for protection of a trade mark in—

(a) any of the Channel Islands or a colony, or

(b) a country or territory in relation to which Her Majesty's Government in the United Kingdom have entered into a treaty, convention, arrangement or engagement for the reciprocal protection of trade marks,

a right to priority, for the purpose of registering the same trade mark under this Act for some or all of the same goods or services, for a specified period from the date of filing of that application.

(2) An Order in Council under this section may make provision corresponding to that made by section 35 in relation to Convention countries or such other provisions as appears to Her Majesty to be appropriate.

(3) A statutory instrument containing an Order in Council under this section shall be subject to annulment in pursuance of a resolution of either House of Parliament.

Registration procedure

Examination of application

37.—(1) The registrar shall examine whether an application for registration of a trade mark satisfies the requirement of this Act (including any requirements imposed by rules).

(2) For that purpose he shall carry out a search, to such extent as he considers necessary, of earlier trade marks.

(3) If it appears to the registrar that the requirements for registration are not met, he shall inform the applicant and give him an opportunity, within such period as the registrar may specify, to make representations or to amend the application.

(4) If the applicant fails to satisfy the registrar that those requirements are met, or to amend the application so as to meet them, or fails to respond before the end of the specified period, the registrar shall refuse to accept the application.

(5) If it appears to the registrar that the requirements for registration are met, he shall accept the application.

Publication, opposition proceedings and observations

38.—(1) When an application for registration has been accepted, the registrar shall cause the application to be published in the prescribed manner.

(2) Any person may, within the prescribed time from the date of the publication of the application, give notice to the registrar of opposition to the registration.

The notice shall be given in writing in the prescribed manner, and shall include a statement of the grounds of opposition.

(3) Where an application has been published, any person may, at any time before the registration of the trade mark, make observations in writing to the registrar as to whether the trade mark should be registered; and the registrar shall inform the applicant of any such observations.

A person who makes observations does not thereby become a party to the proceedings on the application.

Withdrawal, restriction or amendment of application

39.—(1) The applicant may at any time withdraw his application or restrict the goods or services covered by the application.

If the application has been published, the withdrawal or restriction shall also be published.

(2) In other respects, an application may be amended, at the request of the applicant, only by correcting—

(a) the name or address of the applicant,

(b) errors of wording or of copying, or

(c) obvious mistakes,

and then only where the correction does not substantially affect the identity of the trade mark or extend the goods or services covered by the application.

(3) Provision shall be made by rules for the publication of any amendment which affects the representation of the trade mark, or the goods or services covered by the application, and for the making of objections by any person claiming to be affected by it.

Registration

40.—(1) Where an application has been accepted and—

(a) no notice of opposition is given within the period referred to in section 38(2), or

(b) all opposition proceedings are withdrawn or decided in favour of the applicant,

the registrar shall register the trade mark, unless it appears to him having regard to matters coming to his notice since he accepted the application that it was accepted in error.

(2) A trade mark shall not be registered unless any fee prescribed for the registration is paid within the prescribed period.

If the fee is not paid within that period, the application shall be deemed to be withdrawn.

(3) A trade mark when registered shall be registered as of the date of filing of the application for registration; and that date shall be deemed for the purposes of this Act to be the date of registration.

(4) On the registration of a trade mark the registrar shall publish the registration in the prescribed manner and issue to the applicant a certificate of registration.

Registration: supplementary provisions

41.—(1) Provision may be made by rules as to—

(a) the division of an application for the registration of a trade mark into several applications;

(b) the merging of separate applications or registrations;

(c) the registration of a series of trade marks.

(2) A series of trade marks means a number of trade marks which resemble each other as to their material particulars and differ only as to matters of a non-distinctive character not substantially affecting the identity of the trade mark.

(3) Rules under this section may include provision as to—

   (a) the circumstances in which, and conditions subject to which, division, merger or registration of a series is permitted, and

   (b) the purposes for which an application to which the rules apply is to be treated as a single application and those for which it is to be treated as a number of separate applications.

Duration, renewal and alteration of registered trade mark

Duration of registration

42.—(1) A trade mark shall be registered for a period of ten years from the date of registration.

(2) Registration may be renewed in accordance with section 43 for further periods of ten years.

Renewal of registration

43.—(1) The registration of a trade mark may be renewed at the request of the proprietor, subject to payment of a renewal fee.

(2) Provision shall be made by rules for the registrar to inform the proprietor of a registered trade mark, before the expiry of the registration, of the date of expiry and the manner in which the registration may be renewed.

(3) A request for renewal must be made, and the renewal fee paid, before the expiry of the registration.

Failing this, the request may be made and the fee paid within such further period (of not less than six months) as may be prescribed, in which case an additional renewal fee must also be paid within that period.

(4) Renewal shall take effect from the expiry of the previous registration.

(5) If the registration is not renewed in accordance with the above provisions, the registrar shall remove the trade mark from the register.

Provision may be made by rules for the restoration of the registration of a trade mark which has been removed from the register, subject to such conditions (if any) as may be prescribed.

(6) The renewal or restoration of the registration of a trade mark shall be published in the prescribed manner.

Alteration of registered trade mark

44.—(1) A registered trade mark shall not be altered in the register, during the period of registration or on renewal.

(2) Nevertheless, the registrar may, at the request of the proprietor, allow the alteration of a registered trade mark where the mark includes the proprietor's name or address and the alteration is limited to alteration of that name or address and does not substantially affect the identity of the mark.

(3) Provision shall be made by rules for the publication of any such alteration and the making of objections by any person claiming to be affected by it.

Surrender, revocation and invalidity

Surrener of registered trade mark

45.—(1) A registered trade mark may be surrendered by the proprietor in respect of some or all of the goods or services for which it is registered.

(2) Provision may be made by rules—

   (a) as to the manner and effect of a surrender, and

   (b) for protecting the interests of other persons having a right in the registered trade mark.

Revocation of registration

46.—(1) The registration of a trade mark may be revoked on any of the following grounds—

(a) that within the period of five years following the date of completion of the registration procedure it has not been put to genuine use in the United Kingdom, by the proprietor or with his consent, in relation to the goods or services for which it is registered, and there are no proper reasons for non-use;

(b) that such use has been suspended for an uninterrupted period of five years, and there are no proper reasons for non-use;

(c) that, in consequence of acts or inactivity of the proprietor, it has become the common name in the trade for a product or service for which it is registered;

(d) that in consequence of the use made of it by the proprietor or with his consent in relation to the goods or services for which it is registered, it is liable to mislead the public, particularly as to the nature, quality or geographical origin of those goods or services.

(2) For the purpose of subsection (1) use of a trade mark includes use in a form differing in elements which do not alter the distinctive character of the mark in the form in which it was registered, and use in the United Kingdom includes affixing the trade mark to goods or to the packaging of goods in the United Kingdom solely for export purposes.

(3) The registration of a trade mark shall not be revoked on the ground mentioned in subsection (1)(a) or (b) if such use as in referred to in that paragraph is commenced or resumed after the expiry of the five year period and before the application for revocation is made.

Provided that, any such commencement or resumption of use after the expiry of the five year period but within the period of three months before the making of the application shall be disregarded unless preparations for the commencement or resumption began before the proprietor became aware that the application might be made.

(4) An application for revocation may be made by any person, and may be made either to the registrar or to the court, except that —

(a) if proceedings concerning the trade mark in question are pending in the court, the application must be made to the court; and

(b) if in any other case the application is made to the registrar, he may at any stage of the proceedings refer the application to the court.

(5) Where grounds for revocation exist in respect of only some of the goods or services for which the trade mark is registered, revocation shall relate to those goods or services only.

(6) Where the registration of a trade mark is revoked to any extent, the rights of the proprietor shall be deemed to have ceased to that extent as from—

(a) the date of the application for revocation, or

(b) if the registrar or court is satisfied that the grounds for revocation existing at an earlier date, that date.

Grounds for invalidity of registration

47.—(1) The registration of a trade mark may be declared invalid on the ground that the trade mark was registered in breach of section 3 or any of the provisions referred to in that section (absolute grounds for refusal of registration).

Where the trade mark was registered in breach of subsection (1)(b), (c) or (d) of that section, it shall not be declared invalid if, in consequence of the use which has been made of it, it has after registration acquired a distinctive character in relation to the goods or services for which it is registered.

(2) The registration of a trade mark may be declared invalid on the ground—

(a) that there is an earlier trade mark in relation to which the conditions set out in section 5(1), (2) or (3) obtain, or

(b) that there is an earlier right in relation to which the condition set out in section 5(4) is satisfied,

unless the proprietor of that earlier trade mark or other earlier right has consented to the registration.

(3) An application for a declaration of invalidity may be made by any person, and may be made either to the registrar or to the court, except that—

(a) if proceedings concerning the trade mark in question are pending in the court, the application must be made to the court; and

(b) if in any other case the application is made to the registrar, he may at any stage of the proceedings refer the application to the court.

(4) In the case of bad faith in the registration of a trade mark, the registrar himself may apply to the court for a declaration of the invalidity of the registration.

(5) Where the grounds of invalidity exists in respect of only some of the goods or services for which the trade mark is registered, the trade mark shall be declared invalid as regards those goods or services only.

(6) Where the registration of a trade mark is declared invalid to any extent, the registration shall to that extent be deemed never to have been made:

Provided that this shall not affect transactions past and closed.

Effect of acquiescence

48.—(1) Where the proprietor of an earlier trade mark or other earlier right has acquiesced for continuous period of five years in the use of a registered trade mark in the United Kingdom, being aware of that use, there shall cease to be any entitlement on the basis of that earlier trade mark or other right—

(a) to apply for a declaration that the registration of the later trade mark is invalid, or

(b) to oppose the use of the later trade mark in relation to the goods or services in relation to which it has been so used,

unless the registration of the later trade mark was applied for in bad faith.

(2) Where subsection (1) applies, the proprietor of the later trade mark is not entitled to oppose the use of the earlier trade mark or, as the case may be, the exploitation of the earlier right, notwithstanding that the earlier trade mark or right may no longer be invoked against his later trade mark.

Collective marks

Collective marks

49.—(1) A collective mark is a mark distinguishing the goods or services of members of the association which is the proprietor of the mark from those of other undertakings.

(2) The provisions of this Act apply to collective marks subject to the provisions of Schedule 1.

Certification marks

Certification marks

50.—(1) A certification mark is a mark indicating that the goods or services in connection with which it is used are certified by the proprietor of the mark in respect of origin, material, mode of manufacture of goods or performance of services, quality, accuracy or other characteristics.

(2) The provisions of this Act apply to certification marks subject to the provisions of Schedule 2.

Part II

Community Trade Marks and International Matters

Community trade marks

Meaning of "Community trade mark"

51. In this Act —"

Community trade mark" has the meaning given by Article 1(1) of the Community
Trade Mark Regulation; and

"the Community Trade Mark Regulation" means Council Regulation (EC) No. 40/94
of 20th December 1993 on the Community trade mark.

Power to make provision in connection with Community Trade Mark Regulations

52.—(1) The Secretary of State may by regulations make such provision as he considers
appropriate in connection with the operation of the Community Trade Mark Regulation.

(2) Provision may, in particular, be made with respect to—

(a) the making of applications for Community trade marks by way of the Patent
Office;

(b) the procedures for determining a posteriori the invalidity, or liability to revocation,
of the registration of a trade mark from which a Community trade mark claims
seniority;

(c) the conversion of a Community trade mark, or an application for a Community
trade mark, into an application for registration under this Act;

(d) the designation of courts in the United Kingdom having jurisdiction over proceedings arising out of the Community Trade Mark Regulation.

(3) Without prejudice to the generality of subsection (1), provision may be made by
regulations under this section—

(a) applying in relation to a Community trade mark the provisions of—

(i) section 21 (remedy for groundless threats of infringement proceedings);

(ii) sections 89 to 91 (importation of infringing goods, material or articles);
and

(iii) sections 92, 93, 95 and 96 (offences); and

(b) making in relation to the list of professional representatives maintained in
pursuance of Article 89 of the Community Trade Mark Regulation, and persons on
that list, provision corresponding to that made by, or capable of being made under,
sections 84 to 88 in relation to the register of trade mark agents and registered
trade mark agents.

(4) Regulations under this section shall be made by statutory instrument which shall be
subject to annulment in pursuance of a resolution of either House of Parliament.

The Madrid Protocol: international registration

The Madrid Protocol

53. In this Act —

"the Madrid Protocol" means the Protocol relating to the Madrid Agreement concerning the International Registration of Marks, adopted at Madrid on 27th June 1989;

"the International Bureau" has the meaning given by Article 2(1) of that Protocol; and "international trade mark (UK)" means a trade mark which is entitled to protection in the United Kingdom under that Protocol.

Power to make provision giving effect to Madrid Protocol

54.—(1) The Secretary of State may by order make such provisions as he thinks fit for giving effect in the United Kingdom to the provisions of the Madrid Protocol.

(2) Provision may, in particular, be made with respect to—

(a) the making of applications for international registrations by way of the Patent Office as office of origin;

(b) the procedures to be followed where the basic United Kingdom application or registration fails or ceases to be in force;

(c) the procedures to be followed where the Patent Office receives from the International Bureau a request for extension of protection to the United Kingdom;

(d) the effects of a successful request for extension of protection to the United Kingdom;

(e) the transformation of an application for an international registration, or an international registration, into a national application for registration;

(f) the communication of information to the International Bureau;

(g) the payment of fees and amounts prescribed in respect of applications for international registrations, extensions of protection and renewals.

(3) Without prejudice to the generality of subsection (1), provision may be made by regulations under this section applying in relation to an international trade mark (UK) the provisions of—

(a) section 21 (remedy for groundless threats of infringement proceedings);

(b) sections 89 to 91 (importation of infringing goods, material or articles); and

(c) sections 92, 93, 95 and 96 (offences).

(4) An order under this section shall be made by statutory instrument which shall be subject to annulment in pursuance of a resolution of either House of Parliament.

The Paris Convention: supplementary provisions

The Paris Convention

55.—(1) In this Act—

(a) "the Paris Convention" means the Paris Convention for the Protection of Industrial Property of March 20th 1883, as revised or amended from time to time,

(aa) "the WTO agreement" means the Agreement establishing the World Trade Organisation signed at Marrakesh on 15th April 1994, and

(b) a "Convention country" means a country, other than the United Kingdom, which is a party to that Convention.

(2) The Secretary of State may by order make such amendments of this Act, and rules made under this Act, as appear to him appropriate in consequence of any revision or amendment of the Paris Convention or the WTO agreement after the passing of this Act.

(3) Any such order shall be made by statutory instrument which shall be subject to annulment in pursuance of a resolution of either House of Parliament.

Protection of well-known trade marks: Article 6*bis*

56.—(1) References in this Act to a trade mark which is entitled to protection under the Paris Convention or the WTO agreement as a well known trade mark are to a mark which is well-known in the United Kingdom as being the mark of a person who—

(a) is a national of a Convention country, or

(b) is domiciled in, or has a real and effective industrial or commercial establishment in, a Convention country,

whether or not that person carries on business, or has any goodwill, in the United Kingdom. References to the proprietor of such a mark shall be construed accordingly.

(2) The proprietor of a trade mark which is entitled to protection under the Paris Convention or the WTO agreement as a well known trade mark is entitled to restrain by injunction the use in the United Kingdom of a trade mark which, or the essential part of which, is identical or similar to his mark, in relation to identical or similar goods or services, where the use is likely to cause confusion.

This right is subject to section 48 (effect of acquiescence by proprietor of earlier trade mark).

(3) Nothing in subsection (2) affects the continuation of any *bona fide* use of a trade mark begun before the commencement of this section.

National emblems, &c. of Convention countries: Article 6*ter*

57.—(1) A trade mark which consists of or contains the flag of a Convention country shall not be registered without the authorisation of the competent authorities of that country, unless it appears to the registrar that use of the flag in the manner proposed is permitted without such authorisation.

(2) A trade mark which consists of or contains the armorial bearings or any other state emblem of a Convention country which is protected under the Paris Convention or the WTO agreement shall not be registered without the authorisation of the competent authorities of that country.

(3) A trade mark which consists of or contains an official sign or hallmark adopted by a Convention country and indicating control and warranty shall not, where the sign or hallmark is protected under the Paris Convention or the WTO agreement, be registered in relation to goods or services of the same, or a similar kind, as those in relation to which it indicates control and warranty, without the authorisation of the competent authorities of the country concerned.

(4) The provisions of this section as to national flags and other state emblems, and official signs or hallmarks, apply equally to anything which from a heraldic point of view imitates any such flag or other emblem, or sign or hallmark.

(5) Nothing in this section prevents the registration of a trade mark on the application of a national of a country who is authorised to make use of a state emblem, or official sign or hallmark, of that country, notwithstanding that it is similar to that of another country.

(6) Where by virtue of this section the authorisation of the competent authorities of a Convention country is or would be required for the registration of a trade mark, those authorities are entitled to restrain by injunction any use of the mark in the United Kingdom without their authorisation.

Emblems, &c. of certain international organisations: Article 6*ter*

58.—(1) This section applies to—

(a) the armorial bearings, flags or other emblems, and

(b) the abbreviations and names,

of international intergovernmental organisations of which one or more Convention countries are members.

(2) A trade mark which consists of or contains any such emblem, abbreviation or name which is protected under the Paris Convention or the WTO agreement shall not be registered without the authorisation of the international organisation concerned, unless it appears to the registrar that the use of the emblem, abbreviation or name in the manner proposed—

(a) is not such as to suggest to the public that a connection exists between the organisation and the trade mark, or

(b) is not likely to mislead the public as to the existence of a connection between the user and the organisation.

(3) The provisions of this section as to emblems of an international organisation apply equally to anything which from a heraldic point of view imitates any such emblem.

(4) Where by virtue of this section the authorisation of an international organisation is or would be required for the registration of a trade mark, that organisation is entitled to restrain by injunction any use of the mark in the United Kingdom without its authorisation.

(5) Nothing in this section affects the rights of a person whose *bona fide* use of the trade mark in question began before 4th January 1962 (when the relevant provisions of the Paris Convention entered into force in relation to the United Kingdom).

Notification under Article *6ter* of the Convention

59.—(1) For the purpose of section 57 state emblems of a Convention country (other than the national flag), and official signs or hallmarks, shall be regarded as protected under the Paris Convention only if, or to the extent that—

(a) the country in question has notified the United Kingdom in accordance with Article *6ter*(3) of the Convention that it desires to protect that emblem, sign or hallmark,

(b) the notification remains in force, and

(c) the United Kingdom has not objected to it in accordance with Article *6ter*(4) or any such objection has been withdrawn.

(2) For the purposes of section 58 the emblems, abbreviations and names of an international organisation shall be regarded as protected under the Paris Convention only if, or to the extent that—

(a) the organisation in question has notified the United Kingdom in accordance with Article *6ter*(3) of the Convention that it desires to protect that emblem, abbreviation or name,

(b) the notification remains in force, and

(c) the United Kingdom has not objected to it in accordance with Article *6ter*(4) or any such objection has been withdrawn.

(3) Notification under Article *6ter*(3) of the Paris Convention shall have effect only in relation to applications for registration made more than two months after the receipt of the notification.

(4) The registrar shall keep and make available for public inspection by any person, at all reasonable hours and free of charge, a list of —

(a) the state emblems and official signs or hallmarks, and

(b) the emblems, abbreviations and names of international organisations,

which are for the time being protected under the Paris Convention by virtue of notification under Article *6ter*(3).

Acts of agent or representative: Article *6septies*

60.—(1) The following provisions apply where an application for registration of a trade mark is made by a person who is an agent or representative of a person who is the proprietor of the mark in a Convention country.

(2) If the proprietor opposes the application, registration shall be refused.

(3) If the application (not being so opposed) is granted, the proprietor may —

(a) apply for a declaration of the invalidity of the registration, or

(b) apply for the rectification of the register so as to substitute his name as the proprietor of the registered trade mark.

(4) The proprietor may (notwithstanding the rights conferred by this Act in relation to a registered trade mark) by injunction restrain any use of the trade mark in the United Kingdom which is not authorised by him.

(5) Subsections (2), (3) and (4) do not apply if, or to the extent that, the agent or representative justifies his action.

(6) An application under subsection (3)(a) or (b) must be made within three years of the proprietor becoming aware of the registration; and no injunction shall be granted under subsection (4) in respect of a use in which the proprietor has acquiesced for a continuous period of three years or more.

Miscellaneous

Stamp duty

61. Stamp duty shall not be chargeable on an instrument relating to a Community trade mark or an international trade mark (UK), or an application for any such mark, by reason only of the fact that such a mark has legal effect in the United Kingdom.

PART III

ADMINISTRATIVE AND OTHER SUPPLEMENTARY PROVISIONS

The registrar

The registrar

62. In this Act "the registrar" means the Comptroller-General of Patents, Designs and Trade Marks.

The register

The register

63.—(1) The registrar shall maintain a register of trade marks.

References in this Act to "the register" are to that register; and references to registration (in particular, in the expression "registered trade mark") are, unless the context otherwise requires, to registration in that register.

(2) There shall be entered in the register in accordance with this Act—

(a) registered trade marks,

(b) such particulars as may be prescribed of registrable transactions affecting a registered trade mark, and

(c) such other matters relating to registered trade marks as may be prescribed.

(3) The register shall be kept in such manner as may be prescribed, and provisions shall in particular be made for —

(a) public inspection of the register, and

(b) the supply of certified or uncertified copies, or extracts, of entries in the register.

Rectification or correction of the register

64.—(1) Any person having a sufficient interest may apply for the rectification of an error or omission in the register:

Provided that an application for rectification may not be made in respect of a matter affecting the validity of the registration of a trade mark.

(2) An application for rectification may be made either to the registrar or to the court, except that—

(a) if proceedings concerning the trade mark in question are pending in the court, the application must be made to the court; and

(b) if in any other case the application is made to the registrar, he may at any stage of the proceedings refer the application to the court.

(3) Except where the registrar or the court directs otherwise, the effect of rectification of the register is that the error or omission in question shall be deemed never to have been made.

(4) The registrar may, on request made in the prescribed manner by the proprietor of a registered trade mark, or a licensee, enter any change in his name or address as recorded in the register.

(5) The registrar may remove from the register matter appearing to him to have ceased to have effect.

Adaptation of entries to new classification

65.—(1) Provision may be made by rules empowering the registrar to do such things as he considers necessary to implement any amended or substituted classification of goods or services for the purposes of the registration of trade marks.

(2) Provision may in particular be made for the amendment of existing entries on the register so as to accord with the new classification.

(3) Any such power of amendment shall not be exercised so as to extend the rights conferred by the registration, except where it appears to the registrar that compliance with this requirement would involve undue complexity and that any extension would not be substantial and would not adversely affect the rights of any person.

(4) The rules may empower the registrar—

(a) to require the proprietor of a registered trade mark, within such time as may be prescribed, to file a proposal for amendment of the register, and

(b) to cancel or refuse to renew the registration of the trade mark in the event of his failing to do so.

(5) Any such proposal shall be advertised, and may be opposed, in such manner as may be prescribed.

Powers and duties of the registrar

Power to require use of forms

66.—(1) The registrar may require the use of such forms as he may direct for any purpose relating to the registration of a trade mark or any other proceeding before him under this Act.

(2) The forms, and any directions of the registrar with respect to their use, shall be published in the prescribed manner.

Information about applications and registered trade marks

67.—(1) After publication of an application for registration of a trade mark, the registrar shall on request provide a person with such information and permit him to inspect such documents relating to the application, or to any registered trade mark resulting from it, as may be specified in the request, subject, however, to any prescribed restrictions.

Any request must be made in the prescribed manner and be accompanied by the appropriate fee (if any).

(2) Before publication of an application for registration of a trade mark, documents or information constituting or relating to the application shall not be published by the registrar or communicated by him to any person except—

(a) in such cases and to such extent as may be prescribed, or

(b) with the consent of the applicant;

but subject as follows.

(3) Where a person has been notified that an application for registration of a trade mark has been made, and that the applicant will if the application is granted bring proceedings

against him in respect of acts done after publication of the application, he may make a request under subsection (1) notwithstanding that the application has not been published and that subsection shall apply accordingly.

Costs and security for costs

68.—(1) Provision may be made by rules empowering the registrar, in any proceedings before him under this Act—

    (a) to award any party such costs as he may consider reasonable, and

    (b) to direct how and by what parties they are to be paid.

(2) Any such order of the registrar may be enforced—

    (a) in England and Wales or Northern Ireland, in the same way as an order of the High Court;

    (b) in Scotland, in the same way as a decree for expenses granted by the Court of Session.

(3) Provision may be made by rules empowering the registrar, in such cases as may be prescribed, to require a party to proceedings before him to give security for costs, in relation to those proceedings or to proceedings on appeal, and as to the consequences if security is not given.

Evidence before registrar

69. Provision may be made by rules—

    (a) as to the giving of evidence in proceedings before the registrar under this Act by affidavit or statutory declaration;

    (b) conferring on the registrar the powers of an official referee of the Supreme Court as regards the examination of witnesses on oath and the discovery and production of documents; and

    (c) applying in relation to the attendance of witnesses in proceedings before the registrar the rules applicable to the attendance of witnesses before such a referee.

Exclusion of liability in respect of official acts

70.—(1) The registrar shall not be taken to warrant the validity of the registration of a trade mark under this Act or under any treaty, convention, arrangement or engagement to which the United Kingdom is a party.

(2) The registrar is not subject to any liability by reason of, or in connection with, any examination required or authorised by this Act, or any such treaty, convention, arrangement or engagement, or any report or other proceedings consequent on such examination.

(3) No proceedings lie against an officer of the registrar in respect of any matter for which, by virtue of this section, the registrar is not liable.

Registrar's annual report

71.—(1) The Comptroller-General of Patents, Designs and Trade Marks shall in his annual report under section 121 of the Patents Act 1977, include a report on the execution of this Act, including the discharge of his functions under the Madrid Protocol.

(2) The report shall include an account of all money received and paid by him under or by virtue of this Act.

Legal proceedings and appeals

Registration to be *prima facie* evidence of validity

72. In all legal proceedings relating to a registered trade mark (including proceedings for rectification of the register) the registration of a person as proprietor of a trade mark shall be prima facie evidence of the validity of the original registration and of any subsequent assignment or other transmission of it.

Certificate of validity of contested registration

73.—(1) If in proceedings before the court the validity of the registration of a trade mark is contested and it is found by the court that the trade mark is validly registered, the court may give a certificate to that effect.

(2) If the court gives such a certificate and in subsequent proceedings—

(a) the validity of the registration is again questioned, and

(b) the proprietor obtains a final order or judgement in his favour,

he is entitled to his costs as between solicitor and client unless the court directs otherwise.

This subsection does not extend to the costs of an appeal in any such proceedings

Registrar's appearance in proceedings involving the register

74.—(1) In proceedings before the court involving an application for—

(a) the revocation of the registration of a trade mark,

(b) the declaration of the invalidity of the registration of a trade mark, or

(c) the rectification of the register,

the registrar is entitled to appear and be heard, and shall appear if so directed by the court.

(2) Unless otherwise directed by the court, the registrar may instead of appearing submit to the court a statement in writing signed by him, giving particulars of —

(a) any proceedings before him in relation to the matter in issue,

(b) the grounds of any decision given by him affecting it,

(c) the practice of the Patent Office in like cases, or

(d) such matters relevant to the issues and within his knowledge as registrar as he thinks fit;

and the statement shall be deemed to form part of the evidence in the proceedings.

(3) Anything which the registrar is or may be authorised or required to do under this section may be done on his behalf by a duly authorised officer.

The court

75. In this Act, unless the context otherwise requires, "the court" means—

(a) in England and Wales and Northern Ireland, the High Court, and

(b) in Scotland, the Court of Session.

Appeals from the registrar

76.—(1) An appeal lies from any decision of the registrar under this Act, except as otherwise expressly provided by rules.

For this purpose "decision" includes any act of the registrar in exercise of a discretion vested in him by or under this Act.

(2) Any such appeal may be brought either to an appointed person or to the court.

(3) Where an appeal is made to an appointed person, he may refer the appeal to the court if—

(a) it appears to him that a point of general legal importance is involved,

(b) the registrar requests that it be so referred, or

(c) such a request is made by any party to the proceedings before the registrar in which the decision appealed against was made.

Before doing so the appointed person shall give the appellant and any other party to the appeal an opportunity to make representations as to whether the appeal should be referred to the court.

(4) Where an appeal is made to an appointed person and he does not refer it to the court, he shall hear and determine the appeal and his decision shall be final.

(5) The provisions of sections 68 and 69 (costs and security for costs; evidence) apply in relation to proceedings before an appointed person as in relation to proceedings before the registrar.

Persons appointed to hear and determine appeals

77.—(1) For the purposes of section 76 an "appointed person" means a person appointed by the Lord Chancellor to hear and decide appeals under this Act.

(2) A person is not eligible for such appointment unless—

(a) he has a 7 year general qualification, within the meaning of section 71 of the Courts and Legal Services Act 1990;

(b) he is an advocate or solicitor in Scotland of at least 7 years' standing;

(c) he is a member of the Bar of Northern Ireland or solicitor of the Supreme Court of Northern Ireland of at least 7 years' standing; or

(d) he has held judicial office.

(3) An appointed person shall hold and vacate office in accordance with his terms of appointment, subject to the following provisions—

(a) there shall be paid to him such remuneration (whether by way of salary or fees), and such allowances, as the Secretary of State with the approval of the Treasury may determine;

(b) he may resign his office by notice in writing to the Lord Chancellor;

(c) the Lord Chancellor may by notice in writing remove him from office if —

(i) he has become bankrupt or made an arrangement with his creditors or, in Scotland, his estate has been sequestrated or he has executed a trust deed for his creditors or entered into a composition contract, or

(ii) he is incapacitated by physical or mental illness,

or if he is in the opinion of the Lord Chancellor otherwise unable or unfit to perform his duties as an appointed person.

(4) The Lord Chancellor shall consult the Lord Advocate before exercising his powers under this section.

Rules, fees, hours of business, &c.

Power of Secretary of State to make rules

78.—(1) The Secretary of State may make rules—

(a) for the purposes of any provision of this Act authorising the making of rules with respect to any matter, and

(b) for prescribing anything unauthorised or required by any provision of this Act to be prescribed,

and generally for regulating practice and procedure under this Act.

(2) Provision may, in particular, be made—

(a) as to the manner of filing of applications and other documents;

(b) requiring and regulating the translation of documents and the filing and authentication of any translation;

(c) as to the service of documents;

(d) authorising the rectification of irregularities of procedure;

(e) prescribing time limits for anything required to be done in connection with any proceedings under this Act;

(f) providing for the extension of any time limit so prescribed, or specified by the registrar, whether or not it has already expired.

(3) Rules under this Act shall be made by statutory instrument which shall be subject to annulment in pursuance of a resolution of either House of Parliament.

Fees

79.—(1) There shall be paid in respect of applications and registration and other matters under this Act such fees as may be prescribed.

(2) Provision may be made by rules as to—

(a) the payment of a single fee in respect of two or more matters, and

(b) the circumstances (if any) in which a fee may be repaid or remitted.

Hours of business and business days

80.—(1) The registrar may give directions specifying the hours of business of the Patent Office for the purpose of the transaction by the public of business under this Act, and the days which are business days for that purpose.

(2) Business done on any day after the specified hours of business, or on a day which is not a business day, shall be deemed to have been done on the next business day; and where the time for doing anything under this Act expires on a day which is not a business day, that time shall be extended to the next business day.

(3) Directions under this section may make different provision for different classes of business and shall be published in the prescribed manner.

The trade marks journal

81. Provision shall be made by rules for the publication by the registrar of a journal containing particulars of any application for the registration of a trade mark (including a representation of the mark) and such other information relating to trade marks as the registrar thinks fit.

Trade mark agents

Recognition of agents

82. Except as otherwise provided by rules, any act required or authorised by this Act to be done by or to a person in connection with the registration of a trade mark, or any procedure relating to a registered trade mark, may be done by or to an agent authorised by that person orally or in writing.

The register of trade mark agents

83.—(1) The Secretary of State may make rules requiring the keeping of a register of person who act as agent for others for the purpose of applying for or obtaining the registration of trade marks; and in this Act a "registered trade mark agent" means a person whose name is entered in the register kept under this section.

(2) The rules may contain such provisions as the Secretary of State thinks fit regulating the registration of persons, and may in particular—

(a) require the payment of such fees as may be prescribed, and

(b) authorise in prescribed cases the erasure from the register of the name of any person registered in it, or the suspension of a person's registration.

(3) The rules may delegate the keeping of the register to another person, and may confer on that person—

    (a) power to make regulations—

        (i) with respect to the payment of fees, in the cases and subject to the limits prescribed by the rules, and

        (ii) with respect to any other matter which could be regulated by the rules, and

    (b) such other functions, including disciplinary functions, as may be prescribed by the rules.

Unregistered persons not to be described as registered trade mark agents

84.—(1) An individual who is not a registered trade mark agent shall not—

    (a) carry on a business (otherwise than in partnership) under any name or other description which contains the words "registered trade mark agent"; or

    (b) in the course of a business otherwise described or hold himself out, or permit himself to be described or held out, as a registered trade mark agent.

(2) A partnership shall not—

    (a) carry on a business under any name or other description which contains the words "registered trade mark agent"; or

    (b) in the course of a business otherwise describe or hold itself out, or permit itself to be described or held out, as a firm of registered trade mark agents,

unless all partners are registered trade mark agents or the partnership satisfies such conditions as may be prescribed for the purposes of this section.

(3) A body corporate shall not—

    (a) carry on a business (otherwise than in partnership) under any name or other description which contains the words "registered trade mark agent"; or

    (b) in the course of a business otherwise describe or hold itself out, or permit itself to be described or held out, as a registered trade mark agent,

unless all the directors of the body corporate are registered trade mark agents or the body satisfies such conditions as may be prescribed for the purposes of this section.

(4) A person who contravenes this section commits an offence and is liable on summary conviction to a fine not exceeding level 5 on the standard scale; and proceedings for such an offence may be begun at any time within a year from the date of the offence.

Power to prescribe conditions, &c. for mixed partnerships and bodies corporate

85.—(1) The Secretary of State may make rules prescribing the conditions to be satisfied for the purposes of section 84 (persons entitled to be described as registered trade mark agents)—

    (a) in relation to a partnership where not all the partners are qualified persons, or

    (b) in relation to a body corporate where not all the directors are qualified persons,

and imposing requirements to be complied with by such partnerships or bodies corporate.

(2) The rules may, in particular —

    (a) prescribe conditions as to the number or proportion of partners or directors who must be qualified persons;

    (b) impose requirements as to—

        (i) the identification of qualified and unqualified persons in professional advertisements, circulars or letters issued by or with the consent of the partnership or body corporate and which relate to its business, and

(ii) the manner in which a partnership or body corporate is to organise its affairs so as to secure that qualified persons exercise a sufficient degree of control over the activities of unqualified persons.

(3) Contravention of a requirement imposed by the rules is an offence for which a person is liable on summary conviction to a fine not exceeding level 5 on the standard scale.

(4) In this section "qualified person" means a registered trade mark agent.

Use of the term "trade mark attorney"

86.—(1) No offence is committed under the enactments restricting the use of certain expressions in reference to persons not qualified to act as solicitors by the use of the term "trade mark attorney" in reference to a registered trade mark agent.

(2) The enactments referred to in subsection (1) are section 21 of the Solicitors Act 1974, section 31 of the Solicitors (Scotland) Act 1980 and Article 22 of the Solicitors (Northern Ireland) Order 1976.

Privilege for communications with registered trade mark agents

87.—(1) This section applies to communications as to any matter relating to the protection of any design or trade mark, or as to any matter involving passing off.

(2) Any such communication—

(a) between a person and his trade mark agent, or

(b) for the purpose of obtaining, or in response to a request for, information which a person is seeking for the purpose of instructing his trade mark agent,

is privileged from, or in Scotland protected against, disclosure in legal proceedings in the same way as a communication between a person and his solicitor or, as the case may be, a communication for the purpose of obtaining, or in response to a request for, information which a person is seeking for the purpose of instructing his solicitor.

(3) In subsection (2) "trade mark agent" means—

(a) a registered trade mark agent, or

(b) a partnership entitled to describe itself as a firm of registered trade mark agents, or

(c) a body corporate entitled to describe itself as a registered trade mark agent.

Power to registrar to refuse to deal with certain agents

88.—(1) The Secretary of State may make rules authorising the registrar to refuse to recognise as agent in respect of any business under this Act—

(a) a person who has been convicted of an offence under section 84 (unregistered persons describing themselves as registered trade mark agents);

(b) an individual whose name has been erased from and not restored to, or who is suspended from, the register of trade mark agents on the ground of misconduct;

(c) a person who is found by the Secretary of State to have been guilty of such conduct as would, in the case of an individual registered in the register of trade mark agents, render him liable to have his name erased from the register on the ground of misconduct;

(d) a partnership or body corporate of which one of the partners or directors is a person whom the registrar could refuse to recognise under paragraph (a), (b) or (c) above.

(2) The rules may contain such incidental and supplementary provisions as appear to the Secretary of State to be appropriate and may, in particular, prescribe circumstances in which a person is or is not to be taken to have been guilty of misconduct.

Importation of infringing goods, material or articles

Infringing goods, material or articles may be treated as prohibited goods

89.—(1) The proprietor of a registered trade mark, or a licensee, may give notice in writing to the Commissioners of Customs and Excise—

(a) that he is the proprietor or, as the case may be, a licensee of the registered trade mark,

(b) that, at a time and place specified in the notice, goods which are, in relation to that registered trade mark, infringing goods, material or articles are expected to arrive in the United Kingdom—

    (i) from outside the European Economic Area, or
    (ii) from within that Area but not having been entered for free circulation, and

(c) that he requests the Commissioners to treat them as prohibited goods.

(2) When a notice is in force under this section the importation of the goods to which the notice relates, otherwise than by a person for his private and domestic use, is prohibited; but a person is not by reason of the prohibition liable to any penalty other than forfeiture of the goods.

(3) This section does not apply to goods entered, or expected to be entered, for free circulation, export, re-export or for a suspensive procedure in respect of which an application may be made under Article 3(1) of Council Regulation (EEC) No. 3842/86 laying down measures to prohibit the release for free circulation of counterfeit goods.

Power of Commissioners of Customs and Excise to make regulations

90.—(1) The Commissioners of Customs and Excise may make regulations prescribing the form in which notice is to be given under section 89 and requiring a person giving notice —

(a) to furnish the Commissioners with such evidence as may be specified in the regulations, either on giving notice or when the goods are imported, or at both those times, and

(b) to comply with such other conditions as may be specified in the regulations.

(2) The regulations may, in particular, require a person giving such a notice—

(a) to pay such fees in respect of the notice as may be specified by the regulations;

(b) to give such security as may be so specified in respect of any liability or expense which the Commissioners may incur in consequence of the notice by reason of the detention of any goods or anything done to goods detained;

(c) to indemnify the Commissioners against any such liability or expense, whether security has been given or not.

(3) The regulations may make different provision as respects different classes of case to which they apply and may include such incidental and supplementary provisions as the Commissioners consider expedient.

(4) Regulations under this section shall be made by statutory instrument which shall be subject to annulment in pursuance of a resolution of either House of Parliament.

(5) Section 17 of the Customs and Excise Management Act 1979 (general provisions as to Commissioners' receipts) applies to fees paid in pursuance of regulations under this section as to receipts under the enactments relating to customs and excise.

Power of Commissioners of Customs and Excise to disclose information

91. Where information relating to infringing goods, material or articles has been obtained by the Commissioners of Customs and Excise for the purposes of, or in connection with, the exercise of their functions in relation to imported goods, the Commissioners may authorise the disclosure of that information for the purpose of facilitating the exercise by any person of any function in connection with the investigation or prosecution of an offence under section 92 below (unauthorised use of trade mark, &c. in relation to goods) or under the Trade Descriptions Act 1968.

Offences

Unauthorised use of trade mark, &c. in relation to goods

92.—(1) A person commits an offence who with a view to gain for himself or another, or with intent to cause loss to another, and without the consent of the proprietor —

    (a) applies to goods or their packaging a sign identical to, or likely to be mistaken for, a registered trade mark, or

    (b) sells or lets for hire, offers or exposes for sale or hire or distributes goods which bear, or the packaging of which bears, such a sign, or

    (c) has in his possession, custody or control in the course of a business any such goods with a view to the doing of anything, by himself or another, which would be an offence under paragraph (b).

(2) A person commits an offence who with a view to gain for himself or another, or with intent to cause loss to another, and without the consent of the proprietor —

    (a) applies a sign identical to, or likely to be mistaken for, a registered trade mark to material intended to be used—

        (i) for labelling or packaging goods,
        (ii) as a business paper in relation to goods, or
        (iii) for advertising goods, or

    (b) uses in the course of a business material bearing such a sign for labelling or packaging goods, as a business paper in relation to goods, or for advertising goods, or

    (c) has in his possession, custody or control in the course of a business any such material with a view to the doing to anything, by himself or another, which would be an offence under paragraph (b).

(3) A person commits an offence who with a view to gain for himself or another, or with intent to cause loss to another, and without the consent of the proprietor—

    (a) makes an article specifically designed or adapted for making copies of a sign identical to, or likely to be mistaken for, a registered trade mark, or

    (b) has such an article in his possession, custody or control in the course of a business,

knowing or having reason to believe that is has been, or is to be, used to produce goods, or material for labelling or packaging goods, as a business paper in relation to goods, or for advertising goods.

(4) A person does not commit an offence under this section unless —

    (a) the goods are goods in respect of which the trade mark is registered, or

    (b) the trade mark has a reputation in the United Kingdom and the use of the sign takes or would take unfair advantage of, or is or would be detrimental to, the distinctive character or the repute of the trade mark.

(5) It is a defence for a person charged with an offence under this section to show that he believed on reasonable grounds that the use of the sign in the manner in which it was used, or was to be used, was not an infringement of the registered trade mark.

(6) A person guilty of an offence under this section is liable —

    (a) on summary conviction to imprisonment for a term not exceeding six months or a fine not exceeding the statutory maximum, or both;

    (b) on conviction on indictment to a fine or imprisonment for a term not exceeding ten years, or both.

Enforcement function of local weights and measures authority

93.—(1) It is the duty of every local weights and measures authority to enforce within their area the provisions of section 92 (unauthorised use of trade mark, &c. in relation to goods).

(2) The following provisions of the Trade Descriptions Act 1968 apply in relation to the enforcement of that section as in relation to the enforcement of that Act —

section 27 (power to make test purchases)
section 28 (power to enter premises and inspect and seize goods and documents),
section 29 (obstruction of authorised officers), and
section 33 (compensation for loss, &c. of goods seized).

(3) Subsection (1) above does not apply in relation to the enforcement of section 92 in Northern Ireland, but it is the duty of the Department of Economic Development to enforce that section in Northern Ireland.

For that purpose the provisions of the Trade Descriptions Act 1968 specified in subsection (2) apply as if for the references to a local weights and measures authority and any officer of such an authority there were substituted references to that Department and any of its officers.

(4) Any enactment which authorises the disclosure of information for the purpose of facilitating the enforcement of the Trade Descriptions Act 1968 shall apply as if section 92 above were contained in that Act and as if the functions of any person in relation to the enforcement of that section were functions under that Act.

(5) Nothing in this section shall be construed as authorising a local weights and measures authority to bring proceedings in Scotland for an offence.

Falsification of register, &c.

94.—(1) It is an offence for a person to make, or cause to be made, a false entry in the register of trade marks, knowing or having reason to believe that it is false.

(2) It is an offence for a person—

(a) to make or cause to be made anything falsely purporting to be a copy of an entry in the register, or

(b) to produce or tender or cause to be produced or tendered in evidence any such thing,

knowing or having reason to believe that it is false.

(3) A person guilty of an offence under this section is liable—

(a) on conviction on indictment, to imprisonment for a term not exceeding two years or a fine, or both;

(b) on summary conviction, to imprisonment for a term not exceeding six months or a fine not exceeding the statutory maximum, or both.

Falsely representing trade mark as registered

95.—(1) It is an offence for a person—

(a) falsely to represent that a mark is a registered trade mark, or

(b) to make a false representation as to the goods or services for which a trade mark is registered

knowing or having reason to believe that the representation is false.

(2) For the purposes of this section, the use in the United Kingdom in relation to a trade mark—

(a) of the word "registered", or

(b) of any other word or symbol importing a reference (express or implied) to registration,

shall be deemed to be a representation as to registration under this Act unless it is shown that the reference is to registration elsewhere than in the United Kingdom and that the trade mark is in fact so registered for the goods or services in question.

(3) A person guilty of an offence under this section is liable on summary conviction to a fine not exceeding level 3 on the standard scale.

Supplementary provisions as to summary proceedings in Scotland

96.—(1) Notwithstanding anything in section 331 of the Criminal Procedure (Scotland) Act 1975, summary proceedings in Scotland for an offence under this Act may be begun at any time within six months after the date on which evidence sufficient in the Lord Advocate's opinion to justify the proceedings came to his knowledge.

For this purpose a certificate of the Lord Advocate as to the date on which such evidence came to his knowledge is conclusive evidence.

(2) For the purposes of subsection (1) and of any other provision of this Act as to the time within which summary proceedings for an offence may be brought, proceedings in Scotland shall be deemed to be begun on the date on which a warrant to apprehend or to cite the accused is granted, if such warrant is executed without undue delay.

Forfeiture of counterfeit goods, &c.

Forfeiture: England and Wales or Northern Ireland

97.—(1) In England and Wales or Northern Ireland where there has come into the possession of any person in connection with the investigation or prosecution of a relevant offence —

(a) goods which, or the packaging of which, bears a sign identical to or likely to be mistaken for a registered trade mark,

(b) material bearing such a sign and intended to be used for labelling or packaging goods, as a business paper in relation to goods, or for advertising goods, or

(c) articles specifically designed or adapted for making copies of such a sign,

that person may apply under this section for an order for the forfeiture of the goods, material or articles.

(2) An application under this section may be made —

(a) where proceedings have been brought in any court for a relevant offence relating to some or all of the goods, material or articles, to that court;

(b) where no application for the forfeiture of the goods, material or articles has been made under paragraph (a), by way of complaint to a magistrates' court.

(3) On an application under this section the court shall make an order for the forfeiture of any goods, material or articles only if it is satisfied that a relevant offence has been committed in relation to the goods, material or articles.

(4) A court may infer for the purposes of this section that such an offence has been committed in relation to any goods, material or articles if it is satisfied that such an offence has been committed in relation to goods, material or articles which are representative of them (whether by reason of being of the same design or part of the same consignment or batch or otherwise).

(5) Any person aggrieved by an order made under this section by a magistrates' court, or by a decision of such a court not to make such an order, may appeal against that order or decision —

(a) in England and Wales, to the Crown Court;

(b) in Northern Ireland, to the county court;

and an order so made may contain such provisions as appears to the court to be appropriate for delaying the coming into force of the order pending the making and determination of any appeal (including any application under section 111 of the Magistrates' Courts Act 1980 or Article 146 of the Magistrates' Court (Northern Ireland) Order 1981 (statement of case)).

(6) Subject to subsection (7), where any goods, material or articles are forfeited under this section they shall be destroyed in accordance with such directions as the court may give.

(7) On making an order under this section the court may, if it considers it appropriate to do so, direct that the goods, material or articles to which the order relates shall (instead of being destroyed) be released, to such person as the court may specify, on condition that that person—

(a) causes the offending sign to be erased, removed or obliterated, and

(b) complies with any order to pay costs which has been made against him in the proceedings for the order for forfeiture.

(8) For the purposes of this section a "relevant offence" means an offence under section 92 above (unauthorised use of trade mark, &c. in relation to goods) or under the Trade Descriptions Act 1968 or any offence involving dishonesty or deception.

Forfeiture: Scotland

98.—(1) In Scotland the court may make an order for the forfeiture of any —

(a) goods which bear, or the packaging of which bears, a sign identical to or likely to be mistaken for a registered trade mark,

(b) material bearing such a sign and intended to be used for labelling or packaging goods, as a business paper in relation to goods, or for advertising goods, or

(c) articles specifically designed or adapted for making copies of such a sign.

(2) An order under this section may be made —

(a) on an application by the procurator-fiscal made in the manner specified in section 310 of the Criminal Procedure (Scotland) Act 1975, or

(b) where a person is convicted of a relevant offence, in addition to any other penalty which the court may impose.

(3) On an application under subsection (2)(a), the court shall make an order for the forfeiture of any goods, material or articles only if it is satisfied that a relevant offence has been committed in relation to the goods, material or articles.

(4) The court may infer for the purposes of this section that such an offence has been committed in relation to any goods, material or articles if it is satisfied that such an offence has been committed in relation to goods, material or articles which are representative of them (whether by reason of being of the same design or part of the same consignment or batch or otherwise).

(5) The procurator-fiscal making the application under subsection (2)(a) shall serve on any person appearing to him to be the owner of, or otherwise to have an interest in, the goods, material or articles to which the application relates a copy of the application, together with a notice giving him the opportunity to appear at the hearing of the application to show cause why the goods, material or articles should not be forfeited.

(6) Service under subsection (5) shall be carried out, and such service may be proved, in the manner specified for citation of an accused in summary proceedings under the Criminal Procedure (Scotland) Act 1975.

(7) Any person upon whom notice is served under subsection (5) and any other person claiming to be the owner of, or otherwise to have an interest in, goods, material or articles to which an application under this section relates shall be entitled to appear at the hearing of the application to show cause why the goods, material or articles should not be forfeited.

(8) The court shall not make an order following an application under subsection (2)(a) —

(a) if any person on whom the notice is served under subsection (5) does not appear, unless service of the notice on that person is proved; or

(b) if no notice under subsection (5) has been served, unless the court is satisfied that in the circumstances it was reasonable not to serve such notice.

(9) Where an order for the forfeiture of any goods, material or articles is made following an application under subsection (2)(a), any person who appeared, or was entitled to appear, to show cause why goods, material or articles should not be forfeited may, within 21 days of the making of the order, appeal to the High Court by Bill of Suspension; and section 452(4)(a) to (e) of the Criminal Procedure (Scotland) Act 1975 shall apply to an appeal under this subsection as it applies to a stated case under Part II of that Act.

(10) An order following an application under subsection (2)(a) shall not take effect—

(a) until the end of the period of 21 days beginning with the day after the day on which the order is made; or

(b) if an appeal is made under subsection (9) above within that period, until the appeal is determined or abandoned.

(11) An order under subsection (2)(b) shall not take effect—

(a) until the end of the period within which an appeal against the order could be brought under the Criminal Procedure (Scotland) Act 1975; or

(b) if an appeal is made within that period, until the appeal is determined or abandoned.

(12) Subject to subsection (13), goods, material or articles forfeited under this section shall be destroyed in accordance with such directions as the court may give.

(13) On making an order under this section the court may if it considers it appropriate to do so, direct that the goods, material or articles to which the order relates shall (instead of being destroyed) be released, to such person as the court may specify, on condition that that person causes the offending sign to be erased, removed or obliterated.

(14) For the purposes of this section —

"relevant offence" means an offence under section 92 (unauthorised use of trade mark, &c. in relation to goods) or under the Trade Descriptions Act 1968 or any offence involving dishonesty or deception,

"the court" means—

(a) in relation to an order made on an application under subsection (2)(a), the sheriff, and

(b) in relation to an order made under subsection (2)(b), the court which imposed the penalty.

PART IV

MISCELLANEOUS AND GENERAL PROVISIONS

Miscellaneous

Unauthorised use of Royal arms, &c.

99.—(1) A person shall not without the authority of Her Majesty use in connection with any business the Royal arms (or arms so closely resembling the Royal arms as to be calculated to deceive) in such manner as to be calculated to lead to the belief that he is duly authorised to use the Royal arms.

(2) A person shall not without the authority of Her Majesty or of a member of the Royal family use in connection with any business any device, emblem or title in such a manner as to be calculated to lead to the belief that he is employed by, or supplies goods or services to, Her Majesty or that member of the Royal family.

(3) A person who contravenes subsection (1) commits an offence and is liable on summary conviction to a fine not exceeding level 2 on the standard scale.

(4) Contravention of subsection (1) or (2) may be restrained by injunction in proceedings brought by—

(a) any person who is authorised to use the arms, device or emblem or title in question, or

(b) any person authorised by the Lord Chamberlain to take such proceedings.

(5) Nothing in this section affects any right of the proprietor of a trade mark containing any such arms, device, emblem or title to use that trade mark.

Burden of proving use of trade mark

100. If in any civil proceedings under this Act a question arises as to the use to which a registered trade mark has been put, it is for the proprietor to show what use has been made of it.

Offences committed by partnerships and bodies corporate

101.—(1) Proceedings for an offence under this Act alleged to have been committed by a partnership shall be brought against the partnership in the name of the firm and not in that of the partners; but without prejudice to any liability of the partners under subsection (4) below.

(2) The following provisions apply for the purposes of such proceedings as in relation to a body corporate—

(a) any rules of court relating to the service of documents;

(b) in England and Wales or Northern Ireland, Schedule 3 to the Magistrates' Courts Act 1980 or Schedule 4 to the Magistrates' Courts (Northern Ireland) Order 1981 (procedure on charge of offence).

(3) A fine imposed on a partnership on its conviction in such proceedings shall be paid out of the partnership assets.

(4) Where a partnership is guilty of an offence under this Act, every partner, other than a partner who is proved to have been ignorant of or to have attempted to prevent the commission of the offence, is also guilty of the offence and liable to be proceeded against and punished accordingly.

(5) Where an offence under this Act committed by a body corporate is proved to have been committed with the consent or connivance of a director, manager, secretary or other similar officer of the body, or a person purporting to act in any such capacity, he as well as the body corporate is guilty of the offence and liable to be proceeded against and punished accordingly.

Interpretation

Adaptation of expressions for Scotland

102. In the application of this Act to Scotland —

"account of profits" means accounting and payment of profits;
"accounts" means count, reckoning and payment;
"assignment" means assignation;
"costs" means expenses;
"declaration" means declarator;
"defendant" means defender;
"delivery up" means delivery;
"injunction" means interdict;
"interlocutory relief" means interim remedy; and
"plaintiff" means pursuer.

Minor definitions

103.—(1) In this Act —

"business" includes a trade or profession;
"director", in relation to a body corporate whose affairs are managed by its members, means any member of the body;
"infringement proceedings", in relation to a registered trade mark, includes proceedings under section 16 (order for delivery up of infringing goods, &c.);
"publish" means make available to the public, and references to publication —

(a) in relation to an application for registration, are to publication under section 38(1), and

(b) in relation to registration, are to publication under section 40(4);

"statutory provisions" includes provisions of subordinate legislation within the meaning of the Interpretation Act 1978;
"trade" includes any business or profession.

(2) References in this Act to use (or any particular description of use) of a trade mark, or of a sign identical with, similar to, or likely to be mistaken for a trade mark, include use (or that description of use) otherwise than by means of a graphic representation.

(3) References in this Act to a Community instrument include references to any instrument amending or replacing that instrument.

Index of defined expressions

104. In this Act the expressions listed below are defined by or otherwise fall to be construed in accordance with the provisions indicated —

account of profits and accounts (in Scotland)	section 102
appointed person (for purposes of section 76)	section 77
assignment (in Scotland)	section 102
business	section 103(1)
certification mark	section 50(1)
collective mark	section 49(1)
commencement (of this Act)	section 109(2)
Community trade mark	section 51
Community Trade Mark Regulation	section 51
Convention country	section 55(1)(b)
costs (in Scotland)	section 102
the court	section 75
date of application	section 33(2)
date of filing	section 33(1)
date of registration	section 40(3)
defendant (in Scotland)	section 102
delivery up (in Scotland)	section 102
director	section 103(1)
earlier right	section 5(4)
earlier trade mark	section 6
exclusive licence and licensee	section 29(1)
infringement (of registered trade mark)	sections 9(1) and (2) and 10
infringement proceedings	section 103(1)
infringing articles	section 17
infringing goods	section 17
infringing material	section 17
injunction (in Scotland)	section 102
interlocutory relief (in Scotland)	section 102
the International Bureau	section 53
international trade mark (UK)	section 53
Madrid Protocol	section 53
Paris Convention	section 55(1)(a)
plaintiff (in Scotland)	section 102
prescribed	section 78(1)(b)
protected under the Paris Convention	section 56(1)
— well-known trade marks	
— state emblems and official signs or hallmarks	section 57(1)
— emblems, &c. of international organisations	section 58(2)
publish and references to publication	section 103(1)
register, registered (and related expressions)	section 63(1)
registered trade mark agent	section 83(1)
registerable transaction	section 25(2)
the registrar	section 62
rules	section 78
statutory provisions	section 103(1)
trade	section 103(1)
trade mark	
— generally	section 1(1)
— includes collective mark or certification mark	section 1(2)
United Kingdom (references include Isle of Man)	section 108(2)
use (of trade mark or sign)	section 103(2)
well-known trade mark (under Paris Convention)	section 56(1)

Other general provisions

Transitional provisions

105. The provisions of Schedule 3 have effect with respect to transitional matters, including the treatment of marks registered under the Trade Marks Act 1938, and applications for registration and other proceedings pending under that Act, on the commencement of this Act.

Consequential amendments and repeals

106.—(1) The enactments specified in Schedule 4 are amended in accordance with that Schedule, the amendments being consequential on the provisions of this Act.

(2) The enactments specified in Schedule 5 are repealed to the extent specified.

Territorial waters and the continental shelf

107.—(1) For the purposes of this Act the territorial waters of the United Kingdom shall be treated as part of the United Kingdom.

(2) This Act applies to things done in the United Kingdom sector of the continental shelf on a structure or vessel which is present there for purposes directly connected with the exploration of the sea bed or subsoil or the exploitation of their natural resources as it applies to things done in the United Kingdom.

(3) The United Kingdom sector of the continental shelf means the areas designated by order under section 1(7) of the Continental Shelf Act 1964.

Extent

108.—(1) This Act extends to England and Wales, Scotland and Northern Ireland.

(2) This Act also extends to the Isle of Man, subject to such exceptions and modifications as Her Majesty may specify by Order in Council; and subject to any such Order references in this Act to the United Kingdom shall be construed as including the Isle of Man.

Commencement

109.—(1) The provisions of this Act come into force on such day as the Secretary of State may appoint by order made by statutory instrument.

Different days may be appointed for different provisions and different purposes.

(2) The references to the commencement of this Act in Schedules 3 and 4 (transitional provisions and consequential amendments) are to the commencement of the main substantive provisions of Parts I and III of this Act and the consequential repeal of the Trade Marks Act 1938.

Provision may be made by order under this section identifying the date of that commencement.

Short title

110. This Act may be cited as the Trade Marks Act 1994.

APPENDIX B

Trade Mark Directive

First Council Directive 89/104/EEC of December 21, 1988 to approximate the laws of the Member States relating to trade marks

O.J. No. L040

B–01   FIRST COUNCIL DIRECTIVE of December 21, 1988 to approximate the laws of the Member States relating to trade marks (89/104/EEC).

THE COUNCIL OF THE EUROPEAN COMMUNITIES,

Having regard to the Treaty establishing the European Economic Community, and in particular Article 100a thereof,

Having regard to the proposal from the Commission (1),

in co-operation with the European Parliament (2),

Having regard to the opinion of the Economic and Social Committee (3),

Whereas the trade mark laws at present applicable in the Member States contain disparities which may impede the free movement of goods and freedom to provide services and may distort competition within the common market; whereas it is therefore necessary, in view of the establishment and functioning of the internal market, to approximate the laws of Member States.

Whereas it is important not to disregard the solutions and advantages which the Community trade mark system may afford to undertakings wishing to acquire trade marks.

Whereas it does not appear to be necessary at present to undertake full-scale approximation of the trade mark laws of the Member States and it will be sufficient if approximation is limited to those national provisions of law which most directly affect the functioning of the internal market.

Whereas the Directive does not deprive the Member States of the right to continue to protect trade marks acquired through use but takes them into account only in regard to the relationship between them and trade marks acquired by registration.

Whereas Member States also remain free to fix the provisions of procedure concerning the registration, the revocation and the invalidity of trade marks acquired by registration; whereas they can, for example, determine the form of trade mark registration and invalidity procedures, decide whether earlier rights should be invoked either in the registration procedure or in the invalidity procedure or in both and, if they allow earlier rights to be invoked in the registration procedure, have an opposition procedure or an *ex officio* examination procedure or both; whereas Member States remain free to determine the effects of revocation or invalidity of trade marks.

Whereas this Directive does not exclude the application to trade marks of provisions of law of the Member States other than trade mark law, such as the provisions relating to unfair competition, civil liability or consumer protection.

Whereas attainment of the objectives at which this approximation of laws is aiming requires that the conditions for obtaining and continuing to hold a registered trade mark are, in general, identical in all Member States; whereas, to this end, it is necessary to list examples of signs which may constitute a trade mark, provided that such signs are capable of distinguishing the goods or services of one undertaking from those of other undertakings;

whereas the grounds for refusal or invalidity concerning the trade mark itself, for example, the absence of any distinctive character, or concerning conflicts between the trade mark and earlier rights, are to be listed in an exhaustive manner, even if some of these grounds are listed as an option for the Member States which will therefore be able to maintain or introduce those grounds in their legislation; whereas Member States will be able to maintain or introduce into their legislation grounds of refusal or invalidity linked to conditions for obtaining and continuing to hold a trade mark for which there is no provision of approximation, concerning, for example, the eligibility for the grant of a trade mark, the renewal of the trade mark or rules or fees, or related to the non-compliance with procedural rules.

Whereas in order to reduce the total number of trade marks registered and protected in the Community and, consequently, the number of conflicts which arise between them, it is essential to require that registered trade marks must actually be used or, if not used, be subject to revocation; whereas it is necessary to provide that a trade mark cannot be invalidated on the basis of the existence of a non-used earlier trade mark, while the Member States remain free to apply the same principle in respect of the registration of a trade mark or to provide that a trade mark may not be successfully invoked in infringement proceedings if it is established as a result of a plea that the trade mark could be revoked; whereas in all these cases it is up to the Member States to establish the applicable rules of procedure.

Whereas it is fundamental, in order to facilitate the free circulation of goods and services, to ensure that henceforth registered trade marks enjoy the same protection under the legal systems of all the Member States; whereas this should however not prevent the Member States from granting at their option extensive protection to those trade marks which have a reputation.

Whereas the protection afforded by the registered trade mark, the function of which is in particular to guarantee the trade mark as an indication of origin, is absolute in the case of identity between the mark and the sign and goods or services; whereas the protection applies also in case of similarity between the mark and the sign and the goods or services; whereas it is indispensable to give an interpretation of the concept of similarity in relation to the likelihood of confusion; whereas the likelihood of confusion, the appreciation of which depends on numerous elements and, in particular, on the recognition of the trade mark on the market, of the association which can be made with the used or registered sign, of the degree of similarity between the trade mark and the sign and between the goods or services identified, constitutes the specific condition for such protection; whereas the ways in which likelihood of confusion may be established, and in particular the onus of proof, are a matter for national procedural rules which are not prejudiced by the Directive.

Whereas it is important, for reasons of legal certainty and without inequitably prejudicing the interests of a proprietor of an earlier trade mark, to provide that the latter may no longer request a declaration of invalidity nor may he oppose the use of a trade mark subsequent to his own of which he has knowingly tolerated the use for a substantial length of time, unless the application for the subsequent trade mark was made in bad faith.

Whereas all Member States of the Community are bound by the Paris Convention for the Protection of Industrial Property; whereas it is necessary that the provisions of this Directive are entirely consistent with those of the Paris Convention; whereas the obligations of the Member States resulting from this Convention are not affected by this Directive; whereas, where appropriate, the second subparagraph of Article 234 of the Treaty is applicable.

HAS ADOPTED THIS DIRECTIVE:

Article 1

Scope

This Directive shall apply to every trade mark in respect of goods or services which is the subject of registration or of an application in a Member State for registration as an individual trade mark, a collective mark or a guarantee or certification mark, or which is the subject of a registration or an application for registration in the Benelux Trade Mark Office or of an international registration having effect in a Member State.

Article 2

Signs of which a trade mark may consist

A trade mark may consist of any sign capable of being represented graphically, particularly words, including personal names, designs, letters, numerals, the shape of goods or of their packaging, provided that such signs are capable of distinguishing the goods or services of one undertaking from those of other undertakings.

Article 3

Grounds for refusal or invalidity

1. The following shall not be registered or if registered shall be liable to be declared invalid—

(a) signs which cannot constitute a trade mark;

(b) trade marks which are devoid of any distinctive character;

(c) trade marks which consist exclusively of signs or indications which may serve, in trade, to designate the kind, quality, quantity, intended purpose, value, geographical origin, or the time of production of the goods or of rendering of the service, or other characteristics of the goods or service;

(d) trade marks which consist exclusively of signs or indications which have become customary in the current language or in the bona fide and established practices of the trade;

(e) signs which consist exclusively of—

(i) the shape which results from the nature of the goods themselves, or
(ii) the shape of goods which is necessary to obtain a technical result, or
(iii) the shape which gives substantial value to the goods;

(f) trade marks which are contrary to public policy or to accepted principles of morality;

(g) trade marks which are of such a nature as to deceive the public, for instance as to the nature, quality, or geographical origin of the goods or service;

(h) trade marks which have not been authorised by the competent authorities and are to be refused or invalidated pursuant to Article 6*ter* of the Paris Convention for the Protection of Industrial Property, hereinafter referred to as the "Paris Convention".

2. Any Member State may provide that a trade mark shall not be registered or, if registered, shall be liable to be declared invalid where and to the extent that—

(a) the use of that trade mark may be prohibited pursuant to provisions of law other than trade mark law of the Member State concerned or of the Community;

(b) the trade mark covers a sign of high symbolic value, in particular a religious symbol;

(c) the trade mark includes badges, emblems and escutcheons other than those covered by Article 6*ter* of the Paris Convention and which are of public interest, unless the consent of the appropriate authorities to its registration has been given in conformity with the legislation of the Member State;

(d) the application for registration of the trade mark was made in bad faith by the applicant.

3. A trade mark shall not be refused registration or be declared invalid in accordance with paragraph 1(b), (c) or (d) if, before the date of application for registration and following the use which has been made of it, it has acquired a distinctive character. Any Member State may in addition provide that this provision shall also apply where the distinctive character was acquired after the date of application for registration or after the date of registration.

4. Any Member State may provide that, by derogation from the preceding paragraphs, the grounds of refusal of registration or invalidity in force in that State prior to the date on which the provisions necessary to comply with this Directive enter into force, shall apply to trade marks for which application has been made prior to that date.

Article 4

Further grounds for refusal or invalidity concerning conflicts with earlier rights

1. A trade mark shall not be registered or, if registered, shall he liable to be declared invalid:

(a) if it is identical with an earlier trade mark, and the goods or services for which the trade mark is applied for or is registered are identical with the goods or services for which the earlier trade mark is protected;

(b) if because of its identity with, or similarity to, the earlier trade mark and the identity or similarity of the goods or services covered by the trade marks, there exists a likelihood of confusion on the part of the public, which includes the likelihood of association with the earlier trade mark.

2. "Earlier trade marks" within the meaning of paragraph 1 means:

(a) trade marks of the following kinds with a date of application for registration which is earlier than the date of application for registration of the trade mark, taking account, where appropriate, of the priorities claimed in respect of those trade marks —

  (i) Community trade marks;
  (ii) trade marks registered in the Member State or, in the case of Belgium, Luxembourg or the Netherlands, at the Benelux Trade Mark Office;
  (iii) trade marks registered under international arrangements which have effect in the Member State;

(b) Community trade marks which validly claim seniority, in accordance with the Regulation on the Community trade mark, from a trade mark referred to in (a)(ii) and (iii), even when the latter trade mark has been surrendered or allowed to lapse;

(c) applications for the trade marks referred to in (a) and (b), subject to their registration;

(d) trade marks which, on the date of application for registration of the trade mark, or, where appropriate, of the priority claimed in respect of the application for registration of the trade mark, are well known in a Member State, in the sense in which the words "well known" are used in Article 6*bis* of the Paris Convention;

3. A trade mark shall furthermore not be registered, or if registered, shall be liable to be declared invalid if it is identical with, or similar to, an earlier Community trade mark within the meaning of paragraph 2 and is to be, or has been, registered for goods or services which are not similar to those for which the earlier Community trade mark is registered, where the earlier Community trade mark has a reputation in the Community and where the use of the later trade mark without due cause would take unfair advantage of, or be detrimental to, the distinctive character or the repute of the earlier Community trade mark.

4. Any Member State may furthermore provide that a trade mark shall not be registered or, if registered, shall be liable to be declared invalid where, and to the extent that—

(a) the trade mark is identical with, or similar to, an earlier national trade mark within the meaning of paragraph 2 and is to be, or has been, registered for goods or services which are not similar to those for which the earlier trade mark is registered, where the earlier trade mark has a reputation in the Member State concerned and where the use of the later trade mark without due cause would take unfair advantage of, or be detrimental to, the distinctive character or the repute of the earlier trade mark;

(b) rights to a non-registered trade mark or to another sign used in the course of trade were acquired prior to the date of application for registration of the subsequent trade mark, or the date of the priority claimed for the application for registration of the subsequent trade mark and that non-registered trade mark or other sign confers on its proprietor the right to prohibit the use of a subsequent trade mark;

(c) the use of the trade mark may be prohibited by virtue of an earlier right other than the rights referred to in paragraphs 2 and 4(b) and in particular —

    (i) a right to a name;
    (ii) a right of personal portrayal;
    (iii) a copyright;
    (iv) an industrial property right;

(d) the trade mark is identical with, or similar to, an earlier collective trade mark conferring a right which expired within a period of a maximum of three years preceding application;

(e) the trade mark is identical with, or similar to, an earlier guarantee or certification mark conferring a right which expired within a period preceding application the length of which is fixed by the Member State;

(f) the trade mark is identical with, or similar to, an earlier trade mark which was registered for identical or similar goods or services and conferred on them a right which has expired for failure to renew within a period of a maximum of two years preceding application, unless the proprietor of the earlier trade mark gave his agreement for the registration of the later mark or did not use his trade mark;

(g) the trade mark is liable to be confused with a mark which was in use abroad on the filing date of the application and which is still in use there, provided that at the date of the application the applicant was acting in bad faith.

5. The Member States may permit that in appropriate circumstances registration need not be refused or the trade mark need not be declared invalid where the proprietor of the earlier trade mark or other earlier right consents to the registration of the later trade mark.

6. Any Member State may provide that, by derogation from paragraphs 1 to 5, the grounds for refusal of registration or invalidity in force in that State prior to the date on which the provisions necessary to comply with this Directive enter into force, shall apply to trade marks for which application has been made prior to that date.

Article 5

Rights conferred by a trade mark

1. The registered trade mark shall confer on the proprietor exclusive rights therein. The proprietor shall be entitled to prevent all third parties not having his consent from using in the course of trade—

(a) any sign which is identical with the trade mark in relation to goods or services which are identical with those for which the trade mark is registered;

(b) any sign where, because of its identity with, or similarity to, the trade mark and the identity or similarity of the goods or services covered by the trade mark and the sign, there exists a likelihood of confusion on the part of the public, which includes the likelihood of association between the sign and the trade mark.

2. Any Member State may also provide that the proprietor shall be entitled to prevent all third parties not having his consent from using in the course of trade any sign which is identical with, or similar to, the trade mark in relation to goods or services which are not similar to those for which the trade mark is registered, where the latter has a reputation in the Member State and where use of that sign without due cause takes unfair advantage of, or is detrimental to, the distinctive character or the repute of the trade mark.

3. The following, inter alia, may be prohibited under paragraphs 1 and 2 —

(a) affixing the sign to the goods or to the packaging thereof;

(b) offering the goods, or putting them on the market or stocking them for these purposes under that sign, or offering or supplying services thereunder;

(c) importing or exporting the goods under the sign;

(d) using the sign on business papers and in advertising.

4. Where, under the law of the Member State, the use of a sign under the conditions referred to in 1(b) or 2 could not be prohibited before the date on which the provisions necessary to comply with this Directive entered into force in the Member State concerned, the rights conferred by the trade mark may not be relied on to prevent the continued use of the sign.

5. Paragraphs 1 to 4 shall not affect provisions in any Member State relating to the protection against the use of a sign other than for the purposes of distinguishing goods or services, where use of that sign without due cause takes unfair advantage of, or is detrimental to, the distinctive character or the repute of the trade mark.

Article 6

Limitation of the effects of a trade mark

1. The trade mark shall not entitle the proprietor to prohibit a third party from using, in the course of trade—

(a) his own name or address;

(b) indications concerning the kind, quality, quantity, intended purpose, value, geographical origin, the time of production of goods or of rendering of the service, or other characteristics of goods or services;

(c) the trade mark where it is necessary to indicate the intended purpose of a product or service, in particular as accessories or spare parts, provided he uses them in accordance with honest practices in industrial or commercial matters.

2. The trade mark shall not entitle the proprietor to prohibit a third party from using, in the course of trade, an earlier right which only applies in a particular locality if that right is recognised by the laws of the Member State in question and within the limits of the territory in which it is recognised.

Article 7

Exhaustion of the rights conferred by a trade mark

1. The trade mark shall not entitle the proprietor to prohibit its use in relation to goods which have been put on the market in the Community under that trade mark by the proprietor or with his consent.

2. Paragraph 1 shall not apply where there exist legitimate reasons for the proprietor to oppose further commercialisation of the goods, especially where the condition of the goods is changed or impaired after they have been put on the market.

Article 8

Licensing

1. A trade mark may be licensed for some or all of the goods or services for which it is registered and for the whole or part of the Member State concerned. A licence may be exclusive or non-exclusive.

2. The proprietor of a trade mark may invoke the rights conferred by that trade mark against a licensee who contravenes any provision in his licensing contract with regard to its duration, the form covered by the registration in which the trade mark may be used, the scope of the goods or services for which the licence is granted, the territory in which the trade mark may be affixed, or the quality of the goods manufactured or of the services provided by the licensee.

Article 9

Limitation in consequence of acquiescence

1. Where, in a Member State, the proprietor of an earlier trade mark as referred to in Article 4(2) has acquiesced, for a period of five successive years, in the use of a later trade mark registered in that Member State while being aware of such use, he shall no longer be entitled on the basis of the earlier trade mark either to apply for a declaration that the later trade mark is invalid or to oppose the use of the later trade mark in respect of the goods or services for which the later trade mark has been used, unless registration of the later trade mark was applied for in bad faith.

2. Any Member State may provide that paragraph 1 shall apply *mutatis mutandis* to the proprietor of an earlier trade mark referred to in Article 4(4)(a) or another earlier right referred to in Article 4(4)(b) or (c).

3. In the cases referred to in paragraphs 1 and 2, the proprietor of a later registered trade mark shall not be entitled to oppose the use of the earlier right, even though that right may no longer be invoked against the later trade mark.

Article 10

Use of trade marks

1. If, within a period of five years following the date of the completion of the registration procedure, the proprietor has not put the trade mark to genuine use in the Member State in connection with the goods or services in respect of which it is registered, or if such use has been suspended during an uninterrupted period of five years, the trade mark shall be subject to the sanctions provided for in this Directive, unless there are proper reasons for non-use.

2. The following shall also constitute use within the meaning of paragraph 1 —

   (a) use of the trade mark in a form differing in elements which do not alter the distinctive character of the mark in the form in which it was registered;

   (b) affixing of the trade mark to goods or to the packaging thereof in the Member State concerned solely for export purposes.

3. Use of the trade mark with the consent of the proprietor or by any person who has authority to use a collective mark or a guarantee or certification mark shall be deemed to constitute use by the proprietor.

4. In relation to trade marks registered before the date on which the provisions necessary to comply with this Directive enter into force in the Member State concerned—

   (a) where a provision in force prior to that date attaches sanctions to non-use of a trade mark during an uninterrupted period, the relevant period of five years mentioned in paragraph 1 shall be deemed to have begun to run at the same time as any period of non-use which is already running at that date;

   (b) where there is no use provision in force prior to that date, the periods of five years mentioned in paragraph 1 shall be deemed to run from that date at the earliest.

Article 11

Sanctions for non-use of a trade mark in legal or administrative proceedings

1. A trade mark may not be declared invalid on the ground that there is an earlier conflicting trade mark if the latter does not fulfil the requirements of use set out in Article 10(1), (2) and (3) or in Article 10(4), as the case may be.

2. Any Member State may provide that registration of a trade mark may not be refused on the ground that there is an earlier conflicting trade mark if the latter does not fulfil the requirements of use set out in Article 10(1), (2) and (3), or in Article 10(4), as the case may be.

3. Without prejudice to the application of Article 12, where a counterclaim for revocation is made, any Member State may provide that a trade mark may not be successfully invoked in infringement proceedings if it is established as a result of a plea that the trade mark could be revoked pursuant to Article 12(1).

4. If the earlier trade mark has been used in relation to part only of the goods or services for which it is registered, it shall, for purposes of applying paragraphs 1, 2 and 3, be deemed to be registered in respect only of that part of the goods or services.

Article 12

Grounds for revocation

1. A trade mark shall be liable to revocation if, within a continuous period of five years, it has not been put to genuine use in the Member State in connection with the goods or services in respect of which it is registered, and there are no proper reasons for non-use; however, no person may claim that the proprietor's rights in a trade mark should be revoked where, during the interval between expiry of the five-year period and filing of the application for revocation, genuine use of the trade mark has been started or resumed; the commencement or resumption of use within a period of three months preceding the filing of the application for revocation which began at the earliest on expiry of the continuous period of five years of non-use, shall, however, be disregarded where preparations for the commencement or resumption occur only after the proprietor becomes aware that the application for revocation may be filed.

2. A trade mark shall also be liable to revocation if, after the date on which it was registered—

(a) in consequence of acts or inactivity of the proprietor, it has become the common name in the trade for a product or service in respect of which it is registered;

(b) in consequence of the use made of it by the proprietor of the trade mark or with his consent in respect of the goods or services for which it is registered, it is liable to mislead the public, particularly as to the nature, quality or geographical origin of those goods or services.

Article 13

Grounds for refusal or revocation or invalidity relating to only some of the goods or services

Where grounds for refusal of registration or for revocation or invalidity of a trade mark exist in respect of only some of the goods or services for which that trade mark has been applied for or registered, refusal of registration or revocation or invalidity shall cover those goods or services only.

Article 14

Establishment *a posteriori* of invalidity or revocation of a trade mark

Where the seniority of an earlier trade mark which has been surrendered or allowed to lapse, is claimed for a Community trade mark, the invalidity or revocation of the earlier trade mark may be established *a posteriori*.

Article 15

Special provisions in respect of collective marks, guarantee marks and certification marks

1. Without prejudice to Article 4, Member States whose laws authorise the registration of collective marks or of guarantee or certification marks may provide that such marks shall not

be registered, or shall be revoked or declared invalid, on grounds additional to those specified in Articles 3 and 12 where the function of those marks so requires.

2. By way of derogation from Article 3(1)(c), Member States may provide that signs or indications which may serve, in trade, to designate the geographical origin of the goods or services may constitute collective, guarantee or certification marks. Such a mark does not entitle the proprietor to prohibit a third party from using in the course of trade such signs or indications, provided he uses them in accordance with honest practices in industrial or commercial matters; in particular, such a mark may not be invoked against a third party who is entitled to use a geographical name.

Article 16

National provisions to be adopted pursuant to this directive

1. The Member States shall bring into force the laws, regulations and administrative provisions necessary to comply with this Directive not later than December 28, 1991. They shall immediately inform the Commission thereof.

2. Acting on a proposal from the Commission, the Council, acting by qualified majority, may defer the date referred to in paragraph 1 until December 31, 1992 at the latest.

3. Member States shall communicate to the Commission the text of the main provisions of national law which they adopt in the field governed by this Directive.

APPENDIX C

PHOTOGRAPHS

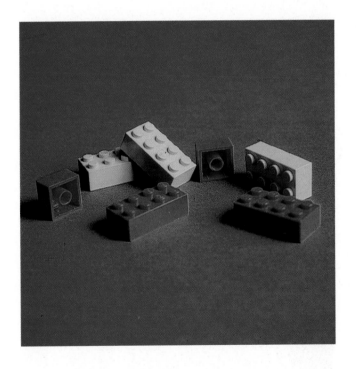

1. Examples of Lego Bricks.

2. The Rubik's Cube puzzle.

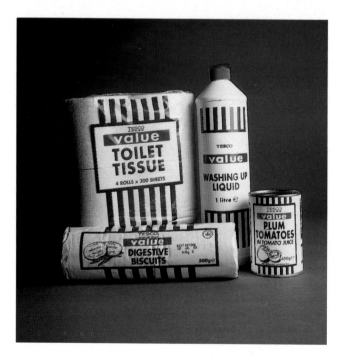

3. Examples of Tesco's Savers range of generic goods.

4. Own brand and branded soap.

5. Own brand and branded wine.

6. Own brand and branded schnapps.

7. Coca-Cola and Sainsbury's Classic Cola.

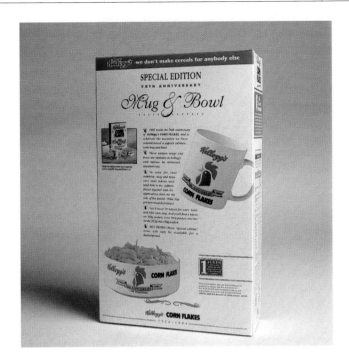

8. Kellogg's Corn Flakes. The warning notice is at the top.

9. Sainsbury's Full Roast and Nescafé coffee.

10. The Flash bottle as illustrated in Proctor & Gamble's trade mark application.

11. Own brand and branded cleaner.

12. JPS and Raffles cigarettes.

13. The Marmite case. At the time of the hearing the cap of Sainsbury's product was yellow.

14. Penguin and Puffin biscuits.

15. A range of colas.

16. Solo lemon drink and Pub Squash.

17. The advertisement for Diclomax Retard.

18. Gillette body spray and a lookalike.

19. Examples of other brands of body spray.

BIBLIOGRAPHY

"Designing for Product Success, essays and case studies from the TRIAD design project exhibition" Design Management Institute, Boston 1989.

"Building Brand Relationships" *Financial Times,* December 4, 1995.

"Unfair Trade Practices-Rubik's Cube under the Marketing Act" [1982] 8 E.I.P.R. D-164.

"Licensing and Merchandising," *Televisual,* June 1997.

"English Football Discovers It's All in the Brand Managing" *Intellectual Property,* October 1997.

"Lego: Building world sales from a single product line" *Marketing Week,* October 28, 1983.

"Brand-Stretching can be fun—and dangerous" *The Economist,* May 5, 1990.

Aaker, *Managing Brand Equity* (Macmillan Free Press, New York, 1991).

Aaker & Keller, "Consumer Evaluations of Brand Extensions" (1990) 54 *Journal of Marketing.*

Abraham & Lodish, "Getting the most of of advertising and promotion" *Harvard Business Review,* May-June 1990.

Abrams, "The Historic Foundation of American Copyright Law: Exploring the Myth of Common Law Copyright" (1983) 29 *Wayne Law Review* 1126.

Adams, "Unfair Competition: Why a Need is Unmet" [1992] 8 E.I.P.R. 259.

Adams, *Character Merchandising,* (Butterworths, London, 2nd ed., 1996).

Annand & Norman, *Blackstone's Guide to the Community Trade Mark* (Blackstone Press Limited, London 1998).

Annand & Norman, *Blackstone's Guide to the Trade Marks Act 1994* (Blackstone Press Limited, London 1994).

Aristotle, "The Nicomacean Ethics" 84-86 *Hippocrates G.Apostle tran.* (1975).

Arnold, *The Handbook Of Brand Management* (FT Pitman Publishing, London, 1993).

Ashley, Granger & Schmalensee, "Advertising and Aggregate Consumption: An Analysis of Causality" (1980) *Econometrica* 48.

Baker (Ed), "Advertising Works No. 7, IPA Advertising Effectiveness Awards 1992" (1993) *NTC Publications Limited* 53.

Bartlett, *Internet: The Legal Tangle Computer Law & Practice* Vol. 11 No. 4, 1995 p. 110.

Becker, "Deserving to Own Intellectual Property" [1993] 68 *Chicago-Kent Law Review* 609.

Becker, Property Rights: Philosophical Foundations.

Belson, "Brand Protection in the Age of the Internet" [1999] E.I.P.R. 481.

Benson, *The Rise of Consumer Society in Britain 1880–1980* (Longman, Harlow, 1994).

Bentley, "Novelty Value" *Marketing Week,* October 11, 1996.

Blaich, *Product Design and Corporate Strategy* (McGraw-Hill, USA, 1993, p.27).

Blakeney, *Trade Related Aspects of Intellectual Property* (Sweet & Maxwell, London, 1996).

Blakeney & McKeough, "Recent Developments in Passing Off" (1994) A.B.L.R. 17.

Boddewyn, "Cigarette Advertising Bans and Smoking: The Flawed Policy Connection" (1994) 13 *International Journal of Advertising* 311.

Boddewyn & Marton, Comparison Advertising and Consumers *Journal of Contemporary Business* 7.

Boddewyn & Morton, *Comparison Advertising—A Worldwide Study* (Hastings House, New York, 1979).

Booy, "A Halfway House for Unfair Competition in the U.K.—A Practitioner's Plea" [1991] 12 E.I.P.R. 439.

Brett, "Unfair Competition—Not Merely an Academic Issue?" [1979] E.I.P.R. 295.

Brewer, *Consumption and the World of Goods* (Routledge, London, 1993).

Brown, "Advertising and the Public Interest: Legal Protection of Trade Symbols" (1948) 57 Yale L.J. 1165.

Brown, "New? Improved?" *Business Week* October 21, 1985.

Buck, "The Continuing Grocery Revolution" *The Journal of Brand Mangement* 4 227.

Butterfield & Haigh, "Understanding the Financial Value of Brands" *IPA Report*, September 1998, p.15 .

Callman, *The Law of Unfair Competition and Trademarks* (Deerfield: Callaghan, 4th ed., 1996).

Callmann, "He Who Reaps Where He Has Not Sown: Unjust Enrichment in the Law of Unfair Competition" [1942] 55 H.L.R. 595.

Callmann, "Unfair Competition Without Competition? The importance of the property concept in the law of trade marks" [1947] 95 U.P.L.R. 443.

Cambell & Yaqub, *European Handbook on Advertising Law* (Cavendish Publishing, London, 1999).

Carty, "Dilution and Passing Off: Cause for Concern" [1996] 112 L.Q.R. 632.

Carty, "Passing Off at the Crossroads" [1996] 11 E.I.P.R. 629.

Chisnell, *Consumer Behaviour* (McGraw Hill, Maidenhead, 1995).

Coleman, "The unauthorised commercial exploitation of the names and likenesses of real persons" [1982] 7 E.I.P.R. 189.

Cornish, *Intellectual Property: Copyright,Trade Marks and Allied Rights* (Sweet & Maxwell, London, 3rd ed., 1986).

Cornish & Phillips, "The Economic Function of Trade Marks: An Analysis with special reference to Developing Countries" (1982) 13 I.I.C. 41.

Coulter, *Property in Ideas: The Patent Question in Mid-Victorian Britian* (The Thomas Jefferson University Press, Kirksville, 1991).

Cowley (ed.), *Understanding Brands* (Kogan Page, London, 1996).

Crown, *Advertising Law and Regulation* (Butterworths, London, 1998).

De Chernatoney, "Categorizing brands: evolutionary process underpinned by two key dimensions" (1993) 9 *Journal of Marketing Management* 173–88.

De Chernatoney, "The Big Brand Challenge" *Esomar seminar* Berlin October 9–11 1996 (Vol. 203).

De Chernatory, *Prospects for Grocery Brands in the Single European Market : A study prepared for the Coca-Cola Retailing Group Europe,* London.

De Chernatory & Dall'olmo Riley, "The Chasm between managers' and consumers' views of brands: the experts' perspectives" (1997) 5 *Journal of Strategic Marketing* 99.

Dinwoodie, "Reconceptualizing the Inherent Distinctiveness of Product Design Trade Dress" (1997) 75 *North Carolina Law Review* 471.

Dreyfuss, "Expressive Genericity: Trademarks as Language in the Pepsi Generation" (1990) 65:397 N.D.L.R.

Dworkin, " 'Knocking Copy' comparative advertising—A Survey of United Kingdom Practice" [1979] E.I.P.R. 41.

Dworkin, "Passing Off & Unfair Competition: An Opportunity Missed [1981] 44 M.L.R. 564.

Dworkin, "Unfair Competition: Is the Common Law Developing?" [1979] E.I.P.R. 41.

Emslie & Lewis, "Passing Off & Image Marketing in the U.K." [1992] E.I.P.R. 270.

Evans, "Passing-Off and the Problem of Product Simulation" Vol. 31 M.L.R. 642.

Fisher-Kellner, "Computer User Interfaces: Trade Dress Protection for 'Look and Feel' " 84 T.M.R. 337.

Fitzgerald, "Self Regulation of Comparative Advertising in the U.K." [1997] ENT.L.R. 250.

Franzen & Hoogerbruuge, The Functions of the Brand (unpublished 1995).

Fraser, The Coming of the Mass Market 1850–1914 (Macmillan, London, 1988).

Frazer, "Appropriation of Personality-A New Tort?" [1983] 99 L.Q.R. 281.

Gielen, "European Trade Mark Legislation: The Statements" [1996] 2 E.I.P.R. 83.

Glemet & Mira, "Solving the Brand Leader's Dilemma" (1993) 4 The McKinsey Quarterley.

Goodenough, "Retheorisng Privacy and Publicity" [1977] I.P.Q. 37.

Goodyear, A Handbook of Market Research Techniques (Kogan Page, London, 1990).

Gordon, "Assertive Modesty: An Economics of Intangibles" [1994] 94 Colum.L.Rev. 2579.

Gordon, Intellectual Property and the Restitutionary Impulse" [1992] 78 Virginia Law Review 149.

Gordon, "A Property Right in Self Expression Equality and Individualism in the Natural Law of Intellectual Property" (1993) 102 Yale L.J. 1533.

Gordon, "An Inquiry into the Merits of Copyright: The Challenges of Consistency, Consent, and Encouragement Theory" (1989) 41 Stanford Law Rev. 1343.

Gordon, "Intellectual Property and the Restitutionary Impulse" [1992] 78 Villanova Law Rev. 151.

Hall, "Brand Development: How design can add value" (1993) 1 The Journal of Brand Management 94.

Hankinson & Cowking, Branding in Action (McGraw-Hill, Maidenhead, 1993).

Harris, Property & Justice (Clarendon Press, Oxford, 1996).

Hartman, "Subliminal Confusion: The Misappropriation of Advertising Value" 78 T.M.R. 506.

Helbling, "Shapes as Trade Marks?—The Struggle to Register Three Dimensional Signs: A Comparative Study of UK and Swiss Law" [1997] I.P.Q. 413.

Henly, "Centre Survey 'Planning for Social Change 1997' " Financial Times, October 13, 1997.

Hettinger, "Justifying Intellectual Property" (1989) 18 Philosophy and Public Affairs 31 at 41.

Hobbs, "Passing Off and the Licensing of Merchandising Rights Part 2" [1980] E.I.P.R. 79.

Holyoak, "United Kingdom Character Rights and Merchandising Rights Today" [1993] J.B.L. 444.

Interbrand, *World's Greatest Brands* (Mercury Books, London, 1992).
Isaac, "Merchandising or Fundraising?: Trade Marks and the Diana, Princess of Wales Memorial Fund" [1998] E.I.P.R. 441.

Jacobs, "The Stephen Stewart Memorial Lecture: Industrial Property—Industry's Enemy?" [1997] 1 I.P.Q. 3.
James, "Only a Trademark Registration Brings Comfort and Joy in the UK" *Trademark World* January, 1998.
Jehoram, "Rubik's Cube-Copyright in Rubik's Cube Under Dutch Law" [1982] 4 E.I.P.R. 117.
Jeremiah, "Passing Off the 'Buzzy Bee': When Get-up Can Be Functional" (1994) E.I.P.R. 355.
Jeremiah, *Merchandising Intellectual Property Rights* (Wiley, 1997).
Jolleymore, "Expiration of the right of publicity when symbolic names and images pass into the public domain", 84 T.M.R. 125.
Jones, *What's in a Name?* (Gower Publishing Co., Aldershot, 1986).

Kamperman Sanders, "The Wagamama Decision: Back to the Dark Ages of Trade Mark Law" [1996] 1 E.I.P.R. 3.
Kamperman Sanders, "The Return to Wagamama" [1996] 10 E.I.P.R. 521.
Kamperman Sanders, "Some frequently Asked Questions About the Trade Marks Act 1994" [1995] E.I.P.R. 3.
Kamperman Sanders, *Unfair Competition Law: The Protection of Intellectual Property and Industrial Creativity* (Clarendon Press, Oxford, 1997).
Karjala, "Misappropriation as a Third Intellectual Property Paradigm" (1994) 94 Columbia Law Rev. 2594.
Kaufman, "The Impact of the Trade Related Aspects of Intellectual Property Rights Agreement on Trademark" (1997) T.M.W.
Keller, "Conceptualizing, Measuring, and Marketing Customer-Based Brand Equity" (1993) 57 *Journal of Marketing*.
Kerly, *The Law of Trade Marks* (Sweet & Maxwell, London, 12th ed., 1984).
Kitchin & Mellor, *The Trade Marks Act 1994* (Sweet & Maxwell, London, 1995).
Kotler, Armstrong, Saunders, *Principles of Marketing* (Prentice Hall European Edition, 1996).
Kyle, "The Impact of Advertising on Markets" (1982) 1 *Journal of Advertising* 345.

Laddie Prescott & Vitoria, *The Modern Law of Copyright & Designs* (Butterworths, London, 2nd ed., 1995).
Lahore, "Product simulation and copying the Get up of Goods" [1979] E.I.P.R. 146.
Lahore, "The Herschel Smith Lecture 1992: Intellectual Property Rights and Unfair Copying: Old Concepts, New Ideas" [1992] 12 E.I.P.R. 428.
Lahore, "The Pub Squash Case Legal Theft or Free Competition" [1981] E.I.P.R. 54.
Landes & Posner, "Trademark Law: An Economic Perspective" (1987) 30 *Journal of Law & Economics* 265.
Lane & Bridge, "The Protection of Formats under English Law" [1990] 3 Ent.L.R. 96 & [1990] 4 Ent.L.R. 131.
Levitt, "Marketing Myopia" *Harvard Business Review* July–August 1960, pp. 45–56.
Lewis, "Easy Money" *Design Week* Retail Supplement, May 1997.

Libling, "The Concept of Property: Property in Intangibles" (1978) 94 L.Q.R. 103.

Locke, *Political Writings* (Penguin, London, 1993).

Loken, Ross & Hinkle, "Consumer confusion of origin and brand similarity perceptions" 7 *Journal of Public Policy and Marketing*.

Macleod, *Inventing the Industrial Revolution* (Cambridge University Press, Cambridge, 1988).

Martino, *Dilution* (Clarendon Press, Oxford, 1996).

Martino & Miskin, "Format Rights: The Price is not Right" [1991] 2 Ent.L.R. 31.

Marwick, *British Society Since 1945* (Penguin, London, 1996).

McCarthy, *Trade Marks and Unfair Competition* (Clark Boardman Callaghan, 1996).

McCormick, "The Future of Comparative Advertising" [1998] E.I.P.R. 41.

McKendrick, *Birth of a Consumer Society* (Europa Publications, London, 1982).

McKitterick, *What is the Marketing Management Concept? The frontiers of marketing thought and action Chicago: American Marketing Association 1957 Mercer Marketing* (Blackwell, Oxford, 1992).

Meyers, "The role of packaging in brand line extensions" 1 *The Journal of Brand Management* 348.

Michaels, *A Practical Guide to Trade Mark Law* (Sweet & Maxwell, London, 2nd ed., 1996).

Mills, "Comparative Advertising—Should it be allowed?" [1985] E.I.P.R. 417.

Morcom, *Guide to the Trade Marks Act 1994*.

Morcom, Zissu & Mostert, "Copyright in Financial Documents" [1994] 1 E.I.P.R. 6.

Morris, "The Strategy of Own Brands" (1971) 13(2) *European Journal of Marketing*.

Mostert, "Trademark Dilution and Confusion in United States, German and English Law" [1986] 17 I.I.C. 80.

Murphy, E. *Branding: A Key Marketing Tool* (Macmillan, London, 1987).

Nevett, *Advertising in Britain* (Heinneman, London, 1982).

Nilson, *Value Added Marketing* (McGraw Hill, Maidenhead, 1992).

Nimmer, (1954) 19 *Law & Contemporary Problems* 203.

Nozick, *Anarchy, State and Utopia* (Blackwell, Oxford, 1974).

Packard, *The Hidden Persuaders* (Puffin, London, 1960).

Paine, "Trade Secrets and the Justification of Intellectual Property: A Comment on Hettinger", *Journal of Philosophy & Public Affairs* 247.

Park, Milberg & Lawson, "Evaluation of Brand Extensions: The Role of Product Similarity and Brand Concept Consistency" (1991) 18 *Journal of Consumer Research*.

Parks, " 'Naked' is Not a Four-Letter Word: Debunking the myth of the 'Quality Control Requirement' in trademark licensing" 1992 82 T.M.R. 531.

Pechmann & Ratneshwar, "The Use of Comparative Advertising for Brand Positioning: Association versus Differentiation (1991) 18 *Journal of Consumer Research*.

Pechmann & Stewart, "The Development of a Contingency Model of Comparative Advertising" Working Paper No. 90–108, Marketing Science Institute, Cambridge, MA.

Perrier (Ed), *Brand Valuation* (Premier Books, London, 3rd ed., 1997).

Phillips, "An Empire Built of Bricks: A Brief Appraisal of 'Lego' " [1987] E.I.P.R. 363.

Phillips & Coleman, "Passing Off and the 'Common Field of Activity' " (1985) 101 L.Q.R. 242.

Pickering, *Trade Marks in Theory and Practice* (Hart, Oxford, 1998).

Pinckaers, "The Right of Persona: A New Intellectual Property Right for the U.S. and E.U. (1997) 68 *Copyright World Issue.*

Poch, "Rubik's Cube—The Austrian Decision" [1982] 8 E.I.P.R. 231.

Prescott, "Has the Benelux Trade Mark Law Been Written into the Directive?" [1997] 3 E.I.P.R. 99.

Prescott, "Analysis: Infringement of Registered Trade Marks: Always a Hypothetical Comparison?" [1997] 1 I.P.Q. 121.

Prescott, "Think Before You Waga Finger" [1996] 6 E.I.P.R. 317.

Radcliffe J., "Comparative Advertising after Barclays Bank v. RBS Advanta" [1996] 4 ENT. L.R. 164.

Randall, Miniard, Barone, Manning & Till, "When Persuasion Goes Undetected: The Case of Comparative Advertising" (1993) *Journal of Market Research* 315.

Rassam, *Design and Corporate Success* (Gower Publishing, Aldershot, 1995).

Reichman, "Legal Hybrids: Between the Patent and Copyright Paradigms" (1994) 94 Colum. L.Rev. 2432.

Richards, *The Commodity Culture of Victorian England* (Verso, London, 1991).

Ricketson, "Reaping Without Sowing: Unfair Competition and Intellectual Property Rights in Anglo-Australian Law" [1984] U.N.S.W.L.J. 1.

Ries & Trout, *Positioning: The Battle for your Mind* (McGraw Hill, Maidenhead, 1st Revised ed.).

Rose, *Authors & Owners—The Invention of Copyright* (Harvard University Press, Cambridge, 1993).

Rose, "Unfair Competition? The problem of lookalike products" *Commercial Lawyer.*

Ruijsenaars, "A Legal Framework to Make Marketing Work" *Managing Intellectual Property* July/August 1997.

Sanders & Maniatis, "A Consumer Trade Mark: Protection Based on Origin and Quality" [1993] 11 E.I.P.R. 406.

Schecter, *The Historical Foundations of the Law Relating to Trademarks* (Columbia, University Press, 1925).

Schecter, "The Rational Basis of Trade Mark Protection" [1927] Harv. L.Rev. 813.

Schricker, "Protection of Famous Trademarks Against Dilution in Germany" (1979) 11 I.I.C. 166, 171.

Sinnot, Gillian and Kyle, "The Relationship between Total Cigarette Advertising and Total Cigarette Consumption" (1994) 13 *Journal of Advertising* 311.

Smith, "Format Rights: Opportunity Knocks" [1991] 3 Ent. L.R. 63.

Southgate, *Total Branding by Design* (Kogan Page, London, 1994).

Spector, "An Outline of a Theory Justifying Intellectual and Industrial Property Rights" [1989] 8 E.I.P.R. 270.

Spence, "Passing Off and the Misappropriation of Valuable Intangibles" (1996) 122 L.Q.R. 472.

Stevenson, *British Society 1914–1945* (Penguin, London, 1984).

Strowel, "Benelux: A Guide to the Validity of Three dimensional Trade Marks in Europe" [1995] E.I.P.R. 154.

Strowel, *Of Authors and Origins* (Clarendon Press, Oxford, 1994).

Sturgess, "Dispelling the Myth: The Effects of Total Advertising Expenditure on Aggregate Consumption" 1(3) *Journal of Advertising: The Quarterly Review of Marketing Communications* 201.

Sullivan, "Further New Zealand Decision on Levi's Pocket Tab Trade Mark" [1994] E.I.P.R. 170.

Swann, "The Configuration Quagmine: Is Protection Anticompetitve or Beneficial to consumers, and The Need to Synthesize Extremes" 87 T.M.R. 253.

Terrell, *Law of Patents* (Sweet & Maxwell, London, 14th ed., 1994).

Terry, Unfair Competition and the Misappropriation of a Competitor's Trade Values" (1988) 51 M.L.R. 296.

Thackara, *Winners! How Today's Successful Companies Innovate by Design* (Gower Publishing, Aldershot, 1997).

Tichane, "The Maturing Trademark Doctrine of Post-Sales Confusion" (1995) 85 T.M.R. 399 Tyerman.

"The Economic Rationale for Copyright Protection for Published Books: A Reply to Professor Breyer" (1971) 18 *UCLA Law Review* 1100.

Wad, Loken, Ross & Hasapopoulos, "The Influence of physical similarity on generalisation of affect and attribute perceptions from national brands to private label brands" in Shrimp *et al* (Eds) American Educator's Proceedings, Series No. 52 (American Marketing Association, Chicago).

Wadlow, *Passing Off* (Sweet & Maxwell, London, 2nd ed., 1995).

Warren & Brandeis (1890) 4 Har.L.Rev. 193, "The Right to Privacy".

Wilkie & Farris, "Comparison Advertising: Problems and Potential" (1975) 39 *Journal of Marketing*

Wilkof, *Trade Mark Licensing* (Sweet & Maxwell, London, 1995).

Wilkof, "Trade Mark Merchandising and the Entertainment Industry: Is quality control still relevant?" (1995) 6 Kent Law Rev. 211.

Willimsky, "Comparative Advertising: An Overview" [1996] E.I.P.R. 649.

Wilson, *The History of Unilever* (Cassell & Co. Ltd, London, 1954).

WIPO, "Protection Against Unfair Competition" *WIPO Publication* No. 725 (1994).

Yen, "Restoring the Natural Law: Copyright as Labor and Possession" (1990) 51 Ohio State Law Journal 517.

Zaichkowsky, *Defending Your Brand Against Imitation* (Quorum Books, Westport).

INDEX

Appearance of product—*cont.*
registered trade marks—*cont.*
form of registration, 3–32
Lego building brick, 3–32, 3–40,
3–43, 3–52
nature of goods, 3–53
registration requirements
3–36—3–39. *See also*
Registration of trade marks
Rubik's Cube puzzle, 3–32, 3–38,
3–39, 3–44, 3–52, 3–81
shapes, 3–33—3–35
technical effect, necessary to achieve,
3–54, 3–55
three dimensional objects, 3–33, 3–34
value of goods, 3–56—3–60
relative novelty of design, 3–19, 3–20
research, 3–03, 3–04
Rubik's Cube puzzle, 3–05, 3–10
copyright, 3–75—3–78
distinctiveness, 3–38, 3–39
eye appeal, 3–17
limitations, 3–74
litigation, 3–74—3–87, 3–97—3–104
passing off, 3–66, 3–76, 3–78, 3–79
patent, 3–67, 3–68
practical protection of, 3–74—3–87
registered design, 3–11—3–20
registered trade marks, 3–32, 3–38,
3–39, 3–44, 3–52, 3–81
success of product, 3–70—3–73
unregistered design right, 3–22, 3–24
shape, 3–13
role of, 3–07
spending by companies on, 3–04
success of product, 3–69—3–73
surface pattern,
registered designs, 3–13
unregistered design right, 3–21, 3–22
Tetley tea bag, 3–02, 3–04
three dimensional objects,
Coca-Cola bottle, 3–33
copyright, 3–27
registered trade marks, 3–32, 3–33
Toblerone, 3–07
Toilet Duck lavatory cleaner, 3–02,
3–04
unregistered design right, 3–21—3–25
commonplace, 3–22
exclusions, 3–21
infringement, 3–25
Lego building brick, 3–22
qualifying individual, 3–23, 3–24
Rubik's Cube puzzle, 3–22, 3–24
shape and configuration, 3–21, 3–22
surface decoration or ornament, 3–21
"utilitarian" articles, 3–27, 3–28
Application,
Community Trade Mark,
advertisement, 2–89
examination, 2–89
opposition, 2–89

Application—*cont.*
European Patent Office, to, 2–80
patents, European Patent Office, to,
2–80
registered design, 2–25
registration of trade marks,
assignment, 2–60
contents, 2–58
examination, 2–59
fee, 2–58
filing, 2–58
multiple, 5–38—5–44
opposition, 2–59
publication of mark, 2–59
Arnold, David,
anatomy of brands 1.20. *See also*
Anatomy of a brand
meaning of brand, 1–12, 1–13, 1–16
Artistic craftsmanship, works of,
2–43—2–45
Artistic works,
See also Copyright
advertisements, 6–25
appearance of product, 3–28
automatic protection, 5–31
Berne Convention, 2–71
copyright, 2–20, 3–28
drawings, 3–28—3–31
logos, 5–30
prototypes, 3–26
signatures, 5–30
Asset,
See also Valuation, brand
brands as, 1–48, 5–99
Assignment,
registered trade marks, 2–60
Augmented product,
definition, 1–05
intangible features, 1–05
meaning, 1–05
meaning of brand, 1–12, 1–18
tangible features, 1–05
variations, 1–05
Australia,
passing off 5–123. *See also* Passing off

Balance sheet,
brands on 1–51, 1–52, 1–53. *See also*
Valuation, brand
Banking sector,
branding, 1–62
Benelux Model,
dissimilar goods, 5–64, 5–65
Trade Mark Harmonisation Directive,
2–85, 2–86, 3–48, 3–49
trade marks registration, refusal of,
3–48, 3–49
Berne Convention, 2–71
artistic works, 2–71
copyright, 2–22, 2–71
GATT-TRIPS Agreement, 2–81, 2–82